LIVING LANGUAGE®
U L T I M A T E
JAPANESE
A D V A N C E D

ULTIMATE
JAPANESE

ADVANCED

BY SUGURU AKUTSU, ED.D.

ASSOCIATE PROFESSOR OF JAPANESE

THUNDERBIRD, AMERICAN GRADUATE SCHOOL

OF INTERNATIONAL MANAGEMENT

EDITED BY

TONY DISTEFANO

AND

MONIQUE LEAHEY SUGIMOTO

LIVING LANGUAGE®
A Random House Company

ACKNOWLEDGMENTS

A special thank-you to Jane Kuo at Thunderbird for her help and encouragement in writing this book.

Thanks also to the staff at Living Language®: Kathy Mintz, Helga Schier, Ana Suffredini, Chris Warnasch, Lisa Alpert, Germaine Ma, Andrea Peabbles, Lenny Henderson, Erin Bekowies. Tom Russell, Elizabeth Bennett, Helen Tang, Zviezdana Verzich, Suzanne McQuade, Sophie Chin, Denise De Gennaro, Linda Schmidt, John Whitman, Alison Skrabek, Arlene Aizer, Helen Kilcullen, and Heather Lanigan. Additional thanks to Monique Leahey Sugimoto, Hiroko Storm, Joseph Essertier, Takeo Kurafuji, Hiroyuki Oshita, and Fuhito Shimoyama.

FREE ACCESS TO MORE
PRACTICE ONLINE

Enhance your *Ultimate Japanese Advanced* learning experience with free extra practice online! Go to **www .livinglanguage.com/bonus/ultimateadvanced/japanese** to get access to 100 additional exercises and answers.

CONTENTS

GLOSSARY

LIVING LANGUAGE®
ULTIMATE
JAPANESE
ADVANCED

INTRODUCTION

Living Language Ultimate Japanese Advanced™ is a continuation of the beginner-intermediate *Ultimate Japanese*™ program. If you have already mastered the basics of Japanese in school, while traveling abroad, or with other Living Language™ courses, then *Ultimate Japanese Advanced*™ is right for you.

The complete course includes this text and eight hours of recordings. However, if you are confident of your pronunciation, you can also use the manual on its own.

With *Ultimate Japanese Advanced*™ you'll continue to learn how to speak, understand, read, and write idiomatic Japanese. The program will also introduce you to some of the more interesting aspects of Japanese culture and business. You'll be able to participate in engaging conversations about a variety of topics, as well as recognize and respond to several styles of formal and informal speech.

The course will take you everywhere, from the office to the trade show to the sushi bar, while teaching useful vocabulary and expressions. You'll become familiar with hundreds of new characters *(kanji)* and will practice translating to and from Japanese. You'll also learn about subtle cultural distinctions in personal interaction, such as the Japanese style of making decisions and taking care of problems, that will help smooth your way in Japan.

THE MANUAL

Living Language® *Ultimate Japanese Advanced* consists of twenty lessons, four reading passages, and two review sections. The reading passages appear every five lessons. There are review sections after Lesson 10 and Lesson 20. In order to accommodate both those readers who feel confident in their ability to read Japanese and those more comfortable with romanized spellings, the manual is further divided into two parts: all Japanese in Section 1 is written in *romaji* (romanized characters), while Section 2 uses *kanji* (Chinese characters) and *hiragana* and *katakana* (the two Japanese syllabaries). The dialogues for each lesson appear in Section 1 in *romaji*, and in Section 2 in Japanese characters. It's best to read and study each lesson in the manual before listening to it on the recordings.

SECTION 1—ROMANJI/ENGLISH

KAIWA (Dialogue): Each lesson begins with a dialogue in standard, idiomatic Japanese, presenting realistic situations—interviewing for a job, finding an apartment, going to see a doctor—set in various locales around Tokyo. All dialogues are written in romaji and translated into colloquial English. Readers not confident in their reading ability in Japanese may want to start by reading the dialogue here first; then, once comfortable with the content, readers may want to move to Section 2 to practice reading Japanese characters.

1

CHUU (Notes): The notes in this section refer to specific expressions, phrases, and other points of interest in the dialogue. They introduce the cultural and historical background relevant to a particular expression and allow you to see grammar rules and vocabulary "in action."

BUNPOO TO YOOHOO (Grammar and Usage): After a brief review of basic Japanese grammar, you'll concentrate on the more advanced grammatical forms and their usages. You'll learn how to express yourself more accurately and appropriately by using idiomatic Japanese. The heading of each topic is listed in the table of contents.

BIJINESU JIKOO (Business Matters): In this section you'll explore different areas of the Japanese business world, as well as cultural and historical information relevant to business etiquette and procedures. Discussing such topics as business connections, contracts, and technology and the generation gap, this section will enable you to conduct business in Japan with confidence.

RENSHUU MONDAI (Exercises): This section allows you to review the grammar and vocabulary covered in the lessons. You can check your answers in the *kotae* (answers) section, immediately following.

FUKUSHUU MONDAI (Review Exercises): The two review sections appear after Lessons 10 and 20. Similar in structure to the *Renshuu Mondai,* these sections allow you to integrate and test your mastery of the material covered in the preceding lessons.

SECTION 2—KANJI/HIRAGANA/KATAKANA/ENGLISH

KAIWA (Dialogue): This section provides the same dialogues as Section 1 written in Japanese script. Readers already confident in their reading ability in Japanese may want to start by reading the dialogue here first, then may want to go on to check their understanding by reading the same dialogue in *romaji* in Section 1.

TANGO (Vocabulary): The words in this section are taken directly from the dialogues, and will help you to understand what you are reading. You'll also be able to increase substantially your Japanese vocabulary in a variety of subjects.

KANJI: This section introduces single *kanji* (Chinese characters), giving both Chinese and Japanese readings (if applicable), and includes examples of the most common *kanji* combinations that use the given character.

RENSHUU MONDAI (Exercises): Similar to the *Renshuu Mondai* in Section 1, these exercises allow you to review what you have covered in the lessons. Practice in translation and using the new *kanji* are emphasized so that you can become more comfortable reading and writing Japanese.

2

YOMU RENSHUU (Reading Practice): The four reading passages, appearing after Lessons 5, 10, 15, and 20, are not translated. The material covered in the preceding lessons and the vocabulary notes on the more difficult words and phrases will enable you to determine the meaning, just as you would when reading a newspaper article or a business report abroad.

GLOSSARY: The extensive two-way glossary will prove an invaluable reference as you work through this program and then apply your knowledge through contact with people in Japan.

RECORDING (SETS A AND B)

This program provides you with eight hours of audio instruction and practice. There are two sets of complementary recordings: the first is designed for use with the manual, while the second may be used independently. By listening to and imitating the native speakers, you'll improve your pronunciation and comprehension while learning to use new phrases and structures.

RECORDINGS FOR USE WITH THE MANUAL (SET A)

This set of recordings gives you four hours of audio practice in Japanese only. It features the complete dialogues of all twenty lessons. The recorded material appears in **boldface** in your manual. You'll first hear native Japanese speakers read the complete dialogue without interruption at normal conversational speed. Then you'll have a chance to listen to the dialogue a second time and repeat each phrase in the pauses provided.

If you wish to practice your comprehension, first listen to the recordings of the dialogue without consulting the translations in the manual. Write down a summary of what you think the dialogue was about, then listen to the recordings a second time, checking how much you understood against the translations in the manual.

After you study each lesson and practice with the recordings, go on to Set B, which can be used on the go—while driving, jogging, traveling, or doing housework.

RECORDINGS FOR USE ON THE GO (SET B)

Set B recordings give you four hours of audio instruction and practice in Japanese and English. Because they are bilingual, these recordings may be used without the manual, wherever it's convenient to learn.

The twenty lessons on Set B correspond to those in the manual. A bilingual narrator leads you through the four sections in each lesson.

The first section presents the most important phrases from the original dialogue. You will first hear the abridged dialogue without interruption at normal conversational speed. You'll then hear it again, phrase by phrase, with English translations and pauses for you to repeat after the native Japanese speakers.

The second section reviews and expands upon the most important vocabulary introduced in the lesson. You will practice words and phrases collected from the *Kaiwa* (Dialogue), *Chuu* (Notes), and *Bijinesu Jikoo* (Business Matters) sections. Additional expressions show how the words may be used in other contexts. Again, you are given time to repeat the Japanese phrases after the native speakers.

In the third section you will explore the lesson's most important grammatical structures. After a quick review of the rules, you can practice with sample phrases and sentences.

The conversational exercises in the last section integrate what you've learned and help you generate sentences in Japanese on your own. You'll take part in brief conversations, ask and respond to questions, transform sentences, and occasionally translate from English into Japanese. After you respond, you'll hear the correct answer from a Japanese native speaker.

The interactive approach on this set of recordings focuses on the idiomatic spoken word and will teach you to speak, understand, and *think* in Japanese.

Now let's begin.

TABLE OF JAPANESE SYLLABLES IN *ROMAJI, HIRAGANA,* AND *KATAKANA*

R = *romaji*; H = *hiragana*; K = *katakana*

An asterisk (*) marks those syllables that, to a speaker of English, appear to have beginning consonants that do not match those of the other syllables in the same row. They do not appear inconsistent from the standpoint of Japanese, which originally lacked such sounds as *si, ti, tu,* etc.

The syllables shown in parentheses are essentially used in Japanese only in words borrowed from other languages.

	R	H	K	R	H	K	R	H	K	R	H	K	R	H	K
	a	あ	ア	*i*	い	イ	*u*	う	ウ	*e*	え	エ	*o*	お	オ
k+vowel	*ka*	か	カ	*ki*	き	キ	*ku*	く	ク	*ke*	け	ケ	*ko*	こ	コ
s	*sa*	さ	サ	**shi*	し	シ	*su*	す	ス	*se*	せ	セ	*so*	そ	ソ
t	*ta*	た	タ	**chi*	ち	チ	**tsu*	つ	ツ	*te*	て	テ	*to*	と	ト
n	*na*	な	ナ	*ni*	に	ニ	*nu*	ぬ	ヌ	*ne*	ね	ネ	*no*	の	ノ
h	*ha*	は	ハ	*hi*	ひ	ヒ	**fu*	ふ	フ	*he*	へ	ヘ	*ho*	ほ	ホ
m	*ma*	ま	マ	*mi*	み	ミ	*mu*	む	ム	*me*	め	メ	*mo*	も	モ
y	*ya*	や	ヤ				*yu*	ゆ	ユ				*yo*	よ	ヨ
r	*ra*	ら	ラ	*ri*	り	リ	*ru*	る	ル	*re*	れ	レ	*ro*	ろ	ロ
w	*wa*	わ	ワ										*wo*	を	ヲ
n'	*n'*	ん	ン												
g	*ga*	が	ガ	*gi*	ぎ	ギ	*gu*	ぐ	グ	*ge*	げ	ゲ	*go*	ご	ゴ
z	*za*	ざ	ザ	**ji*	じ	ジ	*zu*	ず	ズ	*ze*	ぜ	ゼ	*zo*	ぞ	ソ
d	*da*	だ	ダ	**ji*	ぢ	ヂ	**zu*	づ	ヅ	*de*	で	デ	*do*	ど	ド
b	*ba*	ば	バ	*bi*	び	ビ	*bu*	ぶ	ブ	*be*	べ	ベ	*bo*	ぼ	ボ
p	*pa*	ぱ	パ	*pi*	ぴ	ピ	*pu*	ぷ	プ	*pe*	ぺ	ペ	*po*	ぽ	ポ
ky	*kya*	きゃ	キャ				*kyu*	きゅ	キュ				*kyo*	きょ	キョ
sh	*sha*	しゃ	シャ	*shi*	し	シ	*shu*	しゅ	シュ	*(she)*	(しぇ)	(シェ)	*sho*	しょ	ショ
ch	*cha*	ちゃ	チャ	*chi*	ち	チ	*chu*	ちゅ	チュ	*(che)*	(ちぇ)	(チェ)	*cho*	ちょ	チョ
ny	*nya*	にゃ	ニャ				*nyu*	にゅ	ニュ				*nyo*	にょ	ニョ
hy	*hya*	ひゃ	ヒャ				*hyu*	ひゅ	ヒュ				*hyo*	ひょ	ヒョ
my	*mya*	みゃ	ミャ				*myu*	みゅ	ミュ				*myo*	みょ	ミョ
ry	*rya*	りゃ	リャ				*ryu*	りゅ	リュ				*ryo*	りょ	リョ
gy	*gya*	ぎゃ	ギャ				*gyu*	ぎゅ	ギュ				*gyo*	ぎょ	ギョ
j	*ja*	じゃ	ジャ	*ji*	じ	ジ	*ju*	じゅ	ジュ	*(je)*	(じぇ)	(ジェ)	*jo*	じょ	ジョ
by	*bya*	びゃ	ビャ				*byu*	びゅ	ビュ				*byo*	びょ	ビョ
py	*pya*	ぴゃ	ピャ				*pyu*	ぴゅ	ピュ				*pyo*	ぴょ	ピョ

5

Following are *katakana* characters for words borrowed from foreign languages. Owing to their frequent use in words from other languages, the syllables *ti, tu, di,* and *du* have become common both in writing and in speech. However, *va, vi, ve,* and *vo* exist only in writing. These sounds are naturally expressed only in *katakana*, not in *hiragana*.

t			ti	テイ	tu	トゥ/テュ				
d			di	デイ	du	ド゙ゥ/デ゙ュ				
f	fa	ファ	fi	フィ			fe	フェ	fo	フォ
v	va	ブ゙ァ/ヴ゙ァ	vi	ブ゙ィ/ヴ゙ィ			ve	ブ゙ェ/ヴ゙ェ	vo	ブ゙ォ/ヴ゙ォ

LONG VOWELS

a	ああ	i	いい	u	うう	e	ええ	o	おう/おお
	アー		イー		ウー		エー		オー
	あー		いー		うー		えー		おー

SECTION 1

Romaji / English

DAI IKKA
Lesson 1

A. KAIWA (Dialogue)

NIHON NI TOOCHAKU

Bijitekku-sha bijinesu kaihatsu-bu no Neruson-maneejaa wa Tookyoo-shisha ni tenkin ni naru.[1] Kookuugaisha-shain ga messeeji o Neruson-shi ni tsutaeru.

SHAIN: **Neruson-sama[2] desu ne. Suzuki-sama yori messeeji desu ga.[3]**

NERUSON: **Aa, soo desu ka. Nan deshoo ka.**

SHAIN: **Ainiku kyuuyoo ga odeki ni natte, kuukoo ni wa mukae ni irassharenai[4] soo desu.**

NERUSON: **Soo desu ka. Wakarimashita.**

SHAIN: **Sorede, Shinjuku-yuki no rimujin-basu ni notte kudasai to no koto desu. Achira de oai ni naru[5] soo desu.**

NERUSON: **Hai. Doko de basu ni noremasu ka.**

SHAIN: **Hai. Zeikan o deta tokoro de kippu o katte kudasai. Sono sotogawa de sugu noremasu.**

NERUSON: **Arigatoo gozaimashita.**

Neruson-shi wa mondai mo naku nyuukoku, tsuukan o sumasete,[6] hoteru ni iku basu o mitsukeru.

NERUSON: **Sumimasen. Dareka suwatte imasu ka.**

YAMADA: **Iie, daremo. Doozo.**

NERUSON: **Doomo. Shinjuku made dono gurai kakarimasu ka.**

YAMADA: **Soo desu ne. Ichijikan han gurai deshoo. Hoteru wa doko desu ka.**

NERUSON: **Shinjuku-Hiruton desu.**

YAMADA: **Aa, ano Hiruton wa benri de ii desu ne. Chotto takai desu ga, nan ni demo chikai desu kara.**

NERUSON: **Naruhodo.**

YAMADA: **Shitsurei desu ga,[7] Nihon e wa oshigoto desu ka.**

NERUSON: Ee, tenkin desu.

YAMADA: Jaa, Nihon-shisha ni otsutome desu ka.

NERUSON: Hai, raishuu kara hajimemasu.

YAMADA: Doo iu kankei[8] no oshigoto desu ka.

NERUSON: Konpyuutaa kankei desu ga.

YAMADA: Soo desu ka. Jitsu wa[9] watakushi mo konpyuutaa kankei no shigoto o shite iru n desu.[10] Kore,[11] watakushi no meishi desu. Nanika arimashitara, doozo.

NERUSON: Hai. Yamada-san desu ne. Yoroshiku. Neruson to iimasu. Kore wa watakushi no desu.

Neruson-shi, hoteru ni tsuku. Tookyoo-shisha no dooryoo Suzuki-shi, soko de matsu.

SUZUKI: Yaa, Neruson-san, yookoso.[12] Kuukoo[13] made mukae ni ikenakute shitsurei shimashita.

NERUSON: Iie iie, tondemo arimasen.[14] Ohisashiburi desu, Suzuki-san. Osewa ni narimasu.[15] Doozo yoroshiku.[16]

SUZUKI: Kochira koso, yoroshiku. Otsukare ja arimasen ka.[17]

NERUSON: Ee, jisa no kankei de chotto tsukaremashita.

SUZUKI: Jitsu wa, yuushoku demo, to omotte ita n desu ga.

NERUSON: Soo desu ka. Jaa, son'na ni tsukarete imasen. Zehi, onegai shimasu.[18]

SUZUKI: Sorejaa, chekku-in shite, sukoshi yasunde kudasai. Hachiji-goro mukae ni kimasu kara.

Neruson-shi, hoteru ni chekku-in suru.

KURAAKU: Irasshaimase.[19]

NERUSON: Neruson desu ga. Sengetsu no hajime goro yoyaku shi-mashita.

KURAAKU: Shooshoo omachi kudasai. Shinguru de yonpaku[20] no goyoyaku desu ne. Koko ni gojuusho to onamae o onegai shi-masu.

NERUSON: Kin'en-shitsu[21] ga arimasu ka.

KURAAKU: Hai, gozaimasu.[22] Nanakai[23] desu ga, yoroshii desu ka.

NERUSON: Ee. Sorekara taizai ga motto nagaku naru kamoshirenai n desu ga.

KURAAKU: Soo desu ka. Nanpaku gurai desu ka.

NERUSON: **Mada hakkiri wakarimasen ga. Tabun ni, san nichi desu.**

KURAAKU: **Ohayame ni**[25] **oshirase kudasai. Yooi shite okimasu kara.**

NERUSON: **Yoroshiku.**

KURAAKU: **Koko ni sain**[26] **o onegai shimasu.**

NERUSON: **Kore de ii desu ka.**

KURAAKU: **Hai. Kurejitto-kaddo de oshiharai desu ne.**

NERUSON: **Ee, kore doozo.**

ARRIVAL IN JAPAN

Mr. Nelson, a manager of the Business Development Division of BusiTech corporation, has been transferred to a branch office in Tokyo. An airline employee delivers a message to Mr. Nelson.

EMPLOYEE: You are Mr. Nelson, right? I have a message (for you) from Mr. Suzuki.

NELSON: Oh, really? What is it?

EMPLOYEE: Unfortunately, it seems an urgent (business) matter arose, and he cannot come to the airport to meet you.

NELSON: Is that so? (Thank you,) I understand.

EMPLOYEE: Also, he said to please take the limousine bus bound for Shinjuku. He'll meet you there.

NELSON: Okay. Where can I catch that bus? (lit. Where can I ride the bus?)

EMPLOYEE: Well. (lit. Yes, sir.) Please buy your ticket just past (lit. as soon as you pass) the customs area. You can board the bus right outside.

NELSON: Thank you very much.

Mr. Nelson proceeds through immigration and customs without any problems, and finds the bus that will take him to his hotel.

NELSON: Excuse me, is anyone sitting here?

YAMADA: No, nobody. Go ahead.

NELSON: Thanks. (Do you know) about how long it takes to (get to) Shinjuku?

YAMADA: Let me see. Probably about an hour and a half. Which hotel are you staying at? (lit. Where is your hotel?)

NELSON: The Shinjuku Hilton.

YAMADA: Oh, that hotel is (really) convenient, and nice, too. It's a little expensive, but that's because it's close to everything.

NELSON: I see.

YAMADA: Are you in Japan on business?

NELSON: Yes, I've been transferred. (lit. It's a transfer.)

YAMADA: So, will you be working in (your company's) Japanese branch office?

NELSON: Yes, I start (lit. from) next week.

YAMADA: What kind of work (do you do)?

NELSON: (My work is) computer related.

YAMADA: Really? As a matter of fact, I also do computer-related work. This is my business card. If there is anything (that I can do), feel free (to contact me).

NELSON: Thank you. (lit. Yes.) It's Ms. Yamada, right? It is nice to meet you. My name is (lit. I am called) Nelson. Here's my business card. (lit. Here's mine.)

Mr. Nelson arrives at his hotel. Mr. Suzuki, a colleague from the Tokyo branch office, is waiting there (for him).

SUZUKI: Ah, Mr. Nelson, welcome (to Japan). I'm sorry I couldn't go to meet you at the airport. (lit. I was rude.)

NELSON: No, no, not at all. It's been a long time, Mr. Suzuki. I think I am going to need your help (lit. care). I hope that's all right. (lit. Please take care of me.)

SUZUKI: My pleasure. (lit. It is I who should be asking for your help.) Aren't you tired?

NELSON: Yes, I'm a little worn out from the time difference.

SUZUKI: Actually, I was thinking about dinner tonight.

NELSON: Really? Well, I'm not that tired. By all means, let's go.

SUZUKI: Please check in first, and rest a little. I'll come pick you up around eight o'clock.

Mr. Nelson checks into the hotel.

CLERK: Welcome.

NELSON: I'm Mr. Nelson. I made reservations around the beginning of last month.

CLERK: Just one moment, please. (lit. Please wait a little.) Yes, a reservation for a single room for four nights, right? Please (fill in) your address and name here.

NELSON: Do you have a non-smoking room?

CLERK: Yes, we do. It is on the seventh floor. Is that okay?

NELSON: Yes. My stay might turn out to be (lit. become) a little longer (than I had expected).

CLERK: Really? About how many days?

NELSON: I'm not exactly sure yet. Probably two to three days.

CLERK: Please let us know as soon as possible. We will make (the necessary) arrangements.

NELSON: Thank you.

CLERK: Please sign here.

NELSON: Is this okay?

CLERK: Yes. You will be paying by credit card, right?

NELSON: Yes. Please use this one.

B. CHUU (Notes)

1. *Tenkin ni naru* means "to be transferred (to another)." The word *naru* alone means "to become," but when it is preceded by *ni,* it can also denote "It has been decided that." In this sentence, the use of *ni naru* emphasizes that Nelson himself did not make the decision to be transferred. (See Grammar, Lesson 16.)

2. The word *sama* is a more respectful form of *san.* Like *san,* it is attached to a person's last name to show respect in formal situations. It is also commonly used in letters and public speeches.

3. The particle *ga* literally means "but." It is often used, however, in polite conversation to soften sentences, making them more indirect, and to prompt a response from the listener.

4. The expression *irassharenai* literally means "not able to come." *Irassharu* is an honorific form that can be used in place of *kuru* (to come), *iku* (to go), or *iru* (to be, exist). *Irassharenai* is the negative potential form (indicating inability). (See Grammar, Lesson 5.)

5. *Oai ni naru* is a deferential (honorific) equivalent of *au* (to meet someone). This pattern is often used to show respect to people whether they are present or not. It is formed by attaching the honorific prefix *o* to the stem of a verb and then adding *ni naru*.

6. *Sumasete* means "(after) finishing," and is the *te*-form of *sumasu* (to finish).

7. *Shitsurei desu ga* literally means "I will be rude, but . . ." and may also be translated as "Excuse me, but . . ." It is a common expression used before a question to indicate that the question might be considered intrusive or personal. It is formal and is used often in business situations: *Shitsurei desu ga, goshusshin wa.* (Excuse me, but where are you from?) *Shitsurei desu ga, okosan wa nan'nin desu ka.* (Excuse me, but how many children do you have?) *Shitsurei desu ga, oshigoto wa.* (Excuse me, but what do you do?)

8. A question that begins with *Doo iu kankei no* (What kind of . . . ?) is an indirect one that allows the listener to answer in general terms, as in *konpyuutaa kankei* (computer-related), or *jidoosha kankei* (automobile-related). This type of questioning allows one to ask personal questions without making the other party feel too uncomfortable.

9. The expression *jitsu wa* translates as "The fact is . . ." or "Actually . . ." It implies that the speaker is about to disclose something. It is used in more serious or formal situations than these English equivalents, however, so it's important not to overuse it.

10. The non-past (present) progressive form verb (or "V," for short) *te + iru* usually translates as "to be + V + -ing." However, it is sometimes also used in cases, such as this one, where a habitual action is expressed and only the present tense would be used in English.

11. *Kore, watakushi no meishi desu* means "This is my business card." When the context is clear, particles such as *ga, wa,* and *o* are often deleted in conversation.

12. *Yookoso* is a formal expression that means "welcome." It can imply a certain degree of friendliness, indicating that the parties have met before, but this is not always the case.

13. The New Tokyo International Airport (Narita Airport) is in fact not located in the city of Tokyo, but in the city of Narita, Chiba Prefecture, approximately forty miles east of Tokyo. Depending upon the mode of transportation and the time of day, it takes anywhere from one to two hours to travel from the airport to the center of Tokyo.

The airport was named as it was to take advantage of Tokyo's international reputation.

14. *Tondemo arimasen* means "Not at all!" It is used as a means of expressing humility when someone compliments you or apologizes to you.

15. *Osewa ni narimasu* (I will be indebted to you for all the help you will give me) is a very important expression in Japanese. It is used when a newcomer joins a social group, and can also be used as an expression of modesty and humility when seeking friendship or accepting hospitality. Using this expression helps to establish a friendly relationship right from the beginning. *Taihen osewa ni narimashita* (I am indebted to you for all that you have done) is used when one has received assistance and would like to express some sort of gratitude.

16. The phrase *doozo yoroshiku,* which literally means "please handle it in a favorable way," is one of the most frequently used expressions in business. Its translation into English varies greatly according to the situation. The formal form is *doozo yoroshiku onegai itashimasu.*

17. *Otsukare ja arimasen ka* (Aren't you tired?) is an honorific substitute for *Tsukaremasen ka.* Other examples include:

POLITE	HONORIFIC
Kaerimasu ka. (Are you going home?)	*Okaeri desu ka.*
Tomarimasu ka. (Are you staying overnight?)	*Otomari desu ka.*

18. *Onegai shimasu* literally means "I ask you (to do something)," but may be translated hundreds of ways depending on the situation. When using this expression, the request should already be clear based on the context of the dialogue.

19. Employees in the service industries are extremely formal and polite in Japan. They often use such honorific expressions as *Irasshaimase* (Welcome), *Shooshoo omachi kudasai* (Just a moment, please), and *Mooshiwake gozaimasen* (I am extremely sorry). They are trained to think of their customers as "honored guests," and treat them as such.

20. The counter suffix *haku* (or *paku*) is used when indicating the number of nights one plans to stay. It is used by adding the counter after the number, as in *ippaku* (one night), *nihaku* (two nights), *sanpaku* (three nights), *yonpaku* (four nights), or *gohaku* (five nights). As with most counters in the Japanese language, there is no real rule

on when to use *haku* or when to use *paku*. Consequently, the best way to learn them is through memorization.

21. No-smoking rooms are available in most first-rate hotels in Japan. You may request a room in which smoking is allowed by asking for a *kitsuenshitsu* (smoking room).

22. The verb *gozaru* is a humble equivalent of *aru* (to exist, be). When using honorific language, of which humble forms are one type, the speaker is recognizing the difference in social status between himself/herself and the listener: *Hoteru ni ookii kaigishitsu ga gozaimasu.* (There is a large conference room in the hotel.) *Kyoo wa heya ga gozaimasen.* (We do not have any rooms [available] today.) Note that *de gozaimasu* is a humble equivalent of *desu: Ryooshin de gozaimasu.* (These are my parents.)

23. *Nanakai* means "seventh floor." The counter suffix *kai* is used when indicating floors of buildings. The counter is added after the number.

24. The word *yoroshii* is a more polite form of *ii,* meaning "good," or "OK." When used by a superior, however, it conveys a sense of authoritative approval.

25. The phrase *hayame (ni)* means "a little earlier (than usual)." Its meaning is usually slightly different from that of *hayai* (early). *Hayame ni heya o yoyaku shimashoo.* (Let's reserve the room a little earlier than is required [perhaps a few days earlier].) *Hayaku heya o yoyaku shimashoo.* (Let's reserve the room early [as soon as possible].) Note, however, that in an honorific request, as in the dialogue, *hayame (ni)* is simply a more polite way to say *hayaku,* which would sound too direct and demanding.

26. Many words in the Japanese language have been adopted in their foreign form, even though the pronunciation is distinctly Japanese. These words are called *gairaigo* (lit. words coming from outside). *Sain* (sign), *resutoran* (restaurant), and *kurejitto-kaado* (credit card) are just a few examples.

C. BUNPOO TO YOOHOO
(Grammar and Usage)

1. THE COPULA *DESU*

The copula, or linking word, *desu* is roughly equivalent to the English verb "to be." Along with other verbs in Japanese, it normally occurs at the end of a sentence.

Watakushi wa Neruson desu.
   I am (Mr.) Nelson.

Are wa hikooki desu.
   That is an airplane.

Watakushi wa Bijitekku no shain desu.
   I am an employee of BusiTech.

Nan desu ka?
   What is it?

The copula can be used with *na*-adjectives the same way as it is used with nouns.

Kono hoteru wa benri desu.
   This hotel is convenient (conveniently located).

Atarashii kuukoo wa kirei desu ne.
   The new airport is beautiful, isn't it?

The negative form of the copula is *dewa arimasen,* or the contracted form *ja arimasen.* Both forms have the same meaning, but *ja arimasen* is more common in casual, relaxed conversations.

Kore wa kyuuyoo dewa arimasen.
   This is not an urgent matter.

Furui kuukoo wa benri ja arimasen deshita.
   The old airport was not convenient.

When a verb is of secondary importance, or understood by context, it may be replaced by a copula. In the examples below, *arimasu* and *imasu* are regular verbs occurring in questions that can be replaced by the copula *desu* in the answers.

Atarashii meishi wa doko ni arimasu ka.—Asoko desu.
   Where are the new business cards?—They are over there.

Itsu made Nihon ni imasu ka.—Raigetsu made desu.
> How long (lit. until when) will you be in Japan?—I will be here until next month.

The same is true for two declarative sentences.

Watakushi wa Kyooto-Daigaku o sotsugyoo shimashita. Otooto wa Oosaka-Daigaku desu.
> I graduated from Kyoto University. My brother graduated from Osaka University.

The meaning of each of the above sentences may be understood clearly from the context. The same situation can be seen below. The context will clarify which of the three possible meanings is implied.

Oshigoto desu ka.
> Are you going to work?
> Are you going there on business?
> Are you late because of work?

Once one gets used to the concept of using the copula this way, it is quite convenient.

2. *I*-ADJECTIVES

There are two types of adjectives in Japanese: *i*-adjectives and *na*-adjectives. All *i*-adjectives end in *i*.

ii, yoi	good
takai	expensive, tall, high
chikai	near
yoroshii	good
nagai	long

I-adjectives can stand alone, similar to English verbs. Note, however, that the following declarations are appropriate only in informal situations:

Ii.	It is good.
Takai.	It is expensive.
Nagai.	It is long.

The formal form of *i*-adjectives is created by adding *desu* after the adjective. *Desu,* as it is used here, is not a copula but a "formalizer." The meaning of the sentence itself does not change.

18

Ii desu.		It is good.	
Takai desu.		It is expensive.	
Nagai desu.		It is long.	

Unlike adjectives in English, Japanese *i*-adjectives have tenses and both affirmative and negative forms. Below is a chart showing *i*-adjectives in their formal forms. Note that *ii* (good) is irregular.

NON-PAST AFFIRMATIVE	NON-PAST NEGATIVE	PAST AFFIRMATIVE	PAST NEGATIVE
Ii desu	*yoku arimasen*	*yokatta desu*	*yoku arimasen deshita*
takai desu	*takaku arimasen*	*takakatta desu*	*takaku arimasen deshita*
nagai desu	*nagaku arimasen*	*nagakatta desu*	*nagaku arimasen deshita*

I-adjectives can be used as predicates or modifiers. As a predicate:

Hoteru wa kuukoo ni chikai desu.
The hotel is close to the airport.

Kuukoo wa atarashii desu.
The airport is new.

As a modifier:

Takai kippu o kaimashita.
I bought expensive tickets.

Yasui hoteru ga Tookyoo ni arimasu ka.
Are there any inexpensive hotels in Tokyo?

3. *NA*-ADJECTIVES

Unlike *i*-adjectives, most *na*-adjectives do not end with *i* (the exceptions are *kirei,* "pretty, clean," and *kirai,* "dislike"). They can modify nouns by placing *na* between the adjective and the noun. When the *na*-adjective functions as a predicate, it is followed by the copula *desu.*
As a modifier:

Kore wa yuumei na hoteru desu.
This is a famous hotel.

Kore wa kirei na meishi desu ne.
This is a beautiful business card, isn't it?

As a predicate:

When a *na*-adjective is used as a predicate, it functions exactly the same as the pattern "noun *wa* noun *desu*" (see Lesson 1, C1). Below is a chart showing the tenses of *na*-adjectives.

	NON-PAST AFFIRMATIVE	NON-PAST NEGATIVE	PAST AFFIRMATIVE	PAST NEGATIVE
(Yuumei)	*desu*	*dewa arimasen* *(ja arimasen)*	*deshita*	*dewa arimasen deshita* *(ja arimasen deshita)*

Ano yama wa kirei desu.
> That mountain is pretty.

Basu wa totemo fuben desu.
> The bus is very inconvenient.

Please note that *suki* (like; lit. likable) and *kirai* (dislike; lit. dislikable) are not verbs in Japanese, but *na*-adjectives. Of course, when translated into English, verbs should be used.

Watashi wa shigoto ga suki desu.
> I like my job.

Na-adjectives can be used as adverbs by adding *ni* to the end of the word.

Basu ni kantan ni noremasu.
> You can get on a bus easily.

Shizuka ni yasunde kudasai.
> Please rest quietly.

4. PARTICLES AND CONJUNCTIONS

a. *Ka*

The particle *ka* at the end of a sentence transforms a statement into a question. Compare:

Anata wa Nihonjin desu.
> You are Japanese.

Anata wa Nihonjin desu ka.
> Are you Japanese?

Sumisu-san wa kaishain desu.
> Mr. Smith is a company employee.

Sumisu-san wa kaishain desu ka.
> Is Mr. Smith a company employee?

Kore wa Nihon no pasupooto desu.

This is a Japanese passport.

Kore wa Nihon no pasupooto desu ka.

Is this a Japanese passport?

Nihon e tenkin desu.
I have been transferred to Japan.

Nihon e tenkin desu ka.
Have you been transferred to Japan?

Menzeihin o kaimashita.
I bought (some) duty-free goods.

Menzeihin o kaimashita ka.
Did you buy any duty-free goods?

b. *Ne*

The particle *ne* usually appears at the end of a sentence as well. It is used when seeking or expecting agreement or confirmation, or in forming rhetorical questions. It is a common expression, as it is important in Japanese culture to seek or express shared values, beliefs, information, and knowledge.

Are ga Tookyoo-eki desu ne.
That is Tokyo Station, isn't it?

Hoteru wa yoyaku shite arimasu ne.
You have reserved a hotel (room), haven't you?

Kuukoo ni mukae ni ikimasu ne.
You are going to meet him at the airport, aren't you?

c. *De*

When used after nouns, *de* has several meanings. One of them is "because of."

Shigoto de yoku Amerika e ikimasu.
I often go to America on business (lit. because of work).

Kinoo byooki de yasumimashita.
I was absent (lit. rested) yesterday because I was ill.

5. IDIOMATIC EXPRESSIONS

a. *Dekiru*

In general, *dekiru* signifies "can do," but has several meanings that depend on the context.

To be able to

Koko de yoyaku ga dekimasu ka.
Can I make a reservation here?

Koko de ryoogae ga dekimasu ka.
  Can I exchange money here?

To be ready

Meishi wa itsu dekimasu ka.
  When will my business cards be ready?

Kono shigoto wa ashita made ni dekimasu ka.
  Will the job be finished (ready) by tomorrow?

To come into being

Kono kaisha wa itsu dekimashita ka.
  When was this company established?

Juu nen mae ni dekimashita.
  It was established ten years ago.

To be made of

Kono ie wa ki de dekite imasu.
  This house is made of wood.

Kono kaado wa nani de dekite imasu ka.
  What is this card made of?

b. The Phrase *Doo iu* (What kind of?)

Doo iu (what kind of?) is a noun modifier. Answers to *doo iu* questions
can include *koo iu* (this kind of), *soo iu* (that kind of), and *aa iu*
(a kind such as). *Doo iu* is similar in meaning and usage to *don'na*
(what kind of?), and the two phrases can be used interchangeably.
Answers to questions with *don'na* can include *kon'na*, *son'na*, or *an'na*.
Note, however, that *kon'na*, *son'na*, and *an'na* can carry negative con-
notations that *koo iu*, *soo iu*, and *aa iu* do not.

Doo iu (Don'na) nomimono ga hoshii n desu ka.
  What kind of drink do you want?

Doo iu (Don'na) kaisha ni tsutometai desu ka.
  What kind of company do you want to work for?

Koo iu (Kon'na) kotoba wa nakanaka wakarinikui desu.
  These kinds of words are difficult to understand.

Aa iu (An'na) hoteru ni tomaritai desu.
  I would really like to stay at that kind of hotel.

D. BIJINESU JIKOO
(Business Matters)

RYOKOO AN'NAI (TRAVEL TIPS)

American citizens must have a valid U.S. passport to travel to Japan. A short-term visitor (for up to three months) is not required to have a visa in advance, but those who plan to stay longer must apply for visas, preferably before traveling to Japan. This process may take considerable time and should be started well in advance. Some documents, such as a letter from one's company and/or a so-called "letter of guarantee" from someone in Japan, may be required. This letter vouches for your credibility, and states that the guarantor will intervene on your behalf (usually financially) if necessary. This *hoshoonin seido* (guarantee system) acts as a type of insurance that someone in Japan will be liable for any problems. For details on visa requirements, contact the Japanese consulate or embassy in your area.

Upon arrival at Tokyo International Airport (or any other international airport in Japan), an inspector will be waiting at the immigration office (gate) to check passports and stamp visas. Once the passport visa is stamped, you will proceed to the carousel to pick up your luggage, and then pass through customs. Unless it is very crowded, the procedure should take about thirty minutes.

Public transportation is well developed in Japan. Major airports offer fast and convenient transportation (limousine buses, subways, and trains) to city centers, and you can always get advice on this matter at the information desks. The limousine buses will take you to all major hotels, as well as to various train stations. Train and subway systems are convenient, and will get you almost anywhere in the country. Taxis are also available anytime and anywhere, but are rather expensive. To rent a car you will need a valid U.S. driver's license and an international license. Note that in Japan, people drive on the left side of the road.

Hotels are conveniently located virtually everywhere in large cities. Advance reservations are strongly advised, especially during the festival and holiday seasons. First-rate hotels in major cities are considerably more expensive than U.S. hotels and offer exceptional service. American credit cards are accepted in most hotels in major cities such as Tokyo, Kyoto, Osaka, and Nagoya. However, if you are traveling to smaller cities, you should check with the hotel to confirm the methods of payment they accept.

Most restaurants are open from 11 A.M. to 9 P.M. In the larger cities one can find a wide assortment of food. The most popular, moderately priced non-Japanese foods are Chinese, Italian, and American.

For most stores and shops regular business hours are from 9 A.M. to 6 P.M. Twenty-four-hour convenience stores have become very popular, and offer much more in terms of food and other merchandise than their American counterparts.

Until recently, smoking was not an issue and was permitted on public transportation, in restaurants, and in other public areas. However, efforts have been made to prohibit smoking in these areas. Some trains have smoking cars, while many train lines and buses prohibit smoking completely. No-smoking areas also exist in many restaurants and train stations, but do not be surprised if you observe people smoking in these areas.

The dollar-yen exchange rate changes every day and on some days it changes quite drastically. You can exchange money at most banks (usually on the second floor), hotels (for customers only), and in some of the department stores. The rates at these places are the same, but there are some limitations as to how much money you can exchange. A passport is always required for identification.

MISHIRANU HITO TO AU (MEETING WITH STRANGERS)

The Japanese tend not to speak to strangers. You may find that they are rather unfriendly to you and/or the people to whom they have not been properly introduced. Therefore, there is no common, equivalent phrase for "talking to strangers" in the Japanese language. Once the Japanese are engaged in conversation, however, they will open up.

Some Japanese people like to ask personal questions at the beginning of a conversation, such as "Are you married?" "What company do you work for?" "How old are you?" or "What are your hobbies?" This may seem intrusive to a westerner, but the Japanese are not comfortable in conversation until they feel they know something about the person they are talking to. Feel free to be just as forward when asking about your conversation partner's personal life. Any question that you prefer not to answer can be dealt with by speaking in general terms.

During introductions, it is sometimes difficult to tell whether one should bow or shake hands. The fact is that Japanese simply bow when meeting other Japanese. When meeting a non-Japanese person, it is just as acceptable to shake hands. The Japanese also tend to use established greetings when meeting people for the first time. These are illustrated in the dialogues.

Though English is usually the language used to conduct business between Japanese and non-Japanese, your effort and willingness to learn Japanese will instill trust and confidence that will make doing business much easier. Knowledge of the Japanese language itself will help you get to know your colleagues. Making mistakes during efforts to speak the language does not really matter. In fact, the Japanese try very hard to understand a non-native speaker, and even if you do not express yourself correctly, they will interpret what you are saying with generosity, and will not correct your mistakes. If you wish to work for a Japanese corporation in Japan, however, you may be required to be highly proficient in the Japanese language and to have an understanding of the culture.

RENSHUU MONDAI (EXERCISES)

A. *Tsugi no shitsumon ni kotaenasai.* (Answer the following questions.)

1. *Neruson-shi no shigoto wa nan desu ka.*
2. *Neruson-shi wa naze Nihon ni kimashita ka.*
3. *Suzuki-shi wa nan to iu kaisha ni tsutomete imasu ka.*
4. *Neruson-shi wa dooshite tsukarete iru no desu ka.*
5. *Tookyoo Hiruton wa dooshite benri na no desu ka.*

B. *Tekitoo na kotoba o irenasai.* (Insert the appropriate word.)

1. *Basu ni kantan _____ noremasu.*
2. *Hoteru ga kirei _____ totemo benri desu.*
3. *Nihon e wa tenkin _____.*
4. *Otsukare dewa _____ ka.*

C. *Tekitoo na joshi o irenasai.* (Insert the appropriate particle.)

1. *Shisha _____ otsutome desu ka.*
   Do you work at the branch office?
2. *Jisa no kankei _____ tsukaremashita.*
   I'm tired because of the time difference.
3. *Doko _____ dekimasu ka.*
   Where can I do it?
4. *Hoteru de _____ dekimasu.*
   You can even do it at the hotel.

KOTAE (ANSWERS)

A. 1. *Bijitekku no shain maneejaa desu.*   2. *Tenkin desu.*   3. *Bijitekku ni tsutomete imasu.*   4. *Jisa no kankei de tsukarete imasu.*   5. *Nan demo chikai kara desu.*
B. 1. *ni*   2. *de*   3. *desu*   4. *arimasen*
C. 1. *ni*   2. *de*   3. *de*   4. *mo*

DAI NIKA
Lesson 2

A. KAIWA (Dialogue)

NERUSON-SHI NO SHONICHI

Tookyoo de no saisho no shuumatsu ga sugite, getsuyoobi ni natta. Neruson-shi wa shigoto o hajimenakereba naranai. Koofun shinagara mo, kinchoo shite kaisha ni iku.

NERUSON: **Aa, kono biru da.[1] Saa, ganbaranakucha.[2] Nankai ka na.[3] Sumimasen. Bijitekku-sha wa nankai deshoo ka.**

SATOO: **Nanakai desu. Watashi mo soko e ikimasu kara.**

NERUSON: **Aa, soo desu ka. Bijitekku no kata[4] desu ka.**

SATOO: **Hai, soo desu. Satoo to mooshimasu.[5]**

NERUSON: **Aa, Satoo Hiroko-san desu ne. Watakushi wa Neruson desu.[6] Denwa de nankai ka hanashimashita ne.**

SATOO: **Aa, soo deshita ne. Doomo.[7] Itsu Nihon ni irasshatta n desu ka.**

NERUSON: **Senshuu no kinyoobi desu.**

SATOO: **Soo desu ka. Jaa, otsukare deshoo.**

NERUSON: **Chotto bakari. Demo daijoobu desu. Ryokoo wa narete imasu kara.**

SATOO: **Amari muri o shinaide kudasai.[8] Jaa, ikimashoo ka.**

Bijitekku-sha ni tsuku to, Satoo-joo[9] wa Neruson-shi o Suzuki-shi no jimusho ni an'nai suru.[10]

SUZUKI: **Neruson-san, yookoso. Jimusho wa sugu wakarima-shita ka.**

NERUSON: **Hai. Satoo-san ga an'nai shite kuremashita.**

SUZUKI: **Sore wa yokatta desu ne.[11] Kuji ni min'na ni kaigishitsu ni atsumatte moratte imasu. Sono mae ni koohii demo ikaga desu ka.**

NERUSON: **Iie, kekkoo desu.[12]**

SUZUKI: **Jaa, ikimashoo ka.**

Kaigishitsu de.

SUZUKI: **Minasan, sumimasen.**[13] **Kondo honsha kara tenkin no Neruson-san o goshookai shimasu. Eigyoo o tantoo shite moraimasu.**

NERUSON: **Neruson desu. Hajimemashite.**[14] **Kororado-shuu shusshin desu. Irinoi-daigaku o sotsugyoo shite, honsha de wa zutto**[15] **kaihatsu-bu de shigoto o shite kimashita. Minasan to ooi ni ganbaritai to omoimasu. Doozo yoroshiku onegai shimasu.**

ZEN'IN: **Doozo yoroshiku. (hakushu)**

Neruson-shi, Takagi-Jigyoo-Buchoo ni aisatsu ni iku.

NERUSON: **Takagi-buchoo,**[16] **ohisashiburi desu.**

TAKAGI: **Yaa, Neruson-kun, yookoso. Honsha no katagata wa minasan ogenki desu ka.**

NERUSON: **Hai, nanika to**[17] **isogashiku shite imasu.**

TAKAGI: **Sore wa yokatta. Kimi no ashisutanto o shookai shi-mashoo. Kanojo to kyooryoku shite, yatte**[18] **kudasai. Iidakun, chotto. Neruson-kun, Iida-kun desu.**

IIDA: **Ashisutanto no Iida desu. Daigaku o deta bakari de, shin'nyuu shain**[19] **desu. Doozo yoroshiku onegai itashimasu.**[20]

NERUSON: **Kochira koso. Daigaku o dete, hajimete no shigoto desu ka.**

IIDA: **Hai. Demo chichi no kaisha de arubaito**[21] **o sukoshi shita koto wa arimasu ga.**

NERUSON: **Aa, soo. Nan no kaisha desu ka.**

IIDA: **Omocha no kaisha desu. Kikaku-bu no tetsudai o shimashita. Totemo benkyoo ni narimashita.**

NERUSON: **Daigaku de wa nani ka kurabu katsudoo**[22] **demo yattemashita ka.**[23]

IIDA: **Hai. Maaketingu-bu ni haitte imashita.**

NERUSON: **Naruhodo.**[24] **Sore wa jissenteki desu ne. Watakushi wa gorufu-bu ni haitte imashita ga, amari jissenteki jaa arimasen deshita. Demo achira kochira e iku koto ga dekite, yokatta desu yo.**

IIDA: **Jaa, gorufu ga ojoozu nan desu ne.**

NERUSON: **Iya, saikin isogashikute, amari yatte masen kara, dame**[25] **desu.**

IIDA: **Watashi mo chikai uchi ni gorufu o naraitai to omotte imasu. Iroiro oshiete kudasai. Doozo yoroshiku.**[26]

Mr. Nelson's First Day

The first weekend in Tokyo has passed and it is now (lit. has become) Monday. Mr. Nelson must start his job. While he is excited (about starting), he goes to the company nervous.

NELSON: Okay, this is the building. Well, I have to give it my best. I wonder which floor it is ... Excuse me, which floor is BusiTech (located on)?

SATO: It's on the seventh floor. I'm going there also.

NELSON: Oh, really? Are you a BusiTech employee?

SATO: Yes, I am. My name is Sato.

NELSON: Oh, you're Hiroko Sato, aren't you? My name is (lit. I am) Nelson. We have spoken several times on the phone, haven't we?

SATO: Yes, that's right. Nice to meet you. When did you arrive in (lit. come to) Japan?

NELSON: Last Friday.

SATO: Really? Then you're probably tired.

NELSON: Only a little bit. But that's okay. I'm used to traveling.

SATO: Please don't overwork yourself. So, shall we go?

When they arrive at BusiTech, Ms. Sato shows Mr. Nelson the way to Mr. Suzuki's office.

SUZUKI: Mr. Nelson, welcome (to BusiTech). Did you find (lit. understand) the office right away?

NELSON: Yes, Ms. Sato was kind enough to show me the way.

SUZUKI: That's good. I have asked everybody to assemble in the conference room at nine o'clock. Would you like (to get) some coffee beforehand?

NELSON: No, thanks, I'm fine.

SUZUKI: Well then, shall we go (to the meeting)?

In the conference room.

SUZUKI: Excuse me, everyone. I (would like to) introduce Mr. Nelson, who has just (lit. this time) been transferred from our head office. He'll be in charge of sales.

NELSON: My name is Nelson. Pleased to meet all of you. I'm from the state of Colorado. Since graduating from the University of Illinois, I have been working in the development division at the head office. I'm looking forward to working with all of you. (lit. I would like to really do my best with all of you.)

ALL EMPLOYEES: Nice to meet you. (applause)

Mr. Nelson goes to meet (lit. greet) the department director, Mr. Takagi.

NELSON: Mr. Takagi, it's been a long time.

TAKAGI: Oh, Mr. Nelson, welcome! Is everyone at the head office (doing) well?

NELSON: Yes, they're all busy.

TAKAGI: That's good. Let me introduce you to your assistant. Please work in cooperation with her. Ms. Iida, (come over here for) just (a moment). Mr. Nelson, this is Ms. Iida.

IIDA: I'm your assistant, Ms. Iida. I have just graduated from (lit. left) college, and I'm a new employee with the company. It's nice to meet you.

NELSON: My pleasure. Is this your first job after college?

IIDA: Yes, it is. But I have worked part-time at my father's company before.

NELSON: Really? What kind of company is it?

IIDA: It's a toy company. I worked (lit. assisted) in the planning department. It was very educational. (lit. It became learning.)

NELSON: In college were you involved in any extracurricular activities?

IIDA: Yes, I was. I was a member of (lit. I entered) the marketing club.

NELSON: I see. That's practical, isn't it? I was a member of the golf club, but that was not very practical. It was good, however, because I was able to travel here and there.

IIDA: In that case, you must be good at golf, right?

NELSON: No. I've been (too) busy recently. I haven't been playing much, so my game has suffered.

IIDA: I've been thinking that I would also like to learn how to play golf in the near future. Please teach me a few (lit. various) things.

B. CHUU (Notes)

1. Japanese street addresses seem very disorganized when compared to those of other countries. Many streets are unnamed and there are no prominent numbers on houses or buildings. It is often very difficult to locate a building by its address alone because of this complexity. Therefore, Japanese people usually find places by using the names of the buildings they are in. Each building has its own name, such as *Ootemachi biru* (the Otemachi Building) or *Mitsui biru* (the Mitsui Building). An office's specific location in a building is expressed by its floor number: 1F, 2F, or 3F ("F" stands for "floor"), for example.

2. *Ganbaranakucha* is the contracted conversational form of *ganbaranakute wa naranai,* which means "I have to work very hard," or "I have to hang in there."

3. *Nankai ka na* means "I wonder what floor it is." *Ka na* means "I wonder," and is used in informal situations and in speaking to oneself.

4. *Kata* is the polite form of *hito,* meaning "person."

5. *Satoo to mooshimasu* literally means "I call myself Sato." *Moosu* is a humble form of *iu* (to say).

6. In Lesson 1, Mr. Nelson introduced himself to Mr. Yamada by saying *Neruson to iimasu.* This expression is used when speaking to someone for the first time. In this lesson, since Mr. Nelson has spoken to Miss Sato before, he introduces himself with *Neruson desu,* which is appropriate for this situation.

7. *Doomo* has three meanings: "very much," "by any means," and "somehow." Words following *doomo* can be left out because they are understood through sentence context. For example, saying *doomo* alone is sufficient to express *doomo arigatoo.*

8. *Muri* literally means "impossibility" or "unreasonableness." *Muri o suru* signifies "to overdo" or "to overexert."

9. *Satoo-joo* means "Miss Sato." *Joo* is used in writing, instead of *san* or *shi,* when referring to a woman.

10. A typical Japanese office is not divided into individual working cubicles. Except for high-ranking executives, all employees are located in open rooms accommodating anywhere from thirty to forty workers. The desks are arranged in clusters, so that all members of

a particular department *(bu)* or section *(ka)* will face one another. Though it is mainly due to limited space, some suggest that this arrangement creates an atmosphere of teamwork.

11. *Yokatta desu ne* means "That's great." While the English translation is in the non-past tense, since the action being described occurred in the past, the Japanese sentence is in the past tense.

12. *Kekkoo* can have three meanings, depending on the context "good," "fairly," "no thank you" (used when refusing offers).

13. The expression *sumimasen* can be used in many different situations. It can mean "I am sorry (to bother you)," "I am sorry (for what I have done to you)," "Excuse me," or "Thank you." The context will decide which meaning is referred to.

14. *Hajimemashite* literally means "We're starting," but is used only to express "Nice to meet you."

15. *Zutto* means "continuously" or "all the time."

16. Company employees address their superiors by either their name plus their titles, or by their titles alone, as in *Takagi-buchoo,* or just *Buchoo.* Superiors should not be addressed by the standard "name + *san,"* but superiors may refer to their subordinates by using the person's name followed by *kun* or *san. San* is more often used for female employees. *Kun* is attached more to the names of male employees.

17. *Nani ka to* means "in various ways" or "by some means." Often it is hard to translate.

18. *Yaru* can mean "to do," "to perform," or "to play," depending on the context. It is very similar in meaning to *suru* (to do), but is used more often in less formal conversations.

19. *Shin'nyuu-shain* (lit. newly entered employees) has the connotation of "fresh, with no work experience." In April, the time of year that Japanese companies hire new employees, all *shin'nyuu-shain* start work in various corporate training programs.

20. *Itasu* is the humble form of *suru* (to do). *Doozo yoroshiku onegai itashimasu* literally means "May I ask you to treat me favorably."

21. The word *arubaito* is the Japanese pronunciation of the German *Arbeit.* It means "part-time job."

22. *Kurabu katsudoo* (lit. club activities) are an important part of a Japanese student's college experience. Some examples include: rugby club, tennis club, karate club, and rock-climbing club. Many students dedicate more time to these activities than to the regular academic curriculum. The focus of these clubs is more often developing friendships, rather than pure competition.

23. During conversation, the *i* of *imasu* in *te* + *iru* form verbs is often deleted. Thus, *yatte imashita ka* becomes *yattemashita ka.*

24. *Naruhodo* is translated as "I see" or "indeed." However, it does not necessarily mean "I agree with you." The phrase is used only to signal to a conversation partner that his/her opinion is valued and respected. Hence this phrase is often misunderstood by non-Japanese people.

25. *Dame* (no good, bad) is one of the most common words in daily conversation. It is used to describe something that is unacceptable.

26. *Doozo yoroshiku* is usually translated into "please (handle it in a favorable way)." The phrase often adds emphasis to the previous request.

C. BUNPOO TO YOOHOO
(Grammar and Usage)

1. VERBS

Japanese verbs are classified into two types: regular verbs, which end in *eru* or *iru* in their dictionary forms, have one pattern of conjugation; and irregular verbs, which end in *u* (not preceded by *er* or *ir*) in their dictionary forms, have several different patterns of conjugation. In polite sentences (using *masu*), all regular and irregular verbs conjugate in exactly the same manner. Note that *suru* and *kuru* are exceptions.

Regular Verbs: stem (drop the *ru*) + *masu*
Irregular Verbs: change the *u* to *i* + *masu*

DICTIONARY FORM *	NON-PAST AFFIRMATIVE	NON-PAST NEGATIVE	PAST AFFIRMATIVE	PAST NEGATIVE
taberu (to eat)	*tabemasu*	*tabemasen*	*tabemashita*	*tabemasen deshita*
iku (to go)	*ikimasu*	*ikimasen*	*ikimashita*	*ikimasen deshita*
tsukareru (to get tired)	*tsukaremasu*	*tsukaremasen*	*tsukaremashita*	*tsukaremasen deshita*
hajimeru (to begin)	*hajimemasu*	*hajimemasen*	*hajimemashita*	*hajimemasen deshita*
yaru (to do)	*yarimasu*	*yarimasen*	*yarimashita*	*yarimasen deshita*
suru (to do)	*shimasu*	*shimasen*	*shimashita*	*shimasen deshita*
kuru (to come)	*kimasu*	*kimasen*	*kimashita*	*kimasen deshita*

Ashita atarashii shigoto o hajimemasu.
   I will start a new job tomorrow.

Ashita atarashii shigoto o hajimemasen.
   I will not start a new job tomorrow.

Kinoo atarashii shigoto o hajimemashita.
   I started a new job yesterday.

Kinoo atarashii shigoto o hajimemasen deshita.
   I did not start a new job yesterday.

   Please note that "non-past" verbs may refer to either a future action or a habitual action in the present.

Ashita mo kaisha ni ikimasu. (future)
   I will go to work tomorrow, too.

Mainichi ku ji ni kaisha ni ikimasu. (present)
   I go to work at nine o'clock every day.

---

  * The "dictionary form" of verbs is what you will find in a Japanese dictionary. It is similar to the English infinitive.

2. *TE*-FORM OF VERBS

All Japanese verbs may be conjugated in the *te*-form. The *te*-form may be used in combination with the verb *iru* (to be) to express the progress of an action (present progressive tense), similar to the verb + -ing pattern in English.

Tabete imasu.
Someone is eating.

The same pattern can be used to express a state of being.

Okotte imasu.
Someone is angry.

All regular conjugation verbs (those ending with *-eru* or *-iru*) drop the final *ru* and add *te* to the verb stem.

DICTIONARY FORM	STEM	*TE*-FORM
taberu (to eat)	*tabe*	*tabete*
neru (to sleep)	*ne*	*nete*
okiru (to get up)	*oki*	*okite*

With irregular conjugation verbs (*u* verbs) the formation of the *te*-form depends on the ending of the verb.

(a) Verbs ending in *-mu, -bu,* and *-nu* add *nde* to the verb base. Note that "base" is different from "stem." While the stem could also be called the pre-*masu* form, bases vary depending on the verb and just have to be memorized.

DICTIONARY FORM	BASE	*TE*-FORM
yomu (to read)	*yo*	*yonde*
yobu (to call)	*yo*	*yonde*
shinu (to die)	*shi*	*shinde*

(b) Verbs ending in *-u, -tsu,* and *-ru* add *tte* to the verb base.

DICTIONARY FORM	BASE	*TE*-FORM
iu (to say)	*i*	*itte*
matsu (to wait)	*ma*	*matte*
kawaru (to change)	*kawa*	*kawatte*

(c) Verbs ending in *-ku* or *-gu* add *ite* or *ide* to the verb base.

DICTIONARY FORM	BASE	*TE*-FORM
kiku (to listen)	*ki*	*kiite*
oyogu (to swim)	*oyo*	*oyoide*

(d) Verbs ending in *-su* add *shite* to the verb base.

DICTIONARY FORM	BASE	*TE*-FORM
hanasu (to speak)	*hana*	*hanashite*

There are three exceptions.

DICTIONARY FORM	*TE*-FORM
suru (to do)	*shite*
kuru (to come)	*kite*
iku (to go)	*itte*

Here are some examples of the *te*-form used to express the progress of an action.

Suzuki-san o matte imasu ka.
> Are you waiting for Mr. Suzuki?

Doru o en ni kaete imasu.
> I am changing dollars into yen.

Supiichi o yooi shite imasu ka.
> Are you preparing a speech?

Arubaito o shite imasu.
> I am working part-time.

The following are examples of the *te*-form used to show a state of being.

Kuruma de kite imasu.
> I came by car (and the car is still with me).

Hirugohan o moo tabete imasu yo.
> I've already eaten lunch.

Takagi-buchoo o oboete imasu ka.
> Do you remember the department manager, Mr. Takagi?

3. MAKING REQUESTS AND OFFERS

There are several different ways to make a request in Japanese.

a. *Te kudasai*

The *te*-form of a verb plus *kudasai* can be used to make a request in semiformal situations.

Dekiru kagiri ganbatte kudasai.
Please try as hard as you can.

Jimusho ni an'nai shite kudasai.
Please take me (lit. guide me) to the office.

Honbu kara tenkin shita bakari desu kara minasan ni shookai shite kudasai.
I just transferred from the head office, so please introduce me to everyone.

Satoo-san to kyooryoku shite kudasai.
Please work (lit. cooperate) with Ms. Sato.

b. *O* plus Verb plus *Kudasai*

The sentence pattern *o* + verb (stem) + *kudasai* expresses a formal request. It is more formal than the *te*-form + *kudasai*. This pattern cannot, however, be formed with monosyllabic verb stems, like those of *neru* (to sleep), *kuru* (to come), *suru* (to do), or *miru* (to see).

shiraseru (to inform)

> *Oshirase kudasai.*
> Please let me know.

hairu (to enter)

> *Neruson-san, jimusho ni ohairi kudasai.*
> Mr. Nelson, please come in my office.

kaku (to write)

> *Juusho to onamae o okaki kudasai.*
> Please write your address and name.

yoru (to stop by)

> *Zehi jimusho ni o yori kudasai.*
> By all means, please stop by my office.

Because the verbs in the first column cannot form the *o* verb (stem) *kudasai* sentence pattern, use the special verbs in the second column to make a formal request.

neru	*Oyasumi kudasai.*	Good night.
kuru	*Oide kudasai/irasshatte kudasai.*	Please come.
taberu, nomu	*Meshiagatte kudasai.*	Please eat or drink.
suru	*Nasatte kudasai.*	Please do (something).
miru	*Goran kudasai.*	Please look.

c. *O* plus verb plus *suru*

The pattern *o* + verb (stem) + *suru* is one way to make a humble offer.

Takagi-buchoo, sugu oshirase shimasu.
I will let you know immediately, Mr. Takagi.

Kuukoo de omachi shimasu kara.
I will wait for you at the airport.

Watakushi ga tegami o okaki shimasu.
I will write the letter for you.

Note: To make the sentences above more polite, replace *shimasu* with *itashimasu.*

4. CAUSE-AND-EFFECT RELATIONSHIPS

To express a cause-and-effect relationship between two events, use the pattern "Sentence 1 *to*, Sentence 2" (Whenever S1 happens, S2 happens). This pattern is somewhat similar to an English conditional clause ("if" clause). However, in Japanese, whenever S1 happens, S2 always happens, whereas in English this is not necessarily the case. The *to* here can be translated as "whenever," "when," or "if," depending on the context.

Kaze o hiku to, shigoto ga dekimasen.
Whenever I catch cold, I can't work.

Kono michi o massugu iku to, Bijitekku ga miemasu.
If you go straight on this street, you will (lit. can) see BusiTech.

Nihon wa juunigatsu ni naru to, samuku narimasu.
When December comes (lit. When it becomes December), it gets cold in Japan.

Suzuki-san to hanashi o shinai to kono tegami o kaku koto ga dekimasen.
If I don't talk to Mr. Suzuki, then I can't write this letter.

5. *KAMOSHIRENAI* ("MAY" OR "MIGHT")

The phrase *kamoshirenai* is used at the end of a sentence to express either a sense of probability or of doubt in the preceding statement (clause). It is used in the following ways:

verb	(plain form) + *kamoshirenai*
i-adjective	(plain form) + *kamoshirenai*
na-adjective/noun	(plain form, except *da,* which is deleted) + *kamoshirenai*

Zeikan wa konde iru kamoshirenai. (informal sentence)
Customs may be crowded.

Ano hoteru wa takai kamoshiremasen.
That hotel might be expensive.

Ashita wa ame kamoshiremasen ne.
It may rain tomorrow, don't you think?

Kono shashin no hoo ga kirei kamoshiremasen.
(I believe) this picture may be prettier.

Yamada san wa ikanai kamoshirenai.
Mr. Yamada might not go.

D. BIJINESU JIKOO
(Business Matters)

KONE O TSUKURU (MAKING THE CONNECTION)

Generally, it is preferable to know someone in Japan or to be introduced to someone there before visiting. The Japanese distinguish acutely between people who are part of their "in-group" and those who are not. Being part of a particular group or having some sort of connection or contact before you actually go to Japan is therefore to your advantage.

Connections can be made through any governmental office, cultural program, or related organization. However, this is not the most effective—nor the simplest—way. It is easier and more desirable to go through friends and acquaintances to make connections.

In Japan many occasions will require that you introduce yourself or that you be introduced by others in meetings, at parties, and other social gatherings. This is largely due to the fact that the Japanese place great importance on knowing where others are from, what they do for a living, and other such background information. This information influences the kind of language (formal, semiformal, or informal) that will be used. When introducing yourself, you should include where you were born, which college you graduated from, what kinds of interests or hobbies you have, and perhaps a little about your family. Since most Japanese are not familiar with Western-style humor, you should avoid telling complicated jokes, though simple ones will create a friendly atmosphere. Do not forget to show due respect to older people, since age is an important component of status in Japan.

BIJINESU KANKEI (BUSINESS RELATIONSHIPS)

Before you start conducting business in Japan, you would do well to learn the importance of establishing a good "human relationship" *(ningen kankei)* with your Japanese colleagues, especially since this relationship will be the basis for future business ventures. Often, the Japanese will not begin discussing business for days after an initial meeting. Business discussion will start only when they feel comfortable with you as a person and as a potential business partner. This preliminary process may begin by conversations about families, friends, educational backgrounds, hometowns, and any other subject not related to the business at hand. In order to establish mutual understanding, you may be invited to go out for a drink, to play golf, or to participate in some other activity that both you and your colleagues can enjoy together. Many foreigners doing business in Japan do not allow ample time for this preliminary phase and become impatient.

Of course, today's Japanese businesspeople are busier and less concerned with strict adherence to social rituals, but you will still have to spend more time socializing than is common in the United States. Once this relationship is established, business transactions will be much easier to facilitate and, on many occasions, may be considered virtually completed with little real business negotiation.

MEISHI (BUSINESS CARDS)

Business cards are essential in Japan, and you should carry yours with you every day. Everyone in Japan—from the banker to the semi-retired farmer—has a business card ready to give out. They are exchanged when two people meet for the first time in a business context. The person of lower status usually presents his/her card first. The cards contain information considered vital for business: name, address(es), telephone number(s), e-mail address, and most important, the company's name and the person's position or title.

The Japanese appreciate when foreigners present business cards written in both Japanese and English.

RENSHUU MONDAI (EXERCISES)

A. *Tsugi no shitsumon ni kotaenasai.* (Answer the following questions.)

   1. *Neruson-shi wa ima doko ni imasu ka.*
   2. *Kaisha no biru no mae de dare ni aimashita ka.*
   3. *Neruson-shi wa itsu Nihon ni kimashita ka.*
   4. *Iida-san wa shigoto no keiken ga arimasu ka.*

B. *Tekitoo na joshi o irenasai.* (Insert the appropriate particle[s].)

   1. *Watashi mo soko ( ) ikimasu.*
   2. *Denwa ( ) nankai ( ) hanashimashita ne.*
   3. *Honsha ( ) tenkin ( ) Neruson-san desu.*
   4. *Daigaku ( ) nani ( ) kurabu katsudoo ( ) yarimashita ka.*

KOTAE (ANSWERS)

A. 1. *Bijitekku no shisha ni imasu.* 2. *Satoo-san ni aimashita.*
3. *Senshuu no kinyoobi ni kimashita.* 4. *Hai, arubaito o shita koto ga arimasu.*
B. 1. *e* 2. *de, ka* 3. *kara, no* 4. *de, ka, demo*

DAI SANKA
Lesson 3

A. KAIWA (Dialogue)

JUUTAKU JIJOO

Hoteru ni isshuukan taizai shite Neruson-shi, manshon o kariru koto ni suru.
Mazu Suzuki-shi ni soodan suru.

NERUSON: Sassoku apaato o sagashitai n desu ga. Ii tokoro ga
arimasu ka.

SUZUKI: Soo desu ne. Apaato o kariru nara, jimusho kara amari
tooku naku, densha ya chikatetsu no eki kara chikai tokoro o
sagashita hoo ga ii desu ne.

NERUSON: Kaisha kara densha ka chikatetsu de sanjuppun gurai
no tokoro niwa arimasen ka.

SUSUKI: Muri deshoo ne. Don'na apaato o sagashite iru n desu ka.

NERUSON: Yachin ni yorimasu ga,[1] 3LDK[2] ga hoshii desu ne.
Demo Tookyoo wa sugoku takai rashii desu ne.

SUZUKI: Ee, futsuu no wa tsuki juugoman en[3] gurai desu. Chotto ii
apaato wa "manshon"[4] to iu n desu ga, chotto takai no wa
hyakuman en mo shimasu.

NERUSON: Hyakuman en desu ka. Ichiman doru desu ne.
Watakushi wa son'na no wa irimasen. Futsuu de ii desu ga,
tsuukin ni benri na tokoro ga ii desu ne.

SUZUKI: Wakarimashita. Shiriai no fudoosan'ya[5] ni ikutsu ka
shirabete moraimashoo.

NERUSON: Doomo. Sore wa tasukarimasu.[6]

Tsugi no hi, fudoosan'ya yori Neruson-shi ni denwa ga aru.

YOSHIDA: Shinagawa-fudoosan no Yoshida desu. Suzuki-sama
kara odenwa suru yoo ni iwaremashita.[7] Manshon o osagashi
no yoo de.[8]

NERUSON: Hai.

YOSHIDA: Sore de Tookyoo no dono hen ga yoroshii deshoo ka.

NERUSON: Kaisha kara sanjuppun kara ichijikan gurai no tokoro
de, juugoman en kara nijuuman en gurai no o kangaete imasu.

YOSHIDA: Dono gurai no saizu o.

NERUSON: 3LDK ga hoshii n desu ga, 2LDK demo ii desu.

YOSHIDA: Juutaku jijoo wa daibu yoku natte imasu kara, sagaseru deshoo.

NERUSON: Sore wa arigatai desu ne.[9] Semakute mo atarashii no ga ii desu ne. Atarashii 2LDK nara, furui 3LDK yori ii desu.

YOSHIDA: Wakarimashita. Ikutsu ka atatte[10] mimasu. Ashita ni demo tekitoo na no o fakkusu shimasu kara.

NERUSON: Yoroshiku onegai shimasu.

Tsugi no hi, manshon no risuto o uketori, futabukken[11] o mi ni iku.

NERUSON: Kore wa sakki[12] mita no yori yasui desu ne.

YOSHIDA: Ee, kore wa juurokuman gosen en desu. Toshin[13] kara chotto tooi desu kara, yasuku naru wake desu.[14]

NERUSON: Chikaku no eki made nanpun desu ka.

YOSHIDA: Aruite gofun desu. Sorekara Tookyoo-eki made wa san-juppun shika kakaranai soo desu. Warukunai to omoimasu.

NERUSON: Soo desu ne. Tashika ni akarui shi. Sore ni oshare desu ne. Chikaku ni resutoran ya mise mo atte, totemo ii basho desu ne. Nan nen mono desu ka.

YOSHIDA: Hakkiri wakarimasen ga, ninen inai da to omoimasu. Hakkiri shita koto o shirabemashoo ka.

NERUSON: Iie, ii desu.

Neruson-shi ga hotondo kimeyoo to shita toki, totsuzen heya ga ugokidashita.

NERUSON: Waa, jishin desu ka.

YOSHIDA: Iie. Densha deshoo.

NERUSON: Densha desu ka. Senro kara chikai n desu ka.

YOSHIDA: Sono yoo desu ne.

Shindoo ga tomaru.

YOSHIDA: Densha no oto ga ketten desu ne. Dame desu ne.

NERUSON: Iie. Soo to wa iemasen. Yanushi-san ni motto yasuku naranai ka kooshoo shite moraemasu ka.

YOSHIDA: Hai, yatte mimashoo.

NERUSON: **Shikikin sankagetsu, reikin ikkagetsu, yachin** [15] **ga juuy-onman en nara, kariru kamo shiremasen.**

YOSHIDA: **Hontoo desu ka.**

NERUSON: **Hontoo ni nani ka jibun no uchi no yoo na ki ga shite kimashita.**

HOUSING IN JAPAN (LIT. HOUSING SITUATION)

After staying one week in the hotel, Mr. Nelson decides to rent an apartment. First, he discusses it with Mr. Suzuki.

NELSON: I want to look for an apartment right away. Are there any good places (that you can recommend)?

SUZUKI: Let me see. If you're going to rent an apartment, you should look for one that's not too far away from the office, and is close to a train or subway station.

NELSON: Aren't there any about thirty minutes (away) from the company by train or subway?

SUZUKI: I'm afraid not. What kind of apartment are you looking for?

NELSON: It depends on the rent, but I would like a 3LDK. But it seems that Tokyo is really expensive, isn't it?

SUZUKI: Yes, it is. The average (rent for a 3LDK) is about 150,000 yen per month. The better (lit. slightly good) ones are called "mansions," and cost up to (lit. the slightly expensive ones are) one million yen.

NELSON: One million yen! That's (about) ten thousand dollars! I don't think I'll need one like that. An average apartment is fine. I would like a place that is convenient for commuting.

SUZUKI: I understand. I'll have an acquaintance of mine who is a realtor check (things out) for you.

NELSON: Thanks. That will be helpful.

The next day, Mr. Nelson gets a call from the realtor.

YOSHIDA: This is Mr. Yoshida of Shinagawa Realty. I was asked (lit. told) by Mr. Suzuki to give you a call. I understand you are looking for an apartment.

NELSON: Yes.

YOSHIDA: What area of Tokyo is good (for you)?

NELSON: I'm thinking of a place that is between thirty minutes and an hour from my office, and (priced) somewhere around 150,000 to 200,000 yen.

YOSHIDA: About what size (were you thinking)?

NELSON: I want a 3LDK, but a 2LDK is fine, too.

YOSHIDA: Since the housing situation has improved (lit. is improving quite a bit), I can probably find one.

NELSON: I'd appreciate that (very much). Even if it's small (lit. narrow), I would prefer a new one. If it's a new 2LDK, that's better than an old 3LDK.

YOSHIDA: I understand. I'll try to contact (some places). I'll fax you (a list) of possible (lit. appropriate) apartments tomorrow.

NELSON: Thank you.

The next day, Mr. Nelson receives the list of apartments, and goes to look at two of them.

NELSON: This apartment is cheaper than the one we just saw, right?

YOSHIDA: Yes, it is. This one is 165,000 yen. Since it's a bit far from downtown Tokyo, it is (lit. becomes) cheaper.

NELSON: How far (lit. how many minutes) is it to the nearest train station?

YOSHIDA: It's a five-minute walk. Apparently, (the ride) to Tokyo station takes only about thirty minutes. I don't think it's bad (at all).

NELSON: No, it's not. It's certainly very bright. Also stylish. There are restaurants and stores close by, too. It's a really nice place. How old is it?

YOSHIDA: I'm not exactly sure, but I think it's under (lit. within) two years old. Should I find out exactly (what year it was built)?

NELSON: No, that's quite all right.

Mr. Nelson is trying to decide, when suddenly the room begins to move.

NELSON: Oh my gosh, is it an earthquake?

YOSHIDA: No. Probably a train.

NELSON: A train? Are we close to the railroad tracks?

YOSHIDA: Apparently so.

The shaking finally stops.

YOSHIDA: Well, the sound of the train is (quite) a drawback. It's (the apartment) no good, is it?

NELSON: No, I can't say that. Can I get you to negotiate with the landlord about lowering the rent?

YOSHIDA: Yes, I'll try.

NELSON: If (you can get them down to) three months' security deposit, one month's key (lit. courtesy) money, and a (monthly) rent of 140,000 yen, I may take (lit. rent) it.

YOSHIDA: Are you sure?

NELSON: I'm somehow really beginning to feel at home here (lit. that it's my own home).

B. CHUU (Notes)

1. *Yachin ni yorimasu* means "It depends on the rent." The expression (noun) *ni yoru* means "It depends on (noun)."

2. The abbreviations 2LDK and 3LDK indicate a "two-bedroom unit with a combined living/dining/kitchen area" and a "three-bedroom unit with a combined living/dining/kitchen area," respectively.

3. *Juugoman en* means "one hundred fifty thousand yen." The Japanese count in units of 10,000 *(man)*. Thus 20,000 is 2 *man;* 300,000, 30 *man;* and so on. Incidentally, *en* is now used in Japan instead of *"yen,"* which is an archaic term.

4. Apartment buildings with more than two floors and modern features are called *manshon,* whereas buildings with one or two floors are called *apaato. Apaato* are usually older and have fewer units.

5. When you rent an apartment, it is best to rely on a *fudoosan'ya* (realtor). They are usually located near train stations and have comprehensive information on available housing near their places of business. When looking for an apartment, therefore, choose the general area you would like to live in and then ask the realtors to help find a place in that area.

6. *Sore wa tasukarimasu* literally means "That will be a great help." It is used to acknowledge the help that someone has offered to give.

7. *Odenwa suru yoo ni iwaremashita* means "I was told to call you." *Iwaremashita* is the passive form of *iu* (to say). The passive form will be explained in Lesson 8.

8. *Osagashi no yoo de* means "I hear you're looking for (an apartment), but . . ." The sentence is not completed because the speaker expects the listener to fill in the rest of the sentence for himself. In this case, it also prompts the listener to reply with information regarding why he is looking for an apartment.

9. *Arigatai* means "thankful." *Arigatoo gozaimasu* (thank you) has its origins in this word.

10. *Ataru* means "to contact" here, but its literal meaning is "to hit."

11. *Futabukken* means "two houses." *Bukken* (thing, physical object) is often used when referring to houses or apartments.

12. *Sakki* means "a short time ago." The context determines whether the expression refers to a very short length of time or to a longer one (up to an hour).

13. *Toshin* (lit. heart of the capital) refers to the center of Tokyo's metropolitan area. This area is the business center located near Tokyo Station.

14. The distance from a train station greatly determines the price of apartments. Distances that require fifteen minutes or less from train stations on foot are considered good locations.

15. *Yachin* (rent), *shikikin* (deposit), and *reikin* ("key" money) are three important words to remember when renting a house or an apartment in Japan. *Shikikin* and *reikin* are paid only once, when you first rent an apartment or house. *Yachin* is paid on a monthly basis. Depending on the owner, you may have to pay up to six months' rent when you first move in. Recently, "weekly mansions" have become popular. They are expensive, but do not require a deposit or key money.

C. BUNPOO TO YOOHOO
(Grammar and Usage)

1. FORMAL AND INFORMAL SENTENCES

There are two "levels" of speech formality in Japanese. The first is determined by the speaker's relationship with the listener, and the second by the speaker's relationship with the subject of the sentence. (This second level of speech formality will be explained in a later lesson.)

The level of formality is indicated mainly by sentence endings such as *desu* and *masu* for formal speech, and *da* and the plain form of verbs (see Lesson 4) for informal speech.

The following sentences are examples of formal speech. They would be directed to a person of the same or higher status, or to someone the speaker does not know well. Note the formal endings of the sample sentences: *Tanaka desu* (noun *desu*), *tooi desu* (*i*-adjective *desu*), *kirei desu* (*na*-adjective *desu*), and *ikimasu* (verb).

Watakushi ga kachoo no Tanaka desu.
I am Mr. Tanaka, the section manager.

Apaato wa kaisha kara tooi desu.
My apartment is far away from the company.

Kono manshon wa hontoo ni kirei desu.
This apartment is really pretty.

Watakushi wa mainichi kaisha ni ikimasu.
I go to work (lit. the company) every day.

The previous sentences can also be expressed in an informal way. In this case, they would be directed to a person of the same or lower status, or to someone close to the speaker. Note the informal endings of the sentences.

Watakushi ga kachoo no Tanaka da.
I am the section manager, Mr. Tanaka.

Apaato wa kaisha kara tooi. (*I*-adjectives do not require *da*. See Lesson 1.)
My apartment is far away from the company.

Kono manshon wa hontoo ni kirei da.
This apartment is really pretty.

Watakushi wa mainichi kaisha ni iku.
I go to work every day.

2. CONJECTURAL FORM OF THE COPULA *(DESHOO)*

The copula *desu* has a conjectural form, *deshoo,* which is used by the speaker to indicate that he or she is making an assumption, rather than stating a fact. The pattern is as follows:

> verbs (plain form) and *i*-adjectives (plain form) + *deshoo*
> *na*-adjectives and nouns + *deshoo (deshoo* replaces *desu)*

Semai apaato yori hiroi hoo ga ii deshoo.
 A large (lit. wide) apartment is probably better than a small one.

Densha de ichijikan gurai deshoo.
 It will probably (take) one hour.

Tookyoo no apaato wa sekai de ichiban takai deshoo.
 Apartments in Tokyo are probably the most expensive in the world.

Yachin ya shikikin ya reikin ga rokkagetsu bun gurai iru deshoo.
 You will probably need about six months' rent (to cover the first month's rent), the security deposit, and the key money.

3. EXPRESSING HEARSAY AND ASSUMPTIONS

a. *soo desu* (I hear that, I understand that)

The expression *soo desu (soo da)* is used when the speaker is repeating something he or she has heard. It is used in both formal and informal situations, and may follow the plain form of verbs, adjectives, or copulas.

Kyooto wa totemo tanoshii tokoro da soo desu.
 I understand that Kyoto is a really fun place.

Tookyoo no apaato ga Nihon de ichiban takai soo desu.
 I hear that the apartments in Tokyo are the most expensive in Japan.

Nihon dewa apaato no basho to kaisha made no tsuukinjikan ga taisetsu da soo desu.
 I understand that the location of an apartment and commute time to work are important in Japan.

Densha ya chikatetsu no eki wa doko ni demo aru soo desu.
 I hear that there are train and subway stations (almost) everywhere.

b. *rashii (desu)* (It seems that, I understand that)

The expression *rashii (desu)* is used when the speaker wishes to express his or her opinion, impression, or judgment as an objective fact. It is formed as follows:

> plain form of an *i*-adjective or verb + *rashii (desu)*
> *na*-adjective + *rashii (desu)* (Note, however, that the copula is
> deleted after the *na*-adjective.)

Note that *rashii* is followed by *desu* in formal sentences only, and can stand alone in informal speech, similar to *i*-adjectives.

Saikin Amerikajin mo Nihonshoku o taberu rashii desu ne.
I understand that recently Americans have been eating Japanese food also.

Nihon no hoteru wa sugoku takai rashii desu ne.
It seems that Japanese hotels are very expensive.

Kono kinjoo wa shizuka rashii.
I understand that this neighborhood is quiet.

c. *yoo desu* (It seems, I think)

The expression *yoo desu* is used when the speaker expresses subjective opinions, impressions, or judgments. It is often limited to formal conversation and writing. It is formed as follows:

> plain form of an *i*-adjective or verb + *yoo desu (da)*
> noun + copula (affirmative non-past copula is replaced by *no*)
> + *yoo desu (da)*
> *na*-adjective + copula (affirmative non-past copula is replaced
> by *na*) + *yoo desu (da)*

Ano kata wa Nihonjin no yoo desu ne.
He seems Japanese.

Kono resutoran wa yuumei na yoo desu yo.
I think that this restaurant is famous.

Konban mo ame ga furu yoo desu.
It seems like it is going to rain tonight as well.

Nihon dewa unten ga muzukashii yoo desu.
I think that it is difficult to drive in Japan.

Amerika demo apaato ga takai yoo desu ga.
   I understand that apartments in America are also expensive.

d. *mitai desu* (It seems, I think)

The expression *mitai desu* is identical in meaning to *yoo desu,* but it is generally used in more informal situations. Note, however, that it is formed differently and that *mitai* can stand alone at the end of an informal sentence.

> plain form of an *i*-adjective or verb + *mitai desu (da)*
> noun + copula (affirmative non-past copula is deleted)
>   + *mitai desu (da)*
> *na*-adjective + copula (affirmative non-past copula is deleted)
>   + *mitai desu (da)*

Kono apaato wa takai mitai desu.
   This apartment seems expensive.

Basukettobooru o yaru mitai da.
   I think (they) are going to play basketball.

Suzuki-san wa genki mitai.
   Mr. Suzuki looks happy.

Amerikanjin mitai desu.
   (He) seems American.

4. RELATIVE CLAUSES

In Japanese, a relative clause is one that modifies the noun it precedes. Conversely, English relative clauses follow the noun they are referring to. Pronouns such as "who," "which," "where," and "that" are used to introduce clauses that modify nouns, but no such words are used in Japanese. In the sentence "The house that my sister bought" the relative clause is "that my sister bought," which modifies "the house." In Japanese, the word order would be more like "my sister bought house," with the relative clause preceding the noun. Note that in relative clauses the plain form of the verb is used and subjects take *ga* instead of *wa.*

   The nouns being modified in the examples below are *apaato, resutoran, kippu,* and *hoteru:*

Kinoo mita apaato wa ookikatta. (Kinoo mita modifies *apaato.)*
   The apartment I looked at yesterday was big.

Watakushi ga yoku iku resutoran wa totemo konde imasu.
(*Watakushi ga yoku iku* modifies *resutoran*.)
    The restaurant I go to often is very crowded.

Kore wa Nihon de katta kippu desu.
    This is a (train) ticket I bought in Japan.

Koko wa Neruson-san ga yoku tomaru hoteru da soo desu.
    I hear this is the hotel where Mr. Nelson often stays.

5. RECEIVING A FAVOR (*ITADAKU*)

The word *itadaku* (to receive) is used when someone receives something from someone of higher status. The person doing the "giving" is designated by *ni* or *kara*.

Watakushi wa sensei ni kanji no hon o itadakimashita.
    I received a kanji book from the teacher.

Imooto wa haha no shiriai ni omocha o itadakimashita.
    My sister received a toy from my mother's friend.

Takagi-buchoo ni tasuke o itadakimashita.
    I received help from Department Manager Takagi.

The *te*-form of the verb plus *itadakimasu* (to receive the favor of someone doing something for you) is used when the speaker wants to express that someone of higher status has done something, or to ask a person of higher status to do something. This expression clearly demonstrates the differences in social status in Japan, and is used quite often in business.

Yuujin no otoosan ni shigoto o shookai shite itadakimashita.
    My friend's father introduced me to a job.

Takagi-buchoo ni apaato o sagashite itadakimashita.
    I had Department Manager Takagi look for an apartment (for me).

Nanika chuumon shite itadakemasu ka.
    Could you order something (for me)?

Juppun hodo matte itadakemasu ka.
    Could you wait for ten minutes or so?

Sumimasen ga, kite itadakemasu ka.
    I am sorry, but could you come over?

Please note that the last three sentences use the "potential form" of *itadaku (itadakeru)*, which is most commonly used in interrogative sentences.

6. OBLIGATION OR COMMITMENT

The pattern verb (pre-*nai*) + *nakereba naranai* means that you "must do" something because of an obligation or commitment. It generally has a stronger meaning than the English word "must." To form the pre-*nai* form of a verb:

Regular verbs drop the final *ru*. (This is also known as the stem.) For example: *taberu* becomes *tabe* (stem).

Irregular verbs drop the final *u* and add *a*. For example: *iku* becomes *ika*.

Exceptions: *suru* becomes *shi* and *kuru* becomes *ki*.

Ashita wa kuukoo ni ikanakereba narimasen.
I have to go to the airport tomorrow.

Kurasu no tame ni kono hon mo kawanakereba narimasen.
I have to buy this book for the class, too.

Apaato o sagasanakereba naranai. (informal)
I must look for an apartment.

Shiken no junbi no tame motto benkyoo shinakereba naranai. (informal)
I have to study more to prepare for the exam.

Suzuki-san no paati da kara, konakereba naranai.
It's Mr. Suzuki's party, so he has to come.

7. *TE-MIRU* (TRY TO)

The *te*-form of the verb plus *miru* means "try to do," or, more literally, "to do and see how it is."

Fudoosan'ya ni kiite mimasen ka.
Why don't you ask the realtor (and see how he responds)?

Fudoosan'ya ga iroiro atatte mite kureru soo desu.
I understand that the realtor will check various (apartments to see if there are any).

Yachin wa ikura ka o tashikamete mimasu.
I will try to verify how much the rent is.

8. COMPARISONS *(YORI)*

Comparisons can be made using the pattern:

> noun 1 *wa* noun 2 *yori* + adjective (either *i*- or *na*-adjective)
> + *desu (da)*.

52

Using this pattern, noun 1 is more "adjective" than noun 2.

Kono manshon wa ano apaato yori yasui shi akarui desu.
This apartment is cheaper and brighter than the other one.

Toshin wa koogai yori urusai. (informal)
Downtown is (much) noisier than the suburbs.

Narita-kuukoo wa hoka no kuukoo yori benri deshoo.
Narita Airport is probably more convenient than other airports.

9. WAKE (DA)

The word *wake* (lit. reason, meaning) is used to add emphasis. Consider the following patterns:

> plain form of verbs, *i*-adjectives plus *wake (da)*
> *na*-adjectives + copula (affirmative non-past copula becomes *na*)
> plus *wake (da)*

Note that *wake* is usually followed by the copula.

Toshin kara chotto tooi kara, yasuku naru wake desu.
Because (the apartment) is a little far from downtown, it's (lit. becomes) cheaper.

Mondai ga yoku wakaranakatta node, Suzuki-san ni kiita wake desu.
Because I didn't really understand the problem, I asked Mr. Suzuki.

Jibun dewa sagasenai kara, fudoosan'ya ni tanomu wake da.
Since we cannot find (the apartment) by ourselves, we must ask a realtor.

10. "TO GO (COME) TO DO SOMETHING"

The stem form of a verb plus *ni iku* means "to go somewhere to do something." The same pattern ending in *kuru* (to come) means "to come from somewhere to do something."

Denwa shite apaato o mi ni ikimashoo.
Let's call, then go see the apartment.

Fudoosan'ya e apaato o shirabe ni ikimashita.
I went to the real estate agent to look for an apartment.

Manshon o mi ni kimashita.
I came to see the apartment.

11. "NOTHING BUT"

The word *shika,* followed by a verb with a negative ending, means "nothing but" or "only." It is used to emphasize the preceding word and is similar to *dake.* One can even combine the two (*dakeshika* + verb with negative ending) to add more emphasis.

Tookyoo made sanjuppun shika kakarimasen.
It takes only thirty minutes to get to Tokyo.

Manshon no koto wa fudoosan'ya dakeshika wakarimasen.
Only real estate agents will know about apartments.

Apaato wa fakkusu de shika shiraberaremasen.
You can only search for apartments by (sending) faxes.

D. BIJINESU JIKOO
(Business Matters)

JUUTAKU JIJOO (HOUSING IN JAPAN)

Houses in Japan's principal metropolitan areas are often expensive, small, and far from the center of the city. In cities like Tokyo and Osaka, the cost of single-family houses are extremely high, so many Japanese tend to buy *manshon* (condominiums) or opt for the "extended family" situation (two or more generations living in one house), which is considerably more affordable.

The concept of family is changing in Japan. It used to consist of three generations living under the same roof. Home and family were synonymous, and a family would live in the same location for generations. In modern metropolitan life, however, more and more young people establish their lives away from their families, and are less bound by loyalty to their places of residence. If a better place to live can be found, they will move. Since more and more people are moving to metropolitan areas, finding housing near the city center has become increasingly difficult. Therefore, many people commute from forty-five minutes to as long as an hour and a half by train.

In most metropolitan areas, non-Japanese businesspeople can find apartments within an hour of work at a "reasonable" price. However, if you want an American-style apartment (i.e., larger, with bedrooms), you may have to pay quite a bit more. Non-Japanese renters are usually required to have a cosigner, who must be a Japanese citizen. The cosigner must demonstrate an ability to pay the rent for the renter. Some landlords may not rent apartments to non-Japanese people at all because they may feel uncomfortable communicating with foreigners due to language problems and/or cultural differences. Of course, this is illegal.

Rent is usually paid by automatic bank draft. When you sign a lease, you will give the landlord your bank account number, and the bank will transfer the rent to the landlord's account every month.

RENSHUU MONDAI (EXERCISES)

A. *Tsugi no shitsumon ni kotaenasai.* (Answer the following questions.)

1. *Manshon o sagasu toki, nani o kangaenakereba narimasen ka.*
2. *Neruson-san wa don'na manshon ga hoshii desu ka.*
3. *Saikin juutaku jijoo wa yoku natte imasu ka.*
4. *Toshin kara tooku naru to, yachin ga takaku narimasu ka, yasuku narimasu ka.*

B. *Tekitoo na kotoba o irenasai.* (Insert the appropriate word[s].)

1. *Hoteru wa fuben* _____.
2. *Atarashii manshon* _____ *sagashite imasu.*
3. *Donna manshon ga* _____ *ka.*
4. *Juutaku-jijoo wa yoku natte iru* _____ *ne.*
5. *Kinoo mita no* _____ *yasui desu.*

C. *Tekitoo na joshi o irenasai.* (Insert the appropriate particle[s].)

1. *Ookisa wa 2LDK* _____ *3LDK* _____ *hoshii desu.*
2. *Fudoosan'ya* _____ *shirabete moraimashoo.*
3. *Fudoosan'ya* _____ *kiite mimashoo.*
4. *Manshon* _____ *mi* _____ *ikimashoo ka.*
5. *Ichijikan* _____ *kakaranai soo desu.*

KOTAE (ANSWERS)

A. 1. *Basho to tsuukin jikan o kangaenakereba narimasen.* 2. *3LDK no manshon ga hoshii desu.* 3. *Hai, yoku natte imasu.* 4. *Yasuku narimasu.*
B. 1. *deshoo* 2. *o* 3. *ii desu* 4. *soo desu* 5. *yori*
C. 1. *ka, ga* 2. *ni* or *de* 3. *ni* 4. *o, ni* 5. *shika*

DAI YONKA
Lesson 4

A. KAIWA (Dialogue)

Keisatsu ni Jinmon Sareru

Tookyoo ni kite mada ma mo nai node, Neruson-shi wa machigaete, futatsu mae no eki de densha o orita.

NERUSON: Koko wa Tsutsujigaoka ja nai n desu ka.[1]

EKIIN: Tsutsujigaoka wa tsugi no tsugi desu. Tsugi no densha wa juuichiji nijuugo fun desu.[2]

NERUSON: Sanjuppun-go desu ka. Ja, aruita hoo ga hayai desu ka.

EKIIN: Nijuppun gurai kakarimasu ga.

NERUSON: Massugu iku n desu ne.

EKIIN: Ee, massugu desu. Wakariyasui desu. Ima no jikan wa takushii[3] mo nakanaka kimasen shi.

NERUSON: Doomo. Aruite mimasu.

Juppun-go, Neruson-shi wa keisatsukan ni yobikakerareru.[4]

KEISATSUKAN: Moshi moshi, imagoro doko e iku n desu ka.

NERUSON: Tsutsujigaoka ni ikitai n desu ga, michi ni mayotta[5] rashii n desu.

KEISATSUKAN: Soko ni tomatte iru n desu ka.

NERUSON: Hai.

KEISATSUKAN: Ryokoosha desu ka.

NERUSON: Iie. Saikin Amerika kara hikkoshite kimashita.

KEISATSUKAN: Tsutsujigaoka made wa mada daibu arimasu yo. Gaikokujin toorokushoo[6] o motte imasu ka.

NERUSON: Nihon ni tsuita bakari de mada totte imasen ga.

KEISATSUKAN: Sore wa komarimashita ne. Nani ka mibun shoomeisho[7] no yoo na mono wa arimasen ka.

NERUSON: Aa, pasupooto[8] ga arimasu. Kore doozo.

KEISATSUKAN: Hai, Neruson-san desu ka. Washinton-shuu ni sunde ita n desu ne. Ima oshigoto wa.

NERUSON: Bijitekku-sha no Nihon-shisha ni tsutomete iru futsuu no sarariiman desu.

KEISATSUKAN: Kaisha no juusho wa.

NERUSON: Shin-Aoyama biru desu. Nani ka atta n desu ka.

KEISATSUKAN: Jitsu wa saikin wa doroboo toka nozoki nado no jiken ga arimashite.

NERUSON: Soo desu ka. Kono hen wa anzen da to kiite imasu ga.

KEISATSUKAN: Demo ki o tsukenai to ikemasen yo.

NERUSON: Wakarimashita. Doomo.

KEISATSUKAN: Moo osoi shi, abunai kara, okurimashoo. Doozo ushiro ni notte kudasai.

NERUSON: Soo desu ka. Sumimasen ne. Hontoo ni tasukarimasu.

KEISATSUKAN: Nihon ni itsu kita n desu ka.

NERUSON: Senshuu desu.

KEISATSUKAN: Demo Nihongo ga yoku dekimasu ne.

NERUSON: Gakusei-jidai ni Nara[9] ni ninen hodo[10] sunde imashita. Sono toki ni Nihongo o naraimashita.

KEISATSUKAN: Nara wa shizuka deshoo ga, Tookyoo wa urusai deshoo.

NERUSON: Ee. Demo Tookyoo wa ibento ga iroiro attari de,[11] tanoshii desu. Tokorode, kono hen ni wa tanoshii tokoro wa nai n desu ka.

KEISATSUKAN: Karaoke gurai[12] desu ne. Yahari[13] Shinjuku[14] deshoo. Asoko ni wa tanoshii mono ga nan demo arimasu yo.

NERUSON: Jaa kondo itte mimasu.

KEISATSUKAN: Demo, iroiro yuuwaku ga aru kara, ki o tsukete kudasai.

NERUSON: Hai. Aa, soko no kado desu. Doomo go shinsetsu ni arigatoo gozaimashita.

KEISATSUKAN: Iie. Hayai uchi ni gaikokujin toorokushoo o totte kudasai. Kuyakusho de sugu dekimasu kara.

BEING QUESTIONED BY A POLICEMAN

Still new (lit. no time has elapsed since he came) to Tokyo, Mr. Nelson makes a mistake and gets off the train two stops too early (lit. two stations before).

NELSON: This is Tsutsujigaoka (Station), isn't it?

STATION EMPLOYEE: Tsutsujigaoka is two stations away (lit. next after next). The next train (for Tsutsujigaoka) is at 11:25.

NELSON: Half an hour (lit. later) from now? In that case, would it be faster to walk?

STATION EMPLOYEE: It will take about twenty minutes.

NELSON: I just go straight, right?

STATION EMPLOYEE: Yes, straight ahead. It's easy to figure out. At this hour taxis don't come around much either.

NELSON: Thanks. I'll see if I can walk (there).

Ten minutes later, Mr. Nelson is summoned by a policeman.

POLICEMAN: Excuse me, where are you (trying to) go at this time?

NELSON: I want to go to Tsutsujigaoka, but it seems that I'm lost.

POLICEMAN: Is that where you're staying?

NELSON: Yes.

POLICEMAN: Are you a tourist?

NELSON: No, I moved here recently from the United States.

POLICEMAN: You (still) have quite a way (to go) to Tsutsujigaoka. Do you have your foreigner's registration card?

NELSON: I just arrived in Japan, so I haven't gotten mine yet.

POLICEMAN: That is a problem. Do you have any (other) form of identification (lit. showing social status)?

NELSON: Oh, yes. I have my passport. Here you go.

POLICEMAN: Thank you, Mr. Nelson, is it? You used to live in Washington state. What is your occupation now?

NELSON: I am a (lit. normal) businessman working in the Japanese branch office of BusiTech Corporation.

POLICEMAN: What's the address of the company?

NELSON: The Shin-Aoyama building. Is there something (wrong)?

POLICEMAN: Actually, there have been (some) incidences of robbery, Peeping Toms, and such (in this area) recently.

NELSON: Really? I heard that this area is safe.

POLICEMAN: But you still have to be careful.

NELSON: I understand. Thank you.

POLICEMAN: Since it's late and not safe, I'll give you a ride home (lit. I will send you). Please get in the back (seat of the car).

NELSON: Really? Thank you. This sure helps me out.

POLICEMAN: When did you come to Japan?

NELSON: Last week.

POLICEMAN: (That recently?) But your Japanese is really good (lit. can do Japanese well).

NELSON: When I was a student, I lived in Nara for about two years. That's when I learned Japanese.

POLICEMAN: Nara is pretty quiet, but Tokyo is noisy, isn't it?

NELSON: Yes, but Tokyo is a fun place because there are many events (and things) to enjoy. By the way, are there any fun places in this neighborhood?

POLICEMAN: There are some karaoke places (but that's about all). (If you want to go to a fun place), probably Shinjuku (is the place to go). There are all kinds of fun things there.

NELSON: Well, then I'll go there next time.

POLICEMAN: But there are (also) lots of temptations, so please be careful.

NELSON: Yes. Oh, that's the corner! Thank you for your kindness.

POLICEMAN: No, not at all. Please get your foreigner's registration card as soon as possible. You can get one quickly at the ward office.

B. CHUU (Notes)

1. Usually station names on trains and subways are announced in Japanese only. Even people who know all the stations along the train line well may still get off at the wrong stop. During the day, trains run often, so getting off too early or too late is simply a minor inconvenience. However, after eleven at night one may have to wait a long time for the next train.

2. Trains and subways usually run from early in the morning (around 5:30 A.M.) until late at night (around 12:30 A.M.). You should know what time the last train *(saishuu densha)* leaves in order to avoid expensive taxi rides home. If several different trains are involved in your trip, it is important to know the schedule of each of the lines, as Japanese trains are almost always on time.

3. Taxis in Japan are very clean and the drivers are generally very courteous. Be warned, however, that taxis are rather expensive. You can find taxis almost anywhere, except in rural areas. Since many drivers do not understand English, it's best to state your destination in Japanese or show him or her the address written on a piece of paper. There is one thing that bothers taxi drivers: touching the "automatic door" *(jidoo doa)*. All taxis are equipped with a lever that allows the driver to open and close the door automatically. Not only is it dangerous to try to open this door yourself, it also infringes upon the driver's responsibilities.

4. *Yobikakerareru* means "to be summoned." *Yobikakeru* is a compound that combines *yobu* (to call) and *kakeru* (to speak to). *Yobikakerareru* is the passive form.

5. *Michi ni mayou* means "to lose one's way." *Michi* alone can mean "road," "street," or "way" (of the *samurai,* for example), depending on the context.

6. Once foreigners receive a visa to stay in Japan, they are required to obtain a *Gaikokujin toorokushoo* (foreigner's registration card). Registration cards can be applied for at the nearest city hall *(shiyakusho)* or ward office *(kuyakusho)*. Foreigners are usually required to bring a passport and two passport-size photos. It usually takes several weeks before the registration card is ready, so it is advisable to carry a passport at all times.

7. A *Mibun shoomeisho* (identification document) can be a driver's license or any photo I.D.

8. *Pasupooto* is now the most commonly used word for passport in Japan. The official word, however, is *ryoken.*

9. Nara, located just to the southeast of Kyoto, was the ancient capital of Japan. Nara, like Kyoto, is an older, quieter, more tourist-oriented city than Tokyo. Many of the ancient wooden temples, buildings, and palaces are still standing. Tours of these structures are offered, with information in both English and Japanese.

10. The word *hodo* means "approximately" when referring to an amount of time, weight, height, etc.: *Nihongo o ninenkan hodo*

benkyoo shimashita. (I studied Japanese for about two years.) *Jikan o sanjuppun hodo kudasaimasen ka.* (Could you spare about thirty minutes for me?) *Sanshuukan hodo Amerika ni itte imashita.* (I was in the United State for three weeks or so.) *Ramen wa gohyaku en hodo shimasu.* (Ramen costs about 500 yen.)

11. *De* has many functions, including indicating location and expressing "by means of." It is used here to give a reason.

12. *Karaoke gurai* means "only karaoke." *Gurai* is usually used to mean "approximately," but it can also express "only," "at best," or "about as good as."

13. *Yahari* (or *yappari*) means "as expected" or "as you know," and could be said to be one of the Japanese people's favorite expressions.

14. Shinjuku is a well-known entertainment district in Tokyo, as well as home to several government offices and a thriving business community.

C. BUNPOO TO YOOHOO
(Grammar and Usage)

1. PLAIN FORMS OF VERBS (AFFIRMATIVE NON-PAST AND PAST)

We have already studied the polite forms of verbs, that is, forms that end with *-masu, -masen, -mashita,* and *-masen deshita.* Another set of verb forms is called the "plain form." The plain forms of verbs differ according to tense and whether they are affirmative or negative (see Lesson 6 for the negative). Plain forms are used in two different ways: (1) in informal sentences—when speaking with friends, family, or those of lower status; and (2) to build subordinate clauses in sentences. For example, consider *Keizai o senkoo shita soo desu ne.* (I hear you majored in economics.) In this sentence, *shita* (the plain past form of *shimasu*) ends the subordinate clause.

All regular verbs conjugate alike. To go from the polite form to the dictionary form, drop the *masu* ending and add *ru.* To form the past affirmative, drop the *ru* and add *ta.*

POLITE FORM	NON-PAST AFFIRMATIVE (DICTIONARY FORM)	PAST AFFIRMATIVE
tabemasu (to eat)	*taberu*	*tabeta*
mimasu (to watch)	*miru*	*mita*
imasu (to be)	*iru*	*ita*
hajimemasu (to start)	*hajimeru*	*hajimeta*
tsukaremasu (to get tired)	*tsukareru*	*tsukareta*
karimasu (to borrow)	*kariru*	*karita*
tsutomemasu (to work for)	*tsutomeru*	*tsutometa*

Irregular verbs conjugate differently, depending on the particular verb.
To form the non-past affirmative form (dictionary form) from polite forms, drop *i-masu* and add *u:*

yomimasu (to read)	*yomu*
kikimasu (to hear)	*kiku*
iimasu (to say)	*iu*
kaerimasu (to return)	*kaeru*

The past affirmative is formed exactly as the *te*-form of verbs from the dictionary form, except you add *ta,* rather than *te.*

-MU, -BU, AND -NU ENDING   VERB (BASE) + *NDA*

yomu (to read)	*yonda*
yobu (to call)	*yonda*
shinu (to die)	*shinda*

-U, -TSU, -RU ENDING   VERB (BASE) + *TTA*

iu (to say)	*itta*
matsu (to wait)	*matta*
kaeru (to return)	*kaetta*

-KU, -GU ENDING   VERB (BASE) + *ITA* OR *IDA*

kiku (to listen)	*kiita*
oyogu (to swim)	*oyoida*

-*SU* ENDING	VERB (BASE) + *SHITA*
hanasu (to speak)	*hanashita*
kaesu (to return something)	*kaeshita*

There are two exceptions. One of them occurs only in the past affirmative:

	DICTIONARY FORM	PAST AFFIRMATIVE
shimasu (to do)	*suru*	*shita*
kimasu (to come)	*kuru*	*kita*
ikimasu (to go)	*iku*	*itta* (only in past tense)

As mentioned above, the plain form is often used in informal sentences:

Kyoo wa ame ga futteru kara, uchi ni iru.
Because it's raining today, I am going to stay home.

Rainen kekkon suru.
I am going to get married next year.

Daigaku de nani o senkoo shita ka.
What was your major in college?

Again, the plain form is often used in compound/complex sentences to end subordinate and relative clauses:

Neruson-san ga katta omiyage da. (relative clause)
This is the souvenir that Mr. Nelson bought.

Tanaka-san wa moo kaetta rashii desu. (subordinate clause)
It seems that Mr. Tanaka has already gone home.

Satoo-san ga kashite kureta kuruma da soo desu. (relative clause)
I hear that is the car that Ms. Sato loaned (to him).

2. PLAIN FORMS OF THE COPULA *DESU*

Like verbs, the copula *desu* has plain forms. They are used in the construction of informal sentences and in building clauses within sentences. The plain forms of *desu* are:

NON-PAST AFFIRMATIVE	NON-PAST NEGATIVE	PAST AFFIRMATIVE	PAST NEGATIVE
da	*dewa nai* (*ja nai*)	*datta*	*dewa nakatta* (*ja nakatta*)

a. Informal Sentences

Examples of the plain forms of *desu*, as they are used in informal sentences, are given below. Plain forms are used when speaking with friends, family members, subordinates, or to oneself. Consider the following conversation between two coworkers:

A: *Are, dare.* — Who's that?
B: *Ikeda-san da.* — That's Mr. Ikeda.
A: *Dare ka no tomodachi na no.* — Is he someone's friend?
B: *Un, buchoo no daigaku no kurasumeeto da soo da.* — Yeah, I hear he's a classmate of our director.
A: *Nande kita no.* — Why is he here? (lit. Why did he come?)
B: *Tookyoo ni tenkin da soo da.* — I hear he'll be transferred to the Tokyo office.

b. Clause Builders

The second use of plain forms is to build clauses within sentences. Note that plain forms are not necessarily used as the final predicates in such sentences. In the following examples, clauses within sentences are indicated with brackets.

[*Neruson-san wa shisha no shain da*] *soo desu.*
I heard Mr. Nelson is an employee at the branch office.

[*Takagi buchoo wa futsuu no shain ja nai*] *to kiita.*
I heard that Director Takagi is not an average employee.

[*Hiroshima wa kirei na tokoro da*] *to omoimasu ka.*
Do (you) think Hiroshima is a beautiful place?

64

3. HONORIFIC LANGUAGE

Speech in Japanese is modified according to the relationship the speaker has with the person(s) he or she is speaking to, as well as the relationship to the person(s) or thing(s) he or she is talking about. If the speaker is not very close to the person with whom he or she is speaking, *keigo* (honorific language) is used. *Keigo* is very formal and polite, and it is extremely important that you use this form of language to show respect at the appropriate times.

a. Deferential Forms

There are three types of honorific forms: deferential, polite, and humble. Deferential forms are used when speaking to a person of higher status. This type of speech is usually used in very formal situations such as meetings or negotiations.

Some deferential expressions are formed by replacing the verb with a completely different word. Some of the more common ones are:

DICTIONARY FORM	DEFERENTIAL FORM
iku (to go)	*irassharu*
kuru (to come)	*irassharu*
iru (to be)	*irassharu*
iu (to say)	*ossharu*
suru (to do)	*nasaru*
taberu (to eat)	*meshiagaru*
nomu (to drink)	*meshiagaru*

Note that with the exception of *meshiagaru*, none of the verbs above conjugates like other irregular verbs. Consider the following examples:

Kyoo jimusho ni nanji made irasshaimasu ka.
Until what time will you be in your office today?

Keisatsukan ga nan toka osshatte imasu yo.
The policeman is saying something.

Paati de nani o meshiagarimashita ka.
What did you eat at the party?

Ashita wa nani o nasaimasu ka.
What would you like to do tomorrow?

Other ways to make deferential forms will be discussed in Lesson 10.

b. Humble Forms

Humble forms are used when the speaker wishes to lower his or her position or the position of those related to him/her in formal situations.

Similar to the deferential form, separate "humble verbs" exist. Some of the more common ones are:

DICTIONARY FORM	HUMBLE FORM
aru (to be, exist)	*gozaru*
iru (to be, exist)	*oru*
iku (to go)	*mairu*
kuru (to come)	*mairu*

Note that while *aru* and *mairu* conjugate like other irregular verbs, *gozaru* conjugates like *irassharu*.

Ashita wa shigoto ga gozaimasu node, paati ni mairimasen.
Because I have work tomorrow, I will not come to the party.

Ni san nen Nihon ni orimasu.
I will be in Japan for two or three years.

Ryooshin mo mairimasu.
My parents will be coming, too.

c. Polite Forms

Polite forms are represented by verb endings such as *masu* and *desu*. The prefix *o-* may also be attached to words like *ocha* (tea) and *osake* (liquor) to show respect to the item(s) or their owner. Polite forms should be used with people of higher status, equal status, and people not considered close friends. They should also be used whenever there is a doubt about what form is appropriate.

Neruson-san, moo kaerimasu ka.
Mr. Nelson, are you going home already?

Suzuki-san no senmon wa shakaigaku deshita.
Mr. Suzuki's major (lit. specialization) was sociology.

Ocha demo ikaga desu ka.
Would you like to have some tea?

4. EXPRESSING EMPHASIS

The phrase *no desu (ka)*, or *n desu (ka)*, the contracted form, is used to express emphasis or to give an explanation. It is formed as follows:

> plain form verb + *n (no) desu (ka)*

Koko wa Shinjuku-eki janai n desu ka.
This is Shinjuku Station, isn't it?

Massugu iku n da ne.
I should go straight, right?

Nihongo ga zenzen wakaranai n desu ga.
I do not understand Japanese at all.

Konban no paati ni iku n desu ka.
Are you going to the party tonight?

5. GIVING ADVICE

When giving advice, or asking for someone else's advice, use the following pattern:

> past tense plain form verb + *hoo ga ii desu (ka)*

This pattern can be roughly translated as "should do."
When giving advice that contains a negative idea, the non-past negative form of the verb plus *hoo ga ii desu* should be used. This pattern translates as "should not do."

Okane o motte itta hoo ga ii desu ka.
Should I take some money with me?

Keisatsukan to soodan shita hoo ga ii n desu ne.
I should talk with a policeman, right?

Shinkansen no kippu o hayaku katta hoo ga ii desu.
It would be better if you bought the Shinkansen tickets early.

Hikooki ni noranai hoo ga ii desu.
You'd better not take an airplane.

Suzuki-san ni iwanai hoo ga ii.
You should not tell Mr. Suzuki.

6. CONJUNCTIVE PARTICLE *(SHI)*

The particle *shi* connects comparable or similar sentences. It can be translated as "and" or "moreover." A sentence can also end with *shi* when the sentence that follows can be understood through context. The pattern is as follows:

> verb (plain or formal in any tense) + *shi*
> *i*-adjective (any tense) + *shi*
> copula (*da* or *desu* in any tense) + *shi*

Kippu mo katta shi, hoteru mo yoyaku shimashita.
    I bought the tickets and reserved a hotel room.

Hikooki demo ii shi, shinkansen demo ii deshoo.
    Going by airplane is fine, and going by bullet train will be okay, too.

Kono seihin wa yasukatta shi, totemo sugurete imasu.
    This product was inexpensive and, moreover, it is of superior quality (lit. it excels).

Takushii mo nakanaka konai shi.
    Taxis just aren't coming . . .

Kono tokoro wa shizuka da shi, totemo kirei da.
    This place is quiet, and very pretty.

D. BIJINESU JIKOO (Business Matters)

HANZAI TO ANZEN (CRIME AND SAFETY)

Japan is known for being one of the safest countries in the world. You can usually walk around at midnight without much worry for personal safety. Statistics show that Japan's crime rate is less than 10 percent of that in the United States. The Japanese try hard not to violate common rules, because once a person has committed a crime, he or she is likely to be shunned by society, and rehabilitation is extremely difficult.

Historically, Japan has often been preoccupied with security. During the feudal era, the government divided the people of the country into groups consisting of five or six families, and made all members of a given group responsible for the group as a whole. If one individual violated a rule, the entire group was punished. Obviously, in such a system everyone watched over everyone else to make sure that no crimes were committed and no rules violated. While this may seem strange, this system eventually led to the Japanese preoccupation with "in-groups" and strict adherence to rules.

The role of the police force in Japan is the same as that in many other countries: to enforce the laws and to protect the citizens. There are, however, some differences between the police in Japan and those in the rest of the world. For example, in Japan there are small police stations *(kooban)* located approximately every two to three blocks. The police-men stationed at these *kooban* patrol the neighborhood from time to time, usually on bicycle, and respond to calls for assistance. Because their district is relatively small, the policemen are able to develop stong ties with those who live in the neighborhood. This relationship allows many people to feel comfortable enough to contact the police when most people of other countries would not. For example, borrowing an umbrella from the police, or asking for directions, is not unusual. It is widely thought that the close ties that policemen have to their commu-nities in Japan, as well as the large number of *kooban,* is a major reason for the low crime rate.

Nevertheless, the crime rate is rising in large Japanese cities. Some attribute this to the drastic social changes that are taking place due to techonology, the breakup of the traditional Japanese family, and foreign influence. Most likely, the rising crime rate is due to a combination of factors similar to those in other countries.

RENSHUU MONDAI (EXERCISES)

A. *Tsugi no shitsumon ni kotaenasai.* (Answer the following questions.)

1. *Neruson-san wa gaikokujin toorokushoo o motte imashita ka.*
2. *Sore wa naze desu ka.*
3. *Nani ka motte imashita ka.*
4. *Gakusei-jidai ni doko ni sunde imashita ka.*
5. *Tookyoo wa naze tanoshii no desu ka.*

B. *Tekitoo na kotoba o irenasai.* (Insert the appropriate word.)

1. *Koko wa Shinjuku janai _____ ka.*
2. *Kono jikan wa basu mo takushii mo _____ kimasen.*
3. *Michi ni mayotta _____ desu.*
4. *Nihon-shisha _____ tsutomete imasu.*
5. *Nani _____ atta n desu ka.*
6. *Kono hen wa anzen da _____ kiite imasu ga.*
7. *Moo osoi _____, abunai _____, okurimashoo.*
8. *Kyooto wa shizuka _____ ga, Tookyoo wa urusai _____.*
9. *Gaikokujin-toorokushoo wa kuyakusho _____ toremasu.*

KOTAE (ANSWERS)

A. 1. *Iie, motte imasen deshita.* 2. *Nihon ni tsuita bakari desu kara.*
3. *Hai, pasupooto o motte imashita.* 4. *Nara ni sunde imashita.* 5. *Ibento ga aru kara (tanoshii) desu.*
B. 1. *n desu* 2. *nakanaka* 3. *rashii* 4. *ni* 5. *ka* 6. *to* 7. *shi, kara*
8. *deshoo, deshoo* 9. *de*

DAI GOKA
Lesson 5

A. KAIWA (Dialogue)

MAAKETTINGU NI TSUITE NO HANASHIAI

Neruson-shi ga Bijitekku-sha no atarashii denshi-meeru no sofuto ni tsuite hanasu koto ni natte iru. Takagi-buchoo to no hanashiai ni iku tochuu, Suzuki-shi to Neruson-shi wa maakettingu ni tsuite hanasu.

SUZUKI: **Maakettingu-an[1] o misete moraimashita.[2] JT-sha ni zehi tomo[3] kyooryoku shite morau koto ga hitsuyoo na yoo desu ne.**

NERUSON: **Soo omoimasen ka. JT-sha wa denshi-meeru sofuto no hanbaijoo,[4] zettai hitsuyoo na paatonaa ni naru to omoimasu.**

SUZUKI: **Aa, koko desu.**

Maakettingu-bu no sutaffu ga Takagi-buchoo no heya de sude ni[5] matte iru.

TAKAGI: **Neruson-kun, Nihon no seikatsu wa ikaga[6] desu ka.**

NERUSON: **Tookyoo ni tsuita bakari desu[7] kara, mada mezurashii koto bakari desu.**

TAKAGI: **Sugu naremasu yo. Manshon wa doo. Gaman[8] dekiru ka ne.**

NERUSON: **Hai, dekimasu. Semai desu ga, benri ni dekite imasu ne. Asa nanka[9] kao o arai nagara, asagohan mo ryoori dekimasu.**

TAKAGI: **Ahhaha, naruhodo. Jaa, kaigi o hajimemashoo ka. Neruson-kun, Suupaameeru no maakettingu no shikata ni tsuite, kimi[10] no kangae o hanashite moraemasu ka.**

NERUSON: **Eeto, maakettingu puran o tsukuru mae ni, mazu okyaku-san o kangaete iroiro choosa suru hitsuyoo ga aru to omoimasu. Daikigyoo ni shooten o awasete hanbai suru ka, chuushoo kigyoo o yuusen suru ka o kangaeru hitsuyoo ga arimasu. Sorekara don'na bijinesu de, dore gurai[11] shanai renraku ga okonawarete iru ka mo shiranakereba narimasen. Sono wareware no eranda maaketto ni yori, senryaku ga chigatte kuru to omoimasu.**

SATOO: **Sore ni mada ikutsuka no mondai ga aru to omoimasu ga, sore mo shiraberu hitsuyoo ga aru n ja nai ka[12] to omoimasu ga. Tatoeba, Nihon no kigyoo ni wa kanari takusan no nenpai**

no hito ga takai ich ni tsuite ite, shanai renraku ni
denshi-meeru o tsukau koto ni kanari teikoo suru koto mo kan-
gaeraremasu.[13] Maakettingu kyanpeen o suru sai ni[14] kono
koto mo kooryo suru hitsuyoo ga aru n ja nai deshoo ka.

NERUSON: Hai, mattaku soo desu. Shikamo korera[15] no nenpai no
hitotachi ga futsuu kau ka kawanai ka kimeru wake desu kara.

TAKAGI: Kankyoo hogo no koto mo wasurenai yoo ni.[16] Denshi-
meeru o tsukaeba, kanari no kami o tsukawanakute mo yoku
naru.[17] Kono ten wa ooku no Nihon no kaisha ni totte daiji na
koto to omou.

NERUSON: Gomottomo desu.[18]

TAKAGI: Kono seihin o shiten ya kogaisha[19] o tooshite ooi ni uritai
mon[20] da. Sore ni dairiten ni mo kyooryoku shite moratte hanbai o susumeta hoo ga ii to omou.

NERUSON: Tokubetsu na dairiten o kangaete irasshaimasu ka.

TAKAGI: Yahari Toyoda-Shooji[21] no kogaisha no JT-sha ga ii daroo.
Nihon-juu ni totemo tsuyoi seerusu nettowaaku o motte iru
kara ne.[22]

NERUSON: Satoo-san ni motto shirabete moraimashoo.

TAKAGI: Sono hitsuyoo wa nai. Kurasumeeto ga tsutomete ite, moo
hanashi ga shite aru.

NERUSON: Soo desu ka. Jaa, shigoto ga shiyasui desu ne.

TAKAGI: Keiyaku suru mae ni maaketingu maneejaa to hanashite
moraitai. Karera no maakettingu no shikata ga wareware no
hochoo to au ka doo ka tashikamete moraitai n da. Hirai-kun
kara renraku ga aru hazu da kara.

NERUSON: Hai, wakarimashita.

TAKAGI: Jaa, arigatoo.

A DISCUSSION ABOUT MARKETING

(lit. It has been decided that . . .) Mr. Nelson is going to speak about
Busitech's new e-mail software. On their way to the meeting with Director
Takagi, Mr. Suzuki and Mr. Nelson discuss marketing.

SUZUKI: I looked at the marketing plan. It appears that we definitely need
to get JT Corporation's cooperation, doesn't it?

NELSON: Yes, it does. (lit. You don't think so?) In terms of e-mail software
sales, I think JT Corporation would be (lit. become) an absolutely essential partner.

72

SUZUKI: Well, here we are.

The marketing staff is already waiting (for them) in Director Takagi's office.

TAKAGI: Mr. Nelson, how is life in Japan?

NELSON: Since I just got to Tokyo, it is still nothing but strange things.

TAKAGI: (Well,) you'll soon get used to it. How's your condominium? Can you handle (lit. bear) it?

NELSON: Yes, I can. It's small, but conveniently built. In the morning, while I'm washing my face, I can cook breakfast (at the same time).

TAKAGI: Ha ha ha! Indeed! Well, shall we begin the meeting? Mr. Nelson, could you please tell us about your ideas (lit. way of thinking) for marketing SuperMail?

NELSON: Well, before making a marketing plan, I think we first need to consider our customers and examine closely (who they are). We need to think about whether we are going to focus on selling to large companies or give priority to midsized and small companies. After that, we have to know what type of business (we're targeting), and how much internal communication (lit. contacting within the company) is taking place. I think our strategy will change depending on the market we choose.

SATO: In addition, I think we will still have a number of problems. I feel we need to examine those also. For example, (many) Japanese corporations have a sizable number of older employees in high positions who will resist using e-mail for intraoffice communication. When running a marketing campaign, don't we need to consider this also?

NELSON: Yes, absolutely. Especially since these older employees usually decide whether to buy or not.

TAKAGI: Okay, good (lit. I understand). Let's not forget the (issue of) environmental protection. If they use e-mail, they won't have to use as much paper. I think this point will be (really) important to a lot of Japanese companies.

NELSON: I agree entirely.

TAKAGI: We want to sell this product in large numbers through all of our branch offices and subsidiaries. In addition, I believe we should move our sales ahead by getting the cooperation of independent distributors.

NELSON: Were you thinking of a special distributor?

TAKAGI: (I was thinking) Toyoda Trading Company's subsidiary, JT, would be good. They have a very strong sales network throughout Japan.

NELSON: I could have Ms. Sato check them out further.

TAKAGI: That won't be necessary. A classmate (of mine) works there, and I've already spoken with him.

NELSON: Is that right? Well, (our) job will be easy.

TAKAGI: Before we come up with (lit. do) a contract, I would like you to talk to their marketing manager. I want to verify whether or not their way of marketing matches our pace. You should hear from Mr. Hirai.

NELSON: Yes, I understand.

TAKAGI: Good. Thank you.

B. CHUU (Notes)

1. *Maakettingu-an* means "marketing proposal." *An* can also mean "rough draft."

2. *Misete morau* literally means "to have someone allow (me) to see." It's a more polite way of saying "I looked." The V-*te*-form + *morau* pattern will be explained in Grammar in this lesson.

3. *Zehi tomo* means "by all means." *Tomo,* which can mean "of course," is added here for emphasis.

4. As a suffix, *joo* means "in terms of" or "from the viewpoint of."

5. *Sude ni* means "already" or "before."

6. *Ikaga* (how) has the same meaning as *doo,* but is more formal.

7. The expression *bakari (desu)* has two different functions. When it follows the past tense form of a verb, it means "to have just done something." For example: *Tsuita bakari desu.* (I have just arrived.) A noun followed by *bakari (desu)* means "nothing but" or "only." For example: *Chiisai kaisha bakari desu.* (There are nothing but small companies.)

8. *Gaman* means "patience," "perseverance," or "self-control." These qualities are considered virtues in Japanese society.

9. *Asa nanka* literally means "as for in the morning." In this case, *nanka* emphasizes that the action referred to takes place in the morning.

10. *Kimi* means "you." It is used to address younger people by those senior in age.

11. *Dore gurai (dore kurai)* literally means "which degree." It can be translated as "how much" or "how far."

12. *Aru n ja nai ka* means "Isn't there" or "Isn't it the case that." The question has a negative ending, but is usually translated with an affirmative clause.

13. Many Japanese corporations are not fully computerized and continue to operate in a manner that would be considered old-fashioned in the U.S. There is still some resistance among senior members of corporations to changing to computerized operations.

14. *Sai* means "when." It has almost the same meaning as *toki,* but is used in more formal situations, including business.

15. *Korera* is the plural form of *kore* (this).

16. Japan experienced some serious environmental problems from the 1960s to the 1980s, such as mercury poisoning in Minamata City, Kyushu, air pollution in Yokkaichi City, and chemical-laced fog in Tokyo and Osaka. In order to avoid these problems in the future, the government and large corporations along with the Japanese people are trying to cooperate in environmental issues. For example, trash collection has strict rules: both businesses and households must separate their trash into nonburnables (plastics, glass, etc.) and burnables (paper, food items, etc.), which are picked up on separate days of the week. While these efforts are a step in the right direction, one downside is that the burnables are burned in incinerators.

17. Paper is precious and expensive because Japan has to import most of the lumber it needs from such countries as the United States and Canada. In addition, the Japanese management style requires considerable amounts of paperwork. For example, practices such as circulating documents and proposals for general approval by all those involved in the project requires enormous amounts of paper, especially if someone is involved in more than one project. Fortunately, much of this paper is recycled.

18. *Gomottomo desu* means "I certainly agee with you" or "Indeed, I see your point."

19. *Kogaisha* literally means "child company." It is translated as "subsidiary company."

20. *Mon* is a shortened colloquial form of *mono* (thing) used in more informal conversation.

21. *Shooji, shooji-gaisha,* and *bussan* are general terms for trading companies. The ten biggest trading companies are known as *Soogoo Shoosha. Mitsubishi-shooji, Mitsui-bussan,* and *Sumitomo-shooji* are some of the world's largest trading corporations.

22. It's much easier to use existing networks when establishing a new business than to try to develop new relationships. The Japanese use connections *(kone)* as much as possible.

C. BUNPOO TO YOOHOO
(Grammar and Usage)

1. THE POTENTIAL FORM OF THE VERB

The potential form of the verb is used to indicate one's ability to do something or the possibility that an event will occur. It is equivalent to "can" or "to be able to." The potential form of regular verbs is formed as:

> verb stem (drop the *ru*) plus *rareru.*

For irregular verbs, drop the *u* from the dictionary form of the verb and add *eru.*

REGULAR VERBS

taberu	to eat	*taberareru* (can eat)
oshieru	to teach	*oshierareru* (can teach)
kaeru	to exchange	*kaerareru* (can exchange)
shiraseru	to inform	*shiraserareru* (can inform)
kangaeru	to think	*kangaerareru* (can think)

IRREGULAR VERBS

iku	to go	*ikeru* (can go)
yomu	to read	*yomeru* (can read)
hiraku	to open	*hirakeru* (can open)
motsu	to hold	*moteru* (can hold)
kaku	to write	*kakeru* (can write)
okuru	to send	*okureru* (can send)

76

EXCEPTIONS

suru	to do	*dekiru*	(can do)
kuru	to come	*korareru*	(can come)

Maakettingu puran o setusmei dekimasu ka.
Can you explain the marketing plan?

Denshi meeru de sekaijuu no hitobito to hanashiaemasu ka.
Can we talk to people all over the world with e-mail?

Tookyoo to Nara o kuraberaremasu ka.
Can you compare Tokyo with Nara?

Kyoo wa kaigi ni ikemasen ga, asu nara ikemasu.
I cannot go to the meeting today, but I can go tomorrow.

Kono seihin o yasuku uremasu ka.
Can you sell this product inexpensively?

Sugu maakettingu maneejaa ni renraku dekimasu ka.
Can you contact the marketing manager immediately?

2. TE-MORAU

The word *morau* (to receive) is used when the speaker receives something from a person who is lower or equal in status.

Tomodachi ni purezento o moraimashita.
I received a present from a friend.

Chichi ni furui konpyuutaa o moraimashita.
I received an old computer from my father.

The *te*-form of the verb plus *morau* means "to have someone do something." When forming a direct request, the potential form *moraeru* is used. The person being asked to do something is followed by the particle *ni*.

Satoo-san ni shirabete moraimasu.
I'll have Ms. Sato look into it.

Ano kaisha ni kyooryoku shite moraimashita.
I had the company cooperate with us.

Kimi no kangae o hanashite moraemasu ka.
Will you explain your idea? (May I have you explain your idea?)

Seihin o shiten ni utte moraimasu.
We will have our branch offices sell the products.

3. *NONI*

To indicate that something is contrary to what the speaker expected, the expression *noni* is used. *Noni* is equivalent to "despite the fact that" and "even though." It expresses the speaker's surprise and carries an emotional tone. The clause preceding *noni* should be in the plain form. If the clause ends in *da,* it is changed to *na* before *noni.*

Nihon wa semai noni, takusan hito ga imasu.
Though Japan is small, it has many people.

Maakettingu puran o kantan ni setsumei shita noni, wakaranakatta yoo desu.
Even though I explained the marketing plan (very) simply, it appears (the trainees) did not understand it.

Atarashii kaisha na noni, yoku ganbatte imasu.
Even though it is a new company, they are doing well.

Seihin wa sugurete iru noni amari urenai soo desu.
Despite the fact that our product is superior, I understand it is not selling well.

4. *TE-ARU*

We discussed the *te*-form plus *iru* in Lesson 3. When following an action verb, this pattern indicates the continuation of an action (-ing). The *te*-form plus *aru*, however, describes a "steady state" that the verb is in. It implies that the action has already been done by the speaker, or someone else, and is still in that state. For example, compare:

Mado o shimete iru.
I am closing the window.

Mado ga shimete aru.
The window has been closed (by the speaker or someone else, and no one has opened it since).

Note that the direct object of the first sentence, marked by *o,* has now become the subject of the second sentence, marked by *ga.* This change occurs because there is no direct action taking place. (It has already taken place.)

Maaketto-an wa moo kaite arimasu.
The marketing proposal has already been written.

Sono koto wa moo choosa shite arimasu.
That matter has already been looked into.

Kyoosoo mo kooryo shite arimasu.
The competition has also been considered already.

D. BIJINESU JIKOO
(Business Matters)

KAISHA TO JUUGYOOIN (COMPANIES AND EMPLOYEES)

The differences in business practices between the United States and Japan are rooted in the basic differences between the American and Japanese psyche. The American outlook toward work is often based on individualism, while the Japanese mentality leans toward a group effort. Obviously, this creates a difference in the organizational structure of a company. In an American corporation individual performance is usually stressed, whereas in Japanese corporations the overall performance of the group is emphasized. This can also extend to divisions within a company. While each division in an American corporation must perform well individually, individual departments in Japanese companies support each other with the profits of the entire corporation in mind.

Companies are like big families to Japanese employees. Many people believe that they will work for the same company for life and thus develop a very strong sense of loyalty. One practical reason for this is that the salary of Japanese employees is directly related to their seniority within the company. In turn, the companies consider the employees family members and feel somewhat responsible for their welfare. While in countries like the United States it is not uncommon for workers seeking higher compensation or a better position to change employers several times throughout their careers, the Japanese tend to stay even if it is bad for their own careers. Many employees must even take pay cuts when their company is struggling.

KEIYAKU (CONTRACTS)

While the Japanese of the Tokugawa period (1600–1868) are known to have used written documents as key weapons in monetary disputes, the use of written agreements has declined in the modern period. Many Japanese feel that they have little need for explicit or elaborate documentation regarding everyday personal or business interactions. There is a "known" set of standards and common beliefs that exist among and bind most Japanese, a cultural code of behavior that applies to all types of verbal and nonverbal communication.

Non-Japanese people sometimes have trouble understanding this unspoken behavioral code. Therefore, in business dealings with the Japanese it may be advisable to insist upon written business plans and agreements, even though it may not be the standard custom. This may help to avoid confusing and potentially damaging misunderstandings. Because the global market requires the Japanese to adapt to a more Western style of business, they will most likely agree, and may actually prefer written contracts with foreign companies.

TEKUNOROJII TO SEDAI NO SA (TECHNOLOGY AND THE GENERATION GAP)

Japan is a large producer of computers, and is home to several big-name computer manufacturers such as NEC, Fujitsu, and Toshiba.

Many mid- to large-size corporations are computerized, but a number of companies still have not fully utilized the power of their in-house computer systems. The younger generation is more computer literate, having grown up using the latest PC technology, both as it relates to entertainment and the completion of daily tasks. The older generation, on the other hand, has not had as much interaction with computers. And since they are still running the companies, technological advancements may be slower than one would assume. This trend is slowly changing, however, with the proliferation and power of more user-friendly operating systems and software. Japan will see a rapid growth in personal computer use in the near future due to this explosive wave of change.

RENSHUU MONDAI (EXERCISES)

A. *Tsugi no shitsumon ni kotaenasai.* (Answer the following questions.)

1. *Neruson-san wa Suzuki-san to nani ni tsuite hanashite imasu ka.*
2. *Neruson-san to Suzuki-san wa doko de hanashiai o shimasu ka.*
3. *Neruson-san no manshon wa doo desu ka.*
4. *Nihon no kigyoo dewa dare ga kau ka kawanai ka kimemasu ka.*
5. *Denshi-meeru wa naze kankyoo hogo ni ii no desu ka.*

B. *Tekitoo na joshi o irenasai.* (Insert the appropriate particle[s].)

1. *Chotto semai desu _____, benri _____ dekite imasu.*
2. *Mada ikutsu ka _____ mondai _____ aru to omoimasu.*
3. *Asu _____ repooto _____ kimasu.*
4. *Denshi-meeru wa motto hayai _____, sekai no hitobito _____ renraku shiau koto ga dekimasu.*
5. *Yuujin _____ tsutomete ite, hanashi _____ shite aru.*

80

C. *Tsugi o kanookei ni kaenasai.* (Change the following into the "potential form.")

1. *Denshi-meeru o tsukaimasu.*
2. *Sore o kiite, anshin shimashita.*
3. *Nenpai no hito ga kau ka kawanai ka kimemasu.*
4. *Kono seihin wa urimasu.*
5. *Seihin no hanbai o susumemasu.*

KOTAE (ANSWERS)

A. 1. *Maakettingu ni tsuite hanashite imasu.* 2. *Takagi-buchoo no heya de shimashita.* 3. *Semai desu ga, benri ni dekite imasu.* 4. *Nenpai no hito ga kimemasu.* 5. *Kami o tsukawanakutemo yoku narimasu kara.*
B. 1. *ga, ni* 2. *no, ga* 3. *made ni, ga* 4. *shi, ni* 5. *ga, ga*
C. 1. *Denshimeeru o (ga) tsukaemasu.* 2. *Sore o kiite, anshin dekimashita.* 3. *Nenpai no hito ga kau ka kawanai ka kimeraremasu.* 4. *Kono seihin wa uremasu.* 5. *Seihin no hanbai o (ga) susumeraremasu.*

DAI ROKKA
Lesson 6

A. KAIWA

Ohiru no bentoo no okane o harau tame narande matte iru aida ni, Neru-son-shi to Suzuki-shi wa Nihon no shoohisha no okane no tsukaikata ga Amerika to chigau koto ni tsuite chotto hanasu. Jimusho ni modotte, min'na to atsumatte, bentoo o tabenagara hanashiau.

NERUSON: Anoo, kyoo wa saikin no shoohisha no torendo[1] ni tsuite, minasan no okangae o okiki shitai n desu ga.

SUZUKI: Saikin kawatta yoo na ki ga shimasu ga.

NERUSON: Soo desu ka. Tatoeba doo iu koto desu ka.

SUZUKI: Min'na yoku kangaete, mono o kau yoo ni natta to omoimasu.

NERUSON: Mae wa doo datta n desu ka?

SUZUKI: Amari kangaenaide, suki na mono o dondon[2] katte imashita.

NERUSON: Naruhodo ne. Sono keikoo wa aru nendai dake no koto desu ka, soretomo zenpanteki desu ka?

SUZUKI: Nijuu dai kara gojuu dai made de kanari hiroi yoo desu ga.

NERUSON: Satoo-san, Nihon de yoofuku toka ryokoo ni okane o takusan tsukau no wa wakai josei[3] da to kiite iru kedo.

SATOO: Ee, soo nan desu. Kekkon suru mae ni ni san nen shigoto o shite, soshite moratta okane o jiyuu ni tsukatte iru yoo desu.

NERUSON: Dooshite son'na ni tsukaeru n desu ka.

SATOO: Shuushoku shite kara mo ryooshin to issho ni sunde ite, seikatsuhi ga kakarimasen kara.

NEUSON: Naruhodo. Dansei[4] wa doo nan desu ka.

SATOO: Saikin wa dansei mo okane o tsukau yoo ni natta soo desu yo.

NERUSON: Eeto. Wasure nai yoo ni, boodo ni kakimashoo ka? Nedan to hinshitsu[5] no kankei wa doo desu ka?

SATOO: Mae wa "takakutemo ii mono o"[6] to iu kangae deshita ga, saikin wa "ii mono o yasuku" to iu kangaekata ni natta yoo desu.

NERUSON: Naruhodo. Amerika wa daibu mae kara soo desu.

SUZUKI: Satoo-san dattara, don'na seihin o kaimasu ka?

SATOO: Soo desu ne. Watashi wa yahari yasukute shitsu no ii mono, sore ni shin'yoo[7] ga dekiru mono o kaimasu.

NERUSON: Sore wa zuibun muzukashii n ja nai desu ka?

SATOO: Sore wa soo desu ga, saikin wa zasshi[8] nado de yasukute, shitsu ga yokute, shin'yoo dekiru mono ga wariai[9] kantan ni mitsukarimasu yo.

NERUSON: Shitsu to shin'yoo ne. Soo, Nihon de wa shin'yoo ga toku ni taisetsu nan desu ne.

SATOO: Ryuukoo o ou hito mo mada imasu kedo ne.

NERUSON: A, iwayuru neemu burando o konomu hito mo iru wake desu ne.

SATOO: Mada kanari.[10] Tada konpyuutaa nado wa mada hinshitsu ga dai ichi no yoo desu.

NERUSON: Wareware no seihin o katte kureru no[11] wa kigyoo ya yakusho desu kara, sono koto o kangaeta hoo ga genjitsuteki desu ne.

SUZUKI: Kigyoo nado wa nedan yori hinshitsu to saabisu ga taisetsu desu ne.

NERUSON: Yappari ne. Chotto matomete mimasu to, hinshitsu, shin'yoo, saabisu ga taisetsu de, kigyoo nado wa nedan wa takakutemo, mono ga yokereba ii to iu koto desu[12] ne. Daga kojin wa dekiru dake yasui hoo ga ii.

SUZUKI: Sasuga[13] desu ne. Yoku matomemashita ne. Kore kara wa Neruson-san ni kaigi no memo o onegai shimashoo ka.

NERUSON: Tondemo arimasen. Tokoro de shoohisha no torendo to chotto kankei ga aru n desu ga, haiteku no toreedo-shoo ga Makuhari-Messe[14] to iu tokoro de arun desu ga, itte mimasen ka.

SUZUKI: Boku wa mae ni nankai ka itta kara, Satoo-san, goissho shitara doo desu ka.

SATOO: Kekkoo desu yo.

NERUSON: Yokatta. Jaa, soo iu koto de.[15] Arigatoo gozaimashita.

Brainstorming Meeting

While standing in line, waiting to pay for their meals, Mr. Nelson and Mr. Suzuki talk a bit about how Japanese consumer spending habits are different from those in the United States. They go back to the office, get together with everyone else, and talk while eating their "bento" lunches.

NELSON: Today I'd like to hear your opinions on recent consumer trends.

SUZUKI: I think the trends have changed recently.

NELSON: Really? Give me an example. (lit. For example, what things?)

SUZUKI: I think everyone now puts a lot more thought into the things they buy.

NELSON: What did they use to do? (lit. How was it before?)

SUZUKI: People used to (just) buy the things they liked in great quantities without really thinking about it (first).

NELSON: I see. Is this tendency particular to any age group, or is this generally the case?

SUZUKI: There is a really wide (age range), from people in their twenties, to people in their fifties.

NELSON: Ms. Sato, I hear that in Japan it is young women who spend a lot of money on clothes, traveling, and so forth.

SATO: Yes, that's right. Before getting married, they work for two or three years and spend the money they earn freely.

NELSON: How (lit. why) can they spend so much?

SATO: Even after getting jobs, they live with their parents and have no living expenses.

NELSON: I see. How about men?

SATO: It seems like men are spending money these days, too.

NELSON: All right, then. Let's write (some of these points down) on the board so we won't forget them. What about the relationship between price and quality?

SATO: Before, people thought, "high prices for good quality," but now their way of thinking has become, "quality products at a lower price."

NELSON: I see. It has been that way in America for quite a long time (lit. since much before).

SUZUKI: Miss Sato, if it were (up to) you, what kind of products would you buy?

84

SATO: Well, of course I would want things that are inexpensive, of good quality, and also reliable, something I can depend on.

NELSON: That's a pretty difficult thing (to do), don't you think?

SATO: That's true, but these days, it's comparatively easier to find inexpensive quality products in magazines and such.

NELSON: Hmm, quality and dependability (lit. trust). Dependability is especially important in Japan, isn't it?

SATO: (Yes,) but there are still some people who are (just) interested in pursuing fads.

NELSON: Ah, you mean the people who (only) like the so-called "name-brand" goods, right?

SATO: (Yes.) There are still a lot (of people like that). However, for computers and other electronic products (lit. and so on), quality is still the most important factor.

NELSON: Since our customers (lit. those who buy our products) are businesses and government offices, it's probably most realistic for us to think about them.

SUZUKI: (Right,) when it comes to business customers, quality and service are more important than price.

NELSON: I see. So if we try to summarize a bit, (we could say that) quality, reliability, and service are all important, and that businesses (and government) are willing to pay a higher price for quality products (lit. it's okay if the products are good). Individual customers, on the other hand, (prefer products that are) as inexpensive as possible.

SUZUKI: Excellent! You summarized (what we said) very accurately. Should we ask Mr. Nelson (to write up) the minutes for meetings from now on?

NELSON: No, thanks. Oh, by the way, this is something related to consumer trends—there's a high-tech trade show at Makuhari Messe. Would you like to go and see it?

SUZUKI: I've been there a few times already, so, Ms. Sato, why don't you go with him?

SATO: Okay. (That will be fine.)

NELSON: That's great. Then it's all set. Thank you very much.

B. CHUU

1. *Torendo* is a commonly used word meaning "new trend."

2. The word *dondon* means "rapidly" or "in great quantities." It is one of many Japanese onomatopoeic words.

3. Young Japanese women have a reputation for being "rich and big spenders." The primary reason for this is that after graduating from college and finding jobs, many young women continue to live with their parents until they get married. Since they have no living expenses, they have a considerable amount of disposable income to spend on traveling, both domestic and international, as well as high-priced consumer goods.

4. Japanese men traditionally have been known for their simple tastes and needs. This seems to be changing, however, as young men are starting to spend much more money on clothes, sports, entertainment, and other expensive diversions.

5. Japanese consumers have typically demanded high-quality products and were willing to pay high prices for them. However, partly due to the recent slow economy in Japan, consumers have become much more sensitive to prices.

6. *Takakute mo ii mono o* means "(people buy) good things even if they are expensive." The particle *o* indicates a grammatical object, and the verb is omitted because it is understood through context.

7. *Shin'yoo* (trust) in products and producers is extremely important in Japan. Once a product is considered undependable, it is almost impossible for the manufacturer to regain the lost consumer trust.

8. There are thousands of weekly and monthly magazines in Japan. They cover everything from politics and the economy to fashion, food, and entertainment. In addition, many new magazines examine products in terms of price, quality, and practicality. They are much like American consumer guides.

9. *Wariai,* when used as a noun, means "rate" or "proportion." It can also be used as an adverb, meaning "comparatively."

10. *Kanari* means "fairly," "pretty," or "considerably."

11. The word *no* has three uses: a possessive form ('s), as in *tomodachi no* (friend's), an "of" form, as in *Nihon no seihin* (product of Japan), and the nominal form, "one(s)," as in *takai no* (expensive one). It is this latter use that is demonstrated here in *katte kureru no* (those who buy).

12. The phrase *to iu koto desu* means "it means that."

13. The expression *sasuga,* meaning "indeed," "excellent," or "as one might have expected," is used to make a positive statement about someone. This is especially true when expectations concerning the other person have fallen in line with what that person actually did.

14. *Makuhari-Messe* was developed as a new center for trade fairs, complete with convention centers, hotels, restaurants, and commercial offices. It is located in Chiba prefecture, about one hour from central Tokyo.

15. *Soo iu koto de* means "(agreeing) in that way." The expression is used at the end of a discussion to indicate that the speaker agrees with what has been said and is ready to end the conversation.

C. BUNPOO TO YOOHOO

1. PLAIN FORMS OF VERBS (NEGATIVE NON-PAST AND PAST)

In Lesson 4, we started our discussion on the plain forms of verbs. You will recall that we studied the affirmative non-past and past forms. In this lesson, we will cover the negative non-past and past forms. Like the affirmative, the negative non-past and past are used (a) in informal sentences and (b) to build clauses within sentences.

All regular verbs conjugate alike. The negative non-past is formed by adding *nai* to the stem, and the negative past is formed by adding *nakatta* to the stem.

FORMAL	PLAIN	NEGATIVE NON-PAST	NEGATIVE PAST
tabemasu (to eat)	*taberu*	*tabe* (stem) + *nai* (ending) (doesn't eat)	*tabe* (stem) + *nakatta* (ending) (didn't eat)
mimasu (to watch)	*miru*	*minai* (doesn't see)	*minakatta* (didn't see)
imasu (to be)	*iru*	*inai* (is not present)	*inakatta* (was not present)
hajimemasu (to start)	*hajimeru*	*hajimenai* (doesn't start)	*hajimenakatta* (didn't start)
tsukaremasu (to get tired)	*tsukareru*	*tsukarenai* (doesn't get tired)	*tsukarenakatta* (didn't get tired)
karimasu (to borrow)	*kariru*	*karinai* (doesn't borrow)	*karinakatta* (didn't borrow)
tsutomemasu (to work for)	*tsutomeru*	*tsutomenai* (doesn't work for)	*tsutomenakatta* (didn't work for)

Irregular verbs conjugate by dropping the last vowel *u* of the plain form and adding *a-nai* for negative non-past and *a-nakatta* for negative past.

FORMAL	PLAIN	NEGATIVE NON-PAST	NEGATIVE PAST
yomimasu (to read)	*yomu*	*yomanai* (doesn't read)	*yomanakatta* (didn't read)
machimasu (to wait)	*matsu*	*matanai* (doesn't wait)	*matanakatta* (didn't wait)
kaerimasu (to return)	*kaeru*	*kaeranai* (doesn't return)	*kaeranakatta* (didn't return)
dashimasu (to pay)	*dasu*	*dasanai* (doesn't pay)	*dasanakatta* (didn't pay)
shinimasu (to die)	*shinu*	*shinanai* (doesn't die)	*shinanakatta* (didn't die)
tsukaimasu (to use)	*tsukau*	*tsukawanai* (doesn't use)	*tsukawanakatta* (didn't use)
iimasu (to say)	*iu*	*iwanai* (doesn't say)	*iwanakatta* (didn't say)

Please note that the last two verbs add *w*. This is because old forms of *tsukaimasu* and *iimasu* were *tsukawimasu* and *iwimasu (yuwimasu)*, respectively.

There are three exceptions:

FORMAL	PLAIN	NEGATIVE NON-PAST	NEGATIVE PAST
shimasu (to do)	*suru*	*shinai* (doesn't do)	*shinakatta* (didn't do)
kimasu (to come)	*kuru*	*konai* (doesn't come)	*konakatta* (didn't come)
arimasu (to be)	*aru*	*nai* (isn't present)	*nakatta* (was not present)

a. The plain forms of verbs are used in informal sentence constructions.

Kyoo wa kaisha ni ikanai.
I am not going to the office today.

An'na seihin wa kawanai.
I would not buy such a product.

Sono koto o kangaenakatta.
I hadn't thought about that.

Dansei wa mae ni amari okane o tsukawanakatta.
Men did not spend much money before.

b. The plain forms of verbs are also used to build clauses within compound/complex sentences.

Saikin torendo ga amari kawaranai yoo na ki ga shimasu.
I have a feeling that the trends have not been changing lately.

Senshuu okane o zenzen tsukawanakatta to omou.
I don't think I spent any money last week.

Shinbun o yomanakatta deshoo.
You didn't read the paper, did you?

2. *NI TSUITE*

The phrase *ni tsuite* is used after a noun or noun phrase. It means "about," "concerning," or "in regards to."

Sono shoohisha no torendo ni tsuite, minasan no okangae o okiki shitai to omoimasu.
I would like to get everyone's thoughts concerning that consumer trend.

Wakai hitobito no kangaekata ni tsuite ima shirabete imasu.
We are now looking into the way young people think.

Nihon no kaisha ni tsuite iroiro shiritai to omotte imasu.
I would like to know more about Japanese companies.

Suupaa konpyuutaa ni tsuite nani ka shitte imasu ka.
Do you know anything about supercomputers?

3. *TAI TO OMOU*

When you want to express an intention that is unsure, or that you still
have doubts about, use the *tai*-form (desiderative suffix) plus *to omou*.
This form follows the stem of a verb and is also used to express a wish
or desire.

Minasan no iken o kikitai to omoimasu.
(I think) I would like to hear your opinion.

Kekkon suru mae ni sukoshi ryokoo shitai to omoimasu.
(I think) I would like to travel a little, before getting married.

Nedan to hinshitsu no kankei o kangaetai to omoimasu.
I would like to consider the relationship between price and quality.

Hima dattara otsuakiai shitai to omoimasu.
If I have free time, I want to accompany you.

Atarashii seihin ga detara sugu oshirase shitai to omoimasu.
I want to inform you immediately if I get some new products.

4. GRADUAL CHANGE *(YOO NI NARU)*

When you want to express the fact that a change has taken place gradually, use the pattern: plain form, non-past verb + *yoo ni naru*.

Nihongo ga hanaseru yoo ni narimashita.
I have come to be able to speak Japanese. (I could not before.)

Min'na yoku kangaete kau yoo ni narimashita.
Everyone now puts a lot of thought into the things they buy.

Seihin no setsumei ga dekiru yoo ni narimashita.
I have reached the point where I can explain the product.

Atarashii torendo ga wakaru yoo ni natta.
I now understand the new trends.

Okane o tsukawanai yoo ni narimashita.
I do not use much money anymore.

Okane o setsuyaku suru yoo ni narimashita.
We now save money.

5. CONDITIONAL CLAUSES

A conditional clause sets up or states a condition. In English, to set up a condition, the word "if" is often used. In Japanese, this is expressed by adding *ra* to the past forms of verbs and *i*-adjectives, and *dattara* (plain form of *desu* plus *ttara*) to nouns and *na*-adjectives.

VERB	PAST FORM	CONDITIONAL FORM
yaru	*yatta*	*yattara*
(to do)	(did do)	(If ~ did)
hajimaru	*hajimatta*	*hajimattara*
(to begin)	(began)	(If ~ begins)
kuru	*konakatta*	*konakattara*
(to come)	(didn't come)	(If ~ doesn't come)
taberu	*tabenakatta*	*tabenakattara*
(to eat)	(didn't eat)	(If ~ doesn't eat)

Katoo-san dattara, don'na seihin o kaimasu ka.
If it were up to you, Miss Kato, what kind of product would you buy?

Satoo-san ga konakattara, watakushi wa kaerimasu.
If Ms. Sato does not come, I will go home.

Yasukute shitsu ga yokattara, kaitai to omoimasu.
If the product is inexpensive and of high quality, I would like to buy it.

Suki na seihin dattara, dondon kaimasu.
If I like the product, I'll buy a lot.

Hima dattara, otsukiai shimasu.
If I'm free, I will accompany you.

6. *TOKORO DESU*

The present (non-past) tense or past tense of a verb plus *tokoro desu* signifies "in the midst of doing something."

Watakushi mo toreedo-shoo o mitai to omotte ita tokoro desu.
I was just thinking about seeing the trade show myself.

Kaijoo de matte iru tokoro desu.
I am waiting for you in the hall.

Atarashii jimusho o sagashite ita tokoro desu.
We were in the process of looking for a new office.

Zasshi de shirabete iru tokoro desu.
I am in the midst of researching this in some magazines.

D. BIJINESU JIKOO

NEMAWASHI (PRIOR CONSENT)

The Japanese have a very different style of conducting business meetings. Before formal meetings begin, participants have already drawn conclusions regarding information to be presented at the meeting. How is this possible? The Japanese have developed a system known as *nemawashi*, which in its original sense means "smoothing around roots before planting." When a proposal is to be presented to a large group, it will first be discussed with individuals or small groups of people who will be in attendance. The purpose of this is to reach an agreement with all the members of the group beforehand. After significant discussion and once an agreement has been reached, the proposal is presented in a formal meeting. It normally gets formal approval without any problems or adjustment.

This system was developed in order to avoid confrontations in formal meetings and to keep the relationships among group members harmonious. Discussing the issues on a one-to-one basis or in small groups creates an atmosphere in which everyone can express his or her opinion cordially and without reservation.

Nemawashi has advantages and disadvantages. Obviously, discussing an issue in small groups or on an individual basis takes time. However, once a consensus has been reached and a decision has been formally approved, projects are carried out with relative ease.

For westerners accustomed to a decision-making process that includes discussions in formal meetings, this may seem awkward and frustrating. However, an understanding of this decision-making style, and the importance of maintaining a harmonious atmosphere, will definitely help in doing business in Japan.

TAIRITSU O SAKERU (AVOIDING CONFLICT)

The Japanese are often described as being indirect and noncommittal in discussions or negotiations. Although they are often good at listening to the opinions of other people and agreeing fully with what has been said, many Japanese have difficulty expressing their own opinions. As mentioned above, Japanese society places great importance on efforts to avoid conflict. Being critical and challenging is simply not the Japanese way. As a result, such expressions as *"Soo desu ka"* (Is that so?), *"Soo desu ne"* (That is true.), and *"Naruhodo"* (Indeed.) are some of the most commonly used expressions. However, you must recognize that often those who use what are seemingly agreeable phrases may, in fact, not completely agree with you. Rather, they are showing respect for your opinion.

Open criticism is considered socially insensitive and should be avoided. In particular, you should avoid insulting and/or embarrassing others, especially seniors, by challenging their opinions in public. If you disagree with someone, it is best to discuss the matter in private, where you can express yourself in a fairly uninhibited way, as long as the atmosphere remains cordial.

RENSHUU MONDAI

A. _____ *ni tekitoo na kotoba o irenasai.*
(Fill in the blank with the most appropriate word.)

1. *Saikin torendo ga kawatta yoo na* _____ *ga shimasu.*
2. *Minna yoku kangaete mono o kau* _____ *natta to omoimasu.*
3. *Nihonjin* _____, *donna seihin o kaimasu ka.*
4. *Iwayuru neemu-burando o konomu hito mo iru* _____ *desu ne.*
5. *Watakushi mo ikitai to omotte ita* _____ *desu.*

B. *Tekitoo na joshi mata wa setsuzokushi o irenasai.*
(Insert the appropriate particle or conjunction.)

1. *Minasan no okangae o okiki shitai* _____ *omoimasu.*
2. *Okane o takusan tsukau no* _____ *wakai josei da to kikimashita ga.*
3. *Saikin wa zasshi nado* _____ *kantan* _____ *shiraberaremasu.*
4. *Chotto matomete mimasu* _____, *hinshitsu, shinyoo, saabisu* _____ *taisetsu nan desu ne.*

C. *Tadashii kotoba o irenasai.*
(Insert the correct form of the word in parentheses.)

1. *Ryooshin to* _____ *(sumu), seikatsuhi wa irimasen.*
2. *Zasshi de* _____ *(shiraberu), sugu ii seihin ga wakarimasu.*
3. *Shitsu ga* _____ *(ii), takusan urerudeshoo.*
4. *Hinshitsu ga taisetsu* _____ *(da), ii mono o tsukuranakereba narimasen.*

KOTAE

A. 1. *ki*   2. *yoo ni*   3. *dattara*   4. *wake*   5. *tokoro*
B. 1. *to*   2. *wa*   3. *de, ni*   4. *to, ga*
C. 1. *sundara*   2. *shirabetara*   3. *yokattara*   4. *dattara*

DAI NANAKA
Lesson 7

A. KAIWA

Suzuki-shi to Neruson-shi wa rooka de shuumatsu no yotei ni tsuite hanashite iru.

SUZUKI: Neruson-san, konshuu no dooyoobi, nani ka yotei ga arimasu ka.

NERUSON: Iie, nani mo arimasen ga.

SUZUKI: Jaa, uchi[1] de ippai nomimasen ka.[2]

NERUSON: Soo desu ka. Jaa, ukagaimasu.

SUZUKI: Choofu-eki[3] no chikaku desu kara, eki de shichi ji goro matte imasu.

NERUSON: Keioo-sen[4] no Choofu desu ne. Wakarimashita.

Suzuki-san-taku de.

SUZUKI: Saa, doozo, oagari kudasai.[5]

NELSON: Ojama shimasu.[6]

SUZUKI: Junko, Neruson-san ga mieta[7] yo.

JUNKO: Ara, yookoso. Hajimemashite. Kanai de gozaimasu. Kore wa musuko no Ichiroo desu.[8] Ichiroo mo aisatsu shite.

NERUSON: Hajimemashite.

ICHIROO: Kon'nichi wa. Irasshai.[9]

NERUSON: Okusan, kore wa tsumaranai mono desu ga,[10] doozo.

JUNKO: Soo desu ka. Arigatoo gozaimasu.

SUZUKI: Kochira e doozo. Biiru de ii desu ka.

NERUSON: Hai, amari nomemasen kara, sukoshi dake itadakimasu.

SUZUKI: Asahi to Kirin[11] ga arimasu ga, dochira ni shimasu ka.[12]

NERUSON: Eeto Nihon no biiru no koto wa yoku shiranai n desu.

SUZUKI: Jaa, Kirin ni shimashoo.

NERUSON: A, Suzuki-san wa biiru ni urusakatta n desu ne.

SUZUKI: Iya, doomo. Hai, otsugi shimashoo.

Suzuki-shi wa Neruson-shi no gurasu ni biiru o tsugu.[13]

NERUSON: Hai, sumimasen.[14]

SUZUKI: Jaa, kanpai shimashoo. Yookoso.

NERUSON: Arigatoo gozaimasu. Kono hen wa shizuka na juu-takuchi nan desu ne.

SUZUKI: Mae wa soo datta n desu ga, saikin wa soo demo ari-masen.

NERUSON: Nan'nen gurai kochira ni sunde iru n desu ka.

SUZUKI: Juunen gurai ka na.

NERUSON: Doo kawarimashita ka.

SUZUKI: Tookyoo ni hito ga dondon utsutte kite, kono hen ni mo ie ga fuemashita.

NERUSON: Amerika mo onaji desu. Mae ni sunde ita Shiatoru mo jinkoo ga fuemashite, daibu soozooshiku narimashita.

JUNKO: Soo desu ka. Demo chikaku ni kodomo ga fuemashita kara, Ichiroo mo tomodachi ga takusan dekimashita. Tokorode, Neruson-san wa gokekkon wa.

NERUSON: Mada nan desu. Gaarufurendo wa iru n desu ga.

JUNKO: Amerika ni desu ka.

NERUSON: Hai, soo desu. Shiatoru ni sunde imasu.

JUNKO: Jaa, denwadai ga taihen deshoo.

NERUSON: Dekiru dake E-meeru o tsukaoo to omotte imasu.

SUZUKI: Sore dewa, wareware no seihin o jissai ni jikken suru wake desu ne.

NERUSON: Subete o hookoku shimasu kara.

SUZUKI: Kanojo wa Shiatoru de nani o shite iru n desu ka.

NERUSON: Ima daigakuin ni itte iru n desu. Rainen sotsugyoo shi-masu. Sono ato, Nihon ni kitai to itte imasu.

SUZUKI: Nihon ni kita koto wa aru n desu ka.

NERUSON: Kyonen no natsu, isshuukan bakari Kyooto[15] ni taizai shimashita.

SUZUKI: Kyooto ni.

NERUSON: **Hai, seminaa ni shusseki shita n desu. Totemo yokatta to itte imashita.**

JUNKO: **Goryoshin wa ogenki desu ka.**

NERUSON: **Chichi wa sakunen naku narimashita[16] ga, haha wa Arizona-shuu de genki ni shite imasu.**

JUNKO: **Aa, soo desu ka. Watashi mo ni nen mae ni chichi o nakushita n desu.[17]**

NERUSON: **Mattaku byooki ni wa katemasen kara. Suzuki-san-tachi wa ren'ai-kekkon desu ka. Soretomo omiai[18] desu ka.**

JUNKO: **Ara, hazukashii desu wa.[19]**

SUZUKI: **Jitsu wa Junko wa imooto no shinyuu datta n desu. Uchi ni nankai ka asobi ni kite ita kara, nan to naku shitte ita n desu ga.**

JUNKO: **Watashi wa omiai o nankai ka shite ita n desu kedo, nakanaka kimerarenaide ita n desu.**

SUZUKI: **Sore de, aru hi densha no naka de Junko ni guuzen ni ai, hanashi hajimete, sore kara tsukiai hajimeta to iu wake desu.**

NERUSON: **Imooto-san ni wa shiraseta n desu ka.**

SUZUKI: **Hajime wa naisho datta n desu. Kanojo ni shiraseta toki wa bikkuri shite imashita ga, yorokonde kuremashita.**

JUNKO: **Sorede ki ga tsuitara, kekkon shite ita n desu.**

NERUSON: **Naruhodo.**

Yuushokugo, Junko wa teeburu o katazuke, Ichiroo ni furo ni hairu yoo ni iu. Ichiroo wa famikon[20] o shitagatte iru. Neruson-shi wa Ichiroo ni hito-geemu choosen suru.

NERUSON: **Ichiroo-kun wa don'na geemu ga tokui na no.**

ICHIROO: **"Mahjong" to iu geemu ga ichiban suki desu.**

NERUSON: **Jaa, oji-san[21] hito-geemu choosen suru ka na.**

ICHIROO: **Oji-san, honto[22] ni dekiru n desu ka.**

NERUSON: **Daigaku de sono geemu o mainichi shite ita tomodachi ga ite, tokidoki tsukiatteta kara.**

ICHIROO: **Jaa, hajimemashoo. Ii desu ka.**

NERUSON: **Hai, ii desu yo.**

INVITATION

Mr. Suzuki and Mr. Nelson are discussing weekend plans in the hallway.

SUZUKI: Mr. Nelson, do you have any plans for this Saturday?

NELSON: No, I don't have anything (planned).

SUZUKI: Well then, why don't you come over to my place for a drink?

NELSON: Really? I'd love to. (lit. I will pay a visit.)

SUZUKI: It's near Choofu Station, so I'll be waiting for you there around 7 P.M.

NELSON: That's Choofu Station on the Keio Line, right? I got it.

At Mr. Suzuki's house.

SUZUKI: Oh, please come in.

NELSON: Thank you. (lit. I will intrude.)

SUZUKI: Junko, Mr. Nelson has arrived. (lit. Mr. Nelson could be seen.)

JUNKO: Oh! Welcome. It's nice to meet you. I'm Suzuki's wife. This is our son, Ichiro. Ichiro, say hello to Mr. Nelson. (lit. Greet Mr. Nelson.)

NELSON: How do you do?

ICHIRO: Hello. Welcome to our house.

NELSON: Mrs. Suzuki, I brought a little something for you. Here . . . (lit. This is an unworthy thing, but please accept it.)

JUNKO: Really? Thank you very much.

SUZUKI: Right this way. Is beer okay with you?

NELSON: Yes (that's fine). But I can't really drink that much, so I'll have (just) a little.

SUZUKI: We have Asahi and Kirin. Which would you like? (lit. Which will you do?)

NELSON: Hmm, I don't know Japanese beers that well.

SUZUKI: Well, let's start with Kirin.

NELSON: You are a connoisseur of beer, aren't you?

SUZUKI: Not really. Okay, let's fill our glasses.

Mr. Suzuki pours Nelson a glass of beer.

NELSON: Thank you.

SUZUKI: Let's toast. Welcome (to our house).

NELSON: Thank you very much. This sure is a quiet neighborhood, isn't it?

SUZUKI: It used to be, but not recently.

NELSON: About how many years have you been living here?

SUZUKI: About ten years, I guess.

NELSON: How has it changed?

SUZUKI: Well, since more and more people are moving to Tokyo, the number of houses has increased in this area, too.

NELSON: America is the same. In Seattle, where I used to live, the population has grown so much that it is (now) really noisy.

JUNKO: Is that right? But the number of kids nearby also increased, so Ichiro was able (to make) lots of friends. By the way, are you married?

NELSON: No, not yet. But I do have a girlfriend.

JUNKO: Is she in the States?

NELSON: Yes. She lives in Seattle.

JUNKO: So your telephone bills must be terrible.

NELSON: We try to use e-mail as much as possible.

SUZUKI: Well then, you are actually testing our product!

NELSON: I'll give you a complete report!

SUZUKI: What is she doing in Seattle?

NELSON: She's going to graduate school right now. She graduates next year. After that, she says she would like to come to Japan.

SUZUKI: Has she ever been to Japan?

NELSON: Yes. She was in Kyoto for just one week last summer.

SUZUKI: In Kyoto?

NELSON: Yes, she attended a seminar there. She said it (the seminar) was really good.

JUNKO: How are your parents doing?

NELSON: My dad passed away last year, but my mother is doing fine in Arizona.

JUNKO: Is that so? I also lost my father two years ago.

NELSON: Illness (is something) you just can't beat . . . Did you two get married out of love, or through an arranged marriage?

JUNKO: Oh no. It's embarrassing.

SUZUKI: Actually, Junko was my sister's best friend. I knew her a little, since she visited the house a few times.

JUNKO: (At that time,) I had met some guys by arrangement, but I really could not decide (what I should do).

SUZUKI: Then, Junko and I met by chance on a train one day, started talking, and then started dating after that.

NELSON: Did you tell your sister about it?

SUZUKI: We kept it a secret in the beginning. When we told her, she was surprised, but very happy for us.

JUNKO: And then, the next thing we knew (lit. when we noticed), we were married.

NELSON: I see.

After dinner, Junko cleans the table and tells Ichiro to take a bath. Ichiro wants to play his home video game. Mr. Nelson challenges him to a game.

NELSON: Ichiro, what game are you good at?

ICHIRO: I like "Mahjong" the best.

NELSON: All right, I'll challenge you to a game.

ICHIRO: What! You really know how to play that? (lit. Can you really do it?)

NELSON: There was a friend of mine in college who played it every day, and I played a few times with him.

ICHIRO: All right, let's begin. Are you ready?

NELSON: Okay.

B. CHUU

1. *Uchi* means "house." Unless specified to mean someone else's, as in *kare no uchi* (his house), it implies "my house."

2. *Ippai nomimasen ka* literally means "Shall we have one drink?" but usually implies "Shall we have a few drinks?" This phrase can also be used when one expects to eat and drink.

3. When Japanese people invite someone to their home for the first time, they often meet their guests at the train station closest to their house. This is done as a common courtesy, because houses are extremely difficult to find without detailed instructions.

4. The Keio Line starts at Shinjuku Station and is one of several privately owned train lines in Tokyo. The JR (Japan Railways) lines were previously government-owned but have recently been privatized.

5. The phrase *oagari kudasai* (please come in) literally means "please come up." In traditional Japanese homes, guests must take off their shoes before entering the house, and step up onto an elevated floor going into the house.

6. *Ojama shimasu* literally means "I'll disturb you," but is used to indicate that you are entering someone's home or office.

7. *Mieru* literally means "to be able to see." In this case, it refers to the fact that "someone appears" (someone can be seen).

8. *Kore wa musuko no Ichiroo desu* means "This is my son, Ichiro"; it does not mean "This is my son's Ichiro." The *no* here does not signify the possessive "s" introduced previously. It serves to identify or clarify the relationship between two nouns. Other examples include *Kochira wa tomodachi no Tanaka-san desu* (This is a friend of mine, Mr. Tanaka) and *Kanai no Hiroko desu* (This is my wife, Hiroko).

9. *Irasshai* (welcome) is less formal than *yookoso* or *yoku irasshaimashita*. It is often used by males.

10. *Kore wa tsumaranai mono desu ga* (This is an unworthy thing, but please accept it) is a humble expression used by Japanese people to describe presents given to others.

11. *Asahi-biiru* (Asahi beer) and *Kirin-biiru* (Kirin beer) are two of the most popular brands of beer in Japan. They account for 60 to 70 percent of Japanese beer consumption. Other, less popular brands are *Sapporo biiru* (Sapporo beer) and *Ebisu biiru* (Ebisu beer).

12. (Noun) *ni shimasu* means "Someone chooses (noun)." For example: *Kirin-biiru ni shimasu*. (I'll choose Kirin beer.) *Nani ni shimasu ka*. (What do you choose? [What do you want?])

13. In Japan, it is customary to have someone else pour your drinks. This is done as a sign of "concern" from the person pouring the drinks. A guest can even pour the host's drinks once in a while as a sign of concern. One may also note that people often do not start drinking without first saying *kanpai* (cheers) or eating without saying *itadakimasu* (I humbly partake).

14. *Sumimasen* literally means "sorry" or "excuse me." It has an extended meaning of "Thank you for all the trouble you went through for me."

15. Kyoto, located in midwestern Japan, is one of the country's most popular tourist attractions. It is a beautiful city filled with many serene and historic temples and gardens. Kyoto was officially the capital of Japan until it was changed to Tokyo, some one hundred years ago.

16. The word *nakunaru* means "to pass away." It is a euphemism for the verb *shinu* (to die).

17. The word *nakusu* is similar to the English expression "to lose." This can refer to both people and things.

18. *Ren'ai-kekkon* refers to a marriage where the couple meets on their own and falls in love. On the other hand, a *miai-kekkon* is an arranged marriage where the couple is introduced by other people, often their parents.

19. *Wa* is a sentence final particle often used by women. It has no real meaning, but functions to add a little emphasis to the statement.

20. *Famikon,* which originated from "family computer," are game systems for children made by companies like Nintendo and Sega. Personal computers are *pasokon*.

21. *Oji-san* literally means "uncle," but children use the word to address any older man, and use *oba-san* (aunt) to address older ladies. These are considered polite expressions. It is also common to hear *oji-san* refer to themselves as such when they speak to children.

22. *Honto* (really, truly) is a shortened form of *hontoo* and is used only in conversation. Other words that are commonly shortened include *gakkoo* (school) and *sensei* (teacher). The shortened forms are *gakko* and *sense,* respectively.

C. BUNPOO TO YOOHOO

1. INVITATIONS AND REQUESTS

One of the most common patterns used in inviting someone to do something is the negative form of a verb (formal or informal non-past) plus *ka*. The affirmative form of the verb can be used as well, but this is less frequent.

Uchi de ippai nomimasen ka.
Why don't you come to my home for a drink?

Konshuu no kinyoobi paatii o shimasu ga, irasshaimasen ka.
I am going to have a party this Friday, won't you come?

Konban shokuji o issho ni shimasen ka.
Won't you have dinner with me tonight?

Motto biiru o nomimasu ka.
Would you like some more beer?

Note: Because the negative form is not used, this sentence can also mean "Are you going to have more beer?"

Note also that the pattern, verb (stem) plus *tai desu ka* (do you want to), while meaning generally the same thing as the pattern above, is not considered an appropriate form to formally invite someone to do something. *Tai desu* is used to express one's own wants and desires, while the question form, verb (stem) *tai desu ka* is used only in interrogative sentences in more informal situations. For example, when speaking to a friend, it is okay to say *Kyoo wa nani o tabetai desu ka* (What do you want to eat today?). This is a common mistake for native English speakers learning Japanese.

2. FEMALE SPEECH

While in the past many sentence structures and expressions were reserved exclusively for one sex or the other, the trend now is for a more standard syle of speech for both men and women. This is especially true in the workplace.

Some differences in speech between men and women remain, however. Women tend to use a higher pitch and intonate better than men. Women are also more apt to use polite and formal speech. In the past, Japanese women were forced to serve men in public and private life, and consequently used the polite form more often. Even though this is no longer the case, the tradition has continued. Since many foreigners begin by learning formal Japanese, female speech may be easier to understand at first. Following are a few words used mostly by women:

---

wa: Used at the end of a sentence, it signifies mild assertiveness.
no: Used at the end of a sentence, it can signify interrogation, but sometimes has no meaning except to soften the sentence.
kashira: Used at the end of a sentence, it means "I wonder."

Compare the forms in the following conversation between a younger man *(Kenji)* and an older woman *(Keiko)*. Note that *Keiko* uses *wa, no,* and *kashira* at the end of her sentences, yet that she speaks less politely than her younger conversation partner.

KENJI: *Saikin Amerika ni itte iru imooto-san kara denwa ga arimasu ka.*
Have you had a phone call from your sister (living) in America lately?

KEIKO: *Ee. Demo denwadai ga taihen da kara, E-meeru o yoku tsukatte iru wa.*
Yes, but we are using e-mail a lot because the telephone bill is so expensive (lit. terrible).

KENJI: *Aa, soo desu ka. E-meeru o. Sorede okawari arimasen ka.*
Oh, really? (You are using) e-mail. So how is she doing? (lit. has anything changed?)

KEIKO: *Ee, genki mitai. Demo saikin booifurendo ga dekita rashii no.*
She seems fine, but it looks like she recently found a boyfriend.

KENJI: *Amerika-jin desu ka.*
Is he American?

KEIKO: *Saa, doo kashira. Hakkiri itte kurenai kara wakaranai no.*
Hmm, I wonder. She hasn't told me for sure, so I don't know.

KENJI: *Shinpai shinakutemo daijoobu desu yo.*
You don't have to be worried about it.

KEIKO: *Soo kashira. Demo chotto shinpai da wa.*
Really? But I (still) worry a little.

Note that men use *no* as a sentence final question marker in informal (using plain form verbs) situations only. The following might be heard among close male friends:

Ashita wa nani o suru no.
What are you going to do tomorrow?

Ano kaisha de nani o hanashiau no.
What are you going to discuss at that company?

3. *WA* FOR EMPHASIS

There are many ways to stress words, phrases, and sentences. One of the most common is to use the particle *wa*. By using this particle, one stresses the meaning of the preceding words or phrases. (Note: This *wa* is entirely different from the one discussed above.)

Hontoo ni ii seihin wa ooku wa nai.
There are not many really good products.

In this sentence, the speaker wants to emphasize "not many." It normally reads *Hontoo ni ii seihin wa ooku nai.* Other examples are:

Watakushi wa aru teido jishin wa arimasu.
To some degree, I have confidence.

Nihon de wa chiisai konpyuutaa ga ninki ga arimasu.
In Japan small computers are popular.

Kaisha ni wa ikimashita ga, shigoto wa shimasen deshita.
I went to my company, but did not work at all.

4. INTENTION

In Japanese, different forms and sentence patterns are used to express intention. One of them is the *oo*-form of the verb plus *to omou*. In order to form this pattern, you need the plain volitional form (expresses one's will) of the verb. There are both formal and informal (plain) volitional forms.

The formal volitional: verb (stem) + *mashoo* (Let's do)

Hajimemashoo.	Let's begin.
Ikimashoo.	Let's go.

The plain volitional form is also called the *oo*-form. It is constructed as follows:

For regular verbs, add *yoo* to the stem form.

taberu (to eat)	*tabeyoo*
kaeru (to exchange)	*kaeyoo*
shiraberu (to research)	*shirabeyoo*
mitsukeru (to find)	*mitsukeyoo*
kangaeru (to think)	*kangaeyoo*

For irregular verbs, change the *u* of the dictionary form to *oo*.

kaku (to write)	*kakoo*
nomu (to drink)	*nomoo*
hanasu (to talk)	*hanasoo*
iu (to say)	*ioo*
kiku (to listen or hear)	*kikoo*
kau (to buy)	*kaoo*

Exceptions:

suru (to do)	*shiyoo*
kuru (to come)	*koyoo*

The above forms all mean "let's (verb)." When *to omou* is added after the verb, the meaning changes to express personal intention.

Konban ippai nomoo to omou.
I think I will have some drinks tonight.

Rainen Rie to kekkon shiyoo to omoimasu.
I think I will marry Rie next year.

Kyoo denwadai o haraoo to omou.
I think I will pay the telephone bill today.

Tomodachi ni shigoto o tetsudatte moraoo to omoimasu.
I intend to have my friend help me with the work.

Ashita mo shigoto ni koyoo to omoimasu.
I think I will come to work tomorrow, too.

5. INTRANSITIVE AND TRANSITIVE VERBS

All Japanese verbs are either intransitive or transitive. Transitive verbs express actions performed on direct objects.

Watakushi wa mainichi shinbun o yomimasu.
I <u>read</u> the newspaper every day.

In this sentence, *yomimasu* (read) is the transitive verb and *shinbun* (newspaper) is the direct object. The object of the transitive verb is marked by the particle *o*. An intransitive verb does not express an action performed on an object; therefore it does not require a grammatical object.

Ie ga fuemashita.
The (number of) houses has increased.

Whether a verb is transitive or intransitive is just something you will have to memorize. However, if you think of the meaning of the verb in an English sentence, you can usually make an educated guess as to which is which. Verbs like *taberu* (to eat), *kau* (to buy), *suru* (to do), and *toru* (to take) are transitive, and verbs like *iku* (to go), *okiru* (to get up), *kaeru* (to return), and *neru* (to sleep) are intransitive.

Many Japanese verbs have similar spellings and meanings. The intransitive verbs *okiru* and *deru,* for example, look very much like the transitive verbs *okosu* and *dasu.* If you look at these verbs more closely, however, you will see that the intransitive verbs end in *ru* and the transitive verbs end in *su.* This pattern can be helpful when distinguishing between verb types.

INTRANSITIVE	TRANSITIVE
deru (to go out)	*dasu* (to take out)
okiru (to get up)	*okosu* (to wake someone up)
oriru (to get off, go down)	*orosu* (to let down)
sugiru (to elapse [time])	*sugosu* (to spend [time])
kaeru (to return [home])	*kaesu* (to return a [book])

In the examples below, most transitive verbs end with "eru." There are some exceptions, however, that you should memorize.

INTRANSITIVE	TRANSITIVE
aku (to open)	*akeru* (to open)
shimaru (to close)	*shimeru* (to close)
sodatsu (to grow up)	*sodateru* (to raise children)
yogoreru (to get dirty)	*yogosu* (to make dirty)
kowareru (to be broken)	*kowasu* (to break)
agaru (to rise)	*ageru* (to raise)
atsumaru (to gather)	*atsumeru* (to collect, gather)
hajimaru (to begin)	*hajimeru* (to begin)
kimaru (to be decided)	*kimeru* (to decide)
tomaru (to stop)	*tomeru* (to stop)

Look for the particle *o* in the following examples:

Uchi e hayaku kaerimashita.
   I returned home early.

Ano hon o toshokan ni kaeshimashita.
   I returned that book to the library.

Minasan, atsumatte kudasai.
   Everybody, please gather together. (said to a group of people)

Minasan o atsumete kudasai.
   Please gather everybody together. (said to a person)

Kuruma ga tomarimashita.
   A car stopped.

106

Kuruma o tomete kudasai.
Please stop the car.

D. BIJINESU JIKOO

NIHON NO ECHIKETTO (ETIQUETTE IN JAPAN)

When the Japanese visit the home of one of their friends, they customarily bring a gift (*temiyage*) that the host or hostess may enjoy. Liquor, fruit baskets, cookies, and cakes are popular. Recently, flowers have become a standard gift as well. Name-brand products or ones that are nicely packaged are also appreciated.

When Japanese people enter a home, they almost always take off their shoes. The host or hostess will most likely have slippers laid out for their guests' use. Not wearing the provided slippers is considered extremely rude. However, if no slippers are provided, then the guest is not expected to wear any. The Japanese like to keep their homes impeccably clean. Some say this is because they believe the floor is an extension of the bed, and traditionally they sleep on the floor. Westerners, on the other hand, tend to regard the floor as an extension of the street. Nevertheless, foreign visitors are expected to observe the Japanese custom when visiting a home.

Like many Asian people, the Japanese are known for being modest, sometimes too much so. It is believed this custom was borrowed from the Chinese long ago. This is particularly evident when visiting someone's house. For example, when you are invited to dinner, the host or hostess will express apologies for "having nothing to offer," even though the dinner may be very lavish. This may be explained by considering that the emphasis in Japan is on concern for other people's feelings and not one's own. Foreigners in Japan should remember this and try to be as modest as possible in return.

NIHON NO KAZOKU (THE FAMILY IN JAPAN)

The traditional Japanese family consists of three generations: the child, his or her parents, and the child's grandparents. Great pressure is often placed upon the eldest son, as it is his responsibility to take over the family's property and business (if there is one) and to take care of his parents when they are old. This responsibility also weighs heavily upon the eldest son's wife, who shares in the maintenence of the family.

Because the role of eldest son is often considered burdensome, many young Japanese decide to leave the rural areas, where the traditional structure is still maintained by many families, and escape to the big cities. In doing so, they leave the inheritance and responsibility to younger siblings who stay behind. Of course, they often return to the countryside to visit (especially on long national holidays), but their apartments and houses in the cities are often too small to accommodate the entire extended family. Although they usually prefer to live apart from their parents, if they become unable to take care of themselves, the younger generation will usually accept the responsibility. As the Japanese these days are living longer and tending to have smaller families, the issue of caring for the elderly is becoming more problematic, similar to the situation in the United States.

NIHON NO DEETO NO SHIKATA (DATING IN JAPAN)

Until the end of World War II, parents usually selected the person their son or daughter would marry. After the war, Japan adopted a more democratic form of government, and young people were allowed to choose their own spouses. However, families who wished to ensure the future prosperity of their house and young people who did not meet the "appropriate" person on their own made use of *o-miai,* arranged meetings.

Favored by the rich and powerful, the *o-miai* system was designed to match people of equal social status. As part of the procedure, the prospective spouse was thoroughly scrutinized with regard to social position and education. After the mutual investigations satisfied the parents, the two young people could meet and decide for themselves whether to continue dating or not.

Although the practice is still in use today, its format has been modernized and its popularity is declining. What has not changed, however, is the fact that many Japanese people still tend to marry within a small circle of university classmates, coworkers, and friends. They often have difficulty meeting future spouses outside of this group because of a reluctance to develop new relationships with people to whom they have not been properly introduced. In this way, *o-miai* lives on in modern Japan.

RENSHUU MONDAI

A. *Tekitoo na kotoba o irenasai.* (Insert the appropriate word[s].)

1. *Nani* _____ *yotei ga arimasu ka.*
2. *Choofu-eki no chikaku desu* _____, *eki* _____ *matte imasu.*
3. *Kanai* _____ *Junko to musuko* _____ *Ichiroo desu.*
4. *Haha wa Arizona* _____ *genki* _____ *shite imasu.*
5. *Watakushi mo ni nen mae* _____ *chichi* _____ *nakushimashita.*
6. *Konpyuutaa-geemu* _____ *tokui desu.*

B. *Tadashii dooshi o erabinasai.* (Choose the correct verb.)

1. *Saikin Nihon wa doo (kaemashita, kawarimashita) ka.*
2. *Kono hen ni mo ie ga dondon (fuemashita, fuyashimashita).*
3. *Kekkon o (kimenai, kimaranai) de imashita.*
4. *Sorekara tsukiai ga (hajimeta, hajimatta) to iu wake desu.*

KOTAE

A. 1. *ka* 2. *kara, de* 3. *no, no* 4. *de, ni* 5. *ni, o* 6. *ga*
B. 1. *kawarimashita* 2. *fuemashita* 3. *kimenai* 4. *hajimatta*

DAI HACHIKA
Lesson 8

A. KAIWA

TSUKIAI

Neruson-shi to Satoo-joo wa bijitekku ni kite ma mo nai node, boonasu no koto o shiritai. Konban Takagi-Buchoo to shokuji o suru koto ni natte iru node, sono koto ni tsuite kiite miru koto ni suru.

NERUSON: **Kirei na izakaya**[1] **desu ne.**

SUZUKI: **Ee, fun'iki mo kekkoo**[2] **ii shi, ryoori mo oishii n desu. Buchoo wa osoi yoo da kara, biiru demo nomihajimemashoo ka.**

NERUSON: **Ii n desu ka.**

SATOO: **Osoi toki wa hajimete ite kure**[3] **to osshatte imashita.**

SUZUKI: **(Ueitaa ni) Biiru ni san bon onegai shimasu. Aa, buchoo ga miemashita.**

TAKAGI: **Osoku natte sumimasen. Deyoo to shitara, shishachoo ni yobarete shimatte.**[4]

SUZUKI: **Iie. A, choodo biiru ga kimashita. Kanpai shimashoo.**

TAKAGI: **Hai. Jaa, Neruson-kun o kangei shite. Kanpai.**

MIN'NA: **Kanpai.**

SATOO: **Ryoori wa chuumon shite arimasu ga, toku ni gokiboo ga areba tsuika shimasu kara.**

NERUSON: **Hai, wakarimashita. Sore ni shite mo,**[5] **saikin isogashii desu ne. Kyuuryoo o sukoshi agete moraitai desu ne. (Warau.)**

TAKAGI: *(Warau.)* **Sansei.**

NERUSON: **Sore de uchi no kyuuryoo-seido wa kawaru n desu ka.**

TAKAGI: **Iya, soo iu koto wa kiite inai**[6] **kedo. Dooshite.**

SUZUKI: **Buchoo, sore ga kotoshi wa boonasu**[7] **ga deru to iu uwasa desu ga.**

TAKAGI: **Iya, uchi wa gaishikei no kaisha**[8] **da kara, boonasu wa dasanai kyuuyo-seido ni natte iru no de ne.**

SUZUKI: **Jitsu wa, boonasu ga nai kara, nenkyuu**[9] **de keisan shitara hoka no kaisha yori hikui to omoimasu yo.**

110

TAKAGI: Sonna koto wa nai hazu da ga. Choosa shite miyoo.[10]

Ryoori ga ikutsu ka kuru.

NERUSON: Oishi soo desu ne. Nan desu ka.

SATOO: Fugu[11] no karaage[12] desu. Koko wa kore de yuumei nan desu.

TAKAGI: Kore mo oishii kedo, kono aida wa Furansu-ryoori no sugoi tokoro ni shootai saremashita yo.

SATOO: Buchoo wa iroiro suteki na tokoro ni ikeru n desu ne.

TAKAGI: E, booifurendo ni tsurete itte morawanai no.

SATOO: Booifurendo nanka imasen.[13] Sore ni son'na suteki na tokoro nanka ikemasen shi.

SUZUKI: Demo, Satoo-san no yoo ni ryooshin no sewa ni natte iru hito wa raku deshoo.

SATOO: Sonna koto arimasen. Chichioya mo moo intai shite iru shi, sorosoro kekkon no koto mo kangaenakucha naranai shi.

SUZUKI: Soo ieba, Satoo-san, chikai uchi ni kekkon suru to ka kiki-mashita ga.

SATOO: Sonna koto, dare kara kiita n desu ka.

SUZUKI: Itsumo denwa o kakete kuru hito wa.

SATOO: Ano hito wa kookoo jidai no kurasumeeto desu. Zannen nagara koibito nanka ja arimasen. Demo, chikai uchi ni kekkon suru hito o shitte imasu.

SUZUKI: A, hanashi o kaemashita ne. Demo dare ka na.

SATOO: Himitsu mamoremasu ka.

SUZUKI: Daijoobu. Iwanai kara. Demo buchoo wa moo gozonji nan desho.

SATOO: Iida-san desu. Moo sugu gooru-in[14] suru rashii wa yo.

SUZUKI: Hee, honto. Shanai no dare ka ka na.

SATOO: Soko made wa wakarimasen.

SUZUKI: Satoo-san wa kekkon wa.

SATOO: Watashi, hitorikko nan desu. Dakara mondai ga atte.

NERUSON: Dooshite. Aa, shoorai wa ryooshin no sewa o shi-nakereba naranai wake desu ka.[15]

SATOO: Ee, dekireba soo shitai to omoimasu.

Shokuji no ato de, Takagi-Buchoo ga kanjoo o toru.

NERUSON: **Waa, takusan tabemashita ne. Min'na oishikatta desu.**

TAKAGI: **Kyoo wa Neruson-kun no kangei to iu koto de watashi ga mochimasu.**[16]

SUZUKI: **Buchoo, sore wa doomo. Warikan**[17] **ni shiyoo to kangaete ita n desu ga.**

TAKAGI: **Tama ni wa ii deshoo. Maikai to iu wake ni wa ikanai kedo.**

NERUSON: **Arigatoo gozaimasu.**

SATOO: **Gochisoo sama deshita.**[18]

TAKAGI: **Iya, tondemonai. Neruson-kun, nani de kaeru.**

NERUSON: **Suzuki-san to onaji hookoo desu kara, Suzuki-san to densha de kaerimasu.**

TAKAGI: **A, soo. Jaa, ki o tsukete.**

NERUSON: **Buchoo mo oki o tsukete.**

SOCIALIZING

Mr. Nelson and Ms. Sato haven't been with BusiTech for very long, and would like to know about their bonuses. Since they are having dinner tonight with Mr. Takagi, they decide to bring it up then.

NELSON: This is a nice *izakaya* isn't it?

SUZUKI: Yeah, the atmosphere is really nice, and the food is good too. It looks like the boss is going to be late, so why don't we start off with a beer or something.

NELSON: (Are you sure) it's all right (to start without him)?

SATO: He said when he is late to (go ahead) and start (without him).

SUZUKI: (To the waiter) Can we have two or three bottles of beer, please? . . . Oh look, he just arrived.

TAKAGI: Sorry I'm late. I got called in by the branch office manager just as I was on my way out (lit. when I tried to leave).

SUZUKI: No problem at all. Ah, the beer just arrived, so let's have a toast.

TAKAGI: Okay. Let's welcome Mr. Nelson (to our company). Cheers!

ALL: Cheers!

SATO: The food has already been ordered, but if you want something special, I will add it in.

NELSON: Great. Well, we have been busy lately, haven't we? I'd like to get a little pay raise. (laughs)

TAKAGI: (Laughs) I agree.

NELSON: So will the salary system be changing at our company?

TAKAGI: Not that I know of. (lit. I'm not hearing such a thing.) Why?

SUZUKI: Mr. Takagi, there's a rumor that bonuses will be distributed this year.

TAKAGI: I don't think so. (lit. No.) We work for a foreign company, and it has a system of not paying bonuses.

SUZUKI: Actually, since there are no bonuses, if you make the calculations based on our annual salaries, I think our salaries are lower than other companies'.

TAKAGI: That can't be right, but I'll look into it.

Some food arrives.

NELSON: Wow, this looks great. What is it?

SATO: It's fried globefish. This place is well known for it.

TAKAGI: Yes, and it's good, too, but the other day I was invited to a place with wonderful French cuisine.

SATO: You get to go to a lot of nice places, don't you?

TAKAGI: Doesn't your boyfriend take you out?

SATO: I don't have a boyfriend, and I can't (afford to) go to places that are that nice.

SUZUKI: But people like you who live at home (lit. who are taken care of by their parents) probably have it a little easier, right?

SATO: Not really. My dad has just retired, and I also have to start thinking about getting married soon.

SUZUKI: Speaking of that, Ms. Sato, I heard that you actually are getting married soon.

SATO: Who did you hear that from?

SUZUKI: Who is the person who is always calling you?

SATO: He's a classmate of mine from high school. Too bad for you he's not my boyfriend. But I do know someone in the office who is getting married soon.

SUZUKI: You're changing the subject! But who would that be?

SATO: Can you keep a secret?

SUZUKI: It's okay, I won't say anything. But Mr. Takagi probably already knows!

SATO: It's Ms. Iida. It looks like she's getting married soon.

SUZUKI: Wow, really? I wonder if it is someone from the office.

SATO: I don't know about that.

SUZUKI: How about you, Ms. Sato, (do you want to get) married?

SATO: I'm an only child, so I have a problem (concerning marriage).

NELSON: Why is that? Because you will have to take care of your parents in the future?

SATO: Right. If it's possible, I want to.

Mr. Takagi picks up the check (bill) after dinner.

NELSON: Wow, we ate a lot, didn't we? Everything was very good.

TAKAGI: This is Mr. Nelson's welcome (party), so it's my treat (lit. I'll pay it).

SUZUKI: Thanks, (but) we were thinking of dividing the bill equally.

TAKAGI: I don't mind (paying) sometimes, but I can't do it every time.

NELSON: Thanks.

SATO: Thanks for the dinner.

TAKAGI: No problem. So how are you going home, Mr. Nelson?

NELSON: Mr. Suzuki and I live in the same direction, so we're going to take the train together.

TAKAGI: Oh, then take care.

NELSON: You, too.

B. CHUU

1. An *izakaya* is a restaurant where drinks and various foods are served. The atmosphere is informal and can become rather rowdy.

2. As noted earlier, *kekkoo* has several meanings: "good," "okay," "fairly," and "adequate." The meaning depends on the situation. Declining something: *Kekkoo desu.* (Thank you, but no thank you.) As an adverb: *Kekkoo ii desu ne.* (It's fairly good, isn't it?)

3. *Hajimetete kure* (Go ahead and start.) is a shortened form of *hajimete ite kure*. The shortened form is used predominantly by men.

4. *Shishachoo ni yobarete shimatte* means "I was called by the head of the branch office." The sentence is not completed, and the *te*-form here implies that it was done for a reason. This type of incomplete sentence is common in Japanese.

5. *Sore ni shite mo* means something like "in spite of that" or "thinking of the situation," but it doesn't always translate well in English sentences. It often precedes the introduction of a related topic into the conversation.

6. Here, *kiite inai* means "I haven't heard yet." The *te*-form of the verb *tiru* can take on a past tense meaning in certain cases like this. Other examples are: *Mada hanashite inai.* (I have not discussed it yet.) *Moo shootai shite iru.* (I have already invited him.)

7. One of the benefits of working for a Japanese corporation is receiving a bonus every summer and winter. All employees normally receive two to three months' salary in addition to their base salary. As Japanese workers are paid based on their seniority (not ability), they tend to be satisfied if they receive salaries that are comparable to those received by workers of the same approximate age.

8. Joint-venture operations between Japanese and foreign companies often utilize a salary system similar to that of the United States, so employees generally do not receive the big bonuses that most Japanese employers pay.

9. Some Japanese corporations are also considering annual salary systems based on the American model. It appears that many will eventually adopt this type of system.

10. The sentence *Choosa shite miyoo* does not mean "Let's look into it"; rather, it means, "I'll look into it." If the subject of the sentence is singular, even though the verb ending indicates "let's (do)," it usually means "I'll (do)."

11. *Fugu* (globefish) is the name of a fish that is quite tasty, but unless prepared right, lethally poisonous. In Japan, the chef must have a special license in order to cook this fish. Nevertheless, fifty to sixty people still die every year after eating improperly prepared *fugu*.

12. *Karaage* adds the meaning "fried" to foods like fish, chicken, or vegetables. Therefore, *fugu-karaage* means "fried globefish."

13. *Booi-furendo nanka imasen* means "I do not have a boyfriend!" *Nanka* is used to emphasize the preceding word.

14. The slang term *gooru-in* (goal in) is taken from soccer and means a successful event or conclusion, such as "getting married."

15. According to Japanese tradition, children have the responsibility of caring for their parents when they become unable to care for themselves. This issue has become increasingly problematic because young Japanese do not want to accept this responsibility.

16. *Watakushi ga mochimasu* means "It's my treat" or "I'll pay for it." The verb *motsu* sometimes means "to pay" in addition to "to have."

17. The term *warikan* indicates that everyone will pay the same amount regardless of what he or she eats or drinks. When Japanese people go out to eat with coworkers, they usually "go Dutch." However, if one of them holds a higher postion at work, he or she customarily treats his or her subordinates.

18. Even outside the office, Japanese employees typically show the same respect toward their bosses as they do in the workplace, and their language often remains formal in all situations.

C. BUNPOO TO YOOHOO

1. PASSIVE VOICE

The passive voice may be defined as receiving actions from others. The actions can have either a positive or negative effect. In English, for example, you would say "My car was stolen," or "I was praised by my teacher." The Japanese passive voice is similar in usage.

The formation of the passive voice depends on the type of verb you use. The passive voice for regular verbs is formed with the verb (stem) followed by *rareru*. Note that this is the same as the potential form.

kariru (to borrow)	*karirareru* (to be borrowed)
oshieru (to teach)	*oshierareru* (to be taught)
kaeru (to change)	*kaerareru* (to be changed)
shiraseru (to inform)	*shiraserareru* (to be informed)
miru (to see)	*mirareru* (to be seen)
taberu (to eat)	*taberareru* (to be eaten)

For irregular verbs, the passive voice is formed with the verb (pre-*nai* form) plus *reru*. Another way to think about this construction is to drop the *u* from the dictionary form of the verb and add *areru* if a consonant remains at the end, and *wareru* if a vowel is left at the end. Note that for irregular verbs this is different than the potential form.

tanomu (to ask)	*tanomareru* (to be asked)
yomu (to read)	*yomareru* (to be read)
kaku (to write)	*kakareru* (to be written)
hanasu (to talk)	*hanasareru* (to be talked about)
tsukau (to use)	*tsukawareru* (to be used)
harau (to pay)	*harawareru* (to be paid)
omou (to think)	*omowareru* (to be thought of)
shiru (to know)	*shirareru* (to be known)
iu (to say)	*iwareru* (to be said)

There are two exceptions, the verbs *suru* and *kuru:*

suru (to do)	*sareru* (to be done)
kuru (to come)	*korareru* (to have come)

a. The Direct Passive

There are two types of passives in Japanese: the "direct" passive and the "indirect" passive. The direct passive is similar to the English passive in that the direct object is transformed into the subject. Only transitive verbs that require the direct object particle *o* may be transformed into a direct passive. The passive sentence is used to emphasize the subject.

Gakusei o yobimashita.
We called a student.

Gakusei ga yobaremashita.
A student was called.

Atarashii shain ga shookai saremashita.
The new employees were introduced.

Kono seihin wa yoku tsukawarete imasu.
This product is used widely.

Kare wa min'na ni shirarete imasu.
He is known by everyone.

Okyaku-san no koto o kangaete tsukurarete imasu.
It is made with the customer in mind.

b. The Indirect Passive

In the indirect passive, the subject is rarely inanimate. This is due to the fact that the subject is the recipient of an action performed by another. The verbs in the indirect passive form can be either transitive or intransitive. This sentence structure is used when expressing that one has been adversely affected, or has been made to suffer from the actions of another, as in the sentence *Chichi ni shinaremashita.* (My father passed away on me.) Note that the particle *ni* is used to indicate who or what made the subject suffer, and the particle *o* still marks the grammatical object.

Chichi ni tegami o yomaremashita.
My letter (much to my chagrin) was read by my father.

Kyoo wa okyaku-san ni korarete, nani mo dekimasen deshita.
Today, some clients came (by) so I couldn't get anything done. (lit. I was visited by clients and I could not do anything today.)

2. *WAKE DEWA NAI*

The expression *wake dewa nai* (it is not that) is used when clarifying a matter. It follows all parts of speech as follows:

> verbs: plain form + *wake dewa nai*
> *i*-adjectives: plain form + *wake dewa nai*
> nouns and *na*-adjectives + any plain form of the copula
>   *da* + *wake dewa nai*

Please note that in the noun + *da* form, the *da* becomes *no* + *wake dewa nai*. In the *na*-adjective + *da* form, the *da* becomes *na* + *wake dewa nai*.

Uchi no kyuuryoo wa tokubetsu takai wake dewa arimasen.
It's not that our salaries are especially high, or anything.

Keisan shita wake dewa arimasen ga, chigau yoo desu.
I did not actually calculate it, but it seems to be wrong (somehow).

Dame na wake dewa arimasen ga amari yoku arimasen.
It is not that it's bad, but it's not so great (either).

Kekkon shinai wake dewa arimasen ga, mada hayai to omoimasu.
It's not that I will not get married, it's just that it is a little (too) soon.

Pasokon wa takai wake dewa arimasen ga, amari yasuku arimasen.
Personal computers are not too expensive, but they aren't so cheap either.

Yasui kyuuryoo no wake dewa arimasen ga, itsumo tarimasen.
It is not that it's (my salary's) low pay, but I never have enough.

3. *WAKE NIWA IKANAI*

Wake niwa ikanai is equivalent to "there is no reason to" or "can't very well" in English and implies that something cannot be done for social, moral, or psychological reasons. The verbs used before *wake* are always in the plain form.

Boonasu o dasu wake niwa ikimasen.
We just can't be giving out bonuses.

Itsumademo oya no sewa ni naru wake niwa ikimasen.
One can't always be taken care of by one's parents.

Kaisha o yameru wake niwa ikimasen deshita.
It's not like I could have just quit the company.

Itsumademo kekkon shinai wake niwa ikimasen.
One can't stay unmarried forever.

4. *HAZU (DA)*

Hazu is a dependent noun which indicates that the word or phrase preceding it is an expected or logical result. It translates as "I expect that," "It is expected that," or "I am fairly certain that." Since *hazu* is a noun, modifiers (words coming before *hazu*) are in the plain form (with two exceptions):

> verbs: plain form + *hazu (da)*
> *i*-adjectives: plain form + *hazu (da)*
> nouns and *na*-adjectives + any plain form of the copula
>   *da* + *hazu (da)*

Note that in the noun + *da* form, the *da* becomes *no* + *hazu (da)*. In the *na*-adjective + *da* form, the *da* becomes *na* + *hazu (da)*.

Kyuuryoo o hoka no kaisha to kurabetara, takai hazu desu.
If we compare our salaries to those from other companies, ours should be higher.

Ano resutoran no ryoori wa oishii hazu desu.
The food at that restaurant is supposed to be good.

Buchoo wa osake ga amari nomenai hazu desu.
I am fairly certain that the director can't drink much liquor.

Shishachoo mo mieru hazu desu.
The branch manager is also supposed to be coming.

Ano hito wa gaikokujin no hazu da.
He is supposed to be a foreigner.

Kare no koibito wa kirei na hazu da yo.
His girlfriend is supposed to be beautiful.

D. BIJINESU JIKOO

TSUKIAI (SOCIALIZING)

When in Japan on business, you will likely be invited to go out to lunch or dinner quite often. Likewise, there will be ample opportunity to extend similar invitations to colleagues and associates. As elsewhere, conversation over a meal or a few drinks is considered an effective means of developing personal and business relations. However, there are some unstated ground rules you should be aware of.

When a Japanese colleague, customer, or associate invites you out for drinks or a meal, he will most likely take you to an establishment he knows, will do the ordering, and pay for the meal. In this way, the host or hostess of the restaurant knows who is going to pay. When the bill is delivered, simply thank him and tell him politely that next time you will treat him to dinner.

It is important that you somehow "repay" your host for the meal on a later occasion, unless he treated you as remuneration for a favor you had done for him before. However, if someone of much higher status invites you out, it is not necessary to invite him out in return. Finally, there is no "going Dutch" (*warikan* or *betsu betsu*) on business lunches or dinners, even if they are informal.

When a group of friends or colleagues goes out, each person usually pays an equal portion of the bill, no matter how much or how little he or she ordered. You do not pay for only your share. This is a common social practice in Japan. Tips are normally not given at restaurants.

During meals, it is important that you interact properly with your colleagues or other members of your party. It is not wise to begin eating whenever and whatever you like, to finish too soon, or to take too long. In order to interact with one another, the Japanese usually offer to pour each other's drinks and never hesitate to pass common serving dishes around the table.

For more formal gatherings, proper understanding of Japanese protocol will help you to make a good impression. Etiquette at social functions is a mix of manners borrowed from the British and those traditional to the Japanese. The fundamental principles of proper behavior are based on hierarchy and formality. This extends to greetings,

120

seating arrangements, and the order of speakers, among other things.

Seating arrangements are particularly important to the Japanese in formal or semiformal gatherings. These arrangements clearly indicate who is the guest of honor and who is of higher and lower status. The guest of honor or the individual with the highest position should sit in the seat farthest from the door in Western-style rooms and in front of the *tokonoma* (an alcove with scrolls and flowers) in a Japanese-style room. As a courtesy, everyone should stand up upon the arrival of the honored guests. If certain members of the party are meeting for the first time, it is customary to exchange business cards before sitting down.

The person with the highest relative status should start conversations, while persons of lower status customarily do not speak, unless asked to do so. Conversation is usually initiated on general topics such as weather, sports, entertainment, news, and current social and political issues. Issues of business may be discussed, but usually only in general terms. The purpose of such a gathering is to promote relationships among the participants. The language is more relaxed than in the office, and conversations about personal life may also contribute to the feeling of closeness. Drinking a little too much is an accepted behavior among Japanese at these parties, though it is not encouraged.

TATEMAE TO HON'NE ("TWO FACES")

For lack of a better understanding of the so-called two faces of the Japanese, Westerners have sometimes described the Japanese as "inscrutable." Realizing that a Japanese person has "two faces" in almost everything he or she does, however, makes Japanese behavior much more predictable. Casual association with the Japanese reveals only the "first face," and hence only half of the phenomenon.

The two faces are called *tatemae* and *hon'ne*. The concept behind *tatemae* is "official stance" or "organizational posture," whereas *hon'ne* suggests "real, honest feeling." Westerners may often experience the same split personality as a result of being divided between their individual beliefs and their organizational responsibilities, but this phenomenon permeates Japanese interaction much more deeply.

Some believe that Japan's geographical and historical isolation brought about this type of social behavior. The Japanese have traditionally lived together in small, dense communities, and *tatemae* became the solution to the constraints of a highly populated and highly structured society, a way of maintaining harmony, or *wa,* though at the cost of self-expression. It is a cooperative mechanism.

What lies behind the surface is *hon'ne,* the true feelings. These are opinions best reserved for sharing with the appropriate peer group at an appropriate time, and if you get to know someone well enough, you will be able to communicate at this level. However, while everyone has his or her *hon'ne*-self, it is expected that only the *tatemae*-self is presented to the world.

It is important that non-Japanese people understand popular behavior within the context of this system, but not always imitate it. Many Japanese admire the frankness and self-expression of foreigners and find a Westerner's expression of *hon'ne* refreshing—to a degree.

RENSHUU MONDAI

A. *Tekitoo na joshi o irenasai.* (Insert the appropriate particle[s].)

1. *Fuin'iki mo ii _____, ryoori mo oishii desu.*
2. *Buchoo wa osoi yoo da _____, nomihajimemashoo.*
3. *Kyuuryoo ga takai kaisha wa boonasu o dasanakute _____ ii desu.*
4. *Futsuu no kaisha _____ kurabetara, kono kaisha wa takai hazu desu.*
5. *Chikai uchi ni kekkon suru _____ _____ kikimashita.*

B. *Tadashii hyoogen o erabinasai.* (Choose the correct expression.)

1. *Shishachoo ni (yobaremashita, yobimashita).*
2. *Kono kaisha no kyuuryoo wa tokubetsu takai (wake demo arimasen, wake demo arimasu).*
3. *Futsuu no kaisha to kurabetara, (takaku, takai) hazu desu.*
4. *Maikai harau (wake niwa ikimasu, wake niwa ikimasen).*

C. *_____ o shugo ni shite noodootai o judootai ni kaenasai.* (Transform "active voice" to "passive voice," making the underlined words subjects.)

1. *Shishachoo wa buchoo o yobimashita.*
2. *Shain wa Neruson-san o kangei shimashita.*
3. *Tabemono o tsuika shimashita.*
4. *Kyuuryoo-seido o kaemashita.*

KOTAE

A. 1. *shi* 2. *kara* 3. *mo* 4. *to* (or *ni*) 5. *to, ka*
B. 1. *yobaremashita.* 2. *wake demo arimasen* 3. *takai* 4. *wake niwa ikimasen.*
C. 1. *Buchoo ga shishachoo ni yobaremashita.* 2. *Neruson-san ga shain ni kangei saremashita.* 3. *Tabemono ga tsuika saremashita.* 4. *Kyuuryoo-seido ga kaeraremashita.*

DAI KYUUKA
Lesson 9

A. KAIWA

Kyoo wa suiyoobi.[1] Neruson-shi to Satoo-joo wa Makuhari Toreedo Shoo ni iku koto ni natte iru. Neruson-shi, jimusho ni chotto osoku tsuku.

NERUSON: **Satoo-san, osoku natte sumimasen. Kinoo wa hisashiburi ni rirakkusu shite, chotto nomisugite shimatta rashii desu.**

SATOO: **Ara, futsukayoi[2] desu ka. Kyoo Makuhari e iku koto ga dekimasu ka.**

NERUSON: **Maa daijoobu deshoo. Jaa, sorosoro[3] ikimashoo ka.**

SATOO: **Hai. Kanari tooi kara isogimashoo. Ichijikan ijoo kakarimasu.**

NERUSON: **Makuhari wa hajimete desu ga, densha de iku n desu ne.**

SATOO: **Hai. Sakki jikokuhyoo[4] de shirabeta n desu ga, tsugi no kyuukoo wa juuji desu. Isogeba maniau kamo shiremasen.**

Tookyoo-Eki de.

NERUSON: **Furafura de[5] amari hayaku hashiremasen.**

SATOO: **Demo moo sukoshi desu kara, ganbatte.**

NERUSON: **Aa, ma ni atta.**

SATOO: **Asoko ni suwarimashoo ka.**

NERUSON: **Shitsurei. Chotto asupirin o nomimasu.[6] Makuhari-Messe de[7] iroiro na shoo ga aru soo desu ne.**

SATOO: **Hai. Tokyoo kara tooi kedo, totemo kirei na "mirai-toshi"[8] nan desu.**

NERUSON: **Soo rashii desu ne. Mae ni shinbun de yomimashita. Kyoo wa iroiro na shinseihin ga dete iru rashii desu ne.**

SATOO: **Ee, kyoosoo aite no seihin mo miraretara, ii desu ne.**

Makuhari ni tsuku.

SATOO: **Neruson-san, tsukimashita yo.**

NERUSON: **Aa, sukkari nemutte shimatte.[9] Ibiki kaiteta ka naa.[10]**

SATOO: **Ee, chotto.**

NERUSON: **Demo daibu kibun ga yoku narimashita. Gomennasai ne.**

SATOO: **Iie. Koko ga kaijoo desu.**

Toreedo shoo no kaijoo no iriguchi de.

KURAAKU: **Nanmei-sama desu ka.**

SATOO: **Futari desu.**

KURAAKU: **Nimei-sama de sanzen en desu. Kore ga honjitsu tenji shite iru buusu no an'nai de gozaimasu.**

SATOO: **Arigatoo.**

NERUSON: **Waa, kirei na kaijoo da. Sugoi[11] hito desu ne. Koko ni yotte mimasen ka.**

FURUYA: **Kochira ni gokimei o onegai shimasu. Kochira ni saishin no sofuto ga iroiro gozaimasu.**

SATOO: **Kono nichiei hon'yaku no sofuto ni tsuite motto shiritai n desu ga.**

FURUYA: **Kore wa mottomo atarashii mono de, omo ni tegami no hon'yaku ni tsukaimasu. Futsuu no shorui nara kyuujup-paasento seikaku ni hon'yaku dekimasu.**

NERUSON: **Sono nokori no juppaasento no yakushikata ga muzukashii n deshoo.**

FURUYA: **Ee, soo nan desu. Ningen ja nakute, kikai desu kara. Kono sofuto o tsukatte, demonsutoreeshon shite mimashoo ka.**

NERUSON: **Hai.**

FURUYA: **Doozo osuwari ni natte[12] kudasai. Yatte mimashoo.**

NERUSON: **Naruhodo. Bunshoo o iretara, kiiroi aikon o kurikku suru n desu ne. Soo suru to, hon'yaku ga deru to iu wake desu ne. Uumu, nakanaka ii desu ne. Nedan wa dono gurai suru n desu ka.**

FURUYA: **Shijoo ni deta bakari de, chotto takai desu ga. Koko ni kakakuhyoo ga gozaimasu.**

NERUSON: **Waa, kanari ii nedan desu ne. Panfuretto kudasai.**

FURUYA: **Hai. Mochiron intaanetto mo tsunagu koto ga dekimasu.**

SATOO: **Naruhodo. Demo yoo o moraemasu ka.**

FURUYA: **Hai, doozo. Goshitsumon ga arimashitara, koko ni goren-raku kudasai.**

Ichijikan hodo, hoka no demo o mite itara, Satoo-joo, daigaku-jidai no yuujin ni guuzen ni au.

SATOO: **Aa, Keiko[13] ja nai.[14]**

CHIBA: **Hiroko, hisashiburi. Genki!**

SATOO: **Un. Nani shiteru no.[15]**

CHIBA: **NTT de shinseihin koodinetaa o shite iru no.**

SATOO: **Buusu dashiteru no.**

CHIBA: **Un. Asoko na no.**

SATOO: **Shinjirarenai wa. Kon'na tokoro de au nante.[16]**

CHIBA: **Honto. Hiroko wa ima nani shiteru no.**

SATOO: **Bijitekku to iu gaishikei no kaisha ni tsutomete iru no. A, shookai suru wa. Kochira, honsha kara kite iru Neruson desu. Neruson-san, watashi no daigaku no kurasumeeto no Chiba Keiko-san. Suteki na[17] kata deshoo.**

CHIBA: **Yamete.**

NERUSON: **Ee, kirei na kata desu ne. Neruson desu. Doozo yoroshiku.**

CHIBA: **Yoroshiku onegai shimasu. Meishi itadakeru kashira.[18]**

NERUSON: **Aa shitsurei. Kore desu.**

SATOO: **Chuushoku no yotei ga nakattara, issho ni shinai.**

CHIBA: **Soo ne. Zehi.**

NERUSON: **Juuniji ni ano iriguchi de aimashoo.**

CHIBA: **Hai, tanoshimi ni shite iru. Jaa, sono toki ni mata yukkuri.**

MARKET RESEARCH

It's Wednesday. Mr. Nelson and Ms. Sato are supposed to visit the trade show in Makuhari. Mr. Nelson arrives at the office a little late.

NELSON: Ms. Sato, I'm sorry I'm late. Yesterday I relaxed for the first time in a long time and I'm afraid that I had a little too much to drink.

SATO: So, you have a hangover, huh? Will you be able to make it to Makuhari today?

NELSON: Yeah, I think I'll be okay. Shall we get going?

SATOU: Yeah, it is pretty far, so let's hurry. It will take more than an hour.

NELSON: This is my first time to Makuhari. We take the train, right?

SATO: Yes. I checked the timetable and the next express train is at 10 A.M. If we hurry, we may be able to catch it.

At Tokyo Station.

NELSON: I can't run very fast (because) I feel dizzy.

SATO: Well, just a little more. Hang in there!

NELSON: Ah, we made it.

SATO: Shall we sit over there?

NELSON: Excuse me. I'm going to take an aspirin . . . I hear at Makuhari there are all kinds of shows.

SATO: Yes. It is a long way from Tokyo, but it's really a beautiful "city of the future."

NELSON: Yeah, that's what I've heard. (lit. It seems to be so.) I read something about it in the paper (lit. before). I understand that many new products will be on display today.

SATO: That's right. I hope we can also see some of our competitors' products.

They arrive at Makuhari.

SATO: Mr. Nelson, we've arrived.

NELSON: Wow, I fell fast asleep. I wonder if I was snoring.

SATO: Yeah, a little.

NELSON: But I feel much better now. I'm sorry.

SATO: It's okay. This is the meeting place.

At the entrance of the trade show.

CLERK: How many (people)?

SATO: Two.

CLERK: That'll be three thousand yen for both of you. This is a guide to the booths we have on display today.

SATO: Thanks.

126

NELSON: Wow. This is a nice place. There (sure) are a lot of people here. Shall we stop here and take a look (at this booth)?

FURUYA: Could you please register your names here? We have the latest versions of various kinds of software here.

SATO: I'd like to know more about this Japanese-English translation software.

FURUYA: This is our newest (product), and is mainly used for translating letters. For regular documents, it can translate with 90 percent accuracy.

NELSON: It's that remaining 10 percent that's hard to translate, right?

FURUYA: Yes, that's right. After all, it's only a machine, not a person. How about a demonstration of the software? (lit. Shall I give you a demonstration using this software?)

NELSON: Yes, please.

FURUYA: Please sit down. I'll demonstrate it.

NELSON: I see. I input a sentence and click on the yellow icon. Then (lit. when you do that,) the translation will appear. . . . Wow, that's really great, isn't it? About how much is it?

FURUYA: It just came out on the market, so it's (still) pretty expensive. The price list is right here.

NELSON: Wow, that is pretty expensive, isn't it? May I have a pamphlet (for this product)?

FURUYA: Sure. Of course, you can connect with the Internet as well.

SATO: I see. Do you have a demo version that I can have?

FURUYA: Sure, here you are. If you have any questions, please contact me at this number.

After watching other demonstrations for an hour, Sato runs into a friend from her college days.

SATO: Well, if it isn't Keiko!

CHIBA: Hiroko, long time, no see. How are you?

SATO: Fine. What have you been up to?

CHIBA: I'm working for NTT as a new products production coordinator.

SATO: Does (your company) have a booth?

CHIBA: Yes, it's over there.

SATO: I can't believe it! Running into you at a place like this . . .

CHIBA: No kidding. (lit. Really.) What are you doing these days, Hiroko?

SATO: I'm working for a foreign company called BusiTech. Let me introduce you (to someone). This is Mr. Nelson from our home office. Mr. Nelson, this is Keiko Chiba, a former college classmate of mine. She's pretty, don't you think?

CHIBA: Knock it off. (lit. Stop.)

NELSON: Yes, she is pretty. My name is Nelson. It's nice to meet you.

CHIBA: It's nice to meet you, too. May I have one of your business cards?

NELSON: I'm sorry, here you are.

SATO: If you don't have plans for lunch, would you like to join us?

CHIBA: Okay, I'd love to. (lit. By all means.)

NELSON: Let's meet over at that entrance at noon.

CHIBA: Okay, I'm looking forward to it. Let's talk more (over lunch).

B. CHUU

1. *Kyoo wa suiyoobi* means "It's Wednesday today." The copula is omitted because it is clearly understood by context.

2. In Japan there are many occasions to drink. The word *futsuka-yoi* (hangover) (lit. second day drunk) is therefore often heard both in and outside of offices.

3. The expression *sorosoro* translates as "it's about time to" and is used to state the intention of beginning another activity.

4. *Jikokuhyoo* (timetable) is a book listing virtually all the train schedules in Japan.

5. *Furafura* is an onomatopoeic word expressing feelings of dizziness. More examples of onomatopoeia can be found in Lesson 15.

6. While *nomu* means "to drink," it can also mean "to swallow." Therefore, the Japanese use *nomu* for things like medicine and soup.

7. The particle *ni* is used to indicate location with such verbs as *aru* (to be) and *iru* (to exist). However, when *aru* is used to mean "to hold" or "to be held," the particle *de* is used instead.

8. The huge Makuhari Convention Center, along with the surrounding office buildings and hotels, is one of several Japanese government projects built in areas that were previously undeveloped.

Another example is New Kansai International Airport near Osaka, which was constructed on the ocean.

9. Due to the long commutes to and from work, many Japanese sleep on trains and buses.

10. *Ibiki kaiteta ka naa* is an informal sentence meaning "I wonder (if) I was snoring." While the expression "to snore" is really *ibiki o kaku,* particles such as *wa, ga,* and *o* can be omitted in informal sentences like this one. The extra *a* on the end of *ka naa* (I wonder) is used only in informal conversation and makes the sentence more emphatic.

11. The word *sugoi* has many different meanings, depending on the context of the sentence. There are positive meanings such as "wonderful" and "great," as well as negative ones like "awful" and "terrible," which can be extended to express "a terrible amount."

12. The pattern *o* + verb stem + *ni naru* is highly deferential. *Okaeri ni naru* and *oyobi ni naru* mean, respectively, "(Someone with high status) returns" and "(Someone with high status) calls."

13. The Japanese have a long tradition of adding *san, sama, kun,* or other titles to individuals' names to show different levels of respect. Since World War II, this tradition has gradually slipped away, partly due to the influence of Western cultures. Now it is rather common among young people to address their friends without adding such titles.

14. Among friends and family members, Japanese people speak informally, creating an atmosphere of familiarity. Using plain forms of verbs and adjectives is one way of expressing this lack of formality.

15. As you learned in Lesson 7, the particle *no* may be used either to express an interrogative sentence or to end a statement. In the case of a statement, *no* is used only by women, but the interrogative *no* is now used by both men and women.

16. *Nante* is the informal form of *(nan) to wa,* and is used to emphasize the statement that precedes it.

17. *Suteki* means "wonderful," "cute," or "splendid."

18. As mentioned in Lesson 7, *kashira* is an ending that means "I wonder." It is used only in informal situations and only by women. Men use *ka na* to express the same thing.

C. BUNPOO TO YOOHOO

1. REASONS (BECAUSE, SINCE)

The expressions *kara* and *node* are often used to mean "because," "since," or "being that." *Kara* and *node* are sometimes used interchangeably, yet there are subtle differences between the two. *Kara* is used when giving a subjective or personal reason. *Node* is normally used when an objective reason or cause is being given. *Node*, the more polite of the two, is used in more formal situations in business and in written Japanese.

a. *Node*

Node occurs after verbs, adjectives, and nouns in the following way:

verbs	plain form + *node*
i-adjectives	plain form + *node*
nouns and *na*-adjectives + any form of the copula *da* + *node*	

Please note that in the noun or *na*-adjective + *da* forms + *node* pattern, the non-past affirmative copula *(da)* becomes *na* + *node*.

Kanojo wa wakai node, sono shigoto wa chotto muri deshoo.
Since she is young, she may not be able to do that job.

Nemutte shimatta node, oriru eki ni ki ga tsukimasen deshita.
Because I fell asleep, I did not notice the station where I was supposed to get off.

Benri na node, takushii o itsumo tsukatte shimaimasu.
Because it is so convenient, I always end up taking a taxi.

Sono sofuto no tsukaikata wa muzukashikatta node, wakarimasen deshita.
Because the software was difficult to use, I did not understand it.

Suzuki-san wa shinsetsu na hito na node, tasukete kureru deshoo.
Since Mr. Suzuki is a kind person, he will probably help (us).

b. *Kara*

Kara may follow either polite or plain forms of verbs, *i*-adjectives, and nouns or *na*-adjectives plus the copula *da*. There are no exceptions.

Toreedo-shoo ga tooi kara, ikanai koto ni shimashita.
Because the trade show is (so) far away, I decided not to go.

Ningen ja nai kara, sore wa muri deshoo.
  Since they are not human beings, it would be difficult (to perform well).

Kirei na kaijoo da kara, min'na ikimasu.
  Since the hall is a beautiful place, everyone goes there.

Osake ga suki desu kara, tokidoki nomisugite shimaimasu.
  Because I like sake, I end up drinking too much sometimes.

Hon'ya-san ni ikimasu kara, hon o katte agemasu.
  Since I'm going to the bookstore, I'll buy a book for you.

2. SUGIRU

The ending *sugiru* is used to express that something is in a state of excess. This can apply to verbs to mean "to do something too much," as well as to adjectives to express that "something is too much." *Sugiru* follows verbs and adjectives as follows:

verbs	stem + *sugiru*
i-adjectives	stem (without *i*) + *sugiru*
na-adjectives	(without *na*) + *sugiru*

Kinoo wa chotto nomisugimashita.
  I drank a little too much yesterday.

Kyoo wa tabesugita yoo desu.
  It looks like I ate too much today.

Ryoori o tsukurisugite shimaimashita.
  I cooked too much (food).

Nihon no apaato wa takasugimasu ne.
  Apartments in Japan are too expensive, aren't they?

Nihon dewa tabemono ga oishisugite, tabesugite shimaimasu.
  The food in Japan is just too good, so I (usually) eat too much.

Hon'yaku ga seikaku sugiru to iu koto wa arimasen.
  There is no such thing as "the translation is too accurate."

3. KOTO GA DEKIRU

In Lesson 5, you learned that the potential form of verbs indicates "ability" and "probability." You can express almost the same idea using the pattern of verb (plain non-past affirmative) + *koto ga dekiru*. This form is a little more formal and used more often in writing.

Kyoo Makuhari e iku koto ga dekimasu ka.
Can you go to Makuhari today?

Nihongo no shinbun o yomu koto ga dekimasu ka.
Can you read a Japanese newspaper?

Kono sofuto de Nihongo in hon'yaku suru koto ga dekimasu ka.
Can you translate this into Japanese using this software?

Kono sufuto o tsukatte dare demo tanoshiku manabu koto ga dekimasu yo.
Everyone can have fun learning it by using this software.

Hitori de kaeru koto ga dekimasu ka.
Will you be able to go home alone?

Furansu-go o hanasu koto ga dekimasen.
I can't speak French.

4. NEGATIVE *TE*-FORM OF THE COPULA

To negate a previous clause (A) and correct the statement in a second clause (B) the pattern A *dewa nakute/janakute* (derived from *dewa nai* and *janai*) B *da* is commonly used.

Sofuto wa ningen ja nakute, kikai desu kara.
It's because the software is not a human being, but a machine.

Oiwai wa kyoo ja nakute ashita desu yo.
The celebration is not today, but tomorrow.

Sotsugyoo wa kotoshi ja nakute rainen da.
Her graduation is not this year, but next year.

Tenkin dewa nakute shutchoo desu.
It is not a (company) transfer; it's a business trip.

5. *TAME (NI)*

Tame (ni) is a dependent noun (cannot be used alone) and can mean many different things: "in order to do," "for the purpose of something," "because," or "for someone." It follows verbs, adjectives, and nouns in the following way:

verbs	plain non-past + *tame ni*
i-adjectives	plain non-past + *tame ni*
nouns	nouns + *da* become noun + *no* + *tame ni*
na-adjectives	*na*-adjectives + *na* + *tame ni*

Sono sofuto o setsumei suru tame ni kimashita.
I came to explain the software.

Sono shoohin wa nedan ga yasui tame ni yoku uremasu.
Because the products are inexpensive, they sell well.

Shigoto no tame ni mainichi osoku narimasu.
Because of my work, I go home late (lit. it becomes late) every day.

Nan'no tame ni Nihon ni ikimasu ka.
Why (lit. for what purpose) are you going to Japan?

Gaikokujin no tame ni kaihatsu saremashita.
It was developed for non-Japanese people.

D. BIJINESU JIKOO

NIHON NO KONPYUUTAA (COMPUTERS IN JAPAN)

As is the case all over the world, the use of computers is still expanding in Japan. Many businesses are converting to network systems and creating Internet homepages. Japan is by no means new to the computer revolution. Chip-making companies like NEC, Toshiba, and Hitachi have been competing in the computer world for some time. For a long time, Japanese software was imported from companies in the United States, but, with the recent establishment of Japanese software companies, this trend should change. Unlike the United States, most of the computers are purchased and used by businesses, but recently more and more people have been buying home computers, as the younger generation becomes more familiar with them.

Most computer-related vocabulary is borrowed from English, so it's not too difficult for native English speakers who already have some familiarity with computers to learn these words (see the vocabulary list for this chapter in Section 2).

RENSHUU MONDAI

A. *Tekitoo na kotoba o erabinasai.* (Choose the appropriate word.)

1. *Kinoo wa chotto (nomi, nomu) sugimashita.*
2. *Ashita kaisha ni (iki, iku) koto ga dekimasen.*
3. *Kikai (ja nakute, janai), ningen desu.*
4. *Kodomo kara otona made daredemo (tanoshii, tanoshiku) manabemasu.*

B. *Tekitoo na joshi o irenasai.* (Insert the appropriate particle[s].)

1. *Mae ni shinbun* _____ *yomimashita.*
2. *Ibiki kaiteta* _____ *naa.*
3. *Kochira ni saishin no sofuto* _____ *iroiro arimasu.*
4. *Omoni tegami no hon'yaku* _____ *tsukaimasu.*
5. *Gaishikei no kaisha* _____ *tsutomete imasu.*

C. *Tsugi no kaiwa o infoomaru na kaiwa ni kaenasai.* (Change the following dialogue into an informal one.)

1. *Ara, Keiko-san jaa arimasen ka.*
2. *Hiroko-san hisashiburi desu ne.*
3. *Hai, nani o shite imasu ka.*
4. *NTT de shinseihin no koodineetaa o shite imasu.*
5. *Buusu o dashite imasu ka.*
6. *Hai, asoko nan desu no.*

KOTAE

A. 1. *nomi* 2. *iku* 3. *ja nakute* 4. *tanoshiku*
B. 1. *de* 2. *ka* 3. *ga* 4. *ni* 5. *ni*
C. 1. *Aa, Keiko janai.* 2. *Hiroko, hisashiburi, ne.* 3. *Un, nani shiteru no.*
4. *NTT de shinseihin no koodineetaa o shite iru no.* 5. *Buusu dashiteru no.*
6. *Un. Asoko na no.*

DAI JUKKA
Lesson 10

A. KAIWA

Neruson-shi ga Nihon ni kite nikagetsu ni naru. Taihen isogashii seikatsu ga tsuzuki, tsukare ga dete, kaze o hiku.

Denwa de.

IIDA: **Bijitekku de gozaimasu.**

NERUSON: **Moshi moshi, Neruson desu ga.**

IIDA: **Doo saremashita ka. Genki ga nai yoo desu ga.**

NERUSON: **Kyoo wa yasumimasu.[1] Chotto kibun ga warui kara.**

IIDA: **Wakarimashita. Minasan ni tsutaete okimasu.**

NERUSON: **Sore de Satoo-san ni miitingu wa asu suru to tsutaete oite kudasai.**

IIDA: **Hai, wakarimashita.**

NERUSON: **Sore de, doko ka byooin o shitte imasu ka.**

IIDA: **Chotto tooi desu ga, Toranomon-Byooin[2] wa doo desu ka. Shin'yoo ga arimasu.**

NERUSON: **Toranomon-Byooin desu ka. Choofu kara doo ikeba ii n desu ka.**

IIDA: **Shinjuku de chikatetsu ni notte, Toranomon[3] de oriru to soko kara sugu miemasu.**

NERUSON: **Hai. Nani ka attara, gogo renraku shite kudasaru yoo ni itte kudasai. Boku wa kore kara byooin ni itte mimasu kara.**

IIDA: **Hai, odaiji ni.[4]**

Neruson-shi, byooin ni tsuite kara, uketsuke to kaite aru madoguchi ni iku.

NERUSON: **Sumimasen. Kibun ga warui node, oisha-san ni mite itadakitai n desu ga.**

UKETSUKE: **Hai. Jaa, kono mooshikomisho ni kakikonde kudasai. Hoken no kaado[5] wa arimasu ka.**

NERUSON: **Mada Nihon no hoken wa arimasen ga.**

UKETSUKE: Sore dewa zengaku genkin de haratte itadaku koto ni narimasu ga, yoroshii desu ka.

NERUSON: Hai, ii desu. Daibu matanakereba narimasen ka.

UKETSUKE: Iie, juppun gurai deshoo.

Machiaishitsu wa konde ita ga, juppun hodo suru to namae ga yobare shinsatsushitsu ni an'nai sareru.

ISHA: Doo shimashita ka.[6]

NERUSON: Kibun ga yoku arimasen. Sore ni shokuyoku ga nai n desu.

ISHA: Kaoiro ga yokunai desu ne. Chotto kuchi o akete kudasai. Nodo ga chotto akai desu ne.

NERUSON: Soo desu ka. Saikin hidoku tsukareru n desu. Jitsu wa nikagetsu mae ni kochira ni tenkin shite kita n desu ga, yasumi nashi de hataraite ita mono desu kara.

ISHA: Aa, soo. Memai ga shimasen ka.

NERUSON: Ee, chotto. Sore ni atama ga itai desu.

ISHA: Ketsuatsu o hakarimashoo. Sode o makutte kudasai. Amerika kara desu ka.

NERUSON: Hai, Shiatoru kara kimashita.

ISHA: Soo desu ka. Kyonen kaigi de ikimashita yo. Kirei na machi desu ne.

NERUSON: Hai. Demo chotto ame ga ookute.[7]

ISHA: A, soo rashii desu ne. Un, ketsuatsu wa heijoo desu. Netsu ga arimasu ka.

NERUSON: Nai to omoimasu ga.

ISHA: Hakatte mimashoo.

Isha wa taionkei o waki[8] no shita ni ireru.

ISHA: Nihon no seikatsu wa doo desu ka.

NERUSON: Kaiteki de tanoshii desu.

ISHA: Nihon no seikatsu de komaru koto ga arimasen ka.

NERUSON: Soo desu ne. Densha ga komu koto to bukka ga takai koto gurai desu ne.

136

ISHA: **Aa, netsu wa arimasen. Kaze deshoo. Nisan'nichi yukkuri ya-sumeba naorimasu. Kusuri o mikkabun agemasu kara. Sore demo kibun ga warukereba, mata kite kudasai. Moo ichido shirabemasu kara.**

NERUSON: **Hai, soo shimasu.**

ISHA: **Sakki no densha ga komu hanashi desu ga, seiji ga warui n desu[9] yo. Daitoshi ni nan demo tsukuru kara, Tookyoo ya Oosaka ni hito ga atsumatte kimasu.[10]**

NERUSON: **Sekaijuu min'na onaji yoo desu. Tokai ni wa nani ka tanoshii koto ga aru to min'na omotte iru n deshoo.[11]**

ISHA: **Sono yoo desu ne.**

NERUSON: **Doomo arigatoo gozaimashita.**

ISHA: **Odaiji ni.**

HAVING A MEDICAL EXAMINATION

Mr. Nelson has been working in Japan for two months (now). As a result of his terribly busy lifestyle (lit. as his terribly busy lifestyle continues), exhaustion sets in and he catches a cold.

On the telephone:

IIDA: This is BusiTech.

NELSON: Hello, this is Mr. Nelson.

IIDA: What's wrong? You don't sound very good.

NELSON: I'm going to take the day off. I don't feel very well today.

IIDA: I understand. I'll let everyone know.

NELSON: Please tell Ms. Sato that we will have a meeting tomorrow.

IIDA: Yes, certainly.

NELSON: One more thing, (lit. And then,) do you know of a hospital somewhere?

IIDA: It's a little far, but how about Toranomon Hospital? It's a good one. (lit. They are dependable.)

NELSON: Toranomon Hospital? How do I get there from Chofu?

IIDA: Get on the subway at Shinjuku, and when you get off at Toranomon, you will see it right away.

NELSON: Got it. If anything comes up (lit. If there is anything), please let everyone know to contact me in the afternoon. (All right,) I'm going to go to the hospital now.

IIDA: Okay, take care.

After arriving at the hospital, Mr. Nelson goes to the window marked "receptionist."

NELSON: Excuse me. I don't feel well. I'd like to have a doctor examine me.

RECEPTIONIST: Okay. Please fill out this form. Do you have a health insurance card?

NELSON: (No,) I don't have Japanese health insurance yet.

RECEPTIONIST: In that case, you'll have to pay the total in cash. Is that okay?

NELSON: That'll be fine. Will I have to wait long?

RECEPTIONIST: No, it should be about ten minutes or so.

The waiting room is crowded, but after about ten minutes, Mr. Nelson's name is called and he is led to an examination room.

DOCTOR: So, what seems to be the problem?

NELSON: I don't feel well, and I don't have any appetite, either.

DOCTOR: Your complexion isn't good. Open your mouth for a moment, please. Hmm, your throat is a little red.

NELSON: Really? I have been feeling extremely tired lately. You see, I transferred here two months ago, and have been working without a break.

DOCTOR: Oh, I see. Do you have any dizziness?

NELSON: Yes, a little. And I have a headache.

DOCTOR: Let's take your blood pressure. Roll up your sleeve, please. (So,) are you from America?

NELSON: Yes, I'm from Seattle.

DOCTOR: Is that right? I went to a conference there last year. It's a beautiful city, isn't it?

NELSON: Yes, it is. But it rains a little (too) much.

DOCTOR: Yeah, that's what I hear. . . . Hmm, your blood pressure is normal. Do you have a fever?

NELSON: I don't think I do.

138

DOCTOR: Let's take your temperature and see (anyway).

The doctor puts the thermometer in his armpit.

DOCTOR: How do you like living in Japan?

NELSON: I like it very much. (lit. It's comfortable and fun.)

DOCTOR: Are there things about the Japanese lifestyle that bother you?

NELSON: Well, about the only things that bother me are the crowded trains and the high prices.

DOCTOR: Hmm, you don't have a fever. I think it's just a cold. If you rest for two or three days, you'll get better. I'm giving you a three-day dose of medicine. If you're still not feeling well, please come back and I'll examine you again.

NELSON: Yes, I'll do that.

DOCTOR: As for what you said about the crowed trains and high prices, politics are to blame (lit. politics are bad). They make everything in the big cities, so people crowd into places like Tokyo and Osaka.

NELSON: It seems to be the same thing all over the world. Everyone thinks there is something exciting in the city, I suppose.

DOCTOR: It looks that way.

NELSON: Thank you very much.

DOCTOR: Take care.

B. CHUU

1. The basic meaning of *yasumu* is "to rest." It can also mean "to take a day off," or "to cut class or work."

2. Non-Japanese people can get help at any hospital or clinic in Japan. Hospitals such as *Seiroka-Byooin* (also called St. Luke's Hospital) and *Toranomon-Byooin* (Toranomon Hospital) are more accustomed to having patients from foreign countries, and have doctors on staff who speak English. In smaller hospitals, it might be harder to communicate.

3. Toranomon Station is one of the subway stations located near the federal government offices and the American Embassy in Tokyo.

4. *Odaiji ni* means "Take good care of yourself," and is said only to a person who is ill. *Daiji* literally means "important."

5. Health care in Japan is costly. Before you travel there, make sure you have proper health insurance. The usual process is to pay yourself in Japan and then get reimbursed by your insurance company when you return home. The Japanese government provides health insurance to all of its citizens, so minimum health care is quite inexpensive for them. Foreigners can also get on the national health insurance plan if they live and work in Japan.

6. *Doo shimashita ka* literally means "How did you do (it)?" However, in practical usage it means "What seems to be the problem?" It is a polite expression used often by doctors.

7. *Demo chotto ame ga ookute* literally means "But it rains a little (too) much," but because the sentence is left incomplete, it implies "therefore some people may not like it." The Japanese often do not complete their sentences when the context makes the meaning clear.

8. When the Japanese measure body temperature, they put the thermometer in their armpit, unlike in the United States, where people put it in their mouths.

9. *Warui* literally means "bad," but it can also mean "fault." *Watashi ga warukatta.* (It was my fault.)

10. About one-tenth of the Japanese population lives within the city of Tokyo (10.3 million), and another tenth lives in the greater Tokyo metropolitan area. The land size of Japan (380,000 square kilometers) is one twenty-fifth that of the United States, and only 28 percent of that land is habitable because of the many mountains. Japan, with a population of about 125 million, has about half the population of the United States.

11. Tokyo is the center of politics, business, education, and (depending on whom you ask) Japanese culture. While the national and local governments are trying to decentralize, they have been unsuccessful so far.

C. BUNPOO TO YOOHOO

1. -SOO (DA)

The *-soo da* structure (stem form of the verb, *i*-adjective, and *na*-adjective plus *soo da*) can signify a speaker's conjecture based on his or her observations (either visual or circumstantial information). It means "It looks like" or "It seems like." This pattern is different from the *soo da* pattern introduced in Lesson 3, which indicates "rumor" or "hearsay." There are a few exceptions to the formation of this pattern that add *sa soo da* to adjectives. They include *nasa soo* (It seems not to have/be), *yosa soo* (It looks good), and negative forms such as *samuku-nasa soo* (It doesn't seem/look cold).

The pattern can be used as a predicate, functioning like a verb.

Netsu wa nasa soo desu ne.
It looks like you don't have a fever.

Kuuki wa totemo tsumeta soo desu.
It looks really cold outside. (lit. The air looks very cold.)

Ano kaisha no hoken wa yosa soo desu.
The insurance that the company carries looks good.

Pasokon ga sugoku fukyuu shi soo desu.
It looks like personal computers will become really widespread.

Ano byooin wa asa komi soo desu ne.
That hospital looks like it's going to be crowded in the morning.

Kotoba ga wakaranai kara, komari soo desu.
Since I don't understand the language, I may have some difficulties.

This pattern can also be used as a modifier, similar to *na*-adjectives. Just replace the copula *da* with the ending *na*.

Kono seihin o tsukai soo na kaisha o kangaete mimashoo.
Let's think about a corporation that might use this product.

Kantan soo na konpyuutaa o kaimashita.
I bought a computer that looks (rather) simple.

Dare demo hinshitsu ga yosa soo na mono o kaimasu.
Everyone buys things that look good in quality.

2. DEFERENTIAL FORM

As discussed in Lesson 4, there are several different types of honorific forms, including deferential, polite, and humble forms. Deferential forms are used when a speaker wishes to exalt, or honor, the position of a second or third person in formal conversations.

The most commonly used verbs have developed their own deferential forms:

DICTIONARY FORM	DEFERENTIAL FORM
iku (to go)	*irassharu*
iru (to be)	*irassharu*
iu (to say)	*ossharu*
taberu (to eat)	*meshiagaru*
nomu (to drink)	*meshiagaru*
*shitte iru** (to know)	*go zonji (da)*
kuru (to come)	*irassharu*
suru (to do)	*nasaru*
da (to be)	*de irassharu*

For verbs that have not developed their own forms, there are two ways to form deferentials:

a. Add *raremasu (rareru)* to the stem form of regular verbs and add *remasu (reru)* to the pre-*nai* form of irregular verbs. Note that this is the same as the formation of passive forms.

REGULAR VERBS

DICTIONARY FORM	DEFERENTIAL FORM
taberu (to eat)	*taberareru*
tsutomeru (to work)	*tsutomerareru*
tsutaeru (to tell)	*tsutaerareru*
miru (to examine)	*mirareru*
ireru (to insert)	*irerareru*

IRREGULAR VERBS

DICTIONARY FORM	DEFERENTIAL FORM
iku (to go)	*ikareru*
yomu (to read)	*yomareru*
nomu (to drink)	*nomareru*
atsumaru (to get together)	*atsumarareru*
harau (to pay)	*harawareru*
hakaru (to measure)	*hakarareru*

---

* *Shitte iru* is derived from the *te*-form of *shiru* plus *iru*, and is considered a dictionary form.

Note that some verbs that have their own deferential forms, such as *taberu, iku, nomu,* and *iu,* can also take this form. Many people seem to prefer using the *reru* and *rareru* forms at the office and the special forms outside the office.

The following conversation is conducted between a general manager (Mr. Aoki) and a young employee (Mr. Imai). Note the kinds of expressions the young employee uses, as well as those used by the manager.

IMAI: *Aoki Buchoo wa yoku Amerika e <u>ikaremasu</u> ka.*
Mr. Aoki, do you go to America often?

AOKI: *Ichinen ni ni san do iku yo.*
I go there two or three times a year.

IMAI: *Futsuu Amerika dewa nan'nichi gurai <u>taizai saremasu</u> ka.*
About how many days do you usually stay there?

AOKI: *Ishuukan gurai ka naa.*
About one week, I guess.

IMAI: *Buchoo wa Eigo ga joozu <u>de irassharu</u> kara, urayamashii desu.*
I envy you, sir, because you are excellent at English.

AOKI: *Iya, dare demo sugu joozu ni naru yo.*
No, anyone can become good quickly.

IMAI: *Nan'nen gurai <u>narawareta</u> n desu ka.*
About how many years have you been learning?

AOKI: *Boku wa san'nen bakari Hawai ni sunde ita kara.*
I lived in Hawaii for three years, so that's why.

The deferential form of *kuru* is *korareru.* The two deferential forms of *suru* are *sareru* and *nasaru.* It's up to the individual to decide which they prefer to use.

b: The second, more formal way to form the deferential is by combining *o* + verb (stem) + *ni naru.*

Koko ni gojuusho to onamae o okaki ni natte kudasai.
Please write your address and name here.

Don'na byooin o osagashi ni narimasu ka.
What kind of hospital are you going to look for?

3. INDICATING DIRECTION (*IKU* AND *KURU*)

To stress directionality, the Japanese use a pattern constructed with the *te*-form of the verb followed by either *iku* to indicate that someone is going away, or *kuru* to indicate that someone is coming someplace to do something. Consider the following sentences:

Watakushi wa byooin ni ikimasu.
  I will go to the hospital.

Kyoo oisha-san ga kimasu.
  The doctor comes today.

Shokuji o koko de shite ikimashoo.
  Let's go after we finish eating. (lit. Let's have a meal here, and then go.)

Tookyoo ya Oosaka ni hito ga atsumatte kimasu.
  People gather in cities like Tokyo or Osaka (from other places).

Byooin de yasunde itte kudasai.
  Please get some rest at the hospital, and then go (home).

Phrases that convey the same meaning are *motte iku, motte kuru, tsurete iku,* and *tsurete kuru. Motte iku* means "to take something along with (me)" and *motte kuru* means "to bring something along with (me)."

Okane o motte itta hoo ga ii desu ne.
  I should take some money with me, shouldn't I?

Kisha no seihin o motte kite kudasai.
  Please bring your company's product with you.

Hoken no kaado o motte ikimashoo.
  Let's take an insurance card with us.

When you take or bring a person along with you, the phrases *tsurete iku* and *tsurete kuru* are used instead of *motte iku* and *motte kuru.*

Kanai to kodomo o tsurete ikimasu.
  I will take my wife and child along.

Yuujin o tsurete kite mo ii desu ka.
  Is it okay to bring a friend?

Kare wa ryokoo suru toki, oisha-san o tsurete iku soo desu.
  I hear that he takes a doctor with him when he travels.

Byoonin o koko ni tsurete kite kudasai.
  Please bring the sick person here.

144

D. BIJINESU JIKOO

NIHON NO IRYOO-SEIDO
(THE JAPANESE MEDICAL SYSTEM)

The Japanese government provides access to national insurance for every Japanese citizen, except those who are covered by employer-sponsored health insurance. After retirement, the national health insurance takes over for all citizens. Senior citizens also get regular checkups free of charge.

Medical doctors are highly respected not only for their knowledge of medicine, but also for their general knowledge about life. They are called *sensei,* the same title used for teachers and professors who are considered knowledgeable and highly ethical. Like doctors in the United States, Japanese doctors can prescribe medicine, but they are also able to sell medicine to patients. Prescriptions are usually dispensed at either the doctor's office or the hospital dispensary. In some cases, prescriptions can be filled at designated stores. Some general medicines such as vitamins and cold medicines are sold at drugstores. Birth control pills can be prescribed by a doctor.

Although doctors are licensed by a regulatory board ensuring the quality of care, it is always advisable to get an introduction from a friend to a particular doctor. Many doctors perform home visits, but this practice is declining. In large cities, patients usually go to a clinic for the initial examination and, if more tests are required, to a hospital. Of course, a patient can go to a hospital for an initial examination as well. Companies allow people to miss work in order to see a doctor, provided it does not happen too often.

Many Japanese are rather knowledgeable about medicine. There are many television programs and newspaper articles on maintaining good health. Due in part to a diet low in fat, the Japanese are generally a healthy people and have the highest longevity in the world.

Japanese medicine has borrowed from a number of countries throughout its history. Medicine was first introduced from China, and the mainland continued to be the source of learning until the seventeenth century. For all of the seventeenth, eighteenth, and nineteenth centuries, the Japanese learned from the Dutch, who were relegated to an island off Nagasaki in accordance with Japan's closed-country policy during that period. When Japan opened up communication with other countries in the late nineteenth century, Japanese doctors began to study German medicine, which was dominant at that time. Modern Japanese medicine is a mixture of these traditions with American medical practices. *Kanpoo* (Chinese medicine), which mainly uses herbs, is still trusted by many Japanese in combination with modern medicine, but its use is declining.

RENSHUU MONDAI

A. *Tsugi o kanzen na bunshoo ni shinasai.* (Complete the following sentences.)

1. *Dokoka byooin o oshiete* _____.
2. *Ano byooin wa shin'yoo ga* _____.
3. *Kyoo wa shokuyoku ga amari* _____.
4. *Ima memai ga* _____.
5. *Sumu no ni saikoo* _____.

B. *Tekitoo na joshi o irenasai.* (Insert the appropriate particle[s].)

1. *Chotto tooi desu* _____, *ano byooin wa ii desu.*
2. *Shinjuku* _____ *chikatetsu* _____ *notte, Toranomon* _____ *orimasu.*
3. *Kono mooshikomisho* _____ *kakikonde kudasai.*
4. *Hoken* _____ *arimasen* _____, *genkin* _____ *haraimasu.*
5. *Hitobito wa tokai* _____ *tanoshii koto* _____ *aru* _____ *omotte iru.*

KOTAE

A. 1. *kudasai.*   2. *arimasu.*   3. *arimasen.*   4. *shimasu.*   5. *desu* or *deshoo.*
B. 1. *ga*   2. *de, ni, de*   3. *ni*   4. *ga, kara, de*   5. *ni, ga, to*

146

FUKUSHUU 1 (REVIEW 1)

A. *Tekitoo na joshi o irenasai.* (Insert the appropriate particle in the blank.)

1. *Doko _____ basu _____ noremasu ka.*
2. *Shitsurei desu _____, Nihon _____ _____ oshigoto desu ka.*
3. *Daigaku _____ sotsugyoo shite, honsha _____ shigoto _____ shite kimashita.*
4. *Tsuukin _____ benri na tokoro _____ ii desu.*
5. *Moo osoi _____, abunai _____ okurimashoo.*
6. *Kigyoo _____ nedan _____ hinshitsu _____ taisetsu desu.*
7. *Dekiru dake E-meeru _____ tsukaoo _____ omoimasu.*
8. *Guuzen ni densha _____ naka _____ shin'yuu _____ aimashita.*
9. *Kangei _____ iu koto _____, boku _____ mochimasu.*

B. *Tadashi hyoogen o erabinasai.* (Choose the right expression.)

1. *Kore wa yuumei (na, no, de) hoteru desu.*
2. *Jimusho ni an'nai (shita, shite) kudasai.*
3. *Kaze o (hiku, hiki) to, shigoto ga dekimasen.*
4. *Nihon de wa tsuukin jikan ga (taisetsu da, taisetsu no) soo desu.*
5. *Ano kata wa Amerikajin (da, no) yoo desu.*
6. *Watakushi ga yoku (iku, iku no) resutoran wa konde imasu.*
7. *Goryooshin ga (irasshaimasu, mairimasu) ka.*
8. *Raishuu (hima datta kara, hima dattara), otsukiai shimasu.*
9. *Rainen kanojo to kekkon (shimasu, shiyoo) to omoimasu.*

C. *Kakkonai no kotoba o kaenasai.* (Change the word[s] in parentheses to fit the sentence.)

1. *Densha wa benri (desu).* (Informal)
2. *Doozo jimusho ni (hairu) kudasai.*
3. *Kono kinjo wa (shizuka desu) rashii desu.*
4. *Neruson-san ni (iu) hoo ga ii desu.*
5. *Yasukute, hinshitsu ga (ii desu), sore o kaimasu.* (Conditional)
6. *Kono seihin wa yoku (tsukau) imasu.* (Passive)
7. *Yoku Amerika ni (iku) ka.* (Deferential form)
8. *Kono seihin o (tsukau) soo na kaisha o sagashimashoo.*
9. *Buchoo wa amari (nomu) hazu desu.* (Negative)

D. *Tekitoo na hyoogen o irenasai.* (Insert the appropriate expression.)

1. *Jisa no* _____ (because of) *de tsukaremashita.*
2. *Kyoo* _____ (Non-smoking room) *ga arimasu ka.*
3. *Neruson-san wa* _____ (sales) *o tantoo shimasu.*
4. *Honsha de wa* _____ (development department) *de hataraki-mashita.*
5. *Nani ka* _____ (I.D. card) *no yoo na mono ga arimasu ka.*
6. *Nihon no* _____ (life) *wa ikaga desu ka.*
7. _____ (Environment) *hogo mo wasurenai hoo ga ii desu ne.*
8. _____ (Contract) *o hayai uchi ni shimashoo.*

E. *Tsugi no shitsumon ni kotaenasai.* (Answer the following questions.)

1. *Nihon de meishi wa dooshite taisetsu desu ka.*
2. *Kaisha nado de shonichi ni nani o shimasu ka.*
3. *Nihon de sumu tokoro o sagasu toki, nani ga taisetsu desu ka.*
4. *Tookyoo wa hoka no toshi to doo chigaimasu ka.*
5. *Maakettingu puran o tsukuru toki, nani o kangaeru hitsuyoo ga arimasu ka.*
6. *Nihon no shoohisha no torendo wa doo desu ka.*
7. *Nihon de uchi ni shootai sareta toki, nani ka motte itta hoo ga ii desu ka.*
8. *Nihon de tsukiai wa dooshite taisetsu desu ka.*
9. *"Mirai toshi" to iu mono wa nan desu ka.*
10. *Byooki ni naranai tame ni don'na koto ni ki o tsuketara ii desu ka.*

KOTAE

A. 1. *de, ni* 2. *ga, e, wa* 3. *o, de, o* 4. *ni, ga* 5. *shi, kara* 6. *wa, ya (to), ga* 7. *o, to* 8. *no, de, ni* 9. *to, de, ga*
B. 1. *na* 2. *shite* 3. *hiku* 4. *taisetsu da* 5. *no* 6. *iku* 7. *irasshaimasu* 8. *hima dattara* 9. *shiyoo*
C. 1. *da* 2. *haitte* 3. *shizuka* 4. *itta, itta* 5. *yokattara* 6. *tsukawarete* 7. *ikaremasu* or *irasshaimasu* 8. *tsukai* 9. *nomanai*
D. 1. *kankei* 2. *kin'enshitsu* 3. *eigyoo* 4. *kaihatsubu*
5. *mibunshoomeisho* 6. *seikatsu* 7. *kankyoo* 8. *keiyaku*
E. (These are sample answers.) 1. *Nihonjin wa yoku tsukau shi, meishi ni wa iroiro no joohoo ga kaite arimasu kara.* 2. *Jibun o shookai shitari, hoka no hito ni shookai shite morattari shimasu.* 3. *Tsuukin jikan ga taisetsu desu.* 4. *Tookyoo wa iroiro na ibento ga arimasu.* 5. *Okyakusan o kan-gaete, choosa suru hitsuyoo ga arimasu.* 6. *Shitsu to nedan to saabisu ga taisetsu desu.* 7. *Hai, nani ka temiyage o motte itta hoo ga ii desu.*
8. *Ningen kankei wa totemo taisetsu desu kara.* 9. *Atarashii risooteki na machi no koto desu.* 10. *Muri shite amari tsukarenai hoo ga ii desu.*

DAI JUUIKKA
Lesson 11

A. KAIWA

Neruson-shi wa Chiyoda-sangyoo no Fujii-joo ni apointo o toritsukeru[1] tame ni denwa suru. Kare wa uridashichuu[2] no seihin o shookai shitai to omotte iru. Neruson-shi, denwa suru mae ni hanasu koto o matomeru.

NERUSON: **Chiyoda-sangyoo no Fujii-san da na.[3] Shiatoru honsha, sorekara Nihon-denki no Koyama-san kara no shookai no koto.[4] Shoohin no SuupaaMeeru no koto o hanaseba ii n da na. Apointo o toru no o wasurenai yoo ni shiyoo.[5] Yatte miyoo.**

Denwa de.

KOJIMA: **Hai, Kojima-shooji de gozaimasu.**

NERUSON: **Sumimasen. Anoo,[6] Fujii-san o onegai shimasu.**

KOJIMA: **Fujii-san desu ka. Kochira, Kojima-shooji desu ga. Soo iu namae no mono wa orimasen[7] ga.**

NERUSON: **Bangoo wa 737 no 4545 desu ne.[8]**

KOJIMA: **Hai, soo desu ga. Kyokuban wa nanban desu ka.**

NERUSON: **045 desu.**

KOJIMA: **Aa, kochira wa 054 de gozaimasu.**

NERUSON: **Aa, gomen'nasai.[9] Machigaemashita. Taihen shitsurei shimashita.**

KOJIMA: **Iie.**

Neruson-shi, denwa shinaosu.[10]

OOSHIMA: **Hai,[11] Chiyoda-sangyoo de gozaimasu.**

NERUSON: **Moshi moshi, Fujii-san o onegai shimasu.**

OOSHIMA: **Mooshiwake gozaimasen.[12] Fujii[13] wa tadaima[14] gaishutsu shite orimasu.[15] Donata-sama deshoo ka.**

NERUSON: **Neruson to mooshimasu[16] ga, nanji goro okaeri deshoo ka.[17]**

OOSHIMA: **Niji ni wa kaeru hazu desu ga.**

NERUSON: Soo desu ka. Jaa, mata niji sugi ni denwa shimasu.

OOSHIMA: Neruson-sama yori odenwa ga atta koto o tsutaete oki-masu.[18]

NERUSON: Yoroshiku onegai shimasu.[19]

Nijikango, Neruson-shi, mata fuji-shi ni denwa suru.

FUJII: Hai, Fujii desu ga.

NERUSON: Moshi moshi, watakushi, Bijitekku no Neruson to mooshimasu.

FUJII: Aa, doomo.[20] Saki hodo odenwa itadaita soo de.[21]

NERUSON: Ee. Kondo Shiatoru no honsha kara Tookyoo-shisha ni tenkin shite kimashita. Nihon-denki no Koyama-san kara ona-mae o ukagatta no desu ga.

FUJII: Aa, Koyama-san kara no goshookai desu ka. Saikin kanojo ni wa atte imasen ga, ogenki desu ka.

NERUSON: Hai, ogenki desu. Jitsu wa watakushi to wa Amerika no daigaku no doosoosei[22] nan desu.

FUJII: Dochira no daigaku desu ka.

NERUSON: Irinoi-daigaku desu. Yoroshiku to osshatte imashita.[23]

FUJII: Aa, soo desu ka. Jitsu wa kanojo to watakushi wa dookyoo[24] nan desu.

NERUSON: Ee, soo kikimashita. Nagasaki da soo desu ne.

FUJII: Ee, soo desu. Neruson-san wa goshusshin wa.

NERUSON: Umare wa Kororado-shuu no Boorudaa desu. Kookoo sotsugyoo made soko ni imashita.

FUJII: Ee, soo desu ka. Guuzen to iu ka,[25] watakushi, Boorudaa no Kororado-daigaku de ichinen kenshuu shita koto ga aru n desu.

NERUSON: Aa, soo desu ka. Nan'nen mae desu ka.

FUJII: Go, roku nen mae desu. Iroiro omoide ga atte, totemo nat-sukashii desu. Boorudaa wa kirei na machi desu ne.

NERUSON: Hai. Demo watakushi wa saikin itte inai node yoku wakarimasen ga.

FUJII: Mada kirei da to omoimasu yo. Dekireba,[26] kazoku o tsurete ichido sukii ni demo ikitai to omotte iru n desu yo.

NERUSON: Sore wa ii desu ne. Sore de[27] oisogashii yoo desu kara, yooken ni hairasete itadakimasu[28] ga, jitsu wa denshi-meeru no sofuto no goshookai o sasete itadakitai to omoimashite, denwa o sashiageta[29] n desu ga.

FUJII: Denshi-meeru desu ka.

NERUSON: Ee. Gonen mae ni Nihon ni shinshutsu shimashite,[30] iroiro shoohin o atsukatte imasu. Kondo SuupaaMeeru to iu atarashii shoohin o uridashita n desu.

FUJII: Denshi-meeru wa wagasha[31] de wa mada tsukatte imasen ga.

NERUSON: Sorenara, zehi uchi no shoohin o mite kudasai. Chikai shoorai dare demo tsukau yoo ni naru to omoimasu.

FUJII: Soo desu ka. Sore ja, Koyama-san no goshookai de mo aru shi, shoorai no koto mo arimasu kara.

NERUSON: Arigatoo gozaimasu. Itsu ukagattara[32] yoroshii deshoo ka.

FUJII: Watakushi wa asu kara futsuka bakari shucchoo shimasu kara, getsuyoobi wa doo desu ka.

NERUSON: Kekkoo desu yo. Gogo ichiji goro de yoroshii desu ka.

FUJII: Ii desu yo.

NERUSON: Arigatoo gozaimasu. Getsuyoobi no asa kakunin no denwa oire shimasu.[33]

FUJII: Onegai shimasu.

Neruson-shi to Fujii-joo wa denwa o kiru. Neruson-shi wa yakusoku o toritsukeru koto ga dekite taihen ureshikatta.

NERUSON: Yatta zo.[34]

Appointment by Phone

In order to make an appointment, Mr. Nelson calls Ms. Fujii of Chiyoda Industries. He wants to introduce a product (his company) is currently selling. Before calling, Mr. Nelson summarizes what he is going to say.

NELSON: (Let's see,) Ms. Fujii at Chiyoda Industries. (First, I should mention) the Seattle head office, then the introduction by Ms. Koyama at Nihon Denki. (Then) I should talk about (our) product, SuperMail. I can't forget to make (lit. take) an appointment. Here we go! (lit. Let's try.)

On the telephone.

KOJIMA: Hello. This is Kojima Trading Company.

NELSON: Hello. (May I speak to) Ms. Fujii, please?

KOJIMA: Ms. Fujii? This is Kojima Trading Company. There is nobody
here by that name.

NELSON: This is 737-4545, isn't it?

KOJIMA: Yes, it is. What area code (are you dialing)?

NELSON: This is 045, right?

KOJIMA: Ah, this is 054.

NELSON: Oh, I'm sorry. I have the wrong number. (lit. I made a mistake.)
Please excuse me. (lit. I was terribly rude.)

KOJIMA: No problem.

Mr. Nelson tries his call again.

OOSHIMA: Good afternoon, Chiyoda Industries.

NELSON: Hello, (may I speak to) Ms. Fujii, please?

OOSHIMA: I'm sorry, Ms. Fujii is out of the office at the moment. (May I
ask) who's calling?

NELSON: (Yes,) my name is Mr. Nelson. About what time do you expect
her back?

OOSHIMA: She should be back around two o'clock.

NELSON: Oh, in that case, I'll call back after two.

OOSHIMA: I'll tell her that you called, Mr. Nelson.

NELSON: Thank you. (lit. Please do so.)

Two hours later, Nelson calls Ms. Fujii again.

FUJII: Hello, this is Ms. Fujii.

NELSON: Hello, my name is Mr. Nelson of BusiTech.

FUJII: Oh, hello. (lit. Thank you.) I understand that you called me earlier.

NELSON: Yes, I did. I've been transferred to the Tokyo branch office from
our head office in Seattle. I got your name from Ms. Koyama at Nihon
Denki.

FUJII: Oh, an introduction from Ms. Koyama. I haven't seen her for a
while. (lit. I'm not meeting with her recently.) Is she (doing) well?

NELSON: Yes, she's doing just fine. Actually, Ms. Koyama and I went to college together (lit. were classmates) in America.

FUJII: Which university?

NELSON: The University of Illinois. She says hello.

FUJII: Oh, really? Actually, she and I are from the same town.

NELSON: Yes, that's what I heard. (You're from) Nagasaki, right?

FUJII: That's right. Where are you from, Mr. Nelson?

NELSON: I was born in Boulder, Colorado, and I lived there until I graduated from high school.

FUJII: Really? Isn't that a coincidence? I studied (lit. trained) at the University of Colorado at Boulder for a year.

NELSON: Is that right? How many years ago was that?

FUJII: About five or six years ago. I have a lot of memories (of Boulder). I miss it a lot! Boulder is a beautiful town, isn't it?

NELSON: Yes it is, but I haven't been there for a while (lit. not going recently) so I don't really know (what it's like now).

FUJII: I'm sure it's still beautiful. If I can, I think I'd like to take my family there to go skiing or something.

NELSON: That would be nice, wouldn't it? Well, I know you're busy (lit. you seem to be busy), so I'll get right to the point. Actually, I called because I would like to introduce a new e-mail software package to you.

FUJII: Electronic mail?

NELSON: Yes, (my company) expanded into Japan about five years ago and deals in a number of products. Currently, we're promoting (lit. put out for sale) a new product called SuperMail.

FUJII: We're not using electronic mail in our office yet.

NELSON: Well, in that case, by all means, please have a look at our product. We think everybody will be using it in the near future.

FUJII: Really? Well, okay, since you were introduced by Ms. Koyama, and we might have a need for it in the future (lit. it's a thing of the future).

NELSON: Thank you very much. When should I come by your office?

FUJII: Starting tomorrow, I'll be on a business trip for a couple of days. How about Monday?

NELSON: That sounds great. How about around one o'clock?

FUJII: That will be fine.

NELSON: Thank you very much. I'll call and confirm (the meeting) on Monday morning.

FUJII: That would be great. (lit. Please do so.)

Nelson and Fujii hang up. Nelson is very happy that he was able to make an appointment.

NELSON: All right! (lit. I did it!)

B. CHUU

1. *Toritsukeru* is a compound verb that combines the stem form of *toru* (to take) and *tsukeru* (to attach) and means "to acquire."

2. *Uridashichuu* literally means "in the middle of placing (goods) on the market." It is another compound word, made up of *uru* (to sell), *dasu* (to start), and *chuu* (in the middle of doing something).

3. The particle *ne* is used most often when seeking a response from someone during conversation. However, when speaking to oneself, it is common to use *na* to confirm or emphasize a statement. *Na* is also heard in informal conversations, especially among men, and is used more often than *ne* in the Western (Kansai) dialect, which is spoken in the Kyoto-Osaka area.

4. The word *koto* literally means "fact" or "matter." A noun followed by *koto* implies "about noun" or "concerning noun." You can end a sentence with *koto* or with a noun (though it's not a complete sentence) when the missing predicate is understood by context.

5. *Wasurenai yoo ni shiyoo* literally means "Let's try not to forget (it)." The plain non-past negative form of a verb plus *yoo ni shiyoo* means "Let's try not to" or by extension, "I'll try not to." For example: *Niku o amari tabenai yoo ni shiyoo.* (Let's try not to eat too much meat.) *Denwa o amari kakenai yoo ni shiyoo.* (I'll try not to make too many phone calls.) *Jama shinai yoo ni shiyoo.* (Let's try not to disturb [him].)

6. *Anoo* is often used to get someone's attention. It is similar to using "Say . . ." at the beginning of a statement. It can also indicate that the speaker is thinking, similar to "Hmm . . ."

7. *Orimasen* is the humble form equivalent of *imasen*. It is used to indicate that someone within one's in-group is not present. When speaking to someone outside of this group, especially in business, it is customary to refer to people within your company or family using the humble form, even if they are superiors.

8. As in the United States, all Japanese telephone numbers have ten digits, including the area code. The area code in Japan, however, may have from two to five digits, all beginning with 0.

9. *Gomen'nasai* means "I am sorry (for what I have done to you)." It is used to ask forgiveness in informal situations.

10. *Denwa shinaosu* means "to make a telephone call again." The pattern of verb stem + *naosu* means "to do (verb) again."

11. *Hai* is used more often in business for answering the phone than *moshi moshi*. *Moshi moshi* is actually used more by the caller, often accompanied by *sumimasen*. *Moshi moshi* is also used when one can't hear the other person well, or when the connection is bad (Hello . . . ?).

12. *Mooshiwake gozaimasen* also means "I am very sorry (for what I have done to you)" but is more formal than *gomen'nasai* or *sumimasen*.

13. When referring to a person in your in-group to a person of an "out-group," honorific titles after names, such as *san* (or *sama*), are dropped.

14. *Tadaima* means "right now," and is usually used in formal situations. It is also said upon entering a room when a person returns to his or her home or office. In this case it means "I have just now returned."

15. *Gaishutsu shite orimasu* is the humble form of *gaishitsu shite imasu* (being out of the office or home). *Gaishutsu suru* itself means "to go out."

16. (Name) *to mooshimasu* literally means "I call myself." It is translated as "I am," or "My name is." *Moosu* is the humble form of *iu* (to say), and is used when a person meets someone for the first time in a formal situation.

17. *Nanji goro okaeri deshoo ka* means "What time does (he) return?" *O* plus the stem form of a verb plus *desu* is an honorific construction.

18. *Tsutaete okimasu* literally means "I'll inform him in advance." The *te*-form plus *oku* signifies "to do something in advance." It is used when the speaker is doing the action for a perceived future benefit: *Denwa shite okimashoo.* (Let's call him in advance.) *Kakunin shite okimashita.* (I confirmed it in advance.)

155

19. *Yoroshiku,* or the longer *yoroshiku onegai shimasu* (Please do for me), can mean "thank you" when someone is going to do something for you or on your behalf, but not after the favor has been done.

20. *Aa, doomo* (lit. thank you) is a greeting used when you recognize who is calling, or when someone is returning your call and you wish to show some appreciation.

21. *Sakihodo odenwa itadaita soo de* means "I understand you called me and (I appreciate it)." This is a typical "incomplete" sentence, and the ending *de* (*te*-form of *da*) signifies that the rest of the sentence is understood through context.

22. *Doosoosei* means "classmate" or "schoolmate." *Doosoosei* relationships are very important to many Japanese, particularly those who graduate from smaller institutions.

23. *Ossharu* (to say) is the deferential equivalent of *iu* (to say).

24. *Dookyoo* means "of the same hometown" and often implies strong relationships among people, particularly between those from small towns where they share unique customs. This concept is based on the old idea that only people of the same hometown could be trusted during periods of civil war.

25. The expression *"Guuzen to iu ka"* literally means "It can be coincidental."

26. *Dekireba* means "if possible" or "if I can." It consists of *dekiru* (can, do) plus the conditional *ba*-form ending.

27. *Sore de* (and then) can be used to change the course of the conversation. *Tokorode* (by the way) is often used for the same purpose.

28. *Yooken ni hairasete itadakimasu* means "Please let me talk about (lit. enter) the business." The pattern *-sete itadaku* is used in formal situations and is explained in more detail in Lesson 18.

29. *Sashiageru* is the humble equivalent of *ageru* (to give).

30. When you introduce your organization or company, it is important to include the date of establishment, the location of the head office, and your main products. Showing that the company is well established in larger cities adds to your credibility and helps gain the initial trust of the client.

31. *Wagasha* means "our company." The Chinese character *waga* (lit. I) is used in such compounds as *wagakuni* (our country) and *wagaya* (our family).

32. *Ukagau* is a humble form word that can mean "visit," "go," or "come," depending on the context.

33. It is a common business practice in Japan to confirm appointments a few days before the meeting.

34. *Yatta zo* means "I did it," and is used mostly by young Japanese in informal situations. As speech in Japan continues to grow increasingly informal, however, it is not uncommon to hear such expressions from older people now. *Zo* is a sentence-final particle that is used to emphasize a statement.

C. BUNPOO TO YOOHOO

1. HUMBLE FORM

The humble form is used when a speaker wishes to lower his or her position and, consequently, elevate the position of the listener or another person treated as the subject of discussion. For example, the sentence *Watakushi wa Neruson de gozaimasu* is the same in meaning as *Watakushi wa Neruson desu,* but the first sentence has the added implication that Nelson, the speaker, wishes to show his respect for the listener by using *de gozaimasu,* the humble form of *desu.* Below are some commonly used verbs in their plain, polite, and humble forms:

PLAIN FORM	POLITE FORM	HUMBLE FORM
de aru	*desu*	*de gozaimasu* (is)
aru	*arimasu*	*gozaimasu* (there is)
iru	*imasu*	*orimasu* (is)
iku	*ikimasu*	*mairimasu* (go)
kuru	*kimasu*	*mairimasu* (come)
iu	*iimasu*	*mooshimasu* (call)
suru	*shimasu*	*itashimasu* (do)

The following examples show the humble forms of verbs and the copula *desu*, as they would be used when talking to a client or to one's boss:

Iroiro na denshi-meeru no sofuto ga gozaimasu ga.
We have various types of e-mail software available.

Kojima-shooji de gozaimasu.
This is Kojima Trading Company.

Nanji ni mairimashoo ka.
What time should I come?

Watakushi ga itashimasu kara, goshinpai naku.
I will do it, so please don't worry.

2. *YOO NI*

Yoo ni may be translated as "in order to" or "so that." For example, consider the sentence one often hears when getting off a bus or train in Japan, *Wasuremono nai yoo ni go chuui kudasai.* (lit. In order not to have any forgotten items, please be careful.) When *yoo ni* is preceded by a non-past verb and followed by a sentence-ending verb, it can mean "to do" or "not to do."

Apointo no jikan o wasurenai yoo ni shiyoo.
Let's not forget the appointment time.

Neruson-san ni denwa suru yoo ni itte kudasai.
Please tell Mr. Nelson to call me.

Kare ni doosoosei o shookai suru yoo ni iimashita.
I told him to introduce his schoolmate.

Denwa bangoo o machigawanai yoo ni itte kudasai.
Please tell him not to dial the wrong number (lit. make a mistake on the telephone number).

3. *O* AND *GO*

The polite prefixes *o* and *go* are used frequently before nouns in Japanese. *Go* is used before words that are derived from Chinese. Consequently, *go* is used for compound words that consist of more than one *kanji*. *O* precedes words that are inherently Japanese. As it is difficult to differentiate between these different types of words, you may have to memorize some of the more important ones. The most common words that use *o* and *go* may be found below:

Neruson-san wa goshusshin wa.
Where are you from, Mr. Nelson?

Atarashii shoohin o goshookai sasete itadakimasu.
I would like to introduce a new product.

Goyooken wa nan deshoo ka.
May I ask what you want?

Soo iu onamae no kata wa orimasen.
There is no person by that name here.

Nanji goro okaeri deshoo ka.
About what time will he be back?

Odenwa ga atta koto o tsutaete okimasu.
I will tell him that you called.

Other words that occur often are: *ocha* (tea), *oyu* (hot water), *okashi* (cookies, candy), *ohashi* (chopsticks), *goshujin* (husband), *gokazoku* (family), *gotaizai* (stay).

4. EXPERIENCE

To express that you have experienced (or done) something, the plain past form of the verb plus *koto ga aru* is used. To indicate that you have not experienced something, you use the same pattern, but simply change *aru* to the negative, *nai*.

Daigaku de kenshuu shita koto ga arimasu.
In college, I once did some business training.

Apointo o wasureta koto ga arimasu ka.
Have you ever forgotten an appointment?

Denwa bangoo o machigaeta koto ga aru ne.
He has mistakenly dialed the wrong telephone number before, hasn't he?

Shisha ni tenkin shita koto ga arimasen.
I have never been transferred to a branch office.

Denshi-meeru o tsukatta koto ga nai.
I have never used e-mail before.

D. BIJINESU JIKOO

DENWA NO ECHIKETTO (TELEPHONE ETIQUETTE)

Except in conversations between friends or family members, the Japanese initially tend to be quite formal in telephone conversations. When they make calls, they usually identify themselves first and then request the person with whom they wish to speak. The other party also answers formally, identifying him- or herself first and then answering the request. Generally speaking, it's better to be too formal than too casual. When the speaker is not sure with whom he or she is talking, formal speech is used.

Businesspeople are extremely formal on the telephone, especially when expressing their appreciation for a business relationship. *Itsumo osewa ni natte orimasu* (lit. We always receive your care) signifies "Thank you very much for doing business with us," and is a common expression when speaking to business contacts, particularly after giving your name in the beginning of the conversation.

It has become increasingly common for the Japanese to introduce themselves or other people over the telephone, instead of in person. However, it can't be overemphasized that the first introduction by a mutual friend or contact is very important in Japan. It will open many telephone lines for you.

UCHI TO SOTO (IN-GROUPS AND OUT-GROUPS)

Japanese culture is "a culture of human relationships." The Japanese attach great significance to the subtleties of personal interaction. They perceive the world as being composed of things that are either inside or outside one's group. For example, they view their country as *uchi* (inside) and the rest of the world as *soto* (outside).

Japanese relationships can be explained in terms of this *uchi-soto* structure. The diagram below shows the basic relationship of the self with others, based on the degree of closeness or familiarity:

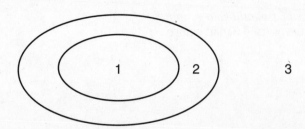

The members of domain 1 include a person's immediate family and close friends. Conversation and interaction with domain 1 members is informal and relaxed. Domain 2 members include associates and acquaintances. Relationships with people in domain 2 are rather formal and somewhat cautious. The members of domain 3 include those considered outsiders or strangers. The relationship with those in domain 3 could be called "noncommittal."

As a non-Japanese person, you will begin interacting with the Japanese from domain 3 and gradually become a member of domain 2. Obviously, you may wish to move within or as near as possible to domain 1. How can this be achieved? Most Japanese tend to establish closer relationships with those who have been formally introduced, or have mutual friends and maintain association through frequent contact. This model for relationships is no more secret or mysterious than those used by people everywhere, just generally a bit more time-consuming and rigid.

The Japanese value the team above all else, and often have little or no concern for strangers. As with many things, this can be explained by Japan's history of political, social, and economic hardships. As a reaction to adversity, people developed strong bonds with their own group and an indifference, or even negative bias, toward outsiders. This is the reason that human relationships take on such importance to foreigners living in Japan, and why foreigners often need connections or proper introductions to enter a more comfortable position in society.

RENSHUU MONDAI

A. *Tsugi no shitsumon ni kotaenasai.* (Answer the following questions.)

1. *Neruson-san wa doko no dare ni denwa o shitai to omotte imasu ka.*
2. *Sono hito wa jimusho ni imashita ka.*
3. *Neruson-san wa Fujii-san no koto o dare ni kikimashita ka.*
4. *Fujii-san wa Koyama-san o dooshite shitte imasu ka.*
5. *Fujii-san wa dooshite Boorudaa o shitte imasu ka.*

B. *Rei ni shitagatte bun o kaenasai.* (Transform the following sentences like the example.)

Example: *Tanaka desu. → Tanaka de gozaimasu.*
Tanaka de gozaimasu. → Tanaka desu.

1. *Chiyoda-sangyoo no Fujii desu.*
2. *Kochira wa san san yon go yon yon go roku de gozaimasu.*
3. *Suzuki wa niji ni kaeru hazu desu.*
4. *Bijitekku no Neruson to mooshimasu.*
5. *Yoroshiku onegai shimasu.*

C. *Tekitoo na kotoba o irenasai.* (Insert the appropriate word.)

1. *Neruson-san yori odenwa ga atta koto* _____ *tsutaemasu.*
2. *Neruson-san yori denwa ga atta* _____ *tsutaemasu.*
3. *Kanojo* _____ *watakushi* _____ *daigaku no doosoosei nan desu.*
4. *Kondo Suupaa-Meeru* _____ *atarashii seihin o uridashite imasu.*
5. *Itsu ukagatta* _____ *ii desu ka.*

KOTAE

A. 1. *Chiyoda-sangyoo no Fujii-san ni denwa o shitai to omotte imasu.*
2. *Iie, gaishutsu shite imashita.* 3. *Nihon-Denki no Koyama-san ni kiki-mashita.* 4. *Dookyoo no hito desu kara.* 5. *Boorudaa de kenshuu shita koto ga arimasu kara.*
B. 1. *Chiyoda-sangyoo no Fujii de gozaimasu.* 2. *Kochira wa san san yon go yon yon go roku desu.* 3. *Suzuki wa niji ni kaeru hazu de gozaimasu.*
4. *Bijitekku no Neruson to iimasu.* 5. *Yoroshiku onegai itashimasu.*
C. 1. *o* 2. *to* 3. *to, wa* 4. *to iu* 5. *ra*

DAI JUUNIKA
Lesson 12

A. KAIWA

SHUUMATSU O ONSENKYOO DE

Neruson-shi to Suzuki-fusai wa shuumatsu o Suzuki-shi no yuujin shoyuu no onsen-ryokan de sugosu. Nagai doraibu no ato, Hakone-onsenkyoo[1,2] ni aru Sekiyoo ni yatto tsuku.

SUZUKI: **Saa, tsukimashita. Keshiki mo nakanaka ii deshoo.**

NERUSON: **Waa, subarashii desu ne. Sekiyoo to iu namae desu ne.**

SUZUKI: **Ee. Kono ryokan wa daigaku-jidai no doosoosei[3] no uchi nan desu. Natsuyasumi ya fuyuyasumi ni yoku ojama shimashita.[4]**

Suzuki-shi, yuujin no okaasan no Onodera-fujin ni aisatsu suru.

SUZUKI: **Gomen kudasai.[5]**

ONODERA: **Ara, Suzuki-san, irasshai. Shibaraku de gozaimasu.[6]**

SUZUKI: **Okaasan,[7] gobusata shite imasu.[8] Kyoo wa kanai to sore kara yuujin o hitori tsurete kimashita. Kanai no Junko desu. Sore kara kaisha no dooryoo no Neruson-san desu.**

JUNKO: **Yoroshiku. Shujin kara taihen osewa ni natta[9] to kiite imasu.**

ONODERA: **Iie, tondemo arimasen.[10]**

NERUSON: **Hajimemashite. Neruson desu. Yoroshiku.**

ONODERA: **Kochira koso[11] yoroshiku. Saa, doozo. Suzuki-san, jitsu wa ne, musuko mo kaette kite iru n desu.**

SUZUKI: **E, soo desu ka. Denwa shita toki wa isogashii to no koto deshita kara.**

ONODERA: **Hai, soo nan desu kedo.[12] Hiroshi, Suzuki-san, otsuki ni narimashita yo.**

Min'na naka ni hairu. Suzuki-shi to Hiroshi, saikai o yorokobu.

HIROSHI: **Yaa, Suzuki. Shibaraku. Genki ka.[13]**

SUZUKI: **Un.[14] Ginkoo-zutome wa doo dai.[15]**

HIROSHI: Sarariiman mo taihen da kedo, maa nan to ka yatte iru.

SUZUKI: Isogashii tte iu kara, aenai to akiramete ita n da.

HIROSHI: Un. Isogashii kedo, tsugoo tsukete[16] tonde kita[17] yo.

SUZUKI: Sore wa sumanai na.[18]

HIROSHI: Kono shuumatsu wa boku no yuujin mo nan'nin ka kuru koto ni natte iru. En'nosuke to okusan mo konban irassharu. Kabuki-yakusha no En'nosuke, shitteru daro.

SUZUKI: Mochiron. Aa, soo.

Min'na sassoku onsen ni hairu.[19] Soshite yuushoku-go, issho ni suwatte zatsu-dan suru.

JUNKO: Ii yu deshita wa.

HIROSHI: Soo deshita ka. Sore wa yokatta.

JUNKO: Sore ni oshokuji mo oishikatta wa.

HIROSHI: Inaka ryoori desu ga.

JUNKO: Son'na koto arimasen wa. Sore ni kon'na ni shizuka na tokoro de seikatsu dekiru hito ga urayamashii wa.

NERUSON: Hontoo ni shizuka de ii tokoro desu ne.

HIROSHI: Shizuka sugite, chotto taikutsu shimasen ka.

NERUSON: Iya, tokai no seikatsu wa benri desu kedo, urusakute, tokidoki iya[20] ni narimasu yo.

HIROSHI: Koo iu inaka ni sumu koto de don'na ii tokoro ga ari-masu ka ne.[21]

NERUSON: Shizukesa. Kanso na seikatsu. Jikan no yoyuu ga aru kara, kangaeru jikan datte[22] motemasu. Shoorai kaisha o yametara, shizuka na tokoro de seikatsu shitai to kangaete imasu.

SUZUKI: Soo. Boku datte, dekiru koto nara, inaka de seikatsu shi-tai desu ne. Kodomo o tokai no gakkoo ni ikasetai[23] kara, ima wa dekimasen ga. Demo teinen[24] ni nattara, tokai kara nigetai desu ne.

NERUSON: Dooshite kodomosan o tokai no gakkoo ni ikasetai n desu ka.

SUZUKI: Yahari tokai ni ii gakkoo ga arimasu. Ii daigaku ni hairu ni wa tokai ni sunde ita hoo ga ii deshoo.

EN'NOSUKE: Watakushi wa tokai no seikatsu no hoo ga suki desu ne. Tookyoo no yoo na tokai no bunka katsudoo wa inaka no shizuka na seikatsu to wa kurabemono ni naranai to omoimasu.

NERUSON: **Kabuki-yakusha-san**[25] **to shite tokai no hoo ga osuki na no wa wakarimasu.**

SUZUKI: **En'nosuke-joo, kabuki no serifu**[26] **o hitokoto onegai dekimasu ka.**

NERUSON: **Ee, zehi onegai shimasu.**

EN'NOSUKE: **Dewa, "Chuushingura" kara hitokusari. "Akoo shijuushichi-shi no hitori, Nakamura Kansuke wa . . ."**

En'nosuke, kabuki no serifu o hiroo suru.

A WEEKEND AT THE HOT SPRINGS

Mr. Nelson and the Suzukis spend the weekend at a hot spring resort owned by Mr. Suzuki's friend. After a long drive, they finally arrive at Sekiyoo, which is in Hakone Hot Springs.

SUZUKI: Well, here we are (lit. we arrived). The view is really great, isn't it?

NELSON: Yeah, it's wonderful. It's (the inn) called Sekiyoo, isn't it?

SUZUKI: Yes. This inn is the house of one of my college friends. I often stayed with them during the summer and winter breaks.

Mr. Suzuki greets Mrs. Onodera, his friend's mother.

SUZUKI: Hello, is anybody home?

ONODERA: Oh, Mr. Suzuki, welcome! It's been such a long time.

SUZUKI: Mrs. Onodera (lit. mother), (I'm sorry) you haven't heard from me (for so long). I brought my wife and a friend with me today. This is my wife, Junko. And this is my colleague, Mr. Nelson.

JUNKO: Nice to meet you. My husband is always telling me (lit. I am hearing from my husband) how good you were to him (lit. took care of him).

ONODERA: How nice of you to say that. (lit. No, not all.)

NELSON: How do you do? My name's Nelson. Nice to meet you.

ONODERA: Nice to meet you, too. Please do come in. Mr. Suzuki, guess what! (lit. Actually!) My son is here (lit. has come home).

SUZUKI: What? Really? When I called him, (he said) he was (too) busy.

ONODERA: Yes, I know . . . Hiroshi, Mr. Suzuki is here.

Everyone goes inside. Suzuki and Hiroshi are happy to see each other again.

HIROSHI: Suzuki, long time, no see. How're you doing?

SUZUKI: Fine. How (do you like) working for a bank?

HIROSHI: (The life of) a salaryman is hard, but, well, I get by (lit. I'm doing it somehow).

SUZUKI: You said you were busy, so I didn't think we'd be able to meet (lit. gave up on meeting).

HIROSHI: Yeah, I am busy, but I made the time and came out here in a hurry.

SUZUKI: I really appreciate that.

HIROSHI: This weekend, a few of my friends are supposed to be coming by. I'm expecting En'nosuke and his wife tonight. You know En'no-suke, the Kabuki actor, don't you?

SUZUKI: Of course. Oh, is that right? (Is he coming?)

Everyone then gets into the hot spring. After dinner, they sit around chatting.

JUNKO: That was a nice hot bath.

HIROSHI: Really? I'm glad. (lit. That was good.)

JUNKO: And the meal was delicious too.

HIROSHI: It's (merely) country cooking.

JUNKO: No, not at all (don't apologize about that). I envy people who can live in such a quiet place.

NELSON: It's really quiet and (just) wonderful here.

HIROSHI: It's too quiet. Don't you (find it) a little boring?

NELSON: No way. Living in the city is convenient, but it's noisy and I get sick of it sometimes.

HIROSHI: So what do you think is so good (lit. what are the good places) about living in this kind of rural area?

NELSON: The quiet. The simple life. It's not so hectic (lit. There is free time) and you even have time to think. In the future, when I retire, I think I'd like to live someplace quiet.

SUZUKI: Right. If it were something I could do, I'd like to live in the country. But I want to send my kids to school in the city, so I can't now. However, when I reach retirement age, I'd like to escape the city.

NELSON: Why do you want your kids to go to school in the city?

SUZUKI: Well, the city has the good schools. In order (for my kids) to get into a good university, it's better to live in the city.

EN'NOSUKE: I prefer city life. I think there is no comparison between the cultural activities in cities like Tokyo and the quiet life of the country.

NELSON: As a Kabuki actor, it's understandable why you like the city better.

SUZUKI: En'nosuke, could you (recite) a few Kabuki lines for us?

NELSON: Yes, please do.

EN'NOSUKE: Well, one line from *Chuushingura*. "Nakamura Kansuke, one of the forty-seven Akaho samurai . . ."

En'nosuke recites (a few) lines from Kabuki.

B. CHUU

1. Hot spring resorts are popular vacation destinations in Japan. Owing to the fact that Japan has many active and inactive volcanoes, there are hundreds of these resorts scattered throughout the country. Many are within an hour from big cities by train or car. An overnight stay ranges from about one hundred to five hundred dollars, and typically includes an elaborate dinner and traditional breakfast. Many hot spring resorts are family-run operations. Recently, however, large companies have also started operating them.

2. The *Hakone Onsenkyo* (Hakone Hot Springs) is one of the most popular resorts in Japan, situated 70 km (50 mi.) to the southwest of Tokyo. Special trains to Hakone take between one and two hours. There are a dozen or so hot springs, as well as several golf courses in the area.

3. *Doosoosei* (classmate) relationships are usually strong and can be important in conducting business.

4. *Ojama shimashita* literally means "I got in the way" or "I disturbed (you)." It is often said when leaving someone's home or office. One can also say *Ojama shimasu* when entering someone's home.

5. *Gomen kudasai* means "Please forgive me (for bothering you)," and is often said upon visiting someone's home or office, when knocking on the door, or entering the room. Once greeted by the host, you should then say *Ojama shimasu*.

6. The word *shibaraku* has two opposite meanings, depending on context. One means "a long time" and the other "a short time": *Shibaraku (buri) desu (de gozaimasu).* (It's been a long time since [I saw you last].) *Shibaraku omachi kudasai.* (Please wait a moment.)

7. When addressing a friend's mother or father, it is not uncommon to call them *Okaasan* (Mother) or *Otoosan* (Father).

8. *Gobusata shite imasu* (I am very sorry for not having contacted you) is said by someone who was supposed to have made contact with another person but has not done so for a long time. This expression is formal and is used both in conversation and writing.

9. *Shujin ga itsumo osewa ni natte imasu* means "Thank you very much for your taking care of my husband." It is a typical expression many Japanese wives say to their husband's friends or associates.

10. The expression *ton demo arimasen,* which means "don't mention it" or "not at all," is said when someone compliments you or tries to do something nice for you.

11. *Kochira koso* literally means "this (side)," but is usually translated as "my pleasure." *Koso* is a particle that functions to emphasize the preceding word.

12. *Kedo* is the shortened form of *keredo* (although, but). It is often said at the end of a sentence to make it more indirect and, therefore, polite.

13. People who were once classmates often maintain their friendships for life. They use informal language when speaking to each other. As in English, they are on a first-name basis (or sometimes, between men only, last name without *san*) and speak in short sentences.

14. *Un* is an informal form of *hai* (yes).

15. *Doo dai* means "How is it?" The use of the copula *da* plus *i* makes a sentence interrogative. The question particle *ka* may also be followed by *i*. *Dai* and *kai* are usually used by men in informal conversations.

16. *Tsugoo tsukeru* means "make every effort to do." Other examples of *tsugoo* are "*tsugoo ga ii* (to be convenient)" and "*tsugoo ga warui* (to be inconvenient)."

17. *Tonde kuru* is a compound verb composed of *tobu* (to fly) and *kuru* (to come). It means "to come in a hurry."

18. *Sore wa sumanai na* literally means "That is inexcusable," or "I am sorry (for what you did for me)," and is very informal. It implies "I am very grateful to you."

19. At hot spring resorts, guests enjoy bathing together in one huge bathtub. There are, of course, private baths available in some resorts at an additional cost.

20. The word *iya (na)* has two meanings: "hateful" and "no." It is one of the first words a Japanese baby will learn, and can be used to indicate dislikes: *Iya da* (I don't like it).

21. *Don'na ii koto ga arimasu ka ne* means "I wonder what kind of benefits (lit. good things) it could have." *Ka ne* at the end of a sentence signifies "I wonder."

22. *Kangaeru jikan datte motemasu* means "(You) even have time to think." The word *datte* here signifies "also" or "even."

23. Many Japanese parents sacrifice their personal lives for the sake of their children's education. When a businessman is transferred to a different city, for example, he often lives alone without his family for several years while the children stay with their mother. One reason Japanese parents do not want their children to transfer to a different school is that moving to a new city will mean leaving their classmates. Some schools also require students to take exams upon transferring, another disadvantage.

24. *Teinen* refers to "age of mandatory retirement." In most organizations, this is between fifty-five and sixty-five years of age.

25. The profession of Kabuki actor is prestigious and well respected. Kabuki actors are addressed with special honorific titles such as *joo,* which is similar to "sir." Kabuki actors' jobs are often handed down from one generation of a certain family to another. The art of Kabuki requires intensive training from a young age, and therefore often only the sons of established actors are able to pursue the profession. All roles, including those of females, are played by men.

26. The word *serifu* means "speech" or "lines," but it often refers to "dialogues" from Kabuki or other theatrical performances.

C. BUNPOO TO YOOHOO

1. A *TO IU* B

The construction A *to iu* B (lit. B called A), in which A is a proper noun and B is a common noun, is used in two ways:

a. Defining the Proper Noun

This is when the speaker assumes that the listener is not familiar with the proper noun and feels that it is necessary to define it.

Sekiyoo to iu ryokan desu.
   It is a Japanese inn called Sekiyoo.

Bijitekku to iu kaisha ni tsutomete imasu.
   I am working for a company called BusiTech.

Fujii-san to iu kata o onegai shimasu.
   May I speak to Mr. Fujii, please?

En'nosuke to iu kabuki-yakusha o shitte imasu ka.
   Do you know a Kabuki actor named En'nosuke?

b. Emphasizing the Proper Noun

To iu is also used when the speaker wishes to emphasize the proper noun.

Tookyoo to iu tokoro wa totemo mushiatsui desu.
   Tokyo is really muggy.

Suzuki-san to iu hito wa omoshiroi hito desu ne.
   Mr. Suzuki is an interesting person, isn't he?

Hakone to iu tokoro ni wa iroiro na mono ga arimasu.
   There are lots of things (to do) in Hakone.

Kariforunia to iu tokoro wa seikatsu shiyasuii tokoro desu.
   California is an easy place to live.

2. RELAYING A MESSAGE

The construction *to no koto desu* is used to relay a message or information learned from a third party.

Ano ryokan wa keshiki ga totemo ii to no koto desu.
   They told me that the inn has a beautiful view.

170

Yasumi ni yoku ojama shita to no koto desu.
They told me that they used to visit them often during vacations.

Buchoo ga matte iru to no koto desu kara isogimashoo.
I heard the director is waiting for us, so let's hurry.

Shiatoru ni honsha ga aru to no koto desu.
They told me that their head office is in Seattle.

Kaisha o yametara, shizuka na seikatsu o shitai to no koto desu.
He told me that when he retires, he would like to live a quiet life.

3. THE CAUSATIVE FORM

Verbs conjugated in the causative form have the meaning "to make someone do something." They are formed as follows:

REGULAR VERBS (STEM + *SASERU*)

taberu (to eat)	*tabesaseru* (to make [someone] eat)
oshieru (to teach)	*oshiesaseru* (to make teach)
kaeru (to exchange)	*kaesaseru* (to make exchange)
miru (to see)	*misaseru* (to make see)
kangaeru (to think)	*kangaesaseru* (to make think)
hajimeru (to begin)	*hajimesaseru* (to make begin)

IRREGULAR VERBS (PRE-*NAI* FORM OF VERB + *SERU*)

tsuka(w)u (to use)	*tsukawaseru* (to make [someone] use)
kiku (to listen)	*kikaseru* (to make listen)
matsu (to wait)	*mataseru* (to make wait)
i(w)u (to say)	*iwaseru* (to make say)
iku (to go)	*ikaseru* (to make go)

EXCEPTIONS

suru (to do)	*saseru* (to make [someone] do)
kuru (to come)	*kosaseru* (to make come)

Kodomo o tokai no gakkoo ni ikasemasu.
I make my child go to school in the city.

Wakai shain o yamesasemashita.
I made the young employees quit.

Kodomo o inaka ni sumasemasu.
I will make my children live in the countryside.

Anata no shigoto o shain ni tetsudawasemasu.
I will have someone from my office assist you with your work.

Kazoku o onsen ni ikasemashita.
I made my family go to the hot spring resort.

Kazoku o shizuka na tokoro de seikatsu sasetai desu.
I want my family to live in a quiet place.

D. BIJINESU JIKOO

INAKA (THE COUNTRYSIDE)

The majority of people who live in big cities such as Tokyo and Osaka are originally from smaller cities and villages. People of the older generation in particular tend to have moved to these larger cities in order to attend a university or technical school, and then decided to stay permanently.

During the holidays, especially at *Obon* (Soul's Day) in the summer, and *Oshoogatsu* (New Year), people return to their hometowns to visit their parents, relatives, and old friends. Many also take this opportunity to pay their respects to their ancestors by visiting the family grave or other such places. The word *inaka* in this situation means "hometown," though it doesn't necessarily mean a small town.

Unfortunately, foreigners in Japan rarely get the opportunity to meet people in the countryside. If a colleague or friend asks you to come along, do accept the invitation. The lifestyle in the country is quite a bit more relaxed, and you'll find that people are more courteous and friendly. People tend to preserve traditional culture and activities, such as festivals and religious ceremonies, more in *inaka*. You will also find that the local dialects in the countryside are quite different from standard spoken Japanese.

Recently, the population in rural areas has been decreasing. This is largely due to the fact that young people prefer the "quality" life they feel the big cities offer. Another trend, however, is that older people are moving to the countryside after they reach retirement age. For them, the quiet and peaceful lifestyle there is more appealing.

RENSHUU MONDAI

A. *Tsugi no shitsumon ni kotaenasai.* (Answer the following questions.)

1. *Neruson-san tachi wa nan to iu ryokan ni tomarimashita ka.*
2. *Sore wa dare no uchi desu ka.*
3. *Sono ryokan wa don'na tokoro ni arimasu ka.*
4. *Suzuki-san wa ima dooshite inaka ni sumenai no desu ka.*
5. *En'nosuke-joo wa dooshite tokai no seikatsu ga suki desu ka.*

B. *Tekitoo na kotoba o irenasai.* (Insert the appropriate word.)

1. *Natsuyasumi ya fuyuyasumi ni yoku* _____ (visited, lit. imposed upon).
2. *Yuujin to kanai o* _____ (brought along).
3. *Tokai no seikatsu wa* _____ (convenient) *desu kedo, tokidoki* _____ (unpleasant) *ni narimasu.*
4. *Jikan no yoyuu ga aru kara,* _____ (time to think) *ga arimasu.*
5. *Dooshite kodomo-san o tokai no gakkoo ni* _____ (want to make them go) *ka.*

KOTAE

A. 1. *Sekiyoo to iu ryokan ni tomarimashita.* 2. *Suzuki-san no yuujin no Onodera Hiroshi to iu hito no uchi desu.* 3. *Shizuka na tokoro ni arimasu.* 4. *Kodomo-san o tokai no gakkoo ni ikasetai kara desu.* 5. *Tokai no bunka-katsudoo wa inaka no shizukesa to kurabemono ni naranai kara desu.*
B. 1. *ojama shimashita* 2. *tsurete kimashita* 3. *benri, iya* 4. *kangaeru jikan* 5. *ikasetai desu*

DAI JUUSANKA
Lesson 13

A. KAIWA

APOINTO NO TORIKESHI[1]

Suzuki-shi to Neruson-shi wa jimusho no rooka de hanasu.

NERUSON: **Tsuyu ga agatta[2] to omoimashita ga, mata ame desu ne.**

SUZUKI: **Taifuu desu yo.**

NERUSON: **Shichigatsu na no ni taifuu ga kuru n desu ka. Natsu no owari ni yoku kuru to kiite imashita ga.**

SUZUKI: **Nihon no taifuu shiizun[3] wa nagai desu kara.**

NERUSON: **Kyoo wa apointo ga aru n desu. Ikeru deshoo ka ne.**

SUZUKI: **Apointo wa doko desu ka.**

NERUSON: **Yokohama desu.**

SUZUKI: **Saa, wakarimasen ne. Terebi de taifuu-sokuhoo o shite imasu yo. Kikimashoo.**

Futari wa kaigishitsu ni itte hoosoo[4] o miru.

ANAUNSAA: **Taifuu-gogoo ga Kantoo-chihoo[5] ni chikazuite imasu. Ima no jookyoo kara suisoku shimasu to, taifuu wa yuugata Tookyoo oyobi[6] Chiba-ken ni jooriku suru kanoosei ga tsuyoku natte imasu. Taifuu ni tomonai[7] ame ga hageshiku furihajimete imasu[8] node, juubun chuui suru yoo kishoochoo wa keikoku shite orimasu. Mata JR oyobi shitetsu[9] mo unten o toriyamete iru tokoro mo arimasu. Odekake no sai wa juubun gochuui kudasai.**

NERUSON: **Kono bun dewa[10] dekakeraremasen ne.**

SUZUKI: **Nanji no apointo desu ka.**

NERUSON: **Ichiji no yakusoku nan desu ga.**

SUZUKI: **Norimono[11] ga ugoite inai tokoro mo aru kara, muri desu yo.**

NERUSON: **Kyanseru shite mo kamaimasen[12] ka. Warui inshoo o ataeru ka na.**

SUZUKI: Iie, daijoobu deshoo. Konna toki wa apointo o torikeshita hoo ga ii desu yo. Aite[13] mo wakatte kuremasu kara. Nihon de wa itsumo kono mondai ga arimasu. Shinpai shinaide.

NERUSON: Jaa, soo shimasu.

Neruson-shi wa Yokohama-shooji no Nakano-joo ni denwa suru.

NERUSON: Moshi moshi, Bijitekku no Neruson desu ga, Nakano-san, onegai shimasu.

NAKANO: Watakushi desu ga.

NERUSON: Aa, Nakano-san. Senshuu odenwa shita Neruson desu ga.

NAKANO: Hai, oboete imasu yo. Kyoo no apointo no koto desu ka.

NERUSON: Ee, Taifuu no kankei de,[14] norimono ga ugoite inai tokoro mo aru soo de. Katte de mooshi wake gozaimasen ga,[15] apointo o enki shite itadakitai no desu ga.

NAKANO: Ichioo junbi wa shite atta n desu ga, shikata ga arimasen[16] ne.

NERUSON: Makoto ni mooshiwake arimasen.

NAKANO: Iie. Sorede doo shimasu ka.

NERUSON: Tooka atari[17] wa ikaga deshoo ka.

NAKANO: Tooka wa mokuyoobi desu nee. Zan'nen desu ga, chotto muri desu.

NERUSON: Kin'yoobi gogo wa.

NAKANO: Ee, kin'yoobi gogo niji ni shimashoo. Tsugoo ga tsukanai[18] toki wa renraku shimasu.

NERUSON: Shoochi itashimashita. Ashisutanto o ni mei tsurete ukagaimasu kara, yoroshiku onegai shimasu.

NAKANO: Sore de, basho wa wakarimasu ka. Chizu o fakkusu shimashoo ka.

NERUSON: Iie, wakaru to omoimasu. Shiyakusho[19] no tonari no biru desu ne.

NAKANO: Soo desu. Jaa, omachi shite imasu.

NERUSON: Doomo arigatoo gozaimasu. Soredewa, shitsurei itashimasu. (Jibun ni) Kore wa dekita. Saa, densha ga nai kara, doo shite uchi ni kaeru ka kangaenakucha.[20]

Canceling an Appointment

Mr. Suzuki and Mr. Nelson are having a discussion in the office hallway.

NELSON: I thought the rainy season was over, but it's raining again.

SUZUKI: It's a typhoon.

NELSON: A typhoon in July (lit. has come even though it's July)? I heard that they come (lit. a lot) at the end of the summer.

SUZUKI: (Well,) Japan's typhoon season is (very) long.

NELSON: I have an appointment today. Do you think I'll be able to go?

SUZUKI: Where is your appointment?

NELSON: In Yokohama.

SUZUKI: Well, I don't know. There's a special typhoon report on TV. Let's watch (lit. listen to) it.

The two of them go to the conference room and watch the news broadcast.

ANNOUNCER: Typhoon #5 is approaching the Kanto area. Judging (lit. if we assume) from the present situation, there is a strong possibility that it will hit the Tokyo and Chiba areas this evening. Heavy rains accompanying the typhoon have started falling (in the area) and the Meteorological Agency has issued a warning to take special (lit. enough) precautions. In addition, both JR and private rail lines have suspended service in (some) areas. (You are advised to) exercise caution when going outdoors.

NELSON: If that's the way it's going to be, I guess I can't go out.

SUZUKI: What time is your appointment?

NELSON: It's at (lit. I promised) one o'clock.

SUZUKI: Well, since the trains aren't even running (lit. not moving) in (some) places, (I think) it'll be impossible (to go).

NELSON: Is it okay to cancel? I wonder if it'll give them a bad impression.

SUZUKI: No, I think it will be okay. At times like these, it's better to cancel. They'll understand. We have these problems constantly in Japan. Don't worry.

NELSON: (Okay,) I'll cancel it, then. (lit. I'll do it.)

Mr. Nelson calls Ms. Nakano of Yokohama Trading Company.

NELSON: Hello, this is Mr. Nelson of BusiTech. May I speak to Ms. Nakano, please?

NAKANO: Speaking. (lit. It is I.)

NELSON: Oh, Ms. Nakano, this is Mr. Nelson. I spoke with you (lit. called) last week.

NAKANO: Yes, I remember. Is this about today's appointment?

NELSON: Yes. Because of the typhoon, it appears that public transportation has been suspended in some areas. I'm sorry, but I'd like to postpone our appointment.

NAKANO: Well, we were prepared, but I guess it can't be helped.

NELSON: I'm very sorry.

NAKANO: It's okay. So what should we (do about the appointment)?

NELSON: Can we reschedule it for (lit. how about) somewhere around the tenth?

NAKANO: (Let's see,) the tenth is a Thursday, right? I'm sorry (lit. It's too bad), but I can't make it then.

NELSON: How about Friday afternoon?

NAKANO: Okay, let's do it at two o'clock on Friday. If I can't make it, I'll get in touch with you.

NELSON: That'll be fine. (lit. I consent.) I'll be bringing two assistants with me. I'll see you then.

NAKANO: Do you know where we're located? Shall I fax you a map?

NELSON: No, I think I know (how to get there). It's the building next to (Yokohama) City Hall, right?

NAKANO: Yes, that's right. Well, I'll see you then (lit. I'm waiting for you.)

NELSON: Thank you very much. Bye. (to himself:) (At least) that's done. Okay, since there are no trains, I have to figure out how to get home.

B. CHUU

1. *Torikeshi* (cancellation), a noun, is actually the stem form of the verb *torikesu,* which in turn is a compound of *toru* (to take) and *kesu* (to erase). This method of forming a noun from the stem of a verb is very common in Japanese.

2. *Tsuyu ga agatta* means "The rainy season has ended." The rainy season, *tsuyu,* usually lasts from early June until the beginning of July. The weather during this time varies greatly, from days when it rains continuously to clear, sunny days.

3. *Taifuu* (typhoons) usually hit Japan in late summer and early fall. A few strong typhoons hit Japan every year and often cause extensive damage. Public transportation is often interrupted, and since many people depend on the trains and buses, they are often forced to stay home during typhoon weather.

4. The language most often used on television, particularly in newscasts, is called "standard Japanese." It is said to most resemble the speech used by the middle class in Tokyo. All Japanese people understand standard Japanese and use it in formal situations, but many speak some kind of dialect at home, or even at school. Dialects have recently been heard more on television because of a revitalization of many regional economies and a subsequent growth in the respect afforded these local cultures. Dialects are also spoken frequently in dramas and comedies.

5. *Kantoo-chihoo* means "the Kanto (eastern) region," which includes Tokyo and six other surrounding prefectures.

6. *Oyobi* means "and," and is used in formal situations and in writing.

7. *Tomonai* means "accompanying" and is used in more formal situations.

8. The expression *furihajimeru* is a compound verb, combining *furu* (to fall) and *hajimeru* (to begin). It means "to start falling" or "to start raining."

9. JR (Japan Railways, pronounced *jee aaru*) used to be a government-owned system, but in the 1980s it was privatized. However, it still has strong government ties. *Shitetsu* means "privately owned railway system." There are many such lines all over Japan and about a dozen major railway systems in the greater Tokyo area.

10. *Kono bun dewa* means "under these circumstances" and is used in both positive and negative situations.

11. *Norimono* literally means "a thing to ride." It refers to modes of transportation such as airplanes, trains, and buses.

12. *Kamaimasen* means "It doesn't matter" or "I don't care," and can extend its meaning to signify "It's okay if."

13. *Aite* can mean "partner," "companion," "the other party," or "opponent," depending on the context.

14. The expression *(no) kankei de* means "because of" or "in relation to." *Kankei* means "relation" or "connection."

15. The expression *Katte de mooshi wake gozaimasen ga* means "I'm terribly sorry to be selfish, but." It is used to cancel appointments, or in similar situations.

16. *Shikata ga arimasen* (It cannot be helped) is heard often in Japanese, and reveals the psychology of many Japanese people. Some believe the phrase originates from the fatalistic attitude that has developed over time in Japan. The idea that something cannot be helped or changed, and thus must be accepted, is typically Japanese. It is believed that this perspective has allowed the Japanese to cope with the frequent natural disasters that occur in their country.

17. *Atari* means "about" or "around" with regard to both time and place. Therefore, *tooka atari* means "around the tenth (day)," while *kono atari* means "around here."

18. *Tsugoo ga tsuku* literally means "when it is convenient," and in this context "to be able to attend."

19. *Shiyakusho* means "city hall." Tokyo, which is divided into twenty-three separate "wards," or districts, has offices similar to the *shiyakusho* called *kuyakusho* (ward office), at which you can tend to business such as getting a foreigner's registration card or applying for national insurance.

20. *Kangaenakucha* is a shortened colloquial equivalent of *kangaenakutewa naranai,* which means "must think about." It is formed by dropping the *i* from the non-past negative and adding *kucha: Yaranakucha.* (I must do [it].) *Asobanakucha.* (I must play.)

C. BUNPOO TO YOOHOO

1. INFORMAL SENTENCES

As we discussed in Lessons 3, 4, and 11, the language you use varies according to whom you are speaking with. Speaking with your boss requires formal speech, while talking to family members, close friends, younger people, and subordinates allows for informal speech. As you become more familiar with the different levels of speech and when each level is appropriate in conversation, you will be able to switch comfortably between both formal and informal speech.

Informal sentences always end with an informal (or plain) form. Following is a summary of the informal forms of all three sentence-ending parts of speech: nouns, adjectives, and verbs.

Nouns and *na*-adjectives plus the copula *da:*

NON-PAST AFFIRMATIVE	NON-PAST NEGATIVE	PAST AFFIRMATIVE	PAST NEGATIVE
Kuruma da	*Kuruma dewa nai.* *Kuruma ja nai.*	*Kuruma datta.*	*Kuruma dewa nakatta. Kuruma ja nakatta.*
It's a car.	It's not a car.	It was a car.	It wasn't a car.
Hana da.	*Hana dewa nai.* *Hana ja nai.*	*Hana datta*	*Hana dewa nakatta. Hana ja nakatta.*
It's a flower	It's not a flower.	It was a flower.	It wasn't a flower.
Kirei da.	*Kirei dewa nai.* *Kirei ja nai.*	*Kirei datta.*	*Kirei dewa nakatta. Kirei ja nakatta.*
It's pretty.	It's not pretty.	It was pretty.	It wasn't pretty.
Shizuka da.	*Shizuka dewa nai.* *Shizuka ja nai.*	*Shizuka datta.*	*Shizuka dewa nakatta. Shizuka ja nakatta.*
It's quiet.	It's not quiet.	It was quiet.	It wasn't quiet.

I-ADJECTIVES

atarashii (new)	*atarashikunai*	*atarashikatta*	*atarashikunakatta*
wakai (young)	*wakakunai*	*wakakatta*	*wakakunakatta*
tanoshii (enjoyable)	*tanoshikunai*	*tanoshikatta*	*tanoshikunakatta*
hazukashii (shy)	*hazukashikunai*	*hazukashikatta*	*hazukashikunakatta*
ii (good)	*yokunai*	*yokatta*	*yokunakatta*

ikeru (to be able to go)	*ikenai*	*iketa*	*ikenakatta*
dekakeru (to go out)	*dekakenai*	*dekaketa*	*dekakenakatta*
kaeru (to change)	*kaenai*	*kaeta*	*kaenakatta*
oshieru (to teach)	*oshienai*	*oshieta*	*oshienakatta*
kangaeru (to think)	*kangaenai*	*kangaeta*	*kangaenakatta*
kimeru (to decide)	*kimenai*	*kimeta*	*kimenakatta*
nomu (to drink)	*nomanai*	*nonda*	*nomanakatta*
yomu (to read)	*yomanai*	*yonda*	*yomanakatta*
hanasu (to talk)	*hanasanai*	*hanashita*	*hanasanakatta*
kimaru (to be decided)	*kimaranai*	*kimatta*	*kimaranakatta*
kanjiru (to feel)	*kanjinai*	*kanjita*	*kanjinakatta*
iu (to say)	*iwanai*	*itta*	*iwanakatta*
komaru (to be a problem)	*komaranai*	*komatta*	*komaranakatta*
damaru (to be silent)	*damaranai*	*damatta*	*damaranakatta*
kuru (to come)	*konai*	*kita*	*konakatta*
suru (to do)	*shinai*	*shita*	*shinakatta*

Moo natsu mo owari da.
  It's already the end of the summer.

Kore wa taifuu-sokuhoo da yo.
  This is a special broadcast on the typhoon.

Norimono ga nai kara muri da.
  It's impossible because there is no transportation (available).

Ikenakute, zan'nen da.
  It's too bad that I can't go.

Taifuu-shiizun wa nagai yo.
  The typhoon season is long.

Kinoo wa totemo zan'nen datta wa. (female speech: note use of *wa*)
  (What happened) yesterday was really too bad.

Taifuu wa kowai.
  Typhoons are scary.

Fakkusu ga tsuita yo.
  The fax came through (lit. arrived).

Taifuu-sokuhoo o kiita yo.
  I listened to a special broadcast on the typhoon.

Ame demo kaisha ni iku no.
  You're going to go to work even if it's raining?

Tsuyu ga agatta to omotta yo.
I thought the rainy season had ended!

The informal form of *mashoo* can be either *yoo* or *oo,* depending on the type of verb to which it is attached. The *yoo* ending is affixed to the stem of regular verbs, and the *oo* ending to the pre-*nai* form of irregular verbs after dropping the *a.*

REGULAR VERBS

FORMAL	STEM + *YOO*	INFORMAL
kaemashoo (let's change)	*kae + yoo*	*kaeyoo*
kimemashoo (let's decide)	*kime + yoo*	*kimeyoo*
tabemashoo (let's eat)	*tabe + yoo*	*tabeyoo*

IRREGULAR VERBS

FORMAL	PRE-*NAI* FORM + *OO*	INFORMAL
hanashimashoo (let's talk)	*hanas(a) + oo*	*hanasoo*
kaerimashoo (let's go home)	*kaer(a) + oo*	*kaeroo*
nomimashoo (let's drink)	*nom(a) + oo*	*nomoo*

EXCEPTIONS

FORMAL	INFORMAL
kimashoo (let's come)	*koyoo*
shimashoo (let's do)	*shiyoo*

Taifuu sokuhoo o kikoo.
Let's listen to the special broadcast on the typhoon.

Apointo o moo sukoshi kangaeyoo.
Let's think about the appointment a little more.

Taifuu ni juubun chuui shiyoo.
Let's be careful during the typhoon.

Such phrases as *kamoshiremasen* (maybe), *rashii desu* (it seems), and *hoshii desu* (want) may be expressed informally, as in the following examples:

Ashita taifuu ga kuru kamoshirenai.
The typhoon may come tomorrow.

Ano kaisha wa katte rashii.
That company seems bent on having its way (lit. seems selfish).

Atarashii joohoo ga hoshii.
    I want the new information.

2. "THERE ARE TIMES WHEN . . ."

Previously, you learned how to talk about things you experienced in
the past by using the past form of a verb plus *koto ga aru*. When either
the affirmative non-past or negative non-past form of a verb is followed
by *koto ga aru,* you can express the idea that "there are times when
something occurs or happens." When used to express this meaning,
koto may also be replaced with *toki* (time).

Tokidoki osoku shokuji o suru koto ga arimasu.
    There are times when I eat late.

Kaisha ni ikenai koto ga arimasu.
    There are times when I can't go to the office (lit. company).

Nihonjin mo apointo o wasureru koto ga arimasu.
    Even the Japanese forget appointments sometimes.

Kaigishitsu o riyoo suru toki ga aru n desu.
    There are times when we use the conference room.

3. *NO NI* (EVEN THOUGH)

"Even though" or "contrary to one's expectation" can be expressed in
Japanese by adding *no ni* to the plain forms of verbs, *i*-adjectives, and
nouns or *na*-adjectives plus the copula *da* (which becomes *na*).

Shichigatsu na no ni taifuu ga kimashita.
    Even though it's July, a typhoon has come.

Apointo no yakusoku ga shite atta no ni ikemasen deshita.
    Even though I had an appointment, I could not go.

Menkai no junbi ga shite atta no ni, dare mo kimasen deshita.
    Even though we were prepared for the meeting, nobody showed up.

Norimono ga ugoite inai no ni, kare wa iku tsumori desu.
    Even though there is no transportation operating, he (still) intends
    to go.

Tenki ga warui no ni, dekakete ikimashita.
    Even though the weather is bad, he went out.

Unten suru no wa muri na no ni, ikanakereba narimasen deshita.
    Even though it was impossible to drive, I had to go.

D. BIJINESU JIKOO

KOOTSUU-KIKAN TO TENKOO (TRANSPORTATION AND WEATHER)

Trains, buses, and other modes of public transportation are essential to the lives of many businesspeople, office employees, plant workers, store clerks, and students. Almost everyone depends on public transportation. Not only is it important to those who commute long distances to and from work, but it is relied upon as a means of travel within the city.

As a result of this dependence on public transportation, the country can literally become paralyzed during times of heavy rain or snow. From time to time, these natural forces compel transportation authorities to suspend their operations, which can cause real problems for the millions who then find themselves stuck. Nevertheless, in general, public transportation is an extremely efficient mode of travel in Japan. (See more on transportation in Lesson 15.)

APOINTO NO TORIKESHI (CANCELING APPOINTMENTS)

In Japan, canceling appointments should be limited to only the most extreme circumstances. Making a request to reschedule an appointment may actually jeopardize the trust between companies. Trust is seen as a delicate and necessary factor in the maintenance of a productive and efficient business relationship.

The primary reason for not breaking appointments in Japan is that the Japanese believe the most effective decisions are made based on information brought forth by numerous parties. As a result, attendance by all who are expected at various meetings is considered extremely important. Of course, rescheduling an appointment is sometimes unavoidable, especially during those difficult times of severe weather, illness, or transportation-related problems. At times like these, it is acceptable to cancel or change the time of an appointment. When it becomes necessary to cancel, it is important to mention the circumstances to blame. In so doing, you will be able to maintain your business relationship.

RENSHUU MONDAI

A. *Tsugi no shitsumon ni kotaenasai.* (Answer the following questions.)

1. *Shichigatsu na no ni, dooshite taifuu ga kimasu ka.*
2. *Taifuu wa doko ni jooriku shimasu ka.*
3. *Neruson-san wa naze apointo o kyanseru shimasu ka.*
4. *Apointo wa itsu ni narimashita ka.*
5. *Apointo no basho wa doko desu ka.*

B. *Tsugi no bunshoo o infoomaru na bunshoo ni kaenasai.* (Transform the following sentences into informal sentences.)

1. *Tsuyu ga agatta to omoimashita ga, mata ame desu ne.*
2. *Nihon no taifuu-shiizun wa nagai desu kara.*
3. *Norimono ga ugoite inai tokoro mo arimasu kara, muri desu yo.*
4. *Ichioo junbi shite atta n desu ga, shikata ga arimasen ne.*
5. *Tsugoo ga tsukanai toki wa renraku shimasu.*

C. *Tadashii kotoba o shita kara erabinasai.* (Select the correct word from below.)

1. *Kyoo wa taisetsu na apointo ga* _____.
   (karu n desu, arun desu)
2. *Kon'na toki wa apointo o* _____ *hoo ga ii desu.*
   (torikesu, torikeshita, torikeshimasu)
3. *Koo iu toki wa aite mo wakatte* _____.
   (agemasu, kuremasu, yarimasu)
4. *Zan'nen desu ga, ashita no apointo wa* _____.
   (daijoobu desu, ii desu, muri desu)

KOTAE

A. 1. *Taifuu no shiizun wa nagai desu kara.* 2. *Tookyoo oyobi Chiba-ken ni jooriku suru kanoosei ga tsuyoi desu.* 3. *Norimono ga ugoite inai tokoro mo arimasu kara.* 4. *Juuichinichi kinyoobi niji ni narimashita.* 5. *Shiyakusho no tonari no biru desu.*
B. 1. *Tsuyu ga agatta to omotta ga, mata ame da ne.* 2. *Nihon no taifuu shiizun wa nagai kara.* 3. *Norimono ga ugoite inai tokoro mo aru kara, muri da yo.* 4. *Ichioo junbi shite atta n da ga, shikata ga nai ne.* 5. *Tsugoo ga tsukanai toki wa, renraku suru.*
C. 1. *aru n desu* 2. *torikeshita* 3. *kuremasu* 4. *muri desu*

DAI JUUYONKA
Lesson 14

A. KAIWA

MACHIGAI NO SHORI

Satoo-joo wa fudan to chigatte kigen ga yokunai. Neruson-shi wa doo shita no ka kangaeru.

NERUSON: Satoo-san wa kyoo doo shita n desu ka. Amari kigen ga yokunai yoo desu ga.

SUZUKI: Jitsu wa kanojo machigatta tokoro ni fakkusu o okutte shimatta rashii n desu yo. Sorede kesa okyaku-san kara boku ni toiawase[1] ga atte, buchoo[2] ni hookoku shitara, buchoo ga kankan ni okotte ne.[3]

NERUSON: Taishita koto ja nai n ja nai n desu ka.[4] Mata fakkusu sureba ii deshoo.

SUZUKI: Sore ga kinoo made ni suru hazu datta n desu.

NERUSON: Kyoo ja[5] osoi n desu ka.

SUZUKI: Ososugiru wake dewa nai n desu ga.

NERUSON: Jaa, dooshite son'na ni oosawagi suru[6] n desu ka.

SUZUKI: Sore ga chigau n desu yo. Buchoo wa shin'yoo no mondai da to iu n desu.

NERUSON: Maa. Sore mo soo desu ga, moo okutte shimatta n desu kara, shikata ga nai deshoo.

SUZUKI: Buchoo wa bu no dareka ga ayamari ni ike[7] to itte iru n desu ga, doo shiyoo ka to kangaete iru n desu.

NERUSON: Denwa de wa ayamarenai n desu ka.

SUZUKI: Buchoo wa seii o shimesu tame ni, wazawaza[8] itte ayamaru beki da to iu n desu.

Amerikajin de aru[9] Neruson-shi wa taishita mondai ja nai to kangae nagara mo, Nihonjin wa koo iu baai, don'na shori no shikata o suru no ka ni kyoomi o motsu. Soshite Neruson-shi wa Satoo-joo to hanasu.

NERUSON: Satoo-san, fakkusu no mondai no koto o kikimashita. Doo shita n desu ka. Fakkusu-bangoo o machigaeta n desu ka.

SATOO: Iie, watashi wa machigaete wa inai n desu.

NERUSON: Jaa, dare ga machigaeta n desu ka.

SATOO: Sore ga wakaranai n desu. Bangoo wa kami ni kaite ari-
mashita kara, sore de okutta n desu. Dare ga sono bangoo o
kaita ka watashi wa shirimasen. Demo Suzuki-san wa watashi
ga sono bangoo o kaita yoo ni buchoo ni hookoku shita n desu.
Sorede chotto kibun o gai shite imasu.[10]

NERUSON: Naruhodo.

SATOO: Sorede buchoo wa watashi no koto o sugoku[11] okotte iru n
desu.

NERUSON: Sorede, doo suru n desu ka. Dare ga ayamari ni iku n
desu ka.

SATOO: Suzuki-san ga tantoo da kara, kare ga iku beki da to omou
n desu. Watashi ga itte mo kamaimasen kedo.

NERUSON: Soo desu ne. Suzuki-san ga itta hoo ga ii kamo ne. Jaa,
Suzuki-san ga ayamari ni iku no ga ichiban ii to iu koto o
watashi ga joozu ni itte agemasu[12] yo. Bangoo no koto mo setsumei shite agemasu yo.

SATOO: Yoroshiku onegai shimasu ne.

NERUSON: Shinpai shinaide. Buchoo mo naze kon'na koto ni natta
ka wakarimasu yo.

*Neruson-shi wa shin'yoo toka "kao"[13] no mondai ni made hatten shite iru
koto ni kizuku. Suzuki-shi, Meiji-hoken no Andoo-kachoo no jimusho made
ayamari ni iku koto ni suru.*

ANDOO: Yaa, doozo, osuwari kudasai.

SUZUKI: Kono tabi wa taihen shitsurei itashimashita. Watakushi-
domo[14] no techigai de taihen gomeiwaku o okake shimashita.[15]

ANDOO: Sore wa wazawaza, goteinei ni arigatoo gozaimasu.[16]

SUZUKI: Chuui wa shite imasu ga, mainichi isogashiku shite iru
mono desu kara.

ANDOO: Iya ne. Kakari no mono o matasete oita shi, soreni amari
koohyoo shitakunai mono desu kara.

SUZUKI: Soo desu ka. Mooshiwake gozaimasen deshita. Kongo[17]
zettai ni kon'na machigai ga nai yoo ni chuui itashimasu kara,
oyurushi kudasai.[18]

ANDOO: Yoku aru koto desu yo.[19] Amari ki ni nasaranaide kudasai.[20] Takagi-buchoo ni yoroshiku osshatte kudasai.

SUZUKI: Wakarimashita. Dewa shitsurei shimasu.

Handling a Mistake

Unlike (her) usual (self), Ms. Sato is not in a good mood. Mr. Nelson wonders what happened (to her).

NELSON: What's wrong with Ms. Sato? She doesn't seem to be in a good mood.

SUZUKI: It seems that she sent a fax to the wrong place. And then I had an inquiry from a client (about it) this morning, and when I reported it to the department manager, he became quite angry.

NELSON: That's not (such) a big deal, is it? If she just sends the fax again, it will be okay, right?

SUZUKI: Well, it was supposed to be done by yesterday.

NELSON: Is it too late to send it today? (lit. If it's today, will it be late?)

SUZUKI: It's not that it's too late . . .

NELSON: So, why are they making such a fuss?

SUZUKI: It's not such a simple matter. (lit. That's wrong.) The department manager says that this is (really) an issue (lit. problem) of trust (between us and the clients).

NELSON: Well, that's (probably) true, but since she has already sent it, there's really not much that can be done about it.

SUZUKI: The department manager told me to send someone from the department to apologize (to the client). I'm still thinking about what to do.

NELSON: Can't we apologize over the phone?

SUZUKI: The department manager says that someone should (lit. on purpose) apologize (in person) in order to show our sincerity.

While Mr. Nelson, an American, does not consider the problem (so) serious, he is interested in how Japanese people solve these kinds of problems (lit. cases). Nelson speaks to Ms. Sato.

NELSON: Ms. Sato, I heard about the fax problem. What happened? Did you make a mistake on the fax number?

SATO: No, I didn't get (the number) wrong.

NELSON: Then who did?

SATO: I don't know. The number was written on the paper, so I (just) sent it. I don't know who wrote the number down. Mr. Suzuki, however, reported to the department manager that I wrote it. That kind of bugs me.

NELSON: I see.

SATO: And the department manager is very upset with me.

NELSON: So what will you do? Who is going to go and apologize?

SATO: Since Mr. Suzuki is responsible for the project (lit. in charge), I think that he should go. I wouldn't mind going myself, though.

NELSON: I think you're right. Maybe Mr. Suzuki should go. I'll tell Mr. Suzuki in a tactful way (lit. skillfully) that (perhaps) it would be best if he went to apologize. I'll also explain the thing about the number to him for you.

SATO: Thank you.

NELSON: Don't worry. I'm sure the department manager will also understand why this (all) happened.

Mr. Nelson discovers that this has developed into a problem of "trust" and "(losing) face." Mr. Suzuki decides to go to Mr. Ando's office at Meiji Insurance Company to offer an apology.

ANDO: Oh, please sit down.

SUZUKI: I am very sorry for what has happened (lit. this time). (I am afraid that) our error has caused you a great deal of trouble.

ANDO: Thank you for coming just to apologize.

SUZUKI: We (try to be) careful, but we are (so) busy every day.

ANDO: That's okay. (lit. No.) I made the person in charge wait and did not want everybody to know about it (lit. make a public announcement).

SUZUKI: Really? I am very, very sorry. We'll be very careful to make sure this kind of mistake doesn't happen again. Please forgive us.

ANDO: It happens all the time. Please, don't worry about it. Please give my regards to Mr. Takagi.

SUZUKI: Yes, I will. Thank you very much and good-bye.

B. CHUU

1. *Toiawase,* a noun, is the root form of the verb *toiawaseru,* which combines *tou* (to ask) and *awaseru* (to match). It means "an inquiry."

2. When addressing a superior or when speaking about that person in conversation with others, it is common to use only his or her title. In the dialogue, Mr. Suzuki calls his boss *Buchoo* instead of Mr. Takagi. You will also hear people use the word *okusan* (wife) when

talking about or addressing a woman who is married, and *dan'na-san* (husband) when referring to or addressing a married man. *Sensei* (teacher) is another common title that is used to address or refer to doctors, professors, famous artists, musicians, and other people who are known for their accomplishments.

3. *Kan kan ni okoru* or *kankan da* means "(Someone) is very angry." It is one of many onomatopoeic expressions. See Grammar, section 3 in this lesson for more on the subject.

4. *Taishita koto ja nai* means "It's not an important thing." The second *ja nai* in *taishita koto ja nai n janai n desu ka* is used in the same way as the particle *ne,* namely to indicate "don't you think?"

5. *Kyoo ja* means "If it is today." When they occur at the end of a clause like this, *dewa* and the contracted form, *ja,* are used to mean "if" when followed by a negative consequence.

6. *Oosawagi* means "uproar." When followed by *suru* it means "to make a big deal."

7. *Ike* is the informal imperative (command) form of *iku* (to go). Therefore, *ayamari ni ike to itte irun desu* literally means "He said, 'Go apologize.'"

8. *Wazawaza* means "on purpose" or "especially."

9. *De aru* is a literary form of the copula *da.*

10. *Kibun o gai suru* literally means "to hurt one's feelings."

11. *Sugoi* has a variety of meanings, such as "great," "weird," "dreadful," "wonderful," "awful." Context determines which meaning is correct. The adverbial form *sugoku* is used to modify adjectives and verbs, and may be translated as "really," "awfully," or "terribly."

12. *Itte agemasu* means "I will explain (lit. say) it for you." The pattern, *te*-form of a verb + *ageru* signifies "to do a favor for someone."

13. It is disgraceful to lose *kao* (face) in Japan. As a result, the Japanese go to great measures to prevent this from happening.

14. The plural forms of "I" *(watakushi)* are *watakushi-tachi, watakushi-domo,* and *wareware.* These, of course, all mean "we." *Watakushi-domo* is used more often in business. For example: *Watakushi-domo wa konpyuutaa kankei no shigoto desu.* (We are involved in computer-related business.) *Watakushi-domo no kaisha dewa sono seihin o atsukatte imasen ga.* (Our company does not handle that product.)

15. *Gomeiwaku o okake shimashita* literally means "I caused you inconvenience," and is frequently used when apologizing to someone for causing them to do something they don't normally do.

16. *Goteinei ni arigatoo gozaimasu* literally means "Thank you politely," and is used to express gratitude to someone for making a special effort to do something.

17. *Kongo* literally means "afterward" or "from now on."

18. *Oyurushi kudasai* means "Please forgive us" and is used in formal situations.

19. The expression *Yoku aru koto desu yo* literally means "It's a thing that often exists," but this is often not the truth. It is said as a means of comforting the other person.

20. *Ki ni suru* means "to worry about." *Nasaru* is the honorific form of *suru*.

C. BUNPOO TO YOOHOO

1. *BEKI DA*

A verb followed by *beki da* is used to express the idea that something should be done. The verb that precedes *beki da* should be in the nonpast affirmative plain form.

Wazawaza itte ayamaru beki desu.
You should go (lit. on purpose) and apologize.

Mondai o min'na de hanasu beki desu.
Everyone should discuss the problem (together).

Machigawanai yoo ni chuui suru beki datta.
We should have been (more) careful not to make any mistakes.

Buchoo ni sore o hookoku suru beki ja nai.
You should not report that to the department manager.

2. THE PARTICLE *KA*

As you know, the particle *ka* occurs at the end of a sentence to make it a question. In addition to this, *ka* also has several other functions.

a. Alternatives

Ka is used between two nouns or sentences in order to indicate alternatives. This function is roughly equivalent to "either . . . or" in English. Examples with nouns are:

Fakkusu ka denshi-meeru de oshirase shimasu.
I will inform you by either fax or e-mail.

Buchoo ka watakushi ga kaigi ni demasu.
Either the department manager or I will attend (lit. leave for) the meeting.

Suzuki-san ka Neruson-san ga tantoo desu.
Either Mr. Suzuki or Mr. Nelson is in charge (but no other persons).

Examples with whole sentences are:

Furansu no wain ni shimasu ka, (soretomo) Amerika no wain ni shimasu ka.
Would you like (lit. will you do) a French wine or an American wine?

Suzuki-san ga ayamari ni ikimasu ka, (soretomo) Satoo-san ga ayamari ni ikimasu ka.
Is Mr. Suzuki or Ms. Sato going to apologize?

Please note that *soretomo* (or) can be inserted between sentences for extra clarity.

b. Embedded Yes/No Questions

Another use of *ka* is as a marker for embedded yes/no questions. This function best translates as "whether (or not)." Quite often, *dooka* is also added without altering the meaning.

Ano konpyuutaa wa seinoo ga ii ka (dooka) shitte imasu ka.
Do you know whether that computer performs well?

Suzuki-san ni hookoku shita ka doo ka oboete imasen.
I don't remember whether I reported it to Mr. Suzuki.

c. Embedded "Wh-" Questions

Another use of *ka* is as a marker for embedded "Wh-" questions (who, what, where, why . . .).

Dare ga sono bangoo o kaita ka shirimasen.
I do not know who wrote that number.

Dare ga iku beki ka buchoo ni kikimashoo.
Let's ask the manager who should go.

3. ONOMATOPOEIA

Onomatopoeic words in English express the sound made by something, such as "bow-wow" to indicate the barking of a dog and "cuckoo" to describe the sound of the bird of the same name. These expressions are very common in Japanese—in fact, the list is practically endless. They're a bit tricky, however, and many of these expressions have little or no apparent connection to sound. Nevertheless, they are often easy to recognize, as they are usually the reduplication of the same word or syllable, and are often followed by either the particle *ni* or *to*. By mastering some of the most commonly used onomatopoeia, you will be able to enrich your Japanese vocabulary and sound more natural.

Buchoo ga kankan ni okotte iru.
The department head is furious!

Suzuki-san wa pekopeko atama o sagete ayamarimashita.
Mr. Suzuki bowed (lit. lowered his head) repeatedly and apologized.

Kanojo wa itsumo buubuu monku bakari itte imasu.
She does nothing but complain.

Kare wa kigen ga yoi toki wa nikoniko waratte imasu.
He smiles a lot when he is in good mood.

Nande nikoniko shite iru n desu ka.
What are you all smiles about?

Kare wa itsumo gyaa gyaa fuhei o iimasu.
He grumbles (about something) all the time.

Dare ni mo kizukare nai yooni sotto hanashite kudasai.
Please tell him secretly not to let anyone notice.

4. *OBOE GA ARU* (RECOLLECTION)

One way to express recollection is by using the past plain affirmative form of the verb plus *oboe ga aru,* which means "have a memory of (doing something)."

Watakushi wa fakkusu shita oboe ga arimasen.
I have no memory of faxing (that).

Buchoo ni hookoku shita oboe ga aru n desu.
I recall reporting (it) to the department manager.

Sore ni tsuite toiawaseta oboe ga arimasu ka.
Do you recall inquiring about it?

Machigatta bangoo o kaita oboe ga nai yo.
I have no memory of writing the wrong number.

D. BIJINESU JIKOO

MACHIGAI NO SHORI (HANDLING A MISTAKE)

In Japan, individual employees are rarely given the opportunity to make big mistakes, because they are constantly supervised and must consult their bosses before making any decisions on how to proceed with a particular project. All members involved in a project, from the managers down, are aware of the activities and progress of each of the other members. This is largely due to the Japanese group decision-making process and to the actual physical arrangement of the offices. That is, the desks of each section in the office face one another in such a way as to encourage interaction among the employees. When a mistake is made, the responsibility will be shared by everyone in the group.

When a mistake is first detected, a Japanese employee immediately talks to his boss. The boss then consults with the other individuals involved in the project, and the group as a whole comes to a consensus on how to rectify the situation. Japanese people generally try to avoid heated arguments or emotional discussions, so if there is a disagreement in solving the problem, the two parties will tend not to attack each other's opinions directly. Rather, it is not uncommon for a person who disagrees with the opinion of his superior to refrain from openly voicing his opinion. As a result, many Japanese subordinates are forced to deal with the resulting frustration and accept being misrepresented. A popular phrase, *Nagai mono ni wa makarero,* which means literally "Be a loser to the stronger power," expresses an important attitude in vertical societies like Japan.

Needless to say, insults are also avoided at all costs. Even bosses are careful not to insult their employees. Personal offenses are taken very seriously, and when someone insults another person, it often takes considerable time for the two parties to reconcile. Foreigners in Japan must be especially careful when using humor, as Western-style jokes can be misunderstood and considered insults.

Just as face-to-face meetings are essential to the smooth and efficient transfer of information, so are they necessary when apologizing. Although there may be times when an apology can be made by phone, it is usually more appropriate to apologize in person. The effort made in such a gesture will help to reestablish a good relationship. The apology is an important gesture in Japanese society and is essential to maintaining harmony.

RENSHUU MONDAI

A. *Tsugi no shitsumon ni kotaenasai.* (Answer the following questions.)

1. *Satoo-san wa dooshite kigen ga warui n desu ka.*
2. *Buchoo wa dooshite okotte imasu ka.*
3. *Buchoo wa doo suru beki da to itte imasu ka.*
4. *Satoo-san wa dare ga machigatta to itte imasu ka.*
5. *Dare ga ayamari ni ikimashita ka.*

B. *Shita ni aru kotoba kara hitotsu erande, bun o kansei shinasai.*
(Choose one of the words below to complete each sentence.)

hazu deshita, beki desu, yoo desu, mono desu, kedo

1. *Satoo-san wa amari kigen ga yokunai* _____.
2. *Fakkusu wa kinoo made ni suru* _____.
3. *Seii o shimesu tame ni wazawaza itte ayamaru* _____.
4. *Watakushi ga itte mo kamaimasen* _____.
5. *Chuui wa shite imasu ga, isogashiku shite iru* _____ *kara.*

C. *Tekitoo na kotoba o irenasai.* (Insert the appropriate word.)

1. *Sore wa kinoo made* _____ *suru hazu datta n desu.*
2. *Ososugiru wake demo* _____ *n desu.*
3. *Dare* _____ *ga ayamari ni ike* _____ *itte imasu.*
4. *Denwa* _____ *wa ayamarenai n desu ka.*
5. *Dare ga sono bangoo o kaita* _____ *shirimasen.*
6. *Sore* _____ *chotto kibun* _____ *gai shite imasu.*
7. *Kongo kon'na machigai ga nai* _____ *chuui shimasu.*

KOTAE

A. 1. *Machigatta tokoro ni fakkusu o okutta to machigaerareta kara.*
2. *Shinyoo no mondai da kara okotte imasu.*   3. *Dareka ga wazawaza ayamari ni iku yoo ni itte imasu.*   4. *Dare ga machigatta ka wakaranai to itte imasu.*   5. *Suzuki-san ga ayamari ni ikimashita.*
B. 1. *yoo desu*   2. *hazu deshita*   3. *beki desu*   4. *kedo*   5. *mono desu*
C. 1. *ni*   2. *nai*   3. *ka, to*   4. *de*   5. *ka*   6. *de, o*   7. *yoo*

DAI JUUGOKA
Lesson 15

A. KAIWA

KYOOTO-RYOKOO KEIKAKU

Neruson-shi wa ikitsuke¹ no sushiya ni iku. Nihon-taizai² wa mijikai ni mo kakawarazu, soko de wa min'na ga kare o yoku shitte iru.

SHEFU: **Irasshai.**

NERUSON: **Konban wa.**

SHEFU: **Maido doomo.³ Kyoo wa ohitori desu ka.**

NERUSON: **Hai. Aikawarazu, konde imasu ne.**

SHEFU: **Okagesama de.⁴ Kazu-chan,⁵ ohitori-sama.**

KAZUKO: **Hai. Irasshaimase.⁶ Onomimono wa itsumo no⁷ osake de yoroshii desu ka.**

NERUSON: **Eeto, kyoo wa nani ni shiyoo ka na. Kyoo wa biiru ni shimasu.**

SHEFU: **Kyoo wa maguro⁸ to uni⁹ ga saikoo¹⁰ desu ga.**

NERUSON: **Hai, tekitoo ni onegai shimasu.¹¹**

SHEFU: **Jaa, maguro no sashimi kara.¹²**

NERUSON: **Itadakimasu. Waa, oishii desu ne.**

Nomimono ga kite, itamae wa sushi o nigitte, Neruson-shi ni dashihajimeru.

NERUSON: **Tokorode, itamae-san wa Kyooto shusshin deshita ne.**

SHEFU: **Boku desu ka. Iie, boku wa Tookyoo umare no Tookyoo sodachi desu. Kazu-chan no koto deshoo. Kanojo wa Kansai¹³ shusshin desu yo. Dooshite desu ka.**

NERUSON: **Jitsu wa raishuu Kyooto ni iku yotei nan desu.**

SHEFU: **Kazu-chan, Kyooto umare datta yo ne.**

KAZUKO: **Hai, Kyooto de umarete, Kyooto de sodachimashita. Kyooto no koto nara, nan demo kiite kudasai.**

NERUSON: **Soo desu ka. Jaa, Kyooto ni tsuite iroiro oshiete ku dasai.¹⁴**

KAZUKO: **Hai. Nani de irasshaimasu ka.**

NERUSON: Shinkansen[15] desu. Yoyaku ga irimasu ka.[16]

KAZUKO: Ima wa ryokoo no shiizun ja arimasen kara, iranai to omoimasu.

NERUSON: Dono hoteru ga ii desu ka.

KAZUKO: Nanpaku nasaimasu ka.

NERUSON: Nihaku-mikka desu. Shigoto wa han'nichi de owaru node, sukoshi kankoo de mo shiyoo to omotte.

KAZUKO: Sore nara, Miyako Hoteru ka Kyooto Kankoo Hoteru ga ii deshoo. Chotto takai kamoshiremasen kedo. Motto yasui hoo ga yokattara, ryokan mo ii deshoo. Katsuratei to iu ryokan nanka ii desu yo. Biiru moo ippon ikaga desu ka.

NERUSON: Hai, onegai shimasu. Wakarimashita. Juusho wa doo shirabetara ii desu ka.

KAZUKO: Min'na Kyooto-eki no chikaku desu.

NERUSON: Aa, soo desu ka. Mochiron kankoo-basu ga arimasu ne.

KAZUKO: Hai, han'nichi kankoo, ichinichi kankoo toka iroiro arimasu. Ichinichi-me wa basu ni notte, tsugi no hi wa jibun de yukkuri[17] mitai tokoro ni iku to iu no ga ii desu.

NERUSON: Naruhodo. Kyooto de oishii mono wa nan desu ka.

KAZUKO: Kyooto tokuyuu no mono o nani ka tameshite mimasu ka. Moshi toofu ga kirai ja nakattara, yudoofu[18] o zehi tabete mite kudasai.

NERUSON: Dooshite toofu ga tokubetsu nan desu ka.

KAZUKO: Kyooto ni wa otera ga sen ijoo mo atte, mukashi oboo-san-tachi wa niku ya sakana o tabenai[19] de, toofu-ryoori o yoku tabetatte kiite imasu.[20]

NERUSON: Aa, sore de. Oishii mise no namae ga wakarimasu ka.

KAZUKO: Achi kochi ni arimasu ga, eeto . . .

SHEFU: Tsugi wa nani ni shimasu ka.

NERUSON: Ebi o onegai.

Soko e Neruson-shi no tonari ni suwatte ita Motoi to iu hito ga kaiwa ni kuwawaru.

MOTOI: Otera toka hoteru no chikaku ni doko de mo arimasu yo. Miyako Hoteru no chikaku ni mo atta to omoimasu.

NERUSON: Kyooto no kata desu ka.

MOTOI: Iie. Demo watakushi, shigoto de yoku ikimasu kara. Kyooto wa ochitsuite ite,[21] hontoo ni ii machi desu yo. Kinkakuji[22] nado yuumei no otera mo ii desu ga, mumei no otera ya mise ni iku no mo ii desu yo. Kawatta mono ga aru shi, min'na shinsetsu ni iroiro oshiete kuremasu yo.

NERUSON: Naruhodo. Mada furui bunka ga nokotte iru wake desu ne.

MOTOI: Ee, nani shiro[23] nagai aida miyako deshita kara, otera dake janakute, omomuki no aru utsukushii tatemono mo takusan taterarete, sore ga mada kanari nokotte imasu. Teien ni kyoomi ga oari dattara, ima wa zekkoo no kisetsu desu. Doozo tanoshii ryokoo o shite kite kudasai.[24]

NERUSON: Ee, hontoo ni tanoshimi desu.

MOTOI: Watakushi wa kore de shitsurei shimasu. Itamae-san, gochisoo sama deshita. Oaiso,[25] onegai shimasu.

SHEFU: Hai, maido arigatoo gozaimasu.

NERUSON: Iroiro oshiete itadaite, hontoo ni arigatoo gozaimashita.

MOTOI: Iie. Jaa osaki ni.[26]

PLANNING A TRIP TO KYOTO

Mr. Nelson goes to his favorite sushi bar. Despite the fact that he has been in Japan (only) a short time, everyone there knows him well.

CHEF: Welcome.

NELSON: Good evening.

CHEF: Thank you for coming again (lit. every time). Are you by yourself today?

NELSON: Yes. As usual, it sure is crowded.

CHEF: Yes, thanks to (regular customers like) you . . . Kazu, party of one.

KAZUKO: Yes, sir. Welcome! Will it be the usual sake today? (lit. Is sake good?)

NELSON: Hmm, what should I have today? Today I'll have a beer.

CHEF: The tuna and sea urchin are very good today.

NELSON: Okay. I'll go with your recommendation.

CHEF: All right then, let's start with tuna sashimi (lit. from sashimi).

NELSON: Thanks. (lit. I will receive.) Oh, it's good, isn't it?

198

The drink comes. The chef (lit. takes hold of the sushi) starts serving sushi to Mr. Nelson.

NELSON: By the way, you're from Kyoto, aren't you?

CHEF: Me? No. I was born and raised in Tokyo. (You must mean) Kazuko. She's from the Kansai area. Why?

NELSON: Actually, I'm planning to go to Kyoto next week.

CHEF: Kazu, you were born in Kyoto, weren't you?

KAZUKO: Yes, I was born and raised in Kyoto. Please ask me anything (you want to know) about Kyoto (lit. if it's Kyoto).

NELSON: Really? Okay, please tell me a few things about Kyoto (lit. teach me a lot).

KAZUKO: Sure. How will you get there?

NELSON: By Shinkansen. Will I need reservations?

KAZUKO: Since it is not the travel season now, I don't think you'll need them.

NELSON: Can you recommend a hotel? (lit. Which hotel would be good?)

KAZUKO: How many nights (are you staying)?

NELSON: Two nights and three days. My work will be finished in half a day, so I was thinking of doing a little sight-seeing.

KAZUKO: In that case (lit. If it's that), I recommend the Miyako, or the Kyoto Kanko Hotel. It might be a bit expensive, though. If cheaper is better, a *ryokan* (Japanese inn) is (pretty) good. An inn called the Katsuratei is pretty nice. How about another beer?

NELSON: Yes, please . . . Okay. How should I find their address?

KAZUKO: They are all (located) near Kyoto station.

NELSON: Oh, really? Of course, there are sight-seeing buses, right?

KAZUKO: Yes, they have half-day tours, full-day tours, and a variety of others. The best thing (to do) is to take a bus tour on the first day, and then on the next day, take your time and go to the places that you want to see on your own.

NELSON: Okay, I see. What's good to eat in Kyoto?

KAZUKO: You should (lit. Will you?) try some Kyoto specialties. If you don't dislike tofu, definitely try (lit. please try) the boiled tofu.

NELSON: Why is tofu a specialty?

KAZUKO: In Kyoto, there are over a thousand temples. I heard that the monks in the past didn't eat meat or fish, but rather, a lot of food made with tofu.

NELSON: Oh, that's why. Do you know the name of a good restaurant?

KAZUKO: They're all over (lit. there and here). Let's see . . .

CHEF: What would you like next?

NELSON: Could I have some shrimp?

A woman sitting next to Mr. Nelson, named Ms. Motoi, joins the conversation.

MOTOI: There are (tofu restaurants) everywhere around the temples and hotels. I think there was one near the Miyako Hotel.

NELSON: Are you (lit. a person) from Kyoto?

MOTOI: No. But I often go (there) on business. Kyoto is (so) relaxed; it's really a nice town. The famous temples like Kinkakuji are nice (to visit), but going to the lesser-known (lit. no name) temples and shops is also great. They have some unusual (lit. changed) things, and everyone is kind and helpful (lit. kindly teaches).

NELSON: I see. You mean the ancient culture is preserved there?

MOTOI: Right. (lit. Anyway,) because Kyoto was the capital (of Japan) for such a long time, it wasn't just temples that were built, but many other tasteful structures as well. Many of them still remain. If you are interested in gardens, now is the ideal season (to visit). Have an enjoyable trip (lit. and come back).

NELSON: Yes, (thank you). I'm really looking forward to it.

MOTOI: Well, I have to go. Mr. Chef, that was a great meal. May I have the check, please?

CHEF: Yes, ma'am. Thanks for coming.

NELSON: Thank you very much for all (the information) you gave me.

MOTOI: You're welcome. All right then, good night. (lit. Ahead of you.)

B. CHUU

1. *Ikitsuke* is a compound verb that combines *iku* (to go) and *tsuke(ru)* (to add), and means "a place one visits often." Examples include *ikitsuke no mise* (the store one goes to often) and *ikitsuke no resutoran* (the restaurant one goes to often).

2. *Nihon taizai* means "stay in Japan."

3. *Maido doomo* means "Thank you very much (for coming) every time." It is often used by people in customer service industries such as shops and restaurants. Similar expressions are *Maido arigatoo gozaimasu* and *Maido arii.*

4. *Okage sama de* means "thanks to (you)" and implies "We are now (happy or successful) due to your continued patronage." It is commonly used when greeting someone who has helped you in some way. It is also a common answer to the question *O genki desu ka* (How are you?).

5. *Chan* is a familiar form of *san* used to address someone who is young, or a person with whom you are very familiar. It is generally not used in offices.

6. *Irasshaimase,* which means "welcome," is the formal form of *irasshai* and is used mainly by people in the service industry.

7. *Itsumo* means "always." The phrase *itsumo no* means "usual" or "the same as usual."

8. *Maguro* means tuna. Japanese distinguishes three distinct parts of the tuna: *toro, chuutoro,* and *akami. Toro* is a fatty part of the tuna, and is considered the most delicious part of the fish by many sushi lovers. *Chuutoro* is less fatty, and *akami* is not fatty at all.

9. *Uni* (sea urchin) is considered a delicacy in Japan, even though many Japanese don't seem to care for it.

10. *Saikoo* literally means "highest," but is used to express "the best" or "excellent."

11. *Tekitoo ni onegai shimasu* literally means "I ask of you (whatever) is appropriate" and implies "I'll leave it to you." This phrase can be used if you are unfamiliar with sushi and don't know what to order, or if you would prefer the chef to make the selection for you.

12. *Maguro no sashimi kara* means "(I want to start) with tuna," (lit. slice of tuna). It is an incomplete sentence, and the unstated portion is understood through context.

13. The term *Kansai* (lit. west of gate) refers to the Osaka-Kyoto area, and is used to differentiate this region from *Kantoo* (lit. east of gate), which is Tokyo and the surrounding area.

14. *Oshiete kudasai* literally means "please teach me," but is used more often to mean "please tell me."

15. *Shinkansen* literally means "new major lines" ("bullet train" in English). It is a convenient and fast means of travel to many parts of Japan.

16. In Japan, advance reservations are usually unnecessary for public transportation. However, during the holiday seasons in January, May, August, and December, reservations are strongly recommended.

17. *Yukkuri* has two meanings: "slowly" and "leisurely."

18. *Yudoofu* is tofu that has been cooked and served in a lightly seasoned broth—nothing more than hot water seasoned with a bit of seaweed. It is usually cooked at the table and served with pickled vegetables and rice.

19. While in the past it was forbidden, today it is not uncommon for monks to have some meat or fish in their diets.

20. *Tabetatte kiite imasu* is an informal form of *tabeta to kiite imasu* (I heard that they ate). *Tte* is a substitution for *to,* and is commonly used in conversation because it is quicker to say.

21. *Ochitsuite iru* means "to be calm."

22. Kinkakuji, Ginkakuji, Kiyomizu-dera, and Ryooanji are the most popular temples in Kyoto. Each is unique and illustrates a different aspect of Kyoto's history.

23. *Nani shiro* means "anyway," "you know," or "because."

24. *Tanoshii ryokoo o shite kite kudasai* literally means "Please have a nice trip and come back." The *te*-form of a verb plus *kuru* signifies "to go do something and come back."

25. *Oaiso* means "check," and is used mostly in sushi restaurants. The term *kaikei* (account) can also be used to refer to the check, regardless of the kind of restaurant.

26. *Osaki ni* can mean "Go ahead" or "I'll go ahead," depending on the situation. The former meaning applies when opening a door for someone, for example, while the latter would be used when you are leaving a place before someone else.

C. BUNPOO TO YOOHOO

1. *NI MO KAKAWARAZU* (DESPITE THE FACT THAT)

Ni mo kakawarazu follows nouns, verbs, and adjectives to express "despite the fact that." In following these parts of speech, the pattern adheres to these rules:

verbs	plain form + *ni mo kakawarazu*
noun + copula	negative and past forms + *ni mo kakawarazu; da* is deleted
i-adjectives	plain form + *ni mo kakawarazu*
na-adjectives + copula	negative and past forms + *ni mo kakawarazu; da* becomes *na no*

Kansai shusshin ni mo kakawarazu, Suzuki-san wa Kantoo no koto o yoku shitte imasu.
>Despite the fact that he is from Kansai, Mr. Suzuki knows a lot about the Kantoo area.

Ryokoo shiizun janai ni mo kakawarzu, Shikansen wa konde imashita.
>Despite the fact that it was not a travel season, the Shinkansen train was crowded.

Kankoo-basu ga takusan atta ni mo kakawarazu, noremasen deshita.
>Despite the fact that there were several tour buses, I could not get a seat (lit. couldn't ride).

Oboo-san wa niku ya sakana o tabenakatta ni mo kakawarazu, genki datta soo desu.
>Despite the fact that monks did not eat meat and fish, they seemed healthy.

2. *TO IU KOTO, TO IU NO*

Much in the same way as *koto* and *no* serve as nominalizers (change verbs to nouns), in such sentences as *Benkyoo suru koto ga suki desu* (I like studying) and *Hashiru no ga kirai desu* (I hate running), *to iu koto* and *to iu no* function to change whole clauses (or sentences) into nominal phrases. When these two phrases follow independent clauses, they best translate as "that."

Kansai shusshin no hito wa sukunai to iu koto o kikimashita.
>I heard that there are (only) a few people from the Kansai region.

Kazuko-san wa Kyooto umare da to iu koto o shirimashita.
I knew that Kazuko was born in Kyoto.

Keiyaku ga dekita to iu no wa hontoo desu ka.
Is it true that you were able (to get) the contract?

Nihonjin wa mae amari niku o tabenakatta to iu koto desu.
(I heard) that Japanese people did not eat much meat in the past (lit. before).

3. *NAI DE* (WITHOUT DOING)

When you want to express the idea that an action is completed (or performed) without first being preceded by another expected action, as in "He went to sleep without brushing his teeth," the pre-*nai* form of the verb followed by *nai de* is used.

Kankoo shinai de, hoteru de yasumimashita.
I rested at the hotel, without doing any sight-seeing.

Yoyaku o shinai de, Shinkansen ni norimashita.
I got on the Shinkansen without making a reservation.

Oboo-san wa niku ya sakana o tabenai de, toofu ryoori o yoku tabemashita.
Monks wouldn't eat meat and fish. They ate a lot of tofu.

Asagohan o tabenai de shigoto ni dekakemashita.
I left for work without eating breakfast.

D. BIJINESU JIKOO

NIHON NO KOOTSUU (TRANSPORTATION IN JAPAN)

Japan is a rather small country, about the size of California, and consists of four main islands, Hokkaido, Honshu, Kyushu, Shikoku, plus the Ryukyu Islands, which include Okinawa. Almost half of the Japanese population lives in the middle part of the main island of Honshu (Pacific Ocean side). As people keep moving into metropolitan areas, the downtown part of most cities is becoming overcrowded, and people are fleeing to the suburbs.

In general, public transportation is extremely well developed and quite convenient for all long-distance and short-distance travel. You can go almost anywhere using public transportation. When you travel long distances to remote places such as Hokkaido and Kyushu, it's best to travel by air, although you can get there easily by train as well. In Japan, trains are heavily relied upon as a means of transportation, much more so than in the United States.

The Shinkansen is the main mode of transportation when traveling between Tokyo and major cities in the Kansai region, such as Osaka, Kyoto, and Kobe. The distance from Tokyo to Osaka is approximately 350 miles and takes about three hours by Shinkansen. The Shinkansen also services the northeastern and southwestern parts of Japan. It is a particularly useful mode of transportation, as it travels at approximately 120 miles per hour.

Within the metropolitan areas, subways and trains are the usual means of getting to and from work. Stations are fairly evenly spaced, making it possible to get reasonably close to your destination. Travel within the city can be quite convenient and comfortable by train, especially during nonpeak hours, but the early-morning and late-afternoon rush hours are extremely crowded and riding the trains at these times can be a test of one's patience.

The largest train system in Japan is called the JR, an abbreviation for Japan Railways. JR train services run on all of the major islands and are relatively inexpensive. There are also dozens of private train systems. In Tokyo, all major JR stations are connected with these smaller private lines, which makes transferring between lines rather easy. Shinjuku Station, for example, has connections to a subway and three large private lines.

Many travel agencies offer sight-seeing tours of Japan. Most of these packages will take care of all the travel arrangements, including hotel, transportation, etc. The tours usually include major tourist attractions such as Nikko, a national park northwest of Tokyo, and Kinkakuji (Golden Pavilion) in Kyoto. The signs in the train stations are clearly marked in Japanese, *romaji* (Roman script), and often in English as well. On some trains and subways in larger cities, announcements over the loudspeaker are made in both Japanese and English. Maps of train routes and charts on ticket prices in English are also available at larger train stations.

For transporting packages in Japan, the postal system is quite efficient. Packages of all sizes can be easily transported anywhere in Japan in a day or two. In fact, sending packages is almost as easy as sending a letter. In addition to the national postal system in Japan, there are numerous delivery companies as well. Actually, this is one area in which U.S. companies like Federal Express have recently begun to gain a presence. Finally, for people moving overseas, there are also many companies specializing in international moving.

RENSHUU MONDAI

A. *Tsugi no shitsumon ni kotaenasai.* (Answer the following questions.)

1. *Neruson-san wa doko ni iku yotei desu ka.*
2. *Dare ga Kyooto no koto o yoku shitte imasu ka.*
3. *Kyooto ni don'na kankoo-basu ga arimasu ka.*
4. *Kyooto tokuyuu no tabemono wa tatoeba nan desu ka.*
5. *Motoi-san ni yoru to, Kyooto wa don'na tokoro desu ka.*

B. *Tekitoo na joshi o irenasai.* (Insert the appropriate particle.)

1. *Onomimono wa osake _____ yoroshii desu ka.*
2. *Kyoo wa maguro to uni _____ ii desu.*
3. *Kyooto no koto nara, nan _____ kiite kudasai.*
4. *Ryokoo no shiizun ja nai _____, konde imasen.*
5. *Kyooto _____ oishii mono wa nan desu ka.*

KOTAE

A. 1. *Kyooto ni iku yotei desu.*   2. *Kazuko to iu juugyooin* (employee) *ga yoku shitte imasu.*   3. *Han'nichi-kankoo toka ichinichi-kankoo toka iroiro arimasu.*   4. *Iroiro aru deshoo ga, toofu wa sono hitotsu desu.*
5. *Ochitsuite ite, ii machi desu.*
B. 1. *de*   2. *ga*   3. *de mo*   4. *kara (node)*   5. *de*

DAI JUUROKKA
Lesson 16

A. KAIWA

NYUUSHA-SHIKEN-MENSETSU

Neruson-shi to Suzuki-shi wa nyuusha shiken[1] no mensetsu o shite iru ga, tekininsha o sagasu no wa nakanaka muzukashii koto ga wakaru.

NERUSON: **Nakanaka tekitoo na hito ga inai desu ne.**

SUZUKI: **Soo desu ne.**

NERUSON: **Majime soo de, yaru ki no aru[2] hito wa imasu ga, sugu shigoto ga dekiru to iu jinzai ga sukunai yoo desu ne.**

SUZUKI: **Sore ni wa riyuu ga aru n desu.**

NERUSON: **To osshaimasu to.[3]**

SUZUKI: **Nihon no wakai hitotachi wa kaisha ni haitte kara shigoto o manaberu to kangaete imasu kara, sukiru[4] o motte iru hito ga sukunai n desu.**

NERUSON: **Naruhodo. Amerika dewa sugu shigoto ga dekiru yoo ni sukiru o motte iru hito no hoo ga shuushoku shiyasui desu ga.**

SUZUKI: **Daigaku kyooiku no chigai mo aru wake desu. Tsumari Nihon no daigakusei wa kurabu katsudoo o shitari, ryokoo shitari shite, nettowaakingu ya tsukiai ni chikara o irete imasu.[5] Benkyoo wa tekitoo ni to iu wake desu.[6,7]**

NERUSON: **Kigyoo wa doo iu kangae nan desu ka?**

SUZUKI: **Sore ga omoshiroi n desu. Jitsu wa kigyoo[8] mo amari chishiki ga ari, kosei no tsuyo sugiru hito wa motomete inai yoo desu. Mushiro majime de yaru ki no aru hito o saiyoo shite kigyoo no hooshin ni shitagatte kyooiku shi naosu to iu kangae desu.**

NERUSON: **Kongo mo soo iu taisei desu ka?**

SUZUKI: **Iya, kawarazaru o enai[9] to omoimasu yo. Kokusaika[10] shitsutsu aru Nihon wa kono mama dewa yatte ikemasen kara. Jijitsu moo daibu kawari tsutsu arimasu.**

NERUSON: **Tsugi no hito mo onaji ka na.**

SUZUKI: **Iya. Keireki ga chotto chigau yoo desu kara.**

Neruson-shi to Suzuki-shi wa kaigishitsu ni haitte kita Yamashita-joo o mensetsu suru.

SUZUKI: Yamashita san desu ne. Doozo okake kudasai.

YAMASHITA: Yoroshiku onegai shimasu.

SUZUKI: Keireki o kantan ni hanashite kudasai.[11]

YAMASHITA: Chiba ni umarete, kookoo made soko ni imashita. Kanagawa daigaku no keiei gakubu ni hairi, san nen no toki Arizona Shuuritsu Daigaku ni ryuugaku shimashita.[12] Eigo no benkyoo no tsumori de itta n desu ga, kekkyoku dookoo ni tenkoo shite sotsugyoo shimashita. Sotsugyoogo, Tookai Denki ni shuushoku shimashita ga, kotoshi jijoo ga atte yamemashita.

SUZUKI: Sashitsukae nakereba,[13] sono jijoo to iu no o hanashite kudasai.

YAMASHITA: Hai. Hitotsu no riyuu wa, gozonji no yoo ni Tookai Denki wa daikigyoo desu.

NERUSON: Ee. Sorede.

YAMASHITA: Mainichi suru koto to ieba, dare demo dekiru yoo na shigoto de, jibun no jitsuryoku o juubun daseru[14] yoo na kankyoo dewa nakatta n desu.

NERUSON: Jaa, uchi no yoo na chiisana[15] kaisha ga anata ni au[16] to kangaete iru n desu ka.

YAMASHITA: Hai. Chiisai kaisha nara, kikaku kara eigyoo made iroiro dekimasu kara, motto jitsuryoku ga daseru to omoimasu.

NERUSON: Naruhodo. (Rirekisho o minagara) Eigyoo[17] no keiken wa zenzen[18] nai yoo desu ne.

YAMASHITA: Ee, jissai ni eigyoo no shigoto wa shita koto wa arimasen ga, Tookai Denki no gyoomu-ka wa eigyoo-bu to kyooryoku shite shigoto o shite imashita kara, iroiro manabimashita.

NERUSON: Eigyoo no shigotoo shitai n desu ne.

YAMASHITA: Hai. Hito to atte hanashitari suru no ga suki desu kara, yareru to omoimasu.

NERUSON: Wakarimashita. Kono shigoto wa seerusu ga omo desu ga, hoka no koto mo shite moraimasu.

YAMASHITA: Hai, sore wa wakatte imasu.

NERUSON: Zangyoo[19] nanka doo kangaete imasu ka.

YAMASHITA: Yamu o enai[20] baai wa yarimasu. Dekireba shitaku arimasen ga. Jikan o yuukoo ni tsukau shugi desu kara.

NERUSON: **Kono shigoto wa konpyuutaa kankei de, konpyuutaa no sofuto no hanbai desu ga, intaanetto toka ofisu no konpyuutaa-ka nado, doo omoimasu ka.**

YAMASHITA: **Sugoku kyoomi ga arimasu.**

NERUSON: **Konpyuutaa ni tsuite no chishiki wa.**

YAMASHITA: **Arizona Shuuritsu de benkyoo shimashita. Uchi ni wa makkintosshu ga arimasu.**

NERUSON: **Hai. Jaa, ni san nichi shite seishiki ni renraku shi-masu.**

YAMASHITA: **Yoroshiku onegai shimasu.**

Yamashita-joo, kaigishitsu o deru.

SUZUKI: **Nakanaka sekkyokuteki de, tanomoshii desu ne.**

NERUSON: **Soo desu ne.**

INTERVIEWING
(LIT. COMPANY ENTRANCE EXAM-INTERVIEW)

Mr. Nelson and Mr. Suzuki are conducting job interviews, but they find the task of searching for a qualified person rather difficult.

NELSON: There just aren't any people who are well suited for the job.

SUZUKI: I know.

NELSON: There seem to be people who have the drive, and are willing to work, but few who are able to work right away.

SUZUKI: There's a reason for that.

NELSON: Oh, What's that? (lit. If you say that . . .)

SUZUKI: Since young Japanese think they will be able to learn the job once they enter a company, there are few people who possess (the necessary) skills.

NELSON: I see. In America, those who have the skills (necessary) to perform the job right away find it easier to get jobs.

SUZUKI: There are also differences in the university education system. That is, Japanese college students engage in club activities, traveling and such, and put their efforts into networking and socializing. They study (only) when it suits them.

NELSON: What do the companies think of this?

SUZUKI: That's what's (really) interesting. The truth is, Japanese companies apparently aren't looking for people who are too knowledgeable or too individualistic. Rather, they think of it this way: hire people who are serious and willing to work, then reeducate them according to company policy.

NELSON: Will that system continue? (lit. Is it that system after now?)

SUZUKI: No. I think that it has to change. Japan, continuing in its internationalization, cannot continue to operate in the same way. In fact, Japan has already changed a great deal.

NELSON: I wonder if the next person will be the same (as the rest).

SUZUKI: No. Her career history looks a little different.

Mr. Nelson and Mr. Suzuki interview Ms. Yamashita, who has entered the conference room.

SUZUKI: Ms. Yamashita, right? Please have a seat.

YAMASHITA: Pleased to meet you.

SUZUKI: Describe briefly your career history, please.

YAMASHITA: I was born in Chiba and lived there through high school. (Later,) I entered the business management department at Kanagawa University, and for my junior year I went to study at Arizona State University. I went there with the intention of studying English, but I ended up transferring (lit. to the same school), and then graduated from there. After graduation, I got a job at Tokai Electric, but this year I quit for (personal) reasons.

SUZUKI: If you don't mind, could you tell us what those reasons are?

YAMASHITA: Sure. One reason is, as you know, Tokai Electric is a huge company.

NELSON: Yes. And . . . ?

YAMASHITA: What I did every day were things anybody could do, and it wasn't the kind of environment where I could perform my best.

NELSON: Well then, do you think a small company like ours would suit you (better)?

YAMASHITA: I think so. In a small company (lit. If it's a small company), one can do various things from planning to marketing, so I think I could perform better.

NELSON: I see. (Looking at her résumé) It appears you don't have any sales experience.

YAMASHITA: That's true. I have never actually had a sales job, but since the business management section of Tokai Electric worked in cooperation with the sales division, I learned a lot (from that).

NELSON: Is sales something you would be interested in? (lit. You'd like to do sales work?)

YAMASHITA: Yes. I like meeting people and talking with them, so I think I would be able to do it.

NELSON: I see. This position is mainly (in) sales, but there are other duties as well (lit. we would have you do other things).

YAMASHITA: Yes, I understand.

NELSON: How do you feel about overtime?

YAMASHITA: If there is no way around it, I'll do it. If it's possible (not to do it), though, I would rather not. My philosophy (lit. principle) is to use time effectively.

NELSON: The work is computer-related, and we sell computer software. What do you think of the Internet and office computerization?

YAMASHITA: I'm very interested (in it).

NELSON: Do you have any knowledge of computers?

YAMASHITA: I studied (computers) at ASU. I have a Macintosh at home.

NELSON: Okay, then. We'll let you know (lit. contact you) officially in two or three days.

YAMASHITA: Thank you.

Ms. Yamashita leaves the conference room.

SUZUKI: She's quite ambitious (lit. positive) and promising, don't you think?

NELSON: Yes, I agree.

B. CHUU

1. *Nyuusha-shiken* means "an entrance examination to a company." It usually consists of both a written examination and an oral interview *(mensetsu)*.

2. *Yaru ki no aru* means "eager to do" or "serious about one's duty." Eagerness and a willingness to work are important qualities in Japan.

3. The phrase *to osshaimasu to* translates literally as "if you say that," but actually is a polite way to ask "What do you mean?"

4. *Sukiru* refers to "skills." The English word has been adopted because there is no equivalent term in Japanese.

5. *Chikara o ireru* literally means "to put (all of your) power (into something)." It is usually translated as "to devote oneself," or "to emphasize." *Kotoshi benkyoo ni chikara o irete imasu.* (I am devoting myself to study this year.) *Nihon wa booeki ni chikara o irete iru.* (Japan is emphasizing international trade.)

6. In the sentence *Benkyoo wa tekitoo ni to iu wake desu,* the word *suru* is omitted after *tekitoo ni.* Omitting verbs that are understood through context is typical syntax in Japanese conversation.

7. Japanese college students are notorious for not taking their studies seriously. (See "Business Matters" in this lesson.)

8. Japanese corporations have special training programs for new employees. After starting work, managers teach the new employees all about the organization and the corporate culture. New employees are rotated to different divisions, and at some point, usually five to seven months after being hired, are assigned to a permanent position. The position is determined by the employee's ability to adapt and by considering which position best utilizes his or her talents.

9. The expression *kawarazaru o enai* means "something has to change." The pre-*nai* form of the verb is followed by *zaru o enai* to express "there is no other way than (verb)." *Manabazaru o enai,* therefore, means "There is no other way but to learn."

10. *Kokusaika* means "internationalization." It is one of the more important agenda items for many Japanese corporations. This is due in large part to limited domestic resources and a lag in domestic demand. Japanese firms believe that internationalization is the only way to overcome these problems.

11. During interviews at Japanese companies, one is rarely asked complicated questions. Interviewers do, however, inquire about personal and non-job-related matters because they like to examine a potential employee's personality and whether he or she possesses "people skills." Because most employers intend to train their new employees in functional skills after hiring, more emphasis is put on a candidate's ability to work with others at this stage.

12. *Ryuugaku* means "studying overseas." Many students go to the United States, Australia, or to countries in Europe to study a variety of subjects.

13. *Sashitsukae nakereba* means "If you have no objections," and is often used before asking personal questions.

14. *Jitsuryoku o dasu* literally means "to show (one's) real ability (power)."

15. *Chiisana* means "small" and is classified as a "pre-nominative." These words modify nouns, just like adjectives. Other pre-nominatives include *ookina* (large) and *chichana* (small).

16. *Au* means "to match," "to fit," or "to be suitable." For example, *Kono shigoto wa watashi ni aimasu.* (This job suits me.) *Sono shattsu wa choodo aimasu.* (That shirt suits you perfectly.)

17. *Eigyoo* literally means "business." In reality, it often implies "marketing and sales," in contrast to *jimu (shoku)*, which means "office work." The *eigyoo-bu* (business department) is often considered the most important department in a company.

18. The pattern *zenzen* plus a negative ending means "not at all."

19. *Zangyoo* (overtime) is an important part of the Japanese work system. Official business hours are generally from 8:30 A.M. to 5:30 P.M., but almost everyone stays past 5:30, even if they don't have much to do. Putting in long hours at the office is expected of employees, and many feel that there is little choice, regardless of whether or not it is necessary.

20. *Yamu o enai* means "unavoidable," "inevitable," or "necessary."

C. BUNPOO TO YOOHOO

1. TEMPORAL EXPRESSIONS

In Japanese, two very important words are used to express when an action occurs. The first, *mae (ni)*, is used to indicate that an action occurs before something else. The second, *ato (de)*, expresses that an action takes place after something else.

Mae is a noun, but it can be used like a conjunction to combine two sentences. It can be preceded by both nouns and verbs, but in the latter case, please note that the verb must always be in the non-past form. Nouns must be connected to *mae (ni)* by adding *no*.

Nihon no gakusei wa, kaisha ni hairu mae ni, amari shigoto no keiken ga arimasen.
Before joining a company, Japanese students do not have much work experience.

Shigoto o hajimeru mae ni, atarashii shain wa kenshuu o ukemasu.
Before starting work, new employees receive training.

Mensetsu no mae ni, rirekisho o okuranakereba narimasen.
Before the interview, I have to send my résumé (to the employer).

Daigakuin ni hairu mae, kookoo no kyooshi o shimashita.
Before entering graduate school, I was a high school teacher.

Ryuugaku suru mae ni, sannen eigo o benkyoo shimashita.
Before studying abroad, I studied English for three years.

Conversely, the word *ato (de)* signifies that something happens after. If *ato (de)* follows a verb, the verb must always be in the past plain form. As with *mae (ni)*, nouns must be connected to *ato de* with *no*.

Sore wa yoku kentoo shita ato, kimemashoo.
Let's decide on that after we have examined it thoroughly.

Sakusen o netta ato de, katsudoo shimashoo.
After creating a plan of attack, let's act on it.

Nagai mensetsu no ato, mata yobaremashita.
After the long interview, I was called again.

Daigaku no ato de, sugu shuushoku shimashita.
After college I found a job immediately.

2. TE-KARA

This clause is similar to *ato (de)* in that both mean "after doing something," but this one specifically means "having done something." It is formed by adding *kara* to the *te*-form of a verb.

Sotsugyoo shite kara, sugu shuushoku shimashita.
After graduating from college, I found a job right away.

Wakai hitotachi wa kaisha ni haitte kara, shigoto o manabimasu.
Young people learn the job after they have entered a company.

Keireki o setsumei shite kara, iroiro hanashiaimashita.
After I explained my work history, we discussed various things.

214

Be careful not to confuse verb + *(te) kara* with verb + *(ta) kara,* which means "because of doing."

Kokusai-bijinesu o benkyoo shita kara, booeki no koto ga yoku wakarimasu.
Because I studied international business, I have a good understanding of international trade.

Eigyoo no shigoto o shita kara, eigyoo no koto wa sukoshi wakarimasu.
Since I worked in marketing, I know a little bit about it.

Majime ni renshuu shita kara, hayaku joozu ni narimashita.
Because he practiced seriously, he improved quickly.

3. ALTERNATING OR REPEATED ACTIONS

When expressing actions that alternate or repeat, the following pattern is used:

```
Plain past tense (affirmative or negative) verb + ri
Past tense i-adjective + ri
Na-adjective + past tense copula (datta) + ri
Noun + past tense copula (datta) + ri
```

Sentences containing this pattern always end with *suru* (to do) and are often translated with "do things like."

Natsu wa ryokoo o shitari, arubaito o shitari shimasu.
In the summer I (do things like) travel and work part-time.

Hito to hanashitari, iken o kiitari suru no ga suki desu.
I like (doing things like) talking with people and listening to (their) opinions.

Hito ga takusan ittari, kitari shite imashita.
Many people were coming and going.

Setsumei ga kuwashikattari, kuwashikunakattari shimasu.
The explanations are sometimes detailed, and sometimes not.

Wakai shain wa majime dattari, fumajime dattari shimasu.
Some young employees are serious, and some are not.

Shigoto wa eigyoo dattari, kikaku dattari shimashita.
My work was in sales one day and in planning the next.

4. SUPPOSITIONAL CLAUSES (BA)

A suppositional clause is one in which a supposition, or a condition on which something is based, is being expressed. In English, suppositions are made by using the word "if." For example, in the sentence "If I leave early, I will make it on time," the conditional clause, "If I leave early," must be fulfilled in order for the main clause, "I will make it on time," to be possible. Japanese uses a construction called the *ba* form to make this type of statement.

The *ba* form for verbs is created by dropping the final vowel of the dictionary form of the verb, and adding *e + ba.*

REGULAR VERBS

miru (to see)	*mireba* (if you see)
taberu (to eat)	*tabereba* (if you eat)
okiru (to get up)	*okireba* (if you get up)
oshieru (to teach)	*oshiereba* (if you teach)
kaeru (to exchange)	*kaereba* (if you exchange)

IRREGULAR VERBS

aru (to be, to have)	*areba* (if there is, if you have)
iku (to go)	*ikeba* (if he goes)
kaeru (to return)	*kaereba* (if you return)
au (to meet)	*aeba* (if you meet)
kaku (to write)	*kakeba* (if she writes)
hanasu (to talk)	*hanaseba* (if they talk)
nomu (to drink)	*nomeba* (if you drink)
yomu (to read)	*yomeba* (if he reads)
tobu (to fly)	*tobeba* (if it flies)
morau (to receive)	*moraeba* (if you receive)
itadaku (to receive)	*itadakeba* (if he receives)
aeru (to be able to meet)	*aereba* (if they can meet)
moraeru (to be able to receive)	*maraereba* (if he can receive)
itadakeru (to be able to receive)	*itadakereba* (if she can receive)
kuru (to come)	*kureba* (if you come)
suru (to do)	*sureba* (if she does)

Yaru ki ga areba, dare demo dekimasu.
   If one has a strong desire to do it, anyone can.

Shigoto no keiken ga areba, motto ii n desu ga.
   It would be better if you had work experience.

Tekitoo na hito ga ireba, sugu saiyoo shimasu.
If we find (lit. If there is) the right person, we will hire him/her immediately.

Kokusaika sureba, Nihon wa kono mama dewa yatte ikemasen.
If Japan is to internationalize, it cannot continue in this way.

Nouns or *na*-adjectives can also form suppositional clauses. In such cases, nouns and *na*-adjectives are followed by *nara(ba)*, while *i*-adjectives add *kereba* to the stem.

Gaikokujin nara(ba), Nihongo ga dekinakereba narimasen.
If one is a foreigner, he/she has to speak (lit. be able to do) Japanese.

Kyuuryoo ga hikukereba, ano kaisha ni hairitakunai.
If the salary is low, I don't want to join that company.

Suki nara(ba), sore o katte kudasai.
If you like it, please buy it.

5. DECISION *(KOTO NI SURU, KOTO NI NARU)*

There are two similar expressions for communicating both one's own decisions and those made by someone else. They are *koto ni suru* and *koto ni naru,* respectively.
To indicate that someone has made his/her own decision, use this form: non-past plain verb + *koto ni suru.*

Rainen shuushoku suru koto ni shimashita.
I have decided to find a job next year.

Kaisha o yameru koto ni shimasu.
She has made up her mind to quit the company.

Rainen tenshoku suru koto ni shimashita.
I have decided to change jobs next year.

Kaisha o kokusaika suru koto ni shimashita.
He has decided to internationalize the company.

The non-past plain form of the verb plus *koto ni naru* indicates that some decision was made by someone other than the speaker. It may also be used when the decision was made by societal pressure (e.g., to get married before age thirty) or when the speaker actually made the decision himself, but wishes to express this in a more humble or indirect way.

Rainen tenshoku suru koto ni narimasu.
They have decided that I will change jobs next year.

Kotoshi no shigatsu tenkin suru koto ni narimashita.
It has been arranged that I will be transferred this April.

Daigaku de oshieru koto ni natta n desu.
It turns out that I will be teaching at a college.

Rainen tenkoo suru koto ni natta.
It has been arranged that I will be transferred to another school next year.

Yaru ki no aru hito o saiyoo suru koto ni narimashita.
It has been decided that we should hire a person who is eager to work.

6. TSUTSU ARU

In Japanese, the progressive form (indicating an action still in progress) is expressed using the *te*-form of the verb plus *iru. Hon o yonde imasu,* for example, means "I am reading a book." However, perhaps contrary to expectation, *Nihon no shakai wa ima kawatte imasu* means "Japanese society has changed"; it does not mean "Japanese society is changing." How, then, does one say "Japanese society is (in the process of) changing"? The correct way is *Nihon no shakai wa ima kawari tsutsu arimasu.* In this sentence, *tsutsu aru* is preceded by the stem form of the verb and expresses the idea of something in the middle of a particular process. This pattern is used to denote gradual change. Sentences with *tsutsu aru* are often translated into English using "in the process of."

Koogyoo ga hattatsu shi tsutsu arimasu.
The manufacturing industry is in the process of developing.

Kaisha wa konpyuutaa-ka shi tsutsu arimasu.
The company is in the process of being computerized.

Pasokon ga fukyuu shi tsutsu arimasu.
Personal computers are becoming widespread.

D. BIJINESU JIKOO

NIHON NO JOSEI (JAPANESE WOMEN)

Although Japanese women have often been depicted as submissive in various media, their role in managing matters such as the family finances and the formal education of their children is not as well publicized. Recent statistics show that more Japanese women attend college than men, and that women tend to read more and are more knowledgeable about social issues.

218

In the 1990s, the status of Japanese women in the workplace has greatly advanced. Many corporations have come to recognize that hiring "career women" makes possible the double benefit of meeting increased business demands and employing a highly educated, able staff. Career-oriented female college graduates have begun to demonstrate that they can work with diligence to satisfy the expectations of top management.

Although more women are now working in corporations, many only stay on until marriage, however, choosing to turn down promotion-oriented transfers or special assignments. For this reason, many organizations are still reluctant to trust women in positions of responsibility. Consequently, those who would welcome the greater responsibility (and greater benefits) associated with promotion must deal with the expected pattern of behavior established by other, less ambitious women, as well as the traditional male attitudes that still dominate Japan. Many able women, for whom marriage and childbirth are not such high priorities, are discouraged by what they feel are forces working against them in the workplace.

Still, much has happened to improve the situation for women in Japan, and more is sure to happen in the near future. Japanese education emphasizes equality in social status and pay for men and women, and legislation has been enacted to enforce this more modern attitude.

NIHON NO KYOOIKU (EDUCATION IN JAPAN)

Education in Japan is based on the American model, and adheres to the so-called "6-3-3-4 system," that is, 6 years of elementary school, 3 years of junior high school, 3 years of high school, and 4 years of college. The first nine years of school are compulsory, and the percentage of students who graduate from high school is approximately 95 percent. About 40 percent of these go on to college.

A distinctive characteristic of Japanese education is that students are primarily motivated to study for various entrance examinations. The most important of these is the university (or college) entrance examination. Starting in elementary school, education focuses on preparation for the university entrance examination because many Japanese believe that admission to a good university in itself determines in large part a student's future. It is a proven fact that graduates from prestigious universities benefit both in their careers and in their social lives through the good reputation and strong alumni networks of their universities. Just being enrolled at a top university is usually sufficient to get a quality job offer by a company. The Japanese education system has been criticized, however, for pushing students to study subjects merely in order to pass university entrance examinations and promoting rote memorization without encouraging creative or individualistic thinking.

Japanese college life has been described as a "four-year vacation," especially when compared to the incessant cramming in secondary school and the serious competition that can be expected in the workplace after graduation. One positive aspect of this time is that students socialize intensively with their classmates, and they have the opportunity to develop strong relationships by participating in various extracurricular activities such as sports and/or cultural clubs. Many of these activities tend to encourage the formation of special circles called *saakuru,* or groups, to which the members often develop strong, lifelong ties. These relationships may also assist a person in his or her future career and business dealings.

SHUUSHOKU (SEEKING EMPLOYMENT)

Many Japanese college and university students find employment during their senior year. They start gathering information and visiting companies early in the summer (in the middle of the April-March academic year), and many get unofficial employment agreements from employers in the late summer or early fall. Several years ago some students started working before graduating, and as a result companies now have agreements among themselves not to accept applications before June or July.

Almost all companies use the same system of hiring. Corporations first choose which colleges or universities they will accept applications from. From these applications they then select a group of candidates through written tests and oral interviews. They are not overly particular about a candidate's qualifications, since corporations will often train new employees according to the various openings within the company. After a student is hired, the corporation will assign him or her to one department, and begin training by rotating the new hires through different departments. This often lasts for several years, after which the employee will be assigned a permanent position based on the needs of the department and the interests of the employee.

This system of employment, however, is now changing considerably, due to changes within the corporations themselves. Many companies are downsizing, and do not hire as many employees as before. They now tend to employ only those people who already have the necessary skills, and not just those freshly graduated from prestigious universities. As a result, 10 to 20 percent of new graduates are not able to find employment upon graduation.

Once employed, a Japanese graduate can expect fairly good job stability. The Japanese have adopted a "permanent employment" system in which the company provides employment for life; in return, the employee is expected to be extremely loyal to the corporation. Thus many Japanese people have worked for only one company. However, with the constant evolution of corporate Japan, this system, too, is changing. Many Japanese people are now changing jobs as they look for better opportunities to advance their careers. Advancement was once based on age and seniority, but many corporations have recently implemented merit-based promotion and salary systems.

RENSHUU MONDAI

A. *Tsugi no shitsumon ni kotaenasai.* (Answer the following questions.)

1. *Dooshite, Nihon dewa sugu shigoto ga dekiru jinzai ga sukunai n desu ka.*
2. *Nihon no daigakusei wa nani ni chikara o irete imasu ka.*
3. *Nihon no kyooiku seido wa kongo kawarimasu ka.*
4. *Yamashita-san wa nani daigaku no nani gakubu ni hairimashita ka.*
5. *Yamashita-san wa dooshite Tookai Denki o yamemashita ka.*

B. *Tekitoo na joshi o irenasai.* (Insert the appropriate particle.)

1. *Sugu shigoto _____ dekiru jinzai _____ sukunai desu.*
2. *Nihon no wakai hitotachi wa kaisha _____ haitte _____, shigoto _____ manaberu _____ kangaete imasu.*
3. *Amerika _____ sugu shigoto _____ dekiru yoo ni sukiru o motte iru hito no hoo _____ shuushoku shi yasui desu.*
4. *Kokusaika shi tsutsu aru Nihon _____ kono mama _____ yatte ikemasen.*
5. *Watakushi wa shigoto _____ suru _____ _____ kirai janai n desu.*

C. *Tekitoo na kotoba o irenasai.* (Insert the appropriate word.)

1. _____ (corporation) *mo* _____ (knowledge) *ga ari,* _____ (individuality) *ga tsuyosugiru hito o motomete inai yoo desu.*
2. _____ (work history) *o hanashite kudasai.*
3. _____ (after graduation) *Tookai Denki ni* _____ (get a job) *shimashita.*
4. _____ (sales) *no shigoto ga dekiru* _____ (confidence) *ga arimasu ka.*

D. *Shita no kotoba yori erabinasai.* (Choose from the words below.)

(mae ni, ato de, kara)

1. *Kaisha ni haitte _____ shigoto o manabimasu.*
2. *Saiyoo shita _____ kyooiku shinaoshimasu.*
3. *Amerika no daigaku ni ryuugaku suru _____ Nihon no daigaku ni imashita.*
4. *Ni, san nichi shite _____ renraku shimasu.*

A. 1. *Kaisha ni haitte kara, shigoto o manaberu to kangaete iru kara desu.*
2. *Nettowaakingu ya tsukiai ni chikara o irete imasu.*   3. *Hai, kawarazaru
o emasen.*   4. *Kanagawa-daigaku no keiei gakubu ni hairimashita.*
5. *Kosei no tsuyoi josei niwa awanai to handan shita kara desu.*
B. 1. *ga, ga*   2. *ni, kara, o(ga), to*   3. *dewa, ga, ga*   4. *wa, dewa*
5. *o, no, ga*
C. 1. *kigyoo, chishiki, kosei*   2. *keireki*   3. *sotsugyoo-go, shuushoku*
4. *eigyoo, jishin*
D. 1. *kara*   2. *ato de*   3. *mae ni*   4. *kara*

DAI JUUNANAKA
Lesson 17

A. KAIWA

PUREZENTEESHON

Neruson-shi, Kobayashi-Sangyoo no Wada-buchoo ni denwa shite, shinseihin o shookai suru tame ni, sono menkai no apointo o toru.

HISHO: Wada-buchoo, Neruson-san to iu kata kara odenwa desu.

WADA: Hai. Soomu-bu no Wada desu ga.

NERUSON: Moshi moshi, JTC no Yamanaka-senmu[1] kara goshookai itadaita[2] Neruson to mooshimasu ga. Ichido ojikan o itadakemashitara arigatai[3] to omoimasu ga.

WADA: Shitsurei desu ga, goyooken wa nan na no deshoo ka.

NERUSON: Jitsu wa Suupaameeru to iu shinseihin o goshookai sasete itadakitai to omoimashite.

WADA: Sore wa doo itta[4] mono desu ka.

NERUSON: E-meeru, sunawachi[5] denshi meeru no sofuto de goza-imasu.

WADA: Naruhodo.

NERUSON: Sorede, sochira sama no hoo de mo konpyuutaa-ka saretsutsu aru to ukagatte orimasu ga.

WADA: Min'na[6] tsukatte wa iru n desu ga, zen'in dewa arimasen.

NERUSON: Sore deshitara, zehi toosha no seihin o gosetsumei sasete itadakemasen ka. Tsukaiyasukute, jimu nooryoku ga koojoo suru koto, machigai arimasen.

WADA: Yamanaka senmu kara no ohanashi demo aru shi,[7] kiku dake demo kiite mimashoo.[8,9]

NERUSON: Hontoo ni arigatoo gozaimasu.[10] Sassoku desu ga, raishuu no sue goro wa ikaga deshoo ka. Aratamete[11] goren-raku sasete itadakimasu ga.

WADA: Iya, mondai nai to omoimasu kara, mokuyoobi no gogo ni kimemashoo.

Neruson-shi, purezenteeshon o suru.

NERUSON: **Bijitekku no Neruson de gozaimasu. Honjitsu wa, oiso-gashii tokoro o oatsumari itadaki,**[12] **arigatoo gozaimasu.**[13] **Kore kara, watakushi-domo de atsukatte**[14] **orimasu**[15] **shoohin "Suu-paameeru" no goshookai o sasete itadakimasu ga, sono mae ni toosha ni tsuite kantan ni gosetsumei shitai to omoimasu.**[16] **Sore kara shoohin setsumei no ato de, minasama no goshit-sumon o oukeshitai to omoimasu. Doozo yoroshiku onegai shimasu.**

Heisha Bijitekku wa sen kyuu hyaku hachijuu nen ni shiatoru ni setsuritsu sare, omo ni konpyuutaa no sofuto no kaihatsu hanbai no gyoomu o okonatte imasu.[17] **Shain wa ima no tokoro**[18] **hyaku nin hodo desu ga, kaigai shinshutsu no tame kotoshi wa daibu fueru yotei desu. Nihon shisha wa san nen mae ni JTC-sha to gyoomu teikei**[19] **shite setsuritsu saremasita. Kokyaku risuto, torihiki ginkoo, uriagedaka**[20] **nado ni tsuite wa, kochira no shiryoo o goran kudasai.**

Honjitsu[21] **goshookai itashimasu "Suupaameeru" wa, shanai no renraku o subete denshi meeru de suru tame no sofuto de gozaimasu. Kore o tsukaimasu to jikan to kami no setsuyaku ga dekimasu shi, ichido ni takusan no katagata ni tanjikan de ren-raku dekimasu. Mochiron gaibu no katagata to mo kantan ni renraku shiaemasu. Gaibu to iimasu no wa sekaijuu no kata-gata to kaiwa dekiru koto desu. Kono seihin no ii tokoro wa Eigo demo Nihongo demo tsukau koto ga dekite, intaanetto to mo tsunageru koto desu. Nihon demo daibu intaanetto ga sakan ni natte iru yoo desu ga, kongo motto motto**[22] **sakan ni naru to omoimasu kara, jikanteki ni taimurii da to iemasu. Kakaku wa iroiro na kinoo ga aru ni mo kakawarazu, hoka no seihin to taisa arimasen. Ijoo, kantan desu ga, gaiyoo o mooshi-agemashita.**[23] **Kore kara puromooshon bideo o goran itadakitai to omoimasu. Sore kara kuwashiku wa shoohin katarogu o goran kudasai. Ato wa minasama no goshitsumon ni okotae shi-nagara hosoku shite ikitai to omoimasu. Arigatoo gozaimashita.**

PRESENTATIONS

Mr. Nelson calls Mr. Wada, a general manager at Kobayashi Industries, in order to make an appointment to introduce his new product.

SECRETARY: Mr. Wada, you have a phone call from a Mr. Nelson.

WADA: Yes, this is Mr. Wada of the General Affairs Department.

NELSON: Hello. My name is Mr. Nelson, I got your name from Mr. Ya-manaka, the managing director of JTC. I would be (really) grateful if you could spare some time (to speak with me).

WADA: I'm sorry, but what does this concern? (lit. What is your business?)

NELSON: Well, I would like to introduce you to our new product, called SuperMail.

WADA: What kind of product is it? (lit. What kind of thing is that?)

NELSON: E-mail—that is, electronic mail software.

WADA: I see.

NELSON: Also, I heard that your company (lit. your side) is in the process of computerizing (your offices).

WADA: A lot of employees are using computers, but not everyone.

NELSON: In that case, won't you please allow me to explain my company's product? It's easy to use and there is no doubt (lit. mistake) that your office productivity (lit. business abilities) will increase.

WADA: Well, since you were referred by (lit. there was the talk with) General Manager Yamanaka, we'll at least listen to what you have to say.

NELSON: Thank you very much. This may be jumping the gun (lit. this is abrupt), but how does the end of next week sound (for a meeting)? I can contact you again (before that).

WADA: No, I don't think there will be a problem, so let's go for (lit. decide on) Thursday afternoon.

Nelson gives his presentation.

NELSON: I'm Mr. Nelson of BusiTech. Thank you very much for taking time out of your busy schedules to meet here today. (lit. Thank you for assembling when you're busy.) Today, (lit. From now,) I would like to introduce the product I am in charge of, called SuperMail, but before that I would like to briefly (lit. simply) explain my company (to you). After the explanation of the product, I would be happy to answer (lit. receive) any questions (you may have). Thank you (for your attention).

My company, BusiTech, was established in 1980 in Seattle, and we are mainly in the business of developing and selling computer software. At the moment, we have about one hundred employees, but we are expecting to increase (the number of employees) this year due to overseas expansion. The Japanese branch was set up three years ago through a joint venture with JTC. For our client list, banking associations, sales, and other (pertinent) information, please look at this data here.

SuperMail, the product I'm introducing today, is software for contacting all (people) within the company by electronic mail. By using this software, you can save both time and paper, and it allows you to contact several people all at once in a short amount of time. Of course, you can easily contact people outside (the office), too. When I say "outside," I mean you can converse with people all over the world. The advantages (lit. good points) of this product include that both English and Japanese can be used, and that it can (be used to) connect to the Internet. It seems like the Internet is growing quite popular in Japan as well (as the rest of the world.) I think the Internet will continue to grow in popularity, so it can be said that this product is quite timely. In spite of the fact that it has various different functions, the price is not much different than that of other products. That's (basically) it . . . It was simple, but I have given you a rough outline (of the product). Now, I would like to have you watch this demo video. For (more) details, please look at the product catalog. Finally, I'd like to supplement this presentation while answering your questions. Thank you very much.

B. CHUU

1. The title *senmu* is the abbreviated form of *senmu-torishimariyaku* (managing director), which is anywhere from the third- to fifth-highest position in most mid- to large-size corporations.

2. Connections and introductions are still important in arranging appointments in Japan. They help make the other party feel more comfortable. Without such connections, appointments may still be made, but you may encounter some difficulties.

3. *Arigatai* means "I am grateful," or "I would be grateful." It is used in formal situations, including business: *Kojinteki na namae mo oshiete itadakereba arigatai desu ne.* (I would be very grateful if he would tell me the names [of the people] he knows.) *Sore wa arigatai desu ne.* (I appreciate that.) *Menkai sasete itadakereba arigatai desu.* (I would appreciate it if you would allow me to see you.)

4. *Doo itta* is a colloquial expression equivalent to *doo iu*, meaning "what kind of."

5. The word *sunawachi* is translated as "namely" or "that is (to say)."

6. *Min'na* is often used to mean "all" or "everyone," but actually means "roughly all" or "almost all."

226

7. *Ohanashi demo aru shi* literally means "There was the talk, and (in addition)." In this case, it refers to the introduction that Mr. Nelson received from Mr. Yamanaka. The particle *shi* connects two sentences, and is often translated as "and" or "and in addition."

8. In the Japanese business world, there is a sense that one is obligated to meet with a person who has been introduced through an acquaintance. This is a standard practice, and is important in maintaining good relationships with all of one's business associates.

9. The sentence *Kiku dake demo kiite mimashoo* literally means "We will listen to you, even though it (may) be only listening." This is a way for the speaker to be noncommittal, expressing that there is not a strong intention of doing business.

10. *Hontoo ni arigatoo gozaimasu* literally means "Really, thank you very much." Adding words like *hontoo ni* (really) or *makoto ni* (sincerely) to *arigatoo gozaimasu* gives emphasis.

11. The word *aratamete* means "again" or "at a different time."

12. *Oatsumari itadaki* (lit. you have done me the favor of gathering, and) has the same meaning as *oatsumari itadaite*. It is a classical form that is still used in formal situations.

13. Presentations are commonly started by expressing one's gratitude to the audience for their attendance and patience. If there are distinguished guests in the audience, they should be recognized at the beginning of the presentation as well.

14. *Atsukau* means "to handle," "to treat," "to manage," or "to deal with."

15. It is not uncommon to use the *masu*-form (instead of plain form) at the end of relative clauses in formal situations.

16. *Gosetsumei shitai to omoimasu* literally means "I think I want to explain." The pattern, verb stem + *tai to omou,* best translates as "I would like to" and is a polite way of saying "I am going to."

17. The verb *okonau* is an old, formal form of *suru* (to do). When used in a sentence, it has the added meaning of "to carry out" or "to perform."

18. The phrase *ima no tokoro* implies "as of now," and suggests that change is expected.

19. The *teikei* or *gyoomu-teikei* (business partnership) has different formats. One of them is the *gooben-gaisha* (joint stock company) in which, for example, an American and Japanese company might share expenses and profits. One advantage of this type of venture is that the American company would be able to make use of the network already established by the Japanese partner. Many successful businesses in Japan are organized according to this format.

20. As a means of gaining the client's trust, it is common to mention the size of the company, the number of employees, the bank(s) it deals with, and perhaps most important, the company's most recognized clients. In addition, mentioning the amount of capital that the organization commands can also be helpful.

21. *Honjitsu* means "today," like *kyoo,* but is used in formal situations and in business.

22. *Motto motto* means "more and more." Much like English, emphasis can be added to many adverbs by repeating the word.

23. *Mooshiagemashita* literally means "said." It is a humble form of *iimashita,* and is used in formal situations, including business.

C. BUNPOO TO YOOHOO

1. COMPLETION OF AN ACTION *(BAKARI DA)*

The phrase *bakari da* may be used to express the completion of an action. It is used when the speaker wishes to indicate that almost no time has passed since the completion of that action. It may be translated as "just." The pattern is as follows:

> verb (past plain) + *bakari da*

Note: Verb (past plain) + *tokoro da* is similar in its usage and meaning (see Lesson 6).

Rainichi shita bakari desu.
    I have just arrived in Japan.

Kare wa ima kaetta bakari desu.
    He has just come back.

Shooshin ni tsuite hanashita bakari desu.
    We have just discussed the promotions.

228

Atarashii sofuto no hanbai o shihajimeta bakari desu.
We have just started selling new software.

2. COUNTERS

As a general rule, there is no plural form in Japanese. The Japanese express the plural, if they have to, by using so-called "counters." One example is the "human counter," which is used in referring to more than one person. There are hundreds of such counters in Japanese, but you need to know only a dozen or so for reasonable fluency. Some of the most frequently used counters are:

	1	2	3	4	5	6	7	HOW MANY?
Persons	*hitori*	*futari*	*san'nin*	*yonin*	*gonin*	*rokunin*	*shichinin*	*nan'nin*
Small things	*hitotsu*	*futatsu*	*mittsu*	*yottsu*	*itsutsu*	*muttsu*	*nanatsu*	*ikutsu*
Slender things	*ippon*	*nihon*	*sanbon*	*yonhon*	*gohon*	*roppon*	*nanahon*	*nanbon*
Flat things	*ichimai*	*nimai*	*sanmai*	*yonmai*	*gomai*	*rokumai*	*nanamai*	*nanmai*
Cars	*ichidai*	*nidai*	*sandai*	*yondai*	*godai*	*rokudai*	*shichidai*	*nandai*
Small animals	*ippiki*	*nihiki*	*sanbiki*	*yonhiki*	*gohiki*	*roppiki*	*nanahiki*	*nanbiki*
Large animals	*ittoo*	*nitoo*	*santoo*	*yontoo*	*gotoo*	*rokutoo*	*nanatoo*	*nantoo*
Cupful	*ippai*	*nihai*	*sanbai*	*yonhai*	*gohai*	*roppai*	*nanahai*	*nanbai*
Houses	*ikken*	*niken*	*sanken*	*yonken*	*goken*	*rokken*	*shichiken*	*nanken*

3. CONTINUATION OF TIME

To indicate that something began in the past and is still continuing in the present, the pattern is: verb (*te*-form) + *kuru*.

Nihon no koogyoo wa sensoo irai hatten shite kimashita.
The Japanese industry has been developing since the war.

Zutto ginkoo no shigoto o shite kimashita.
I have been a banker for a long time.

Ryuutsuu-seido o kenkyuu shite kimashita.
I have been researching distribution systems.

To indicate that something begins now and is going to continue into the future, use the pattern: verb (*te*-form) + *iku*.

Konpyuutaa-sangyoo wa dondon hattatsu shite iku deshoo.
The computer industry will probably continue to develop more and more (in the future).

Kono shigoto o tsuzukete ikitai desu.
I would like to continue this job.

Sekai wa suminikuku natte iku kamoshiremasen.
The world may become harder to live in.

Nihongo o zutto benkyoo shite iku tsumori desu.
I intend to study Japanese for many years to come.

D. BIJINESU JIKOO

PUREZENTEESHON (PRESENTATIONS)

When giving a presentation in Japan, the usual format is to start with a summary that includes an outline of topics to be covered, and follow up with a question-and-answer session. To your surprise, you may find people of various levels attending the presentation, not just upper management. This is largely due to the fact that in Japanese corporations most decisions are based on a consensus among project members.

The Japanese are generally quite serious during business meetings and presentations, and usually remain formal the entire time. Therefore, you should be sensitive to the prevailing business atmosphere in conducting the presentation. Many Japanese are not accustomed to, and do not appreciate, jokes during the first business encounter, so it is advisable not to act overly casual in these situations. Further, it is wise in Japan to avoid direct criticism of competing products, as this could jeopardize the success of your presentation.

The reaction of the audience may be difficult to perceive immediately after the presentation. You may have to "read" the audience's body language to determine if the presentation went over well, since the Japanese tend not to be overly animated in their verbal reactions in business settings. If they do have something to say, it may be quite indirect and not meant to be taken literally. The sentence "Yes, this is very interesting. Let us think about it" may actually mean "We aren't interested." You might also hear such indirect replies as "It's been hard to come to a decision" (*Ketsuron ga nakanaka denaide komatte imasu*) or "We're considering it, but there are differing opinions" (*Kentoochuu desu ga, iroiro iken ga arimashite*). If you do receive a negative response, it is important to answer pleasantly and positively, since you may have to do business with that person again in the future.

In following up your presentation, it is important in Japan not to pursue confirmation of a sale or other definitive responses too aggressively, or you may appear rude and pushy. If a business relationship does develop, the other party will expect it to be for the long term and will expect you to think in the same manner.

If problems arise on your client's end of a deal, it may be wise not to ask for internal details. Discussing another company's problems with someone in that company is inappropriate, and may lead to embarrassment. If it is absolutely necessary to do so, however, the question should be preceded by *Taihen shitsurei desu ga* (I am very sorry to ask, but . . .).

The Japanese tend to avoid answering direct questions regarding prices immediately unless they feel absolutely sure that their superiors will accept any concessions that they may make. A slow or unenthusiastic response may simply be a negotiation tactic, designed to make you come down in price. This is one strategy that is employed, it seems, the world over. Another popular tactic in Japan is simply to mention a competitor's name, reminding you of the buyer's prerogative and pitting you against your competition.

Finally, the presenter should be careful about how technical his or her presentation is. Many upper-management Japanese are not familiar with up-to-date technology, for example, customarily leaving that work to subordinates.

RENSHUU MONDAI

A. *Tsugi no shitsumon ni kotaenasai.* (Answer the following questions.)

1. *Neruson-san no kaisha no seihin wa nan desu ka.*
2. *Neruson-san wa shoohin o shookai suru mae ni nani o setsumei shimashita ka.*
3. *Neruson-san no kaisha wa itsu doko de setsuritsu saremashita ka.*
4. *Shain wa ima nan'nin desu ka.*
5. *Nan to iu kaisha to gyoomu-teikei o shimashita ka.*
6. *Suupaameeru wa nan no tame desu ka.*
7. *Kono seihin o tsukau to nani ga setsuyaku dekimasu ka.*
8. *Intaanetto to tsunagu koto ga dekimasu ka.*
9. *Kakaku wa doo desu ka.*

B. *Tekitoo na joshi o irenasai.* (Insert the appropriate particle.)

1. *Saikin wa iroiro _____ shinseihin _____ dete imasu.*
2. *Yamanaka-senmu kara _____ ohanashi _____ aru shi, kiku dake _____ kikimashoo.*
3. *Toosha _____ tsuite, kantan _____ gosetsumei shitai _____ omoimasu.*

4. *Kore o tsukaimasu* _____ *jikan* _____ *kami no setsuyaku* _____
   dekimasu.
5. *Kono seihin no chigai wa Eigo* _____ *Nihongo* _____ *dekiru koto*
   desu.

C. *Tekitoo na kotoba o irenasai.* (Insert the appropriate word[s].)

Honjitsu wa oisogashii tokoro oatsumari itadaki, _____ *. Kore kara,*
watakushi-domo de atsukatte orimasu _____ *Suupaameeru no shookai*
o sasete itadakimasu ga, sono mae ni _____ *ni tsuite, kantan ni*
_____ *shitai to omoimasu. Toosha wa 1980 nen ni Shiatoru de* _____
sare, omo ni konpuutaa no _____ *no kaihatsu hanbai no* _____ *o*
okonatte imasu. _____ *wa kyoo no tokoro 100 nin desu. Nihon* _____
wa san nen mae ni JTC-sha to _____ *shite setsuritsu saremashita.*

KOTAE

A. 1. *Denshi-meeru no sofuto desu.*   2. *Neruson-san no kaisha ni tsuite set-*
sumei shimashita.   3. *Sen kyuuhyaku hachijuu-nen ni shiatoru de setsuritsu*
saremashita.   4. *Ima hyaku-nin hodo desu.*   5. *JTC-sha to gyoomu-teikei o*
shimashita.   6. *Shanai no renraku o suru tame desu.*   7. *Jikan to kami ga*
setsuyaku dekimasu.   8. *Hai, tsunagu koto ga dekimasu.*   9. *Hoka no seihin*
to taisa arimasen.
B. 1. *na, ga*   2. *no, mo, demo*   3. *ni, na, to*   4. *to, ya (to), ga*   5. *demo,*
demo
C. 1. *arigatoo gozaimasu, shoohin, toosha, setsumei, setsuritsu, sofuto,*
gyoomu, shain, shisha, gyoomu-teikei

DAI JUUHACHIKA
Lesson 18

A. KAIWA

SETTAI[1] GORUFU

Suzuki-shi to Neruson-shi wa senshuu no purezenteeshon no hanashi o tsuzukeru tame, Kobayashi-Sangyoo no Wada-buchoo to Hamanaka-kachoo o gorufu ni shootai suru. Renshuujoo ni ita Wada-buchoo ni Suzuki-shi ga chikazuku.

SUZUKI: **Senjitsu wa arigatoo gozaimashita.**

WADA: **Iie. Kochira koso. Wazawaza oide itadakimashite.**

SUZUKI: **Iie, gomuri o onegai shimashite.[2]**

WADA: **Sore ni shimashite mo, atarashii jidai ni narimashita ne. Wareware mo honkakuteki ni konpyuutaa doonyuu o kangaeru jiki ni kite iru to kanjimashita.**

SUZUKI: **Soo desu ne. Shoorai wa iwayuru "terewaaku"[3] ga fukyuu shite, tsuukin mondai ya jimusho no supeesu mondai ga kanwa sareru to omoimasu.**

WADA: **Zaitaku—kinmu[4] ga kooritsuteki kamoshiremasen.**

SUZUKI: **Mattaku desu.[5] Tokoro de, Buchoo, gorufu no hoo wa yoku saremasu ka.**

WADA: **Tsuki ni kai desu ne. Mae wa motto ookatta n desu ga, saikin sukoshi hikaete imasu.**

SUZUKI: **Naruhodo.**

WADA: **Undoo busoku desu kara, motto yatta hoo ga ii n deshoo ga, jikan ga toremasen. Sore ni hiyoo mo baka ni narimasen[6] kara.**

SUZUKI: **Hai. Tokoro de, kono koosu wa hajimete to ka.[7]**

WADA: **Ee, yoku kikimasu ga, purei suru no wa hajimete desu.**

SUZUKI: **Kono Hakone gorufu koosu wa ichioo[8] meimon—koosu[9] de, kanari nankoosu desu.**

WADA: **Yoku korareru n desu ka.**

SUZUKI: **Tama ni. Jitsu wa yuujin ga kono koosu no yakuin o shite imasu node, tokidoki muri shite[10] yoyaku o totte morattemasu.**

WADA: Sore wa nanika to benri desu ne. Gorufu no yoyaku wa nakanaka taihen desu kara ne.

SUZUKI: Hirayama to iu n desu ga, goshookai shimashoo. Bengi o hakatte kureru[11] yoo ni tanonde okimasu.

WADA: Sore wa arigatai desu ne. Kyuu na toki nado yoyaku ga tore-nakute komaru toki ga arimasu kara.

Soko ni Neruson-shi to Hamanaka-kachoo ga tsuku.

NERUSON: Senjitsu wa doomo arigatoo gozaimashita.

WADA: Iie. Kochira koso. Wazawaza gosokuroo o okake shi-mashite.[12]

NERUSON: Iie.

Min'na renshuu o hajimeru.

HAMANAKA: Yaa, Neruson-kun wa ude ga yosa soo desu ne.

SUZUKI: Kare wa daigaku de gorufubu ni haitte ita soo de, tobasu koto wa tobashimasu.[13]

NERUSON: Demo saikin yatte imasen node, sappari[14] ii shotto ga demasen.

HAMANAKA: Koochi shite kudasai.

NERUSON: Kochira koso, oshiete itadakitai kurai desu. Sore ni Nihon no koosu wa feyaauei ga semaku dekite imasu kara, chotto nigate desu.

WADA: Maa, ii sukoa ga deru yoo ganbarimashoo.

NERUSON: Hai, yoroshiku.

Suujikango, geemu ga owatte kara.

NERUSON: Buchoo, o joozu desu ne.

WADA: Kazu[15] dake wa yatte imasu kara. Katasete itadaki-mashita.[16] Tokoro de, asa hanashita ken desu ga, Hamanaka-kun to mo hanashita n desu ga, otaku[17] no sofuto o tsukatte, konpyuutaaka suru hookoo ni susunde imasu. Yoroshiku tanomimasu.[18]

NERUSON: Arigatoo gozaimasu. Otaku no kaisha ni au yoo na puroguramu o kufuu sasete itadakimasu. Onedan no hoo mo girigiri[19] made benkyoo sasete itadakimasu.[20]

WADA: Kuwashiku wa Hamanaka-kun, sore ni gijutsu buchoo to soodan shinagara hanashi o susumete kudasai.[21]

NERUSON: Hai, kyooshuku desu.[22] Raishuuchuu ni demo go ren-raku shite, oukagai shimasu.

WADA: Kore de, toosha mo ichiryuu kigyoo ni nakama—iri[23] ga dekiru kamoshiremasen.

NERUSON: Meijitsu tomo ni[24] desu ne.

WADA: Arigatoo.

BUSINESS GOLF

In order to continue the discussion on last week's presentation, Mr. Suzuki and Mr. Nelson invite Mr. Wada (a department head) and Mr. Hamanaka (a section chief) of Kobayashi Industries to play golf. Mr. Suzuki approaches Mr. Wada, who is on the practice range.

SUZUKI: Thank you for the other day.

WADA: No, it was my pleasure. Thank you for coming. (lit. You did me the favor of coming on purpose.)

SUZUKI: No, I'm sorry for asking you to do something that might have been difficult. (lit. I asked the impossible.)

WADA: Times have changed, haven't they? (lit. It's become a new era.) I felt (recently) that the time has come for us, too, to seriously think about utilizing (lit. introducing) computers.

SUZUKI: I agree. In the future, so-called "distance working" will become popular (lit. widespread), and I think the problems of commuting (time to work) and (limited) space at the office will be eased (as a result).

WADA: Working at home might be efficient.

SUZUKI: Absolutely. By the way, Mr. Wada, do you play a lot of golf?

WADA: Twice a month. It used to be a lot more, but I've slowed down (lit. I am refraining a bit) recently.

SUZUKI: I see.

WADA: I don't get enough exercise, so I should play more, but I can't find (lit. take) the time. And plus, it's so expensive. (lit. I can't underestimate the expenses.)

SUZUKI: I understand. So, is this your first time on this course?

WADA: I have heard a lot about it, but this is the first time I've played here.

SUZUKI: Hakone Golf Course is, by and large, (one of the more) well-known courses, and it is rather difficult.

WADA: Do you come (here) often?

SUZUKI: Sometimes. The truth is, I have a friend who works here, and sometimes I impose and have him get me reservations.

WADA: That is pretty convenient, isn't it? (Especially) since getting reservations is so difficult.

SUZUKI: His name is Mr. Hirayama. I'll introduce you to him. I'll ask him to help you out, too.

WADA: I appreciate that. There are times when I'm in a hurry, can't get a reservation, and it's a (real) problem.

Mr. Nelson and Mr. Hamanaka arrive.

NELSON: Thank you very much for the other day.

WADA: No, it was my pleasure. Thank you for taking the trouble to come.

NELSON: No problem at all.

Everyone begins to practice.

HAMANAKA: Wow, Mr. Nelson looks like he's got a good arm!

SUZUKI: He was in the golf club in college, so he can really make (the ball) fly (lit. as for making it fly, he makes it fly).

NELSON: But since I haven't been playing lately, I can't get off any good shots.

HAMANAKA: Could you give me some pointers? (lit. Please coach me.)

NELSON: I (am the one who should) ask you to teach me. And the fairways on Japanese golf courses are narrow, so they're not my forte (lit. they are my weak point).

WADA: Well, let's try to get some good scores anyway.

NELSON: Okay.

A few hours later, after the game is over.

NELSON: Mr. Wada, you are really good.

WADA: Only because I've been playing for a long time. You let me win. By the way, regarding what we were talking about this morning, I have already spoken with Mr. Hamanaka, and we are going to try to computerize (lit. advance in the direction of computerization) our offices by using your software. Please help us out.

NELSON: Thank you. I'll try to make (lit. use ingenuity) a program that will suit (the needs of) your company. We'll also do our best to make it as inexpensive as possible.

236

WADA: Please talk to Mr. Hamanaka about the details. Also, while you are consulting with the technology manager, please help him out (advise him).

NELSON: Thank you very much. I'll contact him around the middle of next week for a visit.

WADA: By doing this (computerization), our company might be able to get in among the first-rate companies.

NELSON: Both in name and in reality.

WADA: Thank you.

B. CHUU

1. *Settai* means "entertaining clients," a concept considered very important in Japanese business.

2. *Gomuri o onegai shimashite* literally means "We asked the impossible." Japanese people use these excessively apologetic expressions when they feel they have inconvenienced someone.

3. *Terewaaku* is a "Japanese English" word that means "working from one's home" (instead of going to the office). Some Japanese corporations have started implementing the system but are experiencing difficulties in supervising the employees while they are at home.

4. *Zaitaku-kinmu* has the same meaning as *terewaaku*. The work is done primarily through computers and modems. Due to their experience with computers, the younger generation seems to prefer using this system.

5. *Mattaku desu* means "I agree with you completely" and is an emphatic statement.

6. *Baka ni narimasen* literally means "I won't become a fool" and implies, "I can't ignore," or "I can't underestimate."

7. *Kono koosu wa hajimete to ka* means "Is this your first time on this course?" *To ka* implies "I heard that, but is it true?"

8. *Ichioo* means "tentatively," "once," or "as a formality."

9. *Meimon-koosu* refers to prestigious (and expensive) golf courses.

10. *Muri shite* literally means "to do the impossible." In this case, it means "to make an unreasonable demand" or "against someone's will."

11. *Bengi o hakaru* means "to help" or "to give every convenience." The Japanese usually try very hard to accommodate a request by a friend or an acquaintance.

12. *Gosokuroo o okake shimashite* means "Thank you very much for taking the trouble to come." It is a very polite expression.

13. *Tobasu koto wa tobasu* literally means "As for making it fly, he makes it fly." The pattern, verb (dictionary form) + *koto wa* + the same verb, emphasizes the action of the verb.

14. *Sappari* (plus a verb with a negative ending) is a colloquial expression that means "not at all."

15. *Kazu* literally means "number," but it can refer to an amount of time as well.

16. It is rumored that many Japanese businesspeople lose to their customers on purpose, so as not to embarrass them.

17. *Otaku* means "you" as well as "your home."

18. *Yoroshiku tanomimasu* means "I am asking (you to do something)." It has the same meaning as *yoroshiku onegai shimasu*, but is less formal. Persons of higher status usually say this to those of lower status.

19. *Girigiri* is an onomatopoeic expression that means "barely" or "nearly." In this case, it extends its meaning to signify "lowest possible."

20. One meaning of *benkyoo suru* is "to learn" or "to study," but it can also mean "to sell at a low price."

21. Top management will usually not get involved in the details of a negotiation. Once they agree in principle, they delegate this responsibility to their subordinates.

22. *Kyooshuku* means "to be grateful," "to be sorry for," or "to be ashamed." It is used in very formal situations. For example: *Kyoo wa gorufu ni goshootai itadaki, kyooshuku desu.* (I am much obliged to you for inviting me to a game of golf today.) *Kyooshuku desu ga, odenwa itadakemasu ka.* (I'm sorry to trouble you, but may I ask you to call me.) *Hontoo ni ojoozu nan desu ne.—Iya, kyooshuku*

desu. (You're very good at it, aren't you?—No, not at all.) (lit. I feel ashamed to be mentioned.)

23. *Nakama-iri* means "joining a (special) group."

24. *Meijitsu tomo ni* means "both in name and reality."

C. BUNPOO TO YOOHOO

1. *(SA) SETE ITADAKU/(SA) SETE MORAU* (ASKING FOR PERMISSION)

When asking someone permission to do something, the *te*-form of the causative verb plus *itadaku* is used. This pattern can also be used to state the fact that permission has already been granted.

a. To a person of higher status in formal situations:

Atarashii seihin o shookai sasete itadakimasu.
Please allow me to introduce our new product (to you).

Kare no namae o tsukawasete itadakimashita.
I had him let me use his name (as a reference).

Asu made ni renraku sasete itadakimasu.
Please let me have until tomorrow to contact you.

Kono heya o tsukawasete itadaite mo ii desu ka.
Is it okay to use this room?

b. When talking to a person of equal or lower status in formal situations, replace the *te*-form + *itadaku* with *te*-form + *morau*. (Note: by changing from *itadaku* to *morau,* the sentence becomes much more direct. Thus *morau* should not be used when addressing someone of higher status.)

Kaisha no namae o tsukawasete moraimasu ga, ii desu ka.
I will use your company name (as a reference), is that okay?

Ashita no yoru yorasete moraimasu.
I will drop by tomorrow.

2. NOUN-*SURU*

The verb *suru* (to do) is one of the most frequently used words in Japanese. It is often used in combination with nouns to create verbs such as *kekkon-suru* (to get married), *renshuu-suru* (to practice), and *chuumon-suru* (to order). There are, in fact, hundreds of such "nominal verbs" in

Japanese, many of which are created to translate verbs borrowed from English and other foreign languages. Consider, for example, *fakkusu suru* (to send a fax) and *chekku suru* (to check, examine).

Chikai shoorai wa terewaaku ga fukyuu suru hazu desu.
Distance work is expected to become widespread in the near future.

Gorufu no yoyaku o toru no ni kuroo shite imasu.
I am having difficulty getting golf reservations.

E-meeru no tsukaikata o renshuu shite imasu.
I am practicing how to use e-mail.

Rainen daigakuin o sotsugyoo shimasu.
I will graduate from graduate school next year.

Soomu-buchoo ya gijutsu-buchoo to soodan shite kudasai.
Please consult with the managers of the Human Resources and Technology Departments.

3. *NANI KA TO* (SOMEHOW)

You have already learned that *nani ka* (Lesson 3) means "something," as in, *Nani ka nomimashoo.* (Let's have something to drink.) It can also be used to mean "I feel."

Nani ka atarashii jidai ni natta yoo na ki ga shimasu.
I feel that a new age has begun.

Kare wa nani ka muri shite iru n ja nai desu ka.
I feel that he is overdoing it, don't you?

However, *nani* plus *ka to* is used when the speaker wishes to convey feelings such as "for some reason" or "somehow."

Zaitaku kinmu mo nani ka to taihen desu.
Working at home is also somehow difficult.

Terewaaku o suru to kaisha no koto ga nani ka to shimpai ni naru deshoo.
When you work at home, you probably become worried (for some reason) about what is happening at the office.

Settai wa nani ka to taihen desu.
It is (for some reason) not easy to entertain clients.

D. BIJINESU JIKOO

SETTAI (ENTERTAINING CLIENTS)

The Japanese way of conducting negotiations is unique. The first step is to establish relationships between the groups of people involved. In order to ensure a good working relationship, the Japanese like to get well acquainted with one another so that they feel comfortable enough to discuss business negotiations.

Entertaining clients (called *settai*) after office hours, and even on weekends, could be called one of the Japanese businessperson's unstated duties. Indeed, many consider it part of the job. It often has priority over any other duties in the office or at home. Wives (and sometimes husbands) usually have no power to override their spouse's *settai* appointments.

Playing golf with clients (called *settai gorufu*) is an important business activity. Once the parties get acquainted fairly well and start negotiations, many Japanese invite clients to play golf or to some other activity. While they are actually playing, they usually do not discuss business, and concentrate on the game. Either before or after the game, they briefly touch on the general outline of the negotiations, and a few days later, the client will propose a meeting to finalize the deal.

Other types of entertainment are also considered good activities to promote mutual understanding or to start business relationships. Inviting someone to an upscale restaurant (*ryooriya* or *ryootei*) with private rooms is a common practice. Gifts may even be exchanged following the dinner.

Settai is also used to maintain previously established relationships among business associates. The Japanese periodically invite clients to social activities like company parties. Good customers or clients receive semiannual gifts, every summer and winter. Expenses for these activities are, of course, tax deductible, and top managers or businesspeople in sales and marketing are allocated a fairly large expense account to cover the costs of *settai*. Recently, the Japanese government has been discouraging corporations from *settai,* but it continues to flourish all over Japan.

RENSHUU MONDAI

A. *Tsugi no shitsumon ni kotaenasai.* (Answer the following questions.)

1. *Nani ga fukyuu suru to, tsuukin mondai ya jimusho no supeesu mondai ga kanwa saremasu ka.*
2. *Hakone gorufu koosu wa donna koosu desu ka.*
3. *Suzuki-san wa dooshite muri shite yoyaku shite moraeru no desu ka.*
4. *Hirayama to iu hito wa dare desu ka.*
5. *Wada-buchoo wa konpyuutaa-ka o doo kimemashita ka.*

B. *Tekitoo na kotoba o irenasai.* (Insert the appropriate word in the blank.)

1. *Yoku kikimasu _____, purei suru no _____ hajimete desu.*
2. *Kono koosu wa meimon koosu _____, kanari nan koosu desu.*
3. *Kare wa daigaku _____ gorufu-bu _____ haitte ita soo _____, tobasu koto _____ tobashimasu.*
4. *Otaku no kaisha _____ au yoo na puroguramu _____ kufuu sasete itadakimasu.*

C. *Tekitoo na hyoogen o erabinasai.* (Select the appropriate expression.)

1. *Sore ni shimashite mo, atarashii jidai ni (kimashita, narimashita).*
2. *Konpyuutaa doonyuu o kangaeru jiki ni kite iru to (narimashita, kanjimashita).*
3. *Sore ni keihi mo baka ni (narimasu, narimasen).*
4. *Kare wa tobasu koto wa (tobimasu, tobashimasu).*

KOTAE

A. 1. *Terewaaku ga fukyuu suru to iu koto desu.*   2. *Meimon koosu de kanari nan koosu desu.*   3. *Yuujin ga koosu no yakuin o shite imasu kara.*
4. *Suzuki-san no yuujin de, koosu no yakuin o shite imasu.*   5. *Konpyuutaa-ka suru koto ni shimasu.*
B. 1. *ga, wa*   2. *de*   3. *de, ni, de, wa*   4. *ni, o*
C. 1. *narimashita*   2. *kanjimashita*   3. *narimasen*   4. *tobashimasu*

DAI JUUKYUUKA
Lesson 19

A. KAIWA

NIHON NO SHUUKYOO

Jimusho kara eki ni iku tochuu, Neruson-shi wa Satoo-joo ni kinoo jinja de mita shiroi kami ni tsuite kiku.

NERUSON: Kinoo, sanpo shite itara, jinja[1] ga atte, shiroi kami ga koeda ni takusan burasagatte imashita kedo, are, nan desu ka.

SATOO: Min'na, nani ka negaigoto[2] o shite iru n desu. Are wa hito-bito ga soo natte hoshii to iu yoo na koto o kami ya ita ni kaite asoko ni burasageru n desu.

NERUSON: Negaigoto desu ka.

SATOO: Ee, meishin to wakatte ite mo, iwayuru kami o shinjita-gatte iru wake desu.

NERUSON: Naruhodo. Tatoeba donna koto desu ka.

SATOO: Tatoeba, kenkoo na kodomo ga umareru yoo ni toka, shi-bookoo ni nyuugaku dekiru yoo ni toka, iroiro arimasu.

NERUSON: Kami o shinjite inai koto mo nai n deshoo.[3]

SATOO: Sore wa doo desu ka ne. Shinjite iru hito mo iru deshoo ga, "kurushii toki no kamidanomi"[4] to iu hito mo iru to omoimasu.

NERUSON: Sore wa doo iu imi desu ka.

SATOO: Futsuu wa kami o shinjite inai no ni, komatta toki ni dake kami ni onegai suru wake desu.

NERUSON: Demo Kyooto de yuumei na otera ya jinja de takusan hito o mikakemashita yo.

SATOO: Soo desu yo ne. Watashi no ryooshin nado mo jinja ni yoku omairi[5] ni itte imasu. Neruson-san wa doo na no.

NERUSON: Kodomo no toki, ryooshin ni tsurerarete, kyookai ni iku koto wa itta kedo, saikin wa hotondo ittemasen.

SATOO: Kyookai to ieba, watashi no tomodachi de hitori kurisuchan[6] ga ita wa. Tottemo ii hito datta wa. Doo shite iru ka na.

NERUSON: Demo Nihon ni wa kurisuchan wa sukunai n deshoo.

SATOO: **Nagasaki**[7] **toka ni ooi rashii kedo, futsuu wa sukunai mitai.**[8]

NERUSON: **Nihonjin wa shintoo to bukkyoo o ryoohoo shinjite iru to kiita kedo.**

SATOO: **Maa, oiwai no toki wa shintoo de, osooshiki wa bukkyoo de to iu no ga futsuu desu.**

NERUSON: **Aa, soo desu ka. Ryoohoo o tsukai wakeru n desu ne. Naruhodo. Shuukyoo ni taishite no kangaekata ga oobei no hitotachi to chigau n desu ne.**

SATOO: **Hai, Nihonjin wa kami o shinjite iru to iu ka,**[9] **isshu no tetsugaku mitai ni kangaete iru hito ga ooi mitai desu.**

NERUSON: **Aa, chotto wakarimasen ga.**

SATOO: **Kantan ni wa setsumei dekimasen ga, ooku no Nihonjin wa shirazu shirazu**[10] **bukkyoo nado kara mananda chie o tetsugaku no yoo ni seikatsu ni katsuyoo shite iru yoo desu. Sore ni wa suupaanachuraru tsumari "kami" o hitsuyoo to shinai wake desu.**

NERUSON: **Naruhodo.**

Eki no chikaku de uranaishi o miru.

SATOO: **Asoko ni uranaishi**[11] **ga iru wa. Mite morattara.**

NERUSON: **Soo ne. Rainen wa don'na toshi ni naru ka mite moraoo ka. (Uranaishi ni) Unsei o mite kudasai.**[12]

URANAISHI: **Hai. Rainen desu ga, kenkoo wa joojoo deshoo. Josei kankei wa ketsudan o shinakereba narimasen ne. Shigoto wa "daikichi"**[13] **to dete imasu. Ooi ni atarashii koto o kikaku shite, dondon susumete iku beki desu. Mayotte**[14] **wa ikemasen.**

Densha de.

NERUSON: **Hontoo ni ataru n desu ka.**

SATOO: **Saa, doo deshoo. Demo, anna koto o kiitara, yuuki to yaru ki ga deru n ja nai.**

NERUSON: **Sore mo soo desu ga, warui koto bakari dattara, doo shimasu ka.**

SATOO: **Soo iu toki wa ki o tsukeru yoo ni naru kara, mata ii no yo.**

NERUSON: **Naruhodo ne. Sorezore kooyoo ga aru to iu wake
desu ne.**

RELIGION IN JAPAN

While going from the office to the train station, Mr. Nelson asks Ms. Sato
about the white papers he saw yesterday at a shrine.

NELSON: Yesterday, when I was taking a walk, there was this shrine,
where there were many white pieces of paper hanging from tree
branches. What are those?

SATO: They're wishes (or prayers). People write what they would like to
happen (lit. become so in the future) on paper or pieces of wood, and
hang them there.

NELSON: Wishes?

SATO: Yes, even though they understand it's superstition, they want to
believe in some kind of god (lit. the so-called "gods").

NELSON: I see. For example, what kind of things (are people wishing
for)?

SATO: For example, that they will have a healthy baby, or that they will be
able to get into the school they want . . . things like that.

NELSON: It's not that they don't believe in the gods, right?

SATO: I wonder about that. (lit. How is that?) There are people who
(truly) believe (in gods), but there are also those who are the types to
"ask the gods only in times of difficulty."

NELSON: What does that mean?

SATO: It refers to (those) who normally don't believe in God, but who ask
for his help only during times of trouble.

NELSON: But I saw a lot of people visiting the famous temples and
shrines in Kyoto.

SATO: Yes, that is true. My parents also go to the shrine often to pay their
respects . . . What about you, Mr. Nelson?

NELSON: When I was a kid, I was taken to church by my parents, of
course, but recently I hardly go at all.

SATO: Speaking of church, I had a friend who was a Christian. He was a
really good person. I wonder what he's doing now.

NELSON: But in Japan there aren't that many (lit. there are few) Christians, right?

SATO: In places like Nagasaki there seem to be a lot, but generally speaking, there are not that many (lit. it looks as though there are few).

NELSON: I heard that the Japanese believe in both Shintoism and Buddhism.

SATO: Yeah. Usually it's Shintoism for times of celebration and Buddhism for funerals.

NELSON: Oh really? So they practice (lit. use) them separately. I see. The views (lit. ways of thinking) on religion are quite different from those of European and American people.

SATO: Yes they are. It can be said that the Japanese believe in the gods, but it seems many consider religion a form of philosophy.

NELSON: Oh. I don't really understand.

SATO: I can't explain it in simple (terms), but it appears that many Japanese people unconsciously use the wisdom they learned from Buddhism and Shintoism as (a kind of) philosophy in their lives. What I mean is, they do not need the supernatural, or rather, "the gods."

NELSON: I see.

They see a fortune-teller near the station.

SATO: There's a fortune-teller over there. Why don't you have her read (lit. look at) your future?

NELSON: Okay. I'll have her tell me what kind of year next year will be. (To the fortune-teller) Please tell me what my future holds.

FORTUNE-TELLER: Yes, sir. Next year, you should be healthy. As for your relationships with women, you will have to make a decision (on what you want to do). A "very fortunate" has appeared with regards to your work. You should plan and carry out a lot of new projects. You must not lose focus!

On the train.

NELSON: (Do you think that fortune) was really accurate?

SATO: Well, I wonder. But when you hear that, don't you feel more courageous and encouraged to do something?

NELSON: That's true, too, but what do you do if everything turns out badly (lit. if it's nothing but bad)?

SATO: During those times, you'll be a little more careful, which is also a good (thing).

NELSON: I see. You can utilize that sort of information in different ways for different situations. (lit. There are individual ways of being effective.)

B. CHUU

1. A *jinja* is a Shinto shrine. Most people visit shrines around New Year's to offer wishes for the coming year, and on other holidays and happy occasions. A tall, red gate *(torii)* marks the entrance to a *jinja*.

2. *Negaigoto* means "something one wishes for." It is a combination of the words *negai* (wishing) and *koto* (thing). *Koto* becomes vocalized *(goto)* when the two words are combined. As a general rule, words starting with the consonant sounds *k, t, h, s, sh, ch,* and *ts* become vocalized *(g, d, b, z, j, j,* and *z,* respectively) when they follow other words in a compound.

3. The sentence *Kami o shinjite inai koto mo nai* literally means "It is not that people don't believe in gods. Because it is a sort of double negative" sentence, it also means "Some people believe in gods."

4. *Kurushii toki no kamidanomi* is a phrase that literally means "asking the gods only in times of strife."

5. *Omairi* refers to "visiting a shrine or temple to pray."

6. *Kurisuchan* is the Japanese pronunciation of the word Christian.

7. It is reported that in the city of Nagasaki, about 10 to 15 percent of the population is Christian. This is unusually high for a city in Japan. (See "Business Matters" in this lesson.)

8. *Futsuu wa sukunai mitai* means "Normally, it seems there are few." The word *mitai* means "it seems," and is used in informal conversation.

9. *To iu ka* means "you could say ~ or ~" and is used to express uncertainty.

10. *Shirazu shirazu* literally means "without knowing, without knowing." It is often translated as "unconsciously." *Zu* is a classical form of *nai,* and the repetition is for emphasis.

11. You can find *uranai (shi)* (fortune-tellers) in any large town. They usually have tables set up on the sidewalk in areas where a lot of people pass by.

12. Many Japanese, some quite serious and others just for fun, ask fortune-tellers to predict their futures *(unsei)*. There are special fortune-telling calendars for sale as well, which include all kinds of "information" on predictions.

13. A *daikichi* (big fortune) is the best reading one can receive from a fortune-teller.

14. *Mayou* means "to be lost," as well as "to be at a loss (as to what to do)."

C. BUNPOO TO YOOHOO

1. *(TA) GARU*

As you know, the *tai*-form is mainly used in the first person (I) to express something you want. In informal situations, it is acceptable to use this form for the second (you) or third person (he, she, it, they) as well, especially when it is followed by expressions of uncertainty, like *rashii* and *mitai,* or when it is used in a question.

Ichiryuu daigaku ni nyuugaku shitai desu.
I want to enter a first-rate college.

Nihon no josei wa hayaku kekkon shitai rashii.
It seems that Japanese women prefer to marry early.

Nihon dewa uranaishi ni unsei o mite moraitai hito ga oii mitai.
In Japan, it seems that there are a lot of people who want their fortunes read by fortune-tellers.

Kore ni nani o kakitai desu ka.
What do you want to write on this?

In more formal circumstances, another form is used to indicate wishes or desires in the third person only. The *tagaru*-form signifies that someone is eager to do something. It is actually formed from *tai:* first the *i* is dropped, then *garu* is added.

Dare demo kami o shinjitagarimasu.
Everyone wants to believe in a god.

Nihonjin wa gaikoku ni sumitagarimasu.
Japanese people are eager to live overseas.

Chichi ga uranaishi ni mite moraitagatte iru n desu ga.
My father wants to have a fortune-teller look (at his future).

Yuujin wa kurisuchan ni naritagatte iru rashii.
It seems that my friend wants to become a Christian.

2. NEGATIVE + *KOTO MO NAI*

Japanese grammar permits the use of a pattern that resembles a double negative: negative (verbs, adjectives, clauses) + *koto mo nai*. This may be translated as "It is not that, (but)." The "but" is often implied rather than stated, and the sentence is often followed by an explanation.

Dekinai koto mo arimasen ga muzukashii desu.
It is not that I cannot do it, but it is difficult.

Nihonjin mo shuukyoo o shinjinai koto mo arimasen.
It is not that Japanese people do not believe in religion.

Meishin o shinjinai koto mo arimasen.
It isn't that they don't believe in superstitions.

Eigyoo no keiken ga nai koto mo arimasen ga ooku wa nai desu.
It's not that I don't have any experience in sales, I don't have a lot.

3. AFFIRMATION (VERB + *KOTO WA* + VERB)

When a Japanese person says, *"Iku koto wa itta,"* it implies, "I certainly went." By repeating the same verb, the speaker reaffirms its action, or the situation it dictates. The following construction is used: verb (plain form) + *koto wa* + verb (plain or formal).

Kyookai ni yoku iku koto wa itta n desu ga, naze iku ka wakarimasen deshita.
Indeed, I did go to church often, but I didn't know why.

Nihonjin mo shuukyoo o shinjite iru koto wa shinjite imasu.
Japanese people do indeed believe in religion.

Uranaishi ni shoorai no koto o mite morau koto wa mite moraimashita.
I did indeed have a fortune-teller predict my future.

Renraku suru koto wa renraku shita no desu ga, mada henji ga arimasen.
I certainly did contact him, but I have not received a reply yet.

4. CAUSATIVE-PASSIVE

You have already studied the causative form of verbs (Lesson 7), which indicate "having someone do." To review, this form is constructed by adding *-saseru* to the stems of regular verbs and *-seru* to the pre-*nai* forms of irregular verbs. The two exceptions, *kuru* and *suru,* are *kosaseru* and *saseru,* respectively. You have also studied the passive form (Lesson 4). The causative and passive forms can be combined to indicate that one "is being made (forced) to." The causative-passive is formed by adding *-saserareru* to the stem of regular verbs and *-serareru* (or *sareru*) to the pre-*nai* forms of irregular verbs.

REGULAR VERBS	CAUSATIVE-PASSIVE
taberu (to eat)	*tabesaserareru* (to be made to eat)
shiraberu (to look up)	*shirabesaserareru* (to be made to look up)

IRREGULAR VERBS	CAUSATIVE-PASSIVE
nomu (to drink)	*nomaserareru* (to be made to drink)
yomu (to read)	*yomaserareru* (to be made to read)
matsu (to wait)	*matasareru* (to be made to wait)

EXCEPTIONS	CAUSATIVE-PASSIVE
kuru (to come)	*kosaserareru* (to be made to come)
suru (to do)	*saserareru* (to be made to do)

Kodomo no toki yoku kyookai ni ikaseraremashita.
   When I was a child, I was forced to go to church a lot.

Shuukyoo o benkyoo saseraremashita.
   I was forced to study religion.

Shuukyoo ni tsuite kurasu de kangaesaseraemashita.
   We were made to think about religion in class.

D. BIJINESU JIKOO

NIHON NO SHUUKYOO (RELIGION IN JAPAN)

Japanese beliefs with regard to religion are among the most complicated in the world, due in large part to the fact that they are a reflection of a mixture of several religions. This is exemplified by visits to a Shinto shrine at the beginning of the new year, trips to a Buddhist temple in the spring and fall to visit the family grave, and weddings held in a Christian church. It is common for a Japanese family to have both Shinto and Buddhist altars in their house.

Statistics give evidence of Japanese polytheistic tendencies. According to the Agency for Cultural Affairs' *The Religion Yearbook* (1995), the Japanese polled responded with 220 million declarations of personal religion—nearly double the actual population of 123 million. Although the Japanese tend to avoid identifying with any single religion, they do have an inherent reverence for spirituality that stems from their strongly rooted affinity with nature.

Shintoism *(Shintoo)*, literally the "way of the gods," is the "religion" indigenous to Japan. It is based on Japanese concepts of closeness to nature and ancestor worship, but has no unified doctrine, scriptures, or ancient canon. It teaches that all things on earth were brought forth by the gods and are subsequently governed by the gods. There are numerous Shinto shrines throughout Japan that remain objects of worship. Some Japanese believe that Shintoism constitutes the foundation of the collective sensibility of the Japanese people.

Buddhism *(Bukkyoo)* came to Japan from China in the middle of the sixth century. Proponents of the new religion, supported by the government, built temples in every area and spread the religion throughout the country. Later, in the twelfth century, a number of new leaders appeared who continued to teach the old ways while adding newer ideas that established that *Bukkyoo* was a religion that advocates saving the weak. Zen Buddhism was brought to Japan in the thirteenth century by Japanese priests who had studied it in China. It flourished as the religion of *samurai* (warrior) intellectuals.

There were times throughout Japanese history when one religion or the other won favor with the ruling party. For example, when Japan began to modernize as a state during the Meiji period (1868–1912), the government promoted Shintoism as the main religion. Nonetheless, Shintoism, which is a folk religion, and Buddhism, which came from abroad, continued to coexist, as there were no major contradictions to contend with in synthesizing them. It is still quite common to have a Shinto wedding and a Buddhist funeral. It has been said recently that the religious sense of the Japanese is weakening, but many homes still have Shinto and Buddhist altars, and new sects of religions are emerging and attracting believers every day.

KAKURE KURISUCHAN (HIDDEN CHRISTIANS)

Christianity has a brief but interesting history in Japan. The introduction of Christianity began around the fifteenth century through Catholic missionaries in the city of Nagasaki. As the success of the missionaries grew, the Japanese government began to distrust Christians and worry about the loss of the "Japanese spirit" *(yamatodamashi)* at the expense of becoming more westernized. This problem was further aggravated by the fact that Japanese Christians valued God more than they valued their emperor, or the military rulers *(shogun)* who really governed Japan at this time. This led to the decision in the late sixteenth century to expel the missionaries, along with most other foreigners, and close off Japan to the rest of the world in the seventeenth century. With the missionaries gone, the Japanese Christians were left to harsh persecution. Many of them were forced to step on wooden engravings of Christ *(fumie)* to signify that they had indeed given up their religion. Those who did not comply were either put to death or tortured until they conceded. Of course, not all Christians stepped on the *fumie*. Some went into hiding *(kakure kurisuchan)* and continued to worship and teach the beliefs of Christianity to their families. The "hidden Christians" continued to worship in secret until the religious environment changed with the reopening of the country more than 250 years later, in the late nineteenth century. Today, the number of Christians in Japan is estimated at approximately 0.7 percent of the total population.

RENSHUU MONDAI

A. *Tsugi no shitsumon ni kotaenasai.* (Answer the following questions.)

1. *Jinja de burasagatte iru kami wa nan no tame desu ka.*
2. *Don'na negaigoto desu ka.*
3. *"Kurushii toki no kamidanomi" no imi wa nan desu ka.*
4. *Neruson-san no rainen no unsei wa doo desu ka.*

B. *Tekitoo na joshi o irenasai.* (Insert the appropriate particle.)

1. *Kurushii toki _____ komatta toki ni _____ kami ni onegai shimasu.*
2. *Yuumei na otera ya jinja _____ takusan hito _____ mikakemashita.*
3. *Nihonjin wa shintoo _____ bukkyoo _____ ryoohoo shinjite imasu.*
4. *Oiwai no toki wa shintoo _____, osooshiki wa bukkyoo _____ to iu _____ ga futsuu desu.*
5. *Shuukyoo ni tai shite no kangaekata _____ oobei no hitotachi _____ chigau n desu.*

C. *Tekitoo na kotoba o shita kara erabinasai.* (Select the appropriate word[s] from below.)

1. *Nihonjin wa kami o shinjita* _____ *iru n desu.*
   (gatte, garu)
2. *Kami o shinjite inai koto mo* _____ *deshoo.*
   (nai, ja nai)
3. *Kodomo no toki, kyookai ni iku* _____ *ikimashita.*
   (wa, koto wa)
4. *Yuu ki to yaru ki ga deru n* _____.
   (ja nai, koto)
5. *Sorezore kooyoo ga aru to iu* _____ *desu.*
   (imi, wake)

KOTAE

A. 1. *Negaigoto no tame desu.* 2. *Tatoeba kenkoo na kodomo ga umareru yoo ni to ka kibookoo ni nyuugaku dekiru yoo ni to ka no negaigoto desu.* 3. *Kurushii toki to ka kommatta toki ni dake kami ni onegai suru koto desu.* 4. *Kenkoo to shigoto wa ii desu ga, josei kankei wa ketsudan shinakereba narimasen.*
B. 1. *to ka, dake* 2. *de, o* 3. *to, o* 4. *de, de, no* 5. *ga, to*
C. 1. *gatte* 2. *nai* 3. *koto wa* 4. *ja nai* 5. *wake*

DAI NIJUKKA
Lesson 20

A. KAIWA

BOONENKAI

Nihon dewa juuni gatsu wa totemo isogashiku, boonenkai no kisetsu demo aru.

SATOO: Suzuki-san, kotoshi no boonenkai[1] wa doo shimasu ka.

SUZUKI: Aa, boonenkai ne. Sorosoro nenmatsu[2] desu ne. Sukkari wasurete imashita.

SATOO: Mada junbi shite nai n desu ka. Shikata nai desu yo ne. Isogashikatta n desu kara ne.

SUZUKI: Demo buchoo ni wa boku ga suru to itte aru n desu.

SATOO: Aa, soo. Jaa, watashi choodo shigoto no kugiri ga tsuita kara, otetsudai shimashoo ka.

SUZUKI: Soo desu ka. Sore wa arigatai.

SATOO: Kotoshi no yosan wa ikura gurai kashira.

SUZUKI: Hitori ichi man en gurai ka na.

SATOO: Ichi man en desu ka. Honto. Jaa, ii tokoro ga mitsukaru kamo.[3]

SUZUKI: Jaa, kanji[4] o onegai dekimasu ka.

SATOO: Ee, ii wa. Tekitoo na tokoro ga sagasetara, oshirase shimasu.

SUZUKI: Tayori ni shite imasu.

SATOO: Tanoshii no o kikaku shitai kedo, doo kashira. Un, kotoshi wa "sake nashi no boonenkai"[5] ni shiyoo ka na.

SUZUKI: E, hontoo desu ka.

SATOO: Iie, joodan[6] desu yo. Demo sukoshi shukoo o kaete mo ii desu ka.

SUZUKI: Ee, kyonen made no to chigatte mo ii desu yo. Itsumo to onaji ja,[7] akimasu kara.

SATOO: Doo naru ka wakarimasen ga, keikaku shite mimasu.

SUZUKI: Ja, onegai shimasu. Buchoo ni yoru to, ichijikai[8] no hiyoo wa kaisha ga motsu soo desu kara.[9]

SATOO: Jaa, gooka ni yarimashoo ka.

SUZUKI: Iya ichioo yosan wa aru to omoimasu.

SATOO: Wakarimashita.[10]

Tsugi no hi.

SATOO: Suzuki-san, rei no[11] boonenkai no ken desu ga, kotoshi wa yooshoku de shiyoo to omoimasu ga, doo kashira.

SUZUKI: Ii desu kedo. Takaku tsuku[12] n ja nai desu ka.

SATOO: Chotto ne. Hitori ichiman en gurai ni narimasu.

SUZUKI: Sore gurai nara, daijoobu deshoo.

SATOO: Yuurakuchoo ekimae no Arupusu to iu kookyuu resutoran de kyanseru ga atte, juugo-mei gurai nara, daijoobu da to iu koto desu. Ichioo yoyaku shite okimashita.

SUZUKI: Nanji kaishi desu ka.

SATOO: Shichi ji han ni shimashita. Chotto osoi desu ka.

SUZUKI: Nenmatsu de min'na isogashii kara choodo ii desu yo.

SATOO: Karaoke[13] wa nijikai de shite itadaku to iu koto de, junbi shite imasen.

SUZUKI: Ii desu yo. Jaa, nijikai wa boku no ikitsuke no sunakku ni demo ikimashoo. Saishinshiki no karaoke ga arimasu kara juubun tanoshinde moraemasu. Demo, ichijikai de karaoke ga nai to suru to,[14] jikan o mote amasu[15] n ja nai desu ka.

SATOO: Sore ga mondai na n desu ga, shishachoo ni supiichi demo onegai suru ka, dareka kooshi o maneite hanashi o shite morau ka, myuujishan o yatou ka, nado iroiro kentoo shite imasu.

SUZUKI: Makasemasu.

Boonenkai ga chikazuita no ni, min'na, shigoto ga owaranai.

SUZUKI: Asu wa boonenkai to iu no ni, shigoto ga owari soo mo arimasen yo.

NERUSON: Boku datte soo desu. Demo AP-sha no keiyaku ga tore soo da kara, toshi ga kose soo desu.[16]

SUZUKI: Sore wa yokatta. Wareware no rei no purojekuto mo junchoo ni susunde iru kara, hotto shite iru tokoro desu.

NERUSON: **Mattaku atarashii sofuto o tsukuri dasu no wa nakanaka no kuroo deshoo.**

SUZUKI: **Ee. Demo saiwai ni mo teikeisaki ga tekunorojii no yuushuu na jinzai o motte iru node, uchi no gijutsu to kumiawaseru[17] to sugoi sofuto ga dekiru hazu desu.**

NERUSON: **Sore wa subarashii desu ne. Honsha mo yorokobu deshoo.**

SUZUKI: **Soo ieba, Kurisumasu ni kikoku suru[18] n desu ne.**

NERUSON: **Ee, ni shuukan bakari itte kimasu.[19] Tsuide ni[20] honsha ni mo yotte kimasu. Soshite kochira no jookyoo o iroiro setsumei shite kimasu.**

YEAR-END PARTY

In Japan, the month of December is very busy. It is also the season of year-end parties.

SATO: Mr. Suzuki, what are we going to do for this year's *boonenkai* (year-end party)?

SUZUKI: Oh, the *boonenkai*. It's almost the end of the year, isn't it? I had completely forgotten!

SATO: You haven't prepared yet? (I guess) it can't be helped. You have been busy, haven't you?

SUZUKI: Yes, but I (already) told the department manager that I'd do it.

SATO: Oh, really. Well, I've just wrapped up a project (lit. arrived at a pause in my work). Shall I help you?

SUZUKI: Really? I would appreciate that.

SATO: I wonder what our budget is this year.

SUZUKI: I suppose it's about ten thousand yen a person.

SATO: Ten thousand yen? Really? Well, we might (be able to) find a nice place (to have the party for that much).

SUZUKI: Well then, can I ask you to be the coordinator?

SATO: Sure, that's fine. Once I find (lit. search for) an appropriate place, I'll let you know.

SUZUKI: (I know) I can count on you.

SATO: I want to plan a fun one. Hmm . . . I got it—why don't we make it a "no alcohol" party this year?

SUZUKI: Are you serious? (lit. Is that true?)

256

SATO: No, I'm just kidding. But is it all right to change the theme (lit. plan) a little?

SUZUKI: Sure, having something different from previous years would be fine. After all, if they're always the same, it gets boring.

SATO: I don't know how it will turn out, but I'll start the planning.

SUZUKI: Thank you. (lit. I'll leave it to your care.) According to the department manager, it seems that the company is going to pick up the expenses for the first party.

SATO: In that case, shall we do something extravagant?

SUZUKI: No, I think there is a budget (that we'll have to work within).

SATO: Okay, (lit. I understand.)

The next day.

SATO: Mr. Suzuki. About the year-end party, for this year I was thinking about having Western food. What do you think?

SUZUKI: That's fine, but don't you think it will be expensive?

SATO: Maybe a little. It will cost about ten thousand yen per person.

SUZUKI: If it is around that much, it should be okay.

SATO: There was a cancellation at this ritzy restaurant in front of Yuraku-cho Station called Arupus. They said that a party of fifteen people would be okay, so I went ahead and made a reservation.

SUZUKI: What time will (the party) start?

SATO: I made (the reservation) for seven-thirty. Is that a little late?

SUZUKI: It's the end of the year and everyone will be busy, so that should be just right.

SATO: As far as karaoke goes, that's going to be at the second party, so I haven't done anything to prepare for it (at the first party).

SUZUKI: That's okay. For the second party, let's go to this bar I go to a lot. They have the newest karaoke equipment, so everyone should have a good time (lit. can receive enough fun). But if we don't have karaoke at the first party, won't we have some extra time on our hands?

SATO: Yeah, that's a problem, but I'm considering several things (to fill the time) like having the branch manager give a speech, or having a lecturer, or (even) hiring a musician.

SUZUKI: Okay, I'll leave that to you.

The year-end party has drawn closer, but nobody has finished their work.

SUZUKI: Tomorrow is the year-end party, and it doesn't look like I'm going to finish my work.

NELSON: Me neither. But it looks like we will get the AP contract, so we can head (lit. cross over) comfortably into next year.

SUZUKI: That's great. Our other projects are also proceeding smoothly, so I can relax (lit. I'm feeling relieved).

NELSON: It must be really tough creating completely new software.

SUZUKI: Yes, but fortunately our partner has (some) talented people who are really good with technology. So when we combine them with our (own) technology, we should come up with (lit. be able to do) some great software.

NELSON: That's great. The head office will be happy as well.

SUZUKI: Speaking of that (the home office), you are going home (lit. return to your country) for Christmas, aren't you?

NELSON: Yes, I'll head home for a couple weeks. (lit. I'll go for just two weeks and come back.) While I'm there (lit. while I'm on the subject), I'll also stop by the head office and explain how things are doing here (lit. explain the situation).

B. CHUU

1. Translated literally, *boonenkai* means "forget-the-year party." It is an annual event for most Japanese. From the largest companies to the individual classes at cultural schools, almost every organization holds a party at the end of the year. (See "Business Matters" in this lesson.)

2. *Nenmatsu* (end of the year) has a special meaning in Japan. It is a time to complete the projects and work started during the current year in order to start the new year with a clean slate. Businesses, for example, try to pay off all of their outstanding debts by the end of the year.

3. *Kamo* is a shortened form of *kamoshirenai* (maybe) and is used in informal situations.

4. Whenever the Japanese plan to do something that involves a number of people, they select someone to be in charge. This person is called the *kanji* (coordinator), and he or she plans and oversees the event. Events for which a *kanji* is used include golf tournaments, parties, and group travel.

5. A *sake-nashi-boonenkai* (year-end party without alcohol) would be an unlikely event, unless the party was for children or special groups. Traditionally, *boonenkai* are events at which large amounts of alcohol are consumed.

6. *Joodan* literally means "jest" or "joke," and is used to indicate that someone is just kidding around.

7. *Onaji ja* is a colloquial form of *onaji dewa* and means "if it's the same."

8. It is not unusual to have several parties on the evening of a *boonenkai*. The first and main party *(ichijikai)* is generally attended by all the members of a company. These first parties are rather formal. The second party *(nijikai)* is usually smaller and attended by those in one's immediate group or department, and is therefore a little more relaxed.

9. Since the *boonenkai (ichijikai)* is an official company event, the party is usually paid for by the company. The expenses for the second party are usually divided up among the participants.

10. *Wakarimashita* literally means "I understood." In Japanese, the past tense form is used as soon as something has occurred.

11. *Rei no* can mean "the (thing) in question," "the usual," or "the customary." *Rei* alone can mean "custom," "instance," or "example."

12. *Takaku tsuku* means "prove to be expensive." *Tsuku* usually means "attached to," but in this case it implies "to cost."

13. *Karaoke* literally means "empty orchestra," and is like "singing along." It is still popular in Japan, and its popularity is growing all over the world. (See "Business Matters" in this lesson.)

14. The expression, verb + *to suru to,* means "assuming that" or "suppose that." *Teikeisaki ga nai to suru to, nakanaka taihen deshoo ne.* (Assuming that we don't have a partner, the job should be more difficult.) *Kurisumasu ni kaeru to suru to, kore o hayaku shite shimawanakereba narimasen ne.* (If I'm [going] to go back [to the U.S.] at Christmas, I must finish this soon.)

15. *Jikan o mote amasu* means "to not know how to use the time."

16. *Toshi ga koseru* (to be able to enter the new year) was an important matter in old Japan because one had to pay any debts acquired during the current year before entering a new one.

17. The verb *kumiawaseru* means "to combine" or "to connect."

18. Many foreigners who live in Japan go to their home countries to celebrate the holidays.

19. *Itte kimasu* means "I'll go and come back" and it is said upon leaving a place you are planning to return to, especially home.

20. *Tsuide ni* means "while."

C. BUNPOO TO YOOHOO

1. *TE-OKU*

One of the most important uses of the *te*-form of verbs is its combination with *oku*. The *te*-form plus *oku* means "to do something in advance." In other words, one is doing something for a perceived future benefit.

Boonenkai no junbi o shite okimashoo.
Let's prepare for the year-end party in advance.

Boonenkai no yoyaku o shite okimashoo ka.
Shall we (go ahead and) reserve a room for the year-end party?

Paatii no yosan o kangaete okimashoo.
Let's figure out (lit. think about) a budget for the party in advance.

Nijikai no tame resutoran o yoyaku shite okimashita.
I reserved a restaurant for the second party.

2. SIMULTANEOUS ACTIONS *(NAGARA)*

Japanese has a particular construction to indicate that two actions are occurring simultaneously. It is called the *nagara* form. *Nagara* follows the stem form of a verb and translates roughly as "while doing." Note that the *nagara* form is used for two actions that are performed by one person simultaneously. It cannot be used to indicate actions performed by different people.

Rajio o kikinagara, konpyuutaa o tsukaimasu.
While listening to the radio, I work on (lit. use) the computer.

Shokuji o shinagara, boonenkai no koto o hanashimashoo ka.
Shall we talk about the year-end party over dinner (lit. while eating)?

Kaisha ni tsutomenagara, jibun no bijinesu o shite imasu.
I work at a company and run my own business (at the same time).

Karaoke o kikinagara, osake o nomimasu.
People drink sake while listening to karaoke.

3. *TSUMORI DA*

Tsumori da means "intend to" and follows verbs in the plain, non-past form. It is similar to *oo to omou* and *hazu da,* but it is a bit stronger than these other expressions of intention. One can also add the honorific *o* before *tsumori* when addressing persons of higher status.

Sake nashi no boonenkai o keikaku suru tsumori desu.
I intend to plan a party without alcohol.

Kotoshi wa yooshoku ni suru tsumori desu.
I intend to order (lit. to do) Western food this year.

Seminaa ni kooshi o maneku tsumori desu.
I intend to invite a lecturer to the seminar.

Karaoke o yooi suru (o)tsumori desu ka.
Do you intend to arrange for the karaoke?

Paatii no kanji o suru tsumori desu ka.
Do you intend to be the coordinator for the party?

D. BIJINESU JIKOO

NENMATSU (THE END OF THE YEAR)

In Japan, there are a number of holidays in late December and early January, both official and nonofficial, that involve culturally rich activities. This is the time of year when Japanese people are very busy.

Toward the end of December, the Japanese attend *boonenkai* with their business associates and friends. These are held in the company office or a nearby restaurant, or occasionally in someone's home. If you belong to several organizations or groups, you may be invited to participate in several *boonenkai.* These parties were originally established so that the members of an organization could get together and review the activities of the past year, as well as plan for the year to come. They are now more like annual get-togethers among friends with the purpose of renewing friendships.

A few days before New Year's, most offices have what is called a *nookai,* a gathering of the office members that signifies the last meeting of the year. This is not a normal workday; instead there is often a small party and brief speeches by the managers. The workers usually go home early, as it is assumed that by this time they will have completed all of their work. Employees then have several days off, and many use this time to go back to their hometowns to visit relatives and friends. Former high school or college classmates often get together during this time to renew their friendships.

Several days after New Year's, workers go back to their offices. They usually hold a brief meeting and then have another party called a *shin'nenkai* (New Year's Party). At this party, employees go around to the various departments and greet their bosses and colleagues.

The period between the *boonenkai* and *shin'nenkai* is a time to reflect and to reexamine your work and relationships. It is also a time to renew friendships, build good relations with your family, and in general to renew your energy for the coming year.

RENSHUU MONDAI

A. *Tsugi no shitsumon ni kotaenasai.* (Answer the following questions.)

1. *Nihon de boonenkai wa itsu shimasu ka.*
2. *Satoo-san wa don'na boonenkai o keikaku shimashita ka.*
3. *Ichijikai no hiyoo wa dare ga mochimasu ka.*
4. *Nijikai wa doko de nani o shimasu ka.*
5. *Suzuki-san no purojekuto wa doo desu ka.*

B. *Tekitoo na kotoba o erabinasai.* (Choose the appropriate word.)

1. *Sorosoro boonenkai o (keikaku, kikaku) shitai n desu ga.*
2. *Kotoshi wa "sake nashi no boonenkai" ni (yarimashoo, shimashoo).*
3. *Sukoshi shukoo o (chigaimasu, kaemasu).*
4. *Kotoshi wa yooshoku de (shimashoo, tabemashoo).*
5. *Teikeisaki no jinzai to uchi no gijutsu o kumiawaseru to sugoi sofuto ga dekiru (hazu, tsumori) desu.*

C. *Tekitoo na kotoba o irenasai.* (Insert the appropriate word.)

1. *Juuni gatsu no sue ni suru paatii o _____ to iimasu.*
2. *Paatii nado o keikaku suru hito o _____ to iimasu.*
3. *Osake o nomanai paatii o _____ to iimasu.*
4. *Nibanme no paatii o _____ to iimasu.*
5. *Ichiban atarashii karaoke o _____ karaoke to iimasu.*

D. *Tekitoo na joshi o erabinasai.* (Choose the appropriate particle.)

1. *Anata (ni, o) kanji (ni, o) shite moraemasu ka.*
2. *Kyonen made no (ni, to) chigatte mo ii desu yo.*
3. *Ichijikai no hiyoo (wa, ni) kaisha (ni, ga) motsu soo desu.*

4. *Gooka (de, ni) yarimashoo.*
5. *Nenmatsu (de, ni) dare (ka, demo) isogashii (ga, kara) choodo ii desu.*

KOTAE

A. 1. *Nenmatsu ni shimasu.* 2. *Sukoshi shukoo o kaete yooshooku ni shimashita.* 3. *Kaisha ga mochimasu.* 4. *Suzuki-san no ikitsuke no sunakku de karaoke o shimasu.* 5. *Junchoo ni susunde imasu.*
B. 1. *keikaku* 2. *shimashoo* 3. *kaemasu* 4. *shimashoo* 5. *hazu*
C. 1. *boonenkai* 2. *kanji* 3. *sake nashi paatii* 4. *nijikai* 5. *saishinshiki*
D. 1. *ni, o* 2. *to* 3. *wa, ga* 4. *ni* 5. *de, demo, kara*

FUKUSHUU 2

A. *Tekitoo na joshi o irenasai.* (Insert the appropriate particle in the blank.)

1. *Honsha _____ shisha _____ tenkin shite kimashita.*
2. *Kodomo _____ tokai no gakkoo _____ ikasetai _____, ima dekimasen.*
3. *Tsugoo _____ tsukanai toki _____ denwa shimasu.*
4. *Onomimono _____ itsumo no _____ yoroshii desu _____.*
5. *Hito _____ atte, hanashitari suru no _____ suki desu.*
6. *Senmu kara _____ ohanashi demo aru _____, kiku _____ demo kikimashoo.*
7. *Konpyuutaa _____ doonyuu suru jiki _____ kite iru _____ kanjimashita.*
8. *Shuukyoo _____ taishite _____ kangaekata wa oobei no hitotachi _____ chigaimasu.*
9. *Nenmatsu _____ min'na isogashii _____, choodo ii desu yo.*

B. *Tadashii kotoba o erabinasai.* (Choose the appropriate word.)

1. *Buchoo wa niji ni kaeru (keikoku, hazu) desu.*
2. *Sarariiman mo taihen da (kedo, kara), nan to ka yatte iru.*
3. *Norimono ga ugoite inai (ga, kara, kedo), muri desu yo.*
4. *Kongo chuui shimasu (ga, kara), oyurushi kudasai.*
5. *Kawatta mono mo aru (kara, shi, ga), min'na shinsetsu ni oshiete kuremasu.*
6. *Yuujin ga yakuin o shite iru (noni, node), muri shite yoyaku shite moraimasu.*
7. *Karaoke ga nai to suru (to, kara), jikan o mote amashimasu ne.*

C. *Tekitoo na hyoogen o irenasai* (Insert the appropriate expression in the blank.)

1. *Kaisha de _____ (training) shita koto ga arimasu.*
2. *Shizuka na tokoro de seikatsu dekiru kara _____ (envious) desu.*
3. *Sanji no _____ (appointment) ga arimasu.*
4. *Dare ga _____ (apology) ni ikimasu ka.*
5. *_____ (Address) wa doo shirabetara ii desu ka.*
6. *Iroiro na _____ (reasons) ga aru deshoo.*
7. *Toosha no _____ (product) o setsumei sasete kudasai.*
8. *Mazu _____ (commuting problem) ga kanwa saremasu.*
9. *Atarashii koto o _____ (plan) shite kudasai.*
10. *Ichioo _____ (budget) ga aru to omoimasu.*

KOTAE

A. 1. *yori, ni*   2. *o, ni, kara*   3. *ga, ni*   4. *wa, de, ka*   5. *ni, ga*   6. *no, shi, dake*   7. *o, ni, to*   8. *ni, no, to*   9. *de, kara*
B. 1. *hazu*   2. *kedo*   3. *kara*   4. *kara*   5. *shi*   6. *node*   7. *to*
C. 1. *kenshuu*   2. *urayamashii*   3. *yakusoku*   4. *ayamari*   5. *Juusho*
6. *riyuu*   7. *seihin*   8. *tsuukin mondai*   9. *keikaku*   10. *yosan*

SECTION 2
Kanji / Hiragana
Katakana / English

第一課

A. 会話

日本に到着

ビジテック社 ビジネス開発部のネルソン マネージャーは東京支社に転勤になる。
航空会社社員がメッセージをネルソン氏に伝える。

しゃいん：ネルソン様ですね。鈴木様よりメッセージですが。

ネルソン：ああ、そうですか。何でしょうか。

しゃいん：あいにく急用がお出来になって、空港には迎えにいらっしゃ
　　　　　れないそうです。

ネルソン：そうですか。分かりました。

しゃいん：それで、新宿行きのリムジンバスに乗って下さいとのことで
　　　　　す。あちらでお会いになるそうです。

ネルソン：はい。どこでバスに乗れますか。

しゃいん：はい。税関を出たところで切符を買って下さい。その外 外側
　　　　　ですぐ乗れます。

ネルソン：ありがとうございました。

ネルソン氏は問題もなく入国、通関をすませて、ホテルに行くバスを見つける。

ネルソン：すみません。誰か座っていますか。

やまだ：いいえ。誰も。どうぞ。

ネルソン：どうも。新宿までどのぐらいかかりますか。

やまだ：そうですね。一時間半ぐらいでしょう。ホテルはどこですか。

ネルソン：新宿ヒルトンです。

やまだ：ああ、あのヒルトンは便利でいいですね。ちょっと高いですが、
　　　　何にでも近いですから。

ネルソン：なるほど。

やまだ：失礼ですが、日本へはお仕事ですか。

ネルソン：ええ、転勤です。

やまだ：じゃあ、日本支社にお勤めですか。

ネルソン：はい。来週から始めます。

やまだ：どういう関係のお仕事ですか。

ネルソン：コンピューター関係ですが。

やまだ：そうですか。実は私もコンピューター関係の仕事をしているん
　　　　です。これ、私の名刺です。何かありましたら、どうぞ。

ネルソン：はい。山田さん ですね。よろしく。ネルソンといいます。
　　　　これは私のです。

ネルソン氏、ホテルに着く。東京支社の同僚鈴木氏、そこで待つ。

すずき：やあ、ネルソンさん ようこそ。空港まで迎えに行けなくて、
　　　　失礼しました。

ネルソン：いいえ、いいえ、とんでもありません。お久ぶりです、
　　　　鈴木さん。お世話になります。どうぞよろしく。

270

すずき：こちらこそ、よろしく。お疲れじゃありませんか。

ネルソン：ええ、時差の関係でちょっと疲れました。

すずき：実は、夕食でも、と思っていたんですが。

ネルソン：そうですか。じゃあ、そんなに疲れていません。是非、お願いします。

すずき：それじゃあ、チェックインして、少し休んで下さい。八時ごろ迎えに来ますから。

ネルソン氏、ホテルにチェックインする。

クラーク：いらっしゃいませ。

ネルソン：ネルソンですが。先月の始め頃予約しました。

クラーク：少々お待ち下さい。シングルで四泊のご予約ですね。ここにご住所とお名前をお願いします。

ネルソン：禁煙室がありますか。

クラーク：はい、ございます。七階ですが、よろしいですか。

ネルソン：ええ。それから滞在がもっと長くなるかもしれないんですが。

クラーク：そうですか。何泊ぐらいですか。

ネルソン：まだ、はっきり分かりませんが。多分二、三日です。

クラーク：お早めにお知らせ下さい。用意しておきますから。

ネルソン：よろしく。

クラーク：ここにサインをお願いします。

ネルソン：これでいいですか。

クラーク：はい。クレジット カードでお支払いですね。

ネルソン：ええ、これ どうぞ。

B. 単語

到着	*toochaku*	arrival	開発部	*kaihatsubu*	development, department
支社	*shisha*	branch office	転勤	*tenkin*	transfer
航空	*kookuu*	aviation	あいにく	*ainiku*	unfortunately
急用	*kyuuyoo*	urgent matter	外側	*sotogawa*	outside area
はっきり	*hakkiri*	clearly, definitely	空港	*kuukoo*	airport
迎え	*mukae*	meeting, welcoming	税関	*zeikan*	customs
伝える	*tsutaeru*	to convey, to tell	切符	*kippu*	ticket
入国	*nyuukoku*	entering a country	便利な	*benri na*	convenient
勤める	*tsutomeru*	to work	名刺	*meishi*	business card
同僚	*dooryoo*	colleague	世話	*sewa*	care
疲れ	*tsukare*	fatigue	時差	*jisa*	time difference
是非	*zehi*	certainly	禁煙室	*kin'enshitsu*	no-smoking room
滞在	*taizai*	stay	多分	*tabun*	maybe
用意	*yooi*	preparation	支払い	*shiharai*	payment

C. 漢字

Kanji characters have their origins in Chinese characters. They were introduced into the Japanese writing system over one thousand years ago. In modern Japanese there are about 1,945 frequently used characters, which are referred to as *jooyoo kanji* (commonly used *kanji*) by the Japanese Ministry of Education. Though it would be helpful to master all of them, you can get by knowing approximately 1,000 characters. In addition to those introduced in the *"Kanji"* sections of this book, students are encouraged to familiarize themselves with the other characters used throughout the text.

There are several different ways to read *kanji* characters. One way is to use the *kun-yomi* (*kun* reading). The *kun* reading is strictly Japanese in origin and represents the affixing of a Japanese word to a Chinese character with roughly corresponding meaning. Chinese characters were also introduced and pronounced according to their original Chinese sounds, called *on-yomi* (*on*-reading). Such pronunciations were used only as phonetic symbols, in other words, for their sounds. Later they began to be used as meaningful words as well. *On* readings are usually used in compound words (two characters or more), while *kun* readings are usually used for single characters. Note that not all characters have *kun* readings.

The following is given for each *kanji* character:
1. reading: *on* pronunciation in capitals, *kun* pronunciation in italics
2. meaning
3. examples of usage.

様	YOO *sama*	Mr., Ms., Mrs. appearance	ネルソン様 様子	ネルソンさま ようす	Mr. Nelson appearance
何	NAN *nani*	what	何年 何人	なんねん なんにん	how many years how many people
急	KYUU *iso(gu)*	hurry	急用 急ぐ	きゅうよう いそぐ	urgent business to hurry
用	YOO *mochi(iru)*	use	用事 用意 用いる	ようじ ようい もちいる	errand preparation to use
空	KUU *kara* *sora*	air, sky empty *sky*	空港 空手 空気	くうこう からて くうき	airport "karate" air
港	KOO *minato*	*port*	空港 港	くうこう みなと	airport port
迎	GEI *mukae(ru)*	welcome	歓迎 迎える	かんげい むかえる	welcome to welcome
税	ZEI	tax	税関 税金	ぜいかん ぜいきん	customs tax
関	KAN	relation	関係	かんけい	relation
買	BAI *ka(u)*	buy	売買 買う	ばいばい かう	selling and buying to buy
事	JI *koto*	thing	事業 事実 事件 仕事	じぎょう じじつ じけん しごと	business fact incident work

実	JITSU	truth	実は	じつは	in fact
			実力	じつりょく	capability
名	MEI	name	有名な	ゆうめいな	famous
	na		名刺	めいし	business card
			名前	なまえ	name
時	JI	time	時間	じかん	time
	toki		あの時	あのとき	that time
間	KAN	interval	一週間	いっしゅうかん	one week
	aida		夏の間	なつのあいだ	during the summer
都	TO	capital	東京都	とうきょうと	metropolitan Tokyo
	miyako		京都	きょうと	Kyoto

練習問題

A. 次の文章を英語に訳しなさい。(Translate the following sentences into English.)

   1. どういう関係のお仕事ですか。

   2. 空港から新宿まで何時間かかりますか。

   3. 七階ですがよろしいですか。

   4. クレジットカードは大変便利です。

B. 日本語で書きなさい。(Write in Japanese.)

   1. Are you on business?

   2. Pleased to meet you.

   3. Nice to meet you. (lit. I will need your kindness.)

   4. Is this okay?

答え

A. 1. What kind of work do you do? 2. How long does it take from the airport to Shinjuku? 3. It is on the 7th floor. Is that okay with you? 4. Credit cards are very convenient.

B. 1. お仕事ですか。 2. どうぞよろしく。 3. お世話になります。 4. これでいいで すか。

第二課
だいにか

A. 会話
かいわ

ネルソン氏の初日
しょにち

東京での最初の週末が過ぎて、月曜日になった。ネルソン氏は仕事を始めなければならない。興奮しながらも、緊張して会社に行く。

ネルソン：ああ、このビルだ。さあ、頑張らなくちゃ。何階かな。すみません。ビジテック社は何階でしょうか。

さとう：七階です。私もそこへ行きますから。

ネルソン：ああ、そうですか。ビジテックの方ですか。

さとう：はい、そうです。佐藤と申します。

ネルソン：ああ、佐藤裕子さんですね。私はネルソンです。電話で何回か話しましたね。

さとう：ああ、そうでしたね。どうも。いつ日本にいらっしゃったんですか。

ネルソン：先週の金曜日です。

さとう：そうですか。じゃあ、お疲れでしょう。

ネルソン：ちょっとばかり。でも大丈夫です。旅行はなれていますから。

さとう：あまり無理をしないで下さい。じゃあ行きましょうか。

ビジテック社に着くと、佐藤嬢はネルソン氏を鈴木氏の事務所に案内する。

すずき：ネルソンさん、ようこそ。事務所はすぐ分かりましたか。

ネルソン：はい、佐藤さんが案内してくれました。

すずき：それはよかったですね。9時にみんなに会議室に集まってもらっています。その前にコーヒーでもいかがですか。

ネルソン：いいえ、結構です。

すずき：じゃあ、行きましょうか。

会議室で。

すずき：皆さん、すみません。今度本社から転勤のネルソンさんをご紹介します。営業を担当してもらいます。

ネルソン：ネルソンです。始めまして。コロラド州出身です。イリノイ大学を卒業して、本社ではずっと開発部で仕事をしてきました。皆さんと大いに頑張りたいと思います。どうぞよろしくお願いします。

ぜんいん：どうぞよろしく。（拍手）

ネルソン氏、高木事業部長に挨拶に行く。

ネルソン：高木部長、お久しぶりです。

たかぎ：やあ、ネルソン君、ようこそ。本社の方々は皆さんお元気ですか。

ネルソン：はい、何かと忙しくしています。

たかぎ：それはよかった。君のアシスタントを紹介しましょう。彼女と協力して、やって下さい。飯田君、ちょっと。ネルソン君、飯田君です。

いいだ：アシスタントの飯田です。大学を出たばかりで、新入社員です。どうぞよろしくお願いいたします。

ネルソン：こちらこそ。大学を出て、始めての仕事ですか。

いいだ：はい。でも父の会社でアルバイトを少ししたことはありますが。

ネルソン：ああ、そう。何の会社ですか。

いいだ：おもちゃの会社です。企画部の手伝いをしました。とても勉強になりました。

ネルソン：大学では何かクラブ活動でもやってましたか。

いいだ：はい。マーケティング部に入っていました。

ネルソン：なるほど。それは実践的ですね。私はゴルフ部に入っていましたが、あまり実践的じゃありませんでした。でもあちらこちらへ行くことができて、よかったですよ。

いいだ：じゃあ、ゴルフがお上手なんですね。

ネルソン：いや、最近忙しくて、あまりやってませんから、駄目です。

いいだ：私も近いうちにゴルフを習いたいと思っています。いろいろ教えて下さい。どうぞよろしく。

B. 単語

初日	shonichi	first day	週末	shuumatsu	weekend
興奮	koofun	excitement	緊張	kinchoo	nervousness
頑張る	ganbaru	to persevere	先週	senshuu	last week
旅行	ryokoo	travel	無理な	muri na	impossible
着く	tsuku	to arrive	事務所	jimusho	office
案内	an'nai	guidance	会議室	kaigishitsu	meeting room
集まる	atsumaru	to assemble	結構な	kekkoo na	fine, good
本社	honsha	head office	紹介	shookai	introduction
営業	eigyoo	sales	担当する	tantoo suru	to be in charge of
出身	shusshin	hometown	卒業	sotsugyoo	graduate
事業	jigyoo	business	部長	buchoo	department head
挨拶	aisatsu	greeting	協力	kyooryoku	cooperation
新入社員	shin'nyuushain	new employee	企画部	kikakubu	planning department
手伝い	tetsudai	help	実践的	jissenteki	practical
活動	katsudoo	activity			

278

C. 漢字

階	KAI	floor	二階 三階	にかい さんかい	second floor third floor
社	SHA	association	会社 社会	かいしゃ しゃかい	company society
電	DEN	electricity	電話 電気	でんわ でんき	telephone electricity
話	WA *hanashi*	talk	会話 話題	かいわ わだい	conversation topics
先	SEN *saki*	priority future previous	先生 先週 先月 先見 行き先	せんせい せんしゅう せんげつ せんけん ゆきさき	teacher last week last month foresight destination
週	SHUU	week	週末 来週	しゅうまつ らいしゅう	weekend next week
金	KIN *kane*	gold money	現金 金融 お金	げんきん きんゆう おかね	cash finance money
旅	RYO *tabi*	travel	旅行 旅館 旅行 代理店	りょこう りょかん りょこう だいりてん	travel inn travel agency
無	MU *na(i)*	none	無理な 無駄な 無い	むりな むだな ない	impossible wasteful none
今	KON, KO *ima*	now	今度 今年 今	こんど ことし いま	this time this year now

279

度	DO	degree, time	二度	にど	two times
	tabi		程度	ていど	degree, extent
			度々	たびたび	frequently
転	TEN	turn, change	転勤	てんきん	transfer
	koro(bu)		自転車	じてんしゃ	bicycle
			転ぶ	ころぶ	to fall
営	EI	manage	営業	えいぎょう	business
	itona(mu)		経営	けいえい	management
			営む	いとなむ	to conduct (business)
業	GYOO	vocation	職業	しょくぎょう	occupation
		trade	業務	ぎょうむ	business

練習問題

A. 日本語で書きなさい。(Write the following in Japanese.)

1. When did you come to Japan?

2. I am used to traveling.

3. Please do not overwork yourself.

4. I am from the state of Colorado.

B. 英語に訳しなさい。(Translate into English.)

1. 住所と名前をお願いします。

2. 部屋を用意しましょう。

3. 何でお支払いですか。

C. 次をte-formを使って文にしなさい。(Write the following sentences in Japanese using the "te-form.")

1. I am watching the game.

2. I am waiting for a friend.

3. What are you doing here?

4. Do you remember Department Manager Takagi's letter?

5. Do you know Mr. Suzuki?

D. 次の名刺を日本語にしなさい。 (Translate the following business card into Japanese.)

Busi Tech, Inc.

Planning and Development Dept.

Ed Nelson, Manager

Address: 111 Wilshire Blvd., L.A., CA 90011

答え

A. 1. いつ日本にいらっしゃいましたか。 2. 旅行になれています。 3. あまり無理を
しないで下さい。 4. コロラド州出身です。
B. 1. Please write your name and address. 2. We'll prepare a room for you.
3. How will you be paying?
C. 1. ゲームを見ています。 2. 友人を待っています。 3. ここで何をしていますか。
4. 高木部長の手紙を覚えていますか。 5. 鈴木さんを知っていますか。
D.

ビジテック 会社

開発部企画課

課長 エド・ネルソン

住所 111 Wilshire Blvd., L.A., CA 90011

第三課

A. 会話

住宅事情

ホテルに一週間滞在してネルソン氏、マンションを借りることにする。まず
鈴木氏に相談する。

ネルソン：早速アパートを探したいんですが。いい所がありますか。

すずき：そうですね。アパートを借りるなら、事務所からあまり遠くな
　　　　く、電車や地下鉄の駅から近い所を探した方がいいですね。

ネルソン：会社から電車か地下鉄で三十分ぐらいの所にはありませんか。

すずき：無理でしょうね。どんなアパートを探しているんですか。

ネルソン：家賃によりますが、3LDKがほしいですね。でも東京はすごく
　　　　　高いらしいですね。

すずき：ええ、普通のは月十五万円ぐらいです。ちょっといいアパート
　　　　は「マンション」と言うんですが、ちょっと高いのは百万円もし
　　　　ます。

ネルソン：百万円ですか。一万ドルですね。私はそんなのはいりません。
　　　　　普通でいいですが、通勤に便利な所がいいですね。

すずき：分かりました。知り合いの不動産屋にいくつか調べてもらいま
　　　　しょう。

ネルソン：どうも。それは助かります。

次の日、不動産屋よりネルソン氏に電話がある。

よしだ：品川不動産の吉田です。鈴木様からお電話するように言われま
　　　　した。マンションをお探しのようで。

ネルソン：はい。

よしだ：それで東京のどの辺がよろしいでしょうか。

ネルソン：会社から三十分から一時間ぐらいの所で、十五万円から
　　　　二十万円ぐらいのを考えています。

よしだ：どのぐらいのサイズを。

ネルソン：3LDKがほしいんですが、2LDKでもいいです。

よしだ：住宅事情は大分よくなっていますから、探せるでしょう。

ネルソン：それはありがたいですね。狭くても新しいのがいいですね。
　　　　新しい2LDKなら、古い3LDKよりいいです。

よしだ：分かりました。いくつか当たってみます。明日にでも適当なの
　　　　をファックスしますから。

ネルソン：よろしくお願いします。

次の日、マンションのリストを受け取り、二物件を見に行く。

ネルソン：これはさっき見たのより安いですね。

よしだ：ええ、これは十六万五千円です。都心からちょっと遠いですか
　　　　ら、安くなるわけです。

ネルソン：近くの駅まで何分ですか。

よしだ：歩いて五分です。それから東京駅までは三十分しかかからない
　　　　そうです。悪くないと思います。

ネルソン：そうですね。たしかに明るいし。それにおしゃれですね。近
　　　　くにレストランや店もあって、とてもいい場所ですね。何年ものて
　　　　すか。

よしだ：はっきり分かりませんが、二年以内だと思います。はっきりし
　　　　たことを調べましょうか。

ネルソン：いいえ、いいです。

ネルソン氏がほとんど決めようとした時、突然部屋が動き出した。

ネルソン：わあ、地震ですか。

よしだ：いいえ。電車でしょう。

ネルソン：電車ですか。線路から近いんですか。

よしだ：そのようですね。

振動が止まる。

よしだ：電車の音が欠点ですね。駄目ですね。

ネルソン：いいえ。そうとは言えません。家主さんにもっと安くならな
　　　　　いか交渉してもらえますか。

よしだ：はい、やってみましょう。

ネルソン：敷金三ヵ月、礼金一ヵ月、家賃が十四万円なら、借りるかも
　　　　　しれません。

よしだ：本当ですか。

ネルソン：本当に何か自分の家のような気がしてきました。

B．単語

住宅	juutaku	housing	事情	jijoo	circumstances
借りる	kariru	to borrow	相談	soodan	consultation
早速	sassoku	immediately	探す	sagasu	to search
地下鉄	chikatetsu	subway	普通の	futsuu no	normal
所	tokoro	place	家賃	yachin	rent
通勤	tsuukin	commute	知り合い	shiriai	acquaintance
不動産	fudoosan	real estate	調べる	shiraberu	to look up, investigate

辺	hen	area	狭い	semai	narrow
当たる	ataru	to check out, hit	適当な	tekitoo na	appropriate
受け取る	uketoru	to receive	二物件	futabukken	two homes
都心	toshin	downtown	安い	yasui	cheap
明るい	akarui	bright	突然	totsuzen	suddenly
地震	jishin	earthquake	線路	senro	train tracks
振動	shindoo	vibration	欠点	ketten	weak point
家主	yanushi	landlord	交渉	kooshoo	negotiation
敷金	shikikin	security deposit	礼金	reikin	key money
自分	jibun	own, personal			

C. 漢字

不	FU BU	non-	不便 不利	ふべん ふり	inconvenient disadvantageous
便	BEN	convenient	便利 便所	べんり べんじょ	convenient toilet, bathroom
探	TAN saga(su)	search	探検 探す	たんけん さがす	exploration to look for
環	KAN	ring	環境 環状	かんきょう かんじょう	environment loop
境	KYOO	border	境界 国境	きょうかい こっきょう	boundary border
通	TSUU too(ru)	pass	通勤 通信 通る	つうきん つうしん とおる	commuting communication to pass
勤	KIN tsuto(meru)	work	勤務 勤める	きんむ つとめる	working to work for
会	KAI a(u)	meeting	開会 社会 会う	かいかい しゃかい あう	opening a meeting society to meet

車	SHA *kuruma*	vehicle	自動車 電車 車	じどうしゃ でんしゃ くるま	automobile train car
地	CHI	earth	地下鉄 土地 地球	ちかてつ とち ちきゅう	subway land the earth
家	KA, YA *ie, uchi*	house	家族 家賃 家 家	かぞく やちん いえ うち	family rent house home
東	TOO *higashi*	east	東京 東部 東	とうきょう とうぶ ひがし	Tokyo the East east
動	DOO *ugo (ku)*	move	不動産 動く	ふどうさん うごく	real estate to move
屋	YA	shop, person	不動産屋 パン屋	ふどうさんや パンや	realtor bakery

練習問題

A. 英語に訳しなさい。 (Translate into English.)

1. 地下鉄か電車で一時間ぐらいの所に探せますか。

2. 家賃はかなり高いんでしょう。

3. 環境とか通勤時間を考えると、このアパートはなかなかいいですね。

B. (1), (2), (3), (4)に適当な日本語の言葉を書きなさい。 (Write the appropriate Japanese word for [1], [2], [3], and [4].)

286

家屋マンション賃貸契約書 (Rental Contract)

家屋住所 (Address)
所有者 (Owner)
賃貸者 (Renter)
保証人 (Guarantor)
契約期間 (Contract Period)
(1) (Rent Amount)
(2) (Deposit)
(3) (Key Money)
その他の条件 (Other Items)
(4) 会社 (Realty Agency)
取り扱い者 (Realtor)

答え

A. 1. Can you (or we) find a place within one hour by subway or train?
2. The rent must be fairly high. 3. Considering the location and the
commuting time, this apartment is pretty good.

B. 1. 家賃 2. 敷金 3. 礼金 4. 不動産

第四課
<ruby>第<rt>だい</rt></ruby><ruby>四<rt>よん</rt></ruby><ruby>課<rt>か</rt></ruby>

A. 会話
<ruby>会話<rt>かいわ</rt></ruby>

警察に尋問される
<ruby>警察<rt>けいさつ</rt></ruby>に<ruby>尋問<rt>じんもん</rt></ruby>される

<ruby>東京<rt>とうきょう</rt></ruby>に<ruby>来<rt>き</rt></ruby>てまだ<ruby>間<rt>ま</rt></ruby>もないので、ネルソン<ruby>氏<rt>し</rt></ruby>は<ruby>間違<rt>まちが</rt></ruby>えて、<ruby>二<rt>ふた</rt></ruby>つ<ruby>前<rt>まえ</rt></ruby>の<ruby>駅<rt>えき</rt></ruby>で<ruby>電車<rt>でんしゃ</rt></ruby>を<ruby>降<rt>お</rt></ruby>りた。

ネルソン：ここはつつじが<ruby>丘<rt>おか</rt></ruby>じゃないんですか。

えきいん：つつじが<ruby>丘<rt>おか</rt></ruby>は<ruby>次<rt>つぎ</rt></ruby>の<ruby>次<rt>つぎ</rt></ruby>です。<ruby>次<rt>つぎ</rt></ruby>の<ruby>電車<rt>でんしゃ</rt></ruby>は11<ruby>時<rt>じ</rt></ruby>25<ruby>分<rt>ふん</rt></ruby>です。

ネルソン：<ruby>三十分後<rt>さんじゅっぷんご</rt></ruby>ですか。じゃ、<ruby>歩<rt>ある</rt></ruby>いた<ruby>方<rt>ほう</rt></ruby>が<ruby>早<rt>はや</rt></ruby>いですか。

えきいん：<ruby>二十分<rt>にじゅっぷん</rt></ruby>ぐらいかかりますが。

ネルソン：まっすぐ<ruby>行<rt>い</rt></ruby>くんですね。

えきいん：ええ、まっすぐです。<ruby>分<rt>わ</rt></ruby>かりやすいです。<ruby>今<rt>いま</rt></ruby>の<ruby>時間<rt>じかん</rt></ruby>はタクシーもなかなか<ruby>来<rt>き</rt></ruby>ませんし。

ネルソン：どうも。<ruby>歩<rt>ある</rt></ruby>いてみます。

<ruby>十分後<rt>じゅっぷんご</rt></ruby>、ネルソン<ruby>氏<rt>し</rt></ruby>は<ruby>警察官<rt>けいさつかん</rt></ruby>に<ruby>呼<rt>よ</rt></ruby>びかけられる。

けいさつかん：もしもし、<ruby>今<rt>いま</rt></ruby>ごろどこへ<ruby>行<rt>い</rt></ruby>くんですか。

ネルソン：つつじが<ruby>丘<rt>おか</rt></ruby>に<ruby>行<rt>い</rt></ruby>きたいんですが、<ruby>道<rt>みち</rt></ruby>に<ruby>迷<rt>まよ</rt></ruby>ったらしいんです。

けいさつかん：そこに<ruby>泊<rt>と</rt></ruby>まっているんですか。

ネルソン：はい。

けいさつかん：<ruby>旅行者<rt>りょこうしゃ</rt></ruby>ですか。

ネルソン：いいえ。<ruby>最近<rt>さいきん</rt></ruby>アメリカから<ruby>引<rt>ひ</rt></ruby>っ<ruby>越<rt>こ</rt></ruby>してきました。

けいさつかん：つつじが丘まではまだ大分ありますよ。外国人登録証を持っていますか。

ネルソン：日本に着いたばかりでまだ取っていませんが。

けいさつかん：それは困りましたね。何か身分証明書のようなものはありませんか。

ネルソン：ああ、パスポートがあります。これどうぞ。

けいさつかん：はい、ネルソンさんですか。ワシントン州に住んでいたんですね。今お仕事は。

ネルソン：ビジテック社の日本支社に勤めている普通のサラリーマンです。

けいさつかん：会社の住所は。

ネルソン：新青山ビルです。何かあったんですか。

けいさつかん：実は最近は泥棒とか覗きなどの事件がありまして。

ネルソン：そうですか。この辺は安全だと聞いていますが。

けいさつかん：でも気をつけないといけませんよ。

ネルソン：分かりました。どうも。

けいさつかん：もう遅いし、危ないから、送りましょう。どうぞ後に乗って下さい。

ネルソン：そうですか。すみませんね。本当に助かります。

けいさつかん：日本にいつ来たんですか。

ネルソン：先週です。

けいさつかん：でも日本語がよくできますね。

ネルソン：学生時代に奈良に二年ほど住んでいました。その時に日本語を習いました。

けいさつかん：奈良は静かでしょうが、東京はうるさいでしょう。

ネルソン：ええ。でも東京はイベントがいろいろあったりで、楽しいです。ところで、この辺には楽しい所はないんですか。

けいさつかん：カラオケぐらいですね。やはり新宿でしょう。あそこには楽しいものが何でもありますよ。

ネルソン：じゃあ今度行ってみます。

けいさつかん：でも、いろいろ誘惑があるから、気をつけて下さい。

ネルソン：はい。ああ、そこの角です。どうもご親切にありがとうございました。

けいさつかん：いいえ。早いうちに外国人登録証を取って下さい。区役所ですぐできますから。

B. 単語

駅員	ekiin	station employee	警察官	keisatsukan	police officer
警察	keisatsu	police	尋問	jinmon	interrogation
間違える	machigaeru	to make a mistake	待つ	matsu	to wait
帰る	kaeru	to return	自転車	jitensha	bicycle
乗る	noru	to ride	迷う	mayou	to become lost
泊まる	tomaru	to stay at	旅行者	ryokoosha	vacationer
最近	saikin	recently	引っ越す	hikkosu	to move (residence)
外国人	gaikokujin	foreigner	登録証	toorokushoo	registration card
持つ	motsu	to have, hold	困る	komaru	to be troubled
身分	mibun	social status	証明書	shoomeisho	identification card
住所	juusho	address	泥棒	doroboo	thief
覗く	nozoku	to peep, glance	事件	jiken	incident
安全な	anzen na	safe	遅い	osoi	late
危ない	abunai	dangerous	送る	okuru	to send
習う	narau	to learn	静かな	shizuka na	quiet
誘惑	yuuwaku	temptation	角	kado	corner
親切な	shinsetsu na	kind	区役所	kuyakusho	ward office

C. 漢字

行	KOO, GYOO	go	旅行	りょこう	travel
	i(ku)	carry out	銀行	ぎんこう	bank
			行事	ぎょうじ	event
	okona(u)		行く	いく	to go
			行なう	おこなう	to carry out
来	RAI	come	来年	らいねん	next year
	ku(ru)		来る	くる	to come
道	DOO, TOO		道具	どうぐ	tool
	michi	street, way	道路	どうろ	road
			神道	しんとう	Shinto
			道	みち	street
外	GAI	outside	外国人	がいこくじん	foreigner
	soto, hoka		海外	かいがい	overseas
			外出	がいしゅつ	going out
国	KOKU	country	国内	こくない	domestic
	kuni		国際	こくさい	international
			国	くに	country
登	TOO	climb	登録証	とうろくしょう	registration card
	nobo(ru)		登る	のぼる	to climb
持	JI	hold	持参する	じさんする	to take with
			気持	きもち	feeling
	motsu		持つ	もつ	to have, hold
困	KON	be in trouble	困難	こんなん	difficulty
	koma(ru)		困る	こまる	to have difficulty
身	SHIN	body	身長	しんちょう	height
	mi		身分	みぶん	social status
			身分証明書	みぶんしょうめいしょ	identification card
州	SHUU	state	ワシントン州	ワシントンしゅう	Washington State
		province	アルバータ州	アルバータしゅう	Province of Alberta

住	JUU	live	住所	じゅうしょ	address
	su(mu)		住宅	じゅうたく	housing
			住む	すむ	live
所	SHO	place	場所	ばしょ	location
	tokoro		所	ところ	place
新	SHIN	new	新聞	しんぶん	newspaper
	atara(shii)		新しい	あたらしい	new
安	AN	peacefulness	安全	あんぜん	safety
	yasu(i)	inexpensive	安心	あんしん	peace of mind
			安い	やすい	inexpensive

練習問題

A. 次を日本語で書きなさい。 (Write the following in Japanese.)

1. I moved here recently from the United States.

2. Do you have any form of identification?

3. What is your occupation now?

4. When I was a student, I lived in Nara for about two years.

5. Thank you for your kindness.

B. 次の下線の漢字をひらがなで書きなさい。 (Write the following underlined *kanji* in hiragana.)

1. 今ごろどこへ行きますか。

2. 外国人登録証を持っていますか。

3. ワシントン州に住んでいました。

4. 住所は何ですか。

5. 安全ときいていました。

答え

A. 1. 最近アメリカから引っ越してきました。 2. 何か身分証明書のような
ものがありますか。 3. 今、お仕事は（何ですか）。 4. 学生時代に奈良に
二年ほど住んでいました。 5. どうもご親切にありがとうございました。
B. 1. いま、い 2. がいこくじんとうろくしょう、も 3. しゅう、す 4. じゅ
うしょ、なん 5. あんぜん

第五課

A. 会話

マーケティングについての話し合い

ネルソン氏がビジテック社の新しい電子メールのソフトについて話すことになっている。高木部長との話し合いに行く途中、鈴木氏とネルソン氏はマーケティングについて話す。

すずき：マーケティング案を見せてもらいました。 JT社に是非とも協力してもらうことが必要なようですね。

ネルソン：そう思いませんか。JT社は電子メールソフトの販売上、絶対必要なパートナーになると思います。

すずき：あっ、ここです。

マーケティング部のスタッフが高木部長の部屋ですでに待っている。

たかぎ：ネルソン君、日本の生活は如何ですか。

ネルソン：東京に着いたばかりですから、まだ珍しいことばかりです。

たかぎ：すぐ慣れますよ。マンションはどう。我慢できるかね。

ネルソン：はい、できます。狭いですが、便利にできていますね。朝なんか顔を洗いながら、朝ご飯も料理できます。

たかぎ：あっはは、なるほど。じゃあ、会議を始めましょうか。ネルソン君、スーパーメールのマーケティングのしかたについて、君の考えを話してもらえますか。

ネルソン：えーと、マーケティング プランをつくる前に、まずお客さんを考えていろいろ調査する必要があると思います。大企業に焦点を合わせて販売するか、中小企業を優先するかを考える必要があります。それからどんなビジネスで、どれぐらい社内連絡が行われているかも知らなければなりません。その我々の選んだマーケットにより、戦略が違ってくると思います。

さとう：それにまだいくつかの問題があると思いますが、それも調べる必要があるんじゃないかと思いますが。例えば、日本の企業にはかなり沢山の年輩の人が高い位置についていて、社内連絡に電子メールを使うことにかなり抵抗することも考えられます。マーケティング キャンペーンをする際にこのことも考慮する必要があるんじゃないでしょうか。

ネルソン：はい、全くそうです。しかもこれらの年輩の人たちがふつう買うか買わないか決めるわけですから。

たかぎ：環境保護のことも忘れないように。電子メールを使えば、かなりの紙を使わなくてもよくなる。この点は多くの日本の会社にとって大事なことと思う。

ネルソン：ごもっともです。

たかぎ：この製品を支店や子会社を通して大いに売りたいもんだ。それに代理店にも協力してもらって販売を進めた方がいいと思う。

ネルソン：特別な代理店を考えていらっしゃいますか。

たかぎ：やはり豊田商事の子会社のJT社がいいだろう。日本中にとても強いセールス ネットワークを持っているからね。

ネルソン：佐藤さんにもっと調べてもらいましょう。

たかぎ：その必要はない。クラスメートが勤めていて、もう話がして
　　　ある。

ネルソン：そうですか。じゃあ、仕事がしやすいですね。

たかぎ：契約する前にマーケティングマネージャーと話してもらいたい。
　　　彼らのマーケティングのしかたが我々の歩調と合うかどうか確かめ
　　　てもらいたいんだ。平井君から連絡があるはずだから。

ネルソン：はい、分かりました。

たかぎ：じゃあ、ありがとう。

B. 単語

電子	denshi	electron, electric	話す	hanasu	to talk
話し合い	hanashiai	discussion	途中	tochuu	in the middle of
如何	ikaga	how	珍しい	mezurashii	uncommon
慣れる	nareru	to get used to	安心	anshin	relief
我慢	gaman	patience, endurance	客	kyaku	customer
調査	choosa	investigation	大企業	daikigyoo	large corporations
焦点	shooten	focus	中小	chuushoo	mid and small (size)
優先	yuusen	priority	社内	shanai	within a company
連絡	renraku	contact	行なう	okonau	to perform, take place
我々	wareware	we	選ぶ	erabu	to choose
戦略	senryaku	strategy	地位	chii	position, rank
抵抗	teikoo	resistence	考慮	kooryo	consideration
製品	seihin	product	点	ten	point
方法	hoohoo	way	通信	tsuushin	communication
世界中	sekaijuu	all over the world	強調	kyoochoo	emphasis
保護	hogo	protection	環境	kankyoo	environment
子会社	kogaisha	subsidiary	大事な	daiji na	important
進める	susumeru	to proceed	代理店	dairiten	distributor, agency
歩調	hochoo	pace	契約	keiyaku	contract

296

迷	MEI *mayo(u)*	get lost	迷路 迷う	めいろ まよう	maze to get lost
是	ZE	right	是非	ぜひ	by all means
非	HI	wrong	非常	ひじょう	extreme, emergency
協	KYOO	cooperation	協力 協会	きょうりょく きょうかい	cooperation association
力	RYOKU *chikara*	power	学力 力	がくりょく ちから	scholastic ability power
必	HITSU *kanara(zu)*	certain	必要 必ず	ひつよう かならず	need by all means
販	HAN	sell	販売	はんばい	selling
売	BAI *u(ru)*	sell	売買 売る	ばいばい うる	buying and selling to sell
部	BU HE	part, department	部長 販売部 部分 部屋	ぶちょう はんばいぶ ぶぶん へや	department head sales department part room
長	CHOO *naga(i)*	long, chief	課長 長い	かちょう ながい	section head long
生	SEI *i(kiru)* *u(mareru)*	life	生活 生きる 生まれる	せいかつ いきる うまれる	daily life to live to be born
活	KATSU	activity	活動	かつどう	activities
慣	KAN *nare(ru)*	get used to	習慣 慣れる	しゅうかん なれる	custom to get used to

違	I	difference	相違	そうい	difference
	chiga(u)		違う	ちがう	to differ, be wrong
我	GA	myself	我慢	がまん	patience, endurance
	ware		我々	われわれ	we

練習問題

A. 次を日本語で書きなさい。(Write the following in Japanese.)

1. I've come to enjoy the Japanese way of life.

2. Do you find Tokyo very different from Nara?

3. We need to do (more) research into our customer (base).

4. Let's not forget about environmental protection.

B. 次の下線の漢字をひらがなで書きなさい。 (Write the following underlined *kanji* in hiragana.)

1. 是非とも協力しましょう。
2. 絶対必要なパートナーです。
3. 大企業に販売しましょう。
4. 高木部長はもう待っています。
5. もう生活に慣れました。

答え

A. 1. 日本の生活が好きになったんです。 2. 東京は奈良と大分違います か。 3. お客さんを考えて、調査する必要があります。 4. 環境保護のこと を忘れないように。

B. 1. ぜひ、きょうりょく 2. ひつよう 3. はんばい 4. ぶちょう
5. せいかつ、な

日本語学習者と敬語

日本語を学ぶ学生や一般の人々が最近どんどん増えています。年齢的にも十代から四十代五十代までの学習者がいます。勉強のしかたにも、楽しく学習している人、苦労している人、などいろいろいるようです。そう言った学習者の中には、他の言語と比べて日本語はかなり難しいという人が多くいます。

学習者は日本語の発音はやさしいが、文法と漢字が難しいと言います。そしてかなり日本語を使いこなせる上級学習者も敬語で時々困ると言います。確かに発音はスペイン語やイタリア語（大抵の学習者はスペイン語やイタリア語の言葉をいくつか知っているものとして）などとよく似ているし、それほど苦労もしないでしょう。文法はどうでしょう。これはいろいろ意見もあるようですが、最初の何か月かは誰でも苦労するようです。しかし、一旦原則を覚えてしまえば、それほどむずかしくもない、というのがすでに学習した多くの人々の感想です。

では、漢字はどうでしょう。沢山の漢字を覚えるのは時間がかかるし、一旦覚えてもすぐ忘れることも多いです。しかも例外が多くて、似たような漢字がたくさんあることは事実です。しかし、どの言語を勉強するにしても、綴りを覚えなければならないし、多くの言語は発音通りの綴りではありません。ですから、毎日の生活に必要な漢字の読みだけなら、何とか学べるでしょう。

さて、かなり上手に日本語を話す人の多くは敬語が難しいと言いますが、なぜではうか。日本語を子供の時から話していない学習者には、日本の

上下関係や内と外の関係などは全く新しい考え方であるからでしょう。したがって、理論は分かっても使うことになるとそうは簡単ではないということです。大体上下関係などあまり気にしないで育ってきているわけですから、こういう考え方を「実行」するのは容易ではないはずです。

では外国人にその敬語が必要でしょうか。これについては必要だと主張する人、必要ではないという両極端の意見があって、それぞれにポイントがあります。必要と考える人は「敬語は人を思う優しさだ」と言います。必要ないという人は「敬語は自己表現の障害だ」と主張します。これからも議論される話題となりそうです。

上下関係や内と外の関係などは全く新しい考え方であるからでしょう。したがって、理論は分かっても使うことになるとそうは簡単ではないということです。大体上下関係などあまり気にしないで育ってきているわけですから、こういう考え方を「実行」するのは容易ではないはずです。

では外国人にその敬語が必要でしょうか。これについては必要だと主張する人、必要ではないという両極端の意見があって、それぞれにポイントがあります。必要と考える人は「敬語は人を思う優しさだ」と言います。必要ないという人は「敬語は自己表現の障害だ」と主張します。これからも議論される話題となりそうです。

単語

敬語	けいご	honorifics
学習者	がくしゅうしゃ	learner, student
年齢的	ねんれいてき	age-wise
苦労	くろう	hardship, trouble
言語	げんご	language
発音	はつおん	pronunciation
文法	ぶんぽう	grammar
使いこなせる	つかいこなせる	to be able to use fully
上級	じょうきゅう	advanced
確か(に)	たしか(に)	definite(ly), certainly
似ている	にている	to resemble
一旦	いったん	once
原則	げんそく	prinicples
感想	かんそう	impression
例外	れいがい	exception
綴り	つづり	spelling
上下	じょうげ	upper and lower
関係	かんけい	relationship
内	うち	inside
外	そと	outside
理論	りろん	theory, logic, reason
育つ	そだつ	to be raised
実行	じっこう	to actually do
容易な	よういな	easy
主張する	しゅちょうする	to insist, to emphasize
両極端	りょうきょくたん	both extremes
優しい	やさしい	gentle, tender, nice, polite
自己表現	じこひょうげん	self-expression
障害	しょうがい	barrier
議論	ぎろん	argument
話題	わだい	subject, topic

第六課

A. 会話

戦略会議

お昼の弁当のお金を払うため並んで待っている間に、ネルソン氏と鈴木氏は日本の消費者のお金の使い方がアメリカと違うことについてちょっと話す。
事務所に戻って、みんなと集まって、弁当を食べながら話し合う。

ネルソン：あのう、きょうは最近の消費者のトレンドについて、皆さんのお考えをお聞きしたいんですが。

すずき：最近変わったような気がしますが。

ネルソン：そうですか。例えばどういうことですか。

すずき：皆よく考えて、ものを買うようになったと思います。

ネルソン：前はどうだったんですか。

すずき：あまり考えないで、好きなものをどんどん買っていました。

ネルソン：なるほどね。その傾向はある年代だけのことですか、それとも全般的ですか。

すずき：20代から50代まででかなり広いようですが。

ネルソン：佐藤さん、日本で洋服とか旅行にお金をたくさん使うのは若い女性だと聞いているけど。

さとう：ええ、そうなんです。結婚する前に二三年仕事をして、そしてもらったお金を自由に使っているようです。

ネルソン：どうしてそんなに使えるんですか。

さとう：就職してからも両親と一緒に住んでいて、生活費がかかりませんから。

301

ネルソン：なるほど。男性はどうなんですか。

さとう：最近は男性もお金を使うようになったそうですよ。

ネルソン：ええと。忘れないように、ボードに書きましょうか。値段と
　　　品質の関係はどうですか。

さとう：前は「高くてもいいものを」という考えでしたが、最近は「い
　　　いものを安く」という考え方になったようです。

ネルソン：なるほど。アメリカは大分前からそうです。

すずき：佐藤さんだったら、どんな製品を買いますか。

さとう：そうですね。私はやはり安くて質のいいもの、それに信用がで
　　　きるものを買います。

ネルソン：それはずいぶん難しいんじゃないですか。

さとう：それはそうですが、最近は雑誌などで安くて、質がよくて、
　　　信用できるものが割合簡単に見つかりますよ。

ネルソン：質と信用ね。そう、日本では信用が特に大切なんですね。

さとう：流行を追う人もまだいますけどね。

ネルソン：あ、いわゆるネームブランドを好む人もいる訳ですね。

さとう：まだかなり。ただコンピューターなどはまだ品質が第一のよう
　　　です。

ネルソン：我々の製品を買ってくれるのは企業や役所ですから、そのこ
　　　とを考えた方が現実的ですね。

すずき：企業などは値段より品質とサービスが大切ですね。

ネルソン：やっぱりね。ちょっとまとめてみますと、品質、信用、サービスが大切で、企業などは値段は高くても、ものがよければいいということですね。だが個人はできるだけ安い方がいい。

すずき：さすがですね。よくまとめましたね。これからはネルソンさんに会議のメモをお願いしましょうか。

ネルソン：とんでもありません。ところで消費者のトレンドとちょっと関係があるんですが、ハイテクのトレードショーが幕張メッセというところであるんですが、行ってみませんか。

すずき：僕は前に何回か行ったから、佐藤さん、ご一緒したらどうですか。

さとう：結構ですよ。

ネルソン：よかった。じゃあ、そういうことで。ありがとうございました。

B. 単語

弁当	*bentoo*	lunch(box)	払う	*harau*	to pay
消費者	*shoohisha*	consumer	事務所	*jimusho*	office
戻る	*modoru*	to return	傾向	*keikoo*	trend
年代	*nendai*	age	全般的な	*zenpanteki na*	general
洋服	*yoofuku*	Western clothes	女性	*josei*	female
自由な	*jiyuu na*	free	就職	*shuushoku*	finding a job
生活費	*seikatsuhi*	living expenses	値段	*nedan*	price
品質	*hinshitsu*	quality	関係	*kankei*	relation
考え	*kangae*	idea	製品	*seihin*	product
質	*shitsu*	quality	信用	*shin'yoo*	trust
割合	*wariai*	rate	流行	*ryuukoo*	fad
役所	*yakusho*	government office	企業	*kigyoo*	company
現実的	*genjitsuteki*	realistic	個人	*kojin*	individual
会議	*kaigi*	meeting	付き合いする	*tsukiai suru*	to accompany

C. 漢字

最	SAI *motto(mo)*	most	最近 最初 最小 最も	さいきん さいしょ さいしょう もっとも	recent beginning minimum most
近	KIN *chika(i)*	near close	近所 近眼 近い	きんじょ きんがん ちかい	neighborhood nearsighted close
消	SHOO *ke(su)*	erase, extinguish to put out	消費者 消防署 消す	しょうひしゃ しょうぼうしょ けす	consumer fire station to erase
費	HI *tsuiya(su)*	expense	費用 会費 費やす	ひよう かいひ ついやす	expenses membership fee to spend
趣	SHU	taste	趣向 趣味	しゅこう しゅみ	trend hobby
考	KOO *kanga(eru)*	idea	参考 考え 考える	さんこう かんがえ かんがえる	reference thought to think
聞	BUN *ki(ku)*	listen	新聞 聞く	しんぶん きく	newspaper to listen
気	KI	feeling, spirit	気持 天気 気がする 気がつく 気にいる	きもち てんき きがする きがつく きにいる	feeling weather to feel to notice to like
使	SHI *tsuka(u)*	use	使用者 使う	しようしゃ つかう	user to use
男	DAN *otoko*	male	男性 男	だんせい おとこ	male man

女	JO	female	女性	じょせい	female
	on'na		女の子	おんなのこ	girl
値	CHI	price	価値	かち	value
	ne		値段	ねだん	price
			値打ち	ねうち	value
			値上げ	ねあげ	price-hike
品	HIN	article	商品	しょうひん	product
	shina		品質	ひんしつ	quality
			品物	しなもの	things
製	SEI	made	製品	せいひん	product
			日本製	にほんせい	made in Japan
者	SHA	person	学者	がくしゃ	scholar
	mono		記者	きしゃ	reporter
			変わり者	かわりもの	strange person

練習問題

A. 次の質問に答えなさい。 (Answer the following questions.)

1. ネルソンさんは何についてみなさんに聞いていますか。

2. ものをよく買うのはどの年代ですか。

3. 日本の企業は値段や品質より何が大切ですか。

4. 幕張に何がありますか。

B. 次を日本語で書きなさい。 (Write the following in Japanese.)

1. I think the trends have changed recently.

2. It seems like men are spending money these days, too.

3. What kind of products would you buy?

4. Dependability is especially important in Japan.

5. Quality and service are more important than price.

答え

A. 1. 最近の消費者のトレンドについて聞いています。2. ものを買うのは二十代から五十代までです。3. サービスが大切です。4. トレードショーがあります。

B. 1. 最近トレンドが変わったような気がします。2. 最近は男性もお金を使うようになったそうです。3. どんな製品を買いますか。4. 日本では信用が特に大切です。5. 値段より品質とサービスが大切です。

第七課
<ruby>第<rt>だい</rt>七<rt>なな</rt>課<rt>か</rt></ruby>

A. 会話
<ruby>会<rt>かい</rt>話<rt>わ</rt></ruby>

招待
<ruby>招待<rt>しょうたい</rt></ruby>

<ruby>鈴木氏<rt>すずきし</rt></ruby>とネルソン<ruby>氏<rt>し</rt></ruby>は<ruby>廊下<rt>ろうか</rt></ruby>で<ruby>週末<rt>しゅうまつ</rt></ruby>の<ruby>予定<rt>よてい</rt></ruby>について<ruby>話<rt>はな</rt></ruby>している。

すずき：ネルソンさん、<ruby>今週<rt>こんしゅう</rt></ruby>の<ruby>土曜日<rt>どようび</rt></ruby>、<ruby>何<rt>なに</rt></ruby>か<ruby>予定<rt>よてい</rt></ruby>がありますか。

ネルソン：いいえ、<ruby>何<rt>なに</rt></ruby>もありませんが。

すずき：じゃあ、<ruby>家<rt>うち</rt></ruby>でいっぱい<ruby>飲<rt>の</rt></ruby>みませんか。

ネルソン：そうですか。じゃあ、<ruby>伺<rt>うかが</rt></ruby>います。

すずき：<ruby>調布駅<rt>ちょうふえき</rt></ruby>の<ruby>近<rt>ちか</rt></ruby>くですから、<ruby>駅<rt>えき</rt></ruby>で7<ruby>時頃<rt>じごろ</rt></ruby><ruby>待<rt>ま</rt></ruby>っています。

ネルソン：<ruby>京王線<rt>けいおうせん</rt></ruby>の<ruby>調布<rt>ちょうふ</rt></ruby>ですね。<ruby>分<rt>わ</rt></ruby>かりました。

<ruby>鈴木<rt>すずき</rt></ruby>さん<ruby>宅<rt>たく</rt></ruby>で。

すずき：さあ、どうぞ、お<ruby>上<rt>あ</rt></ruby>がり<ruby>下<rt>くだ</rt></ruby>さい。

ネルソン：お<ruby>邪魔<rt>じゃま</rt></ruby>します。

すずき：<ruby>順子<rt>じゅんこ</rt></ruby>、ネルソンさんが<ruby>見<rt>み</rt></ruby>えたよ。

じゅんこ：あら、ようこそ。はじめまして。<ruby>家内<rt>かない</rt></ruby>でございます。これは<ruby>息子<rt>むすこ</rt></ruby>の<ruby>一郎<rt>いちろう</rt></ruby>です。<ruby>一郎<rt>いちろう</rt></ruby>も<ruby>挨拶<rt>あいさつ</rt></ruby>して。

ネルソン：はじめまして。

いちろう：<ruby>今日<rt>こんにち</rt></ruby>は。いらっしゃい。

ネルソン：<ruby>奥<rt>おく</rt></ruby>さん、これはつまらないものですが、どうぞ。

じゅんこ：そうですか。ありがとうございます。

すずき：こちらへどうぞ。ビールでいいですか。

ネルソン：はい、あまり飲めませんから、少しだけいただきます。

すずき：アサヒとキリンがありますが、どちらにしますか。

ネルソン：えーと、日本のビールのことはよく知らないんです。

すずき：じゃあ、キリンにしましょう。

ネルソン：あっ、鈴木さんはビールにうるさかったんですね。

すずき：いや、どうも。はい、お注ぎしましょう。

鈴木氏はネルソン氏のグラスにビールを注ぐ。

ネルソン：はい、すみません。

すずき：じゃあ、乾杯しましょう。ようこそ。

ネルソン：ありがとうございます。この辺は静かな住宅地なんですね。

すずき：前はそうだったんですが、最近はそうでもありません。

ネルソン：何年ぐらいこちらに住んでいるんですか。

すずき：十年ぐらいかな。

ネルソン：どう変わりましたか。

すずき：東京に人がどんどん移ってきて、この辺にも家が増えました。

ネルソン：アメリカも同じです。前に住んでいたシアトルも人口が増え
　　　　 まして、大分騒々しくなりました。

じゅんこ：そうですか。でも近くに子供が増えましたから、一郎も友達がたくさんできました。ところで、ネルソンさんはご結婚は。

ネルソン：まだなんです。ガールフレンドはいるんですが。

じゅんこ：アメリカにですか。

ネルソン：はい、そうです。シアトルに住んでいます。

じゅんこ：じゃあ、電話代が大変でしょう。

ネルソン：できるだけE-メールを使おうと思っています。

すずき：それでは、我々の製品を実際に実験するわけですね。

ネルソン：総てを報告しますから。

すずき：彼女はシアトルで何をしているんですか。

ネルソン：今大学院に行っているんです。来年卒業します。そのあと、日本に来たいと言っています。

すずき：日本に来たことはあるんですか。

ネルソン：去年の夏、一週間ばかり京都に滞在しました。

すずき：京都に。

ネルソン：はい、セミナーに出席したんです。とてもよかったと言っていました。

じゅんこ：ご両親はお元気ですか。

ネルソン：父は昨年亡くなりましたが、母はアリゾナ州で元気にしています。

じゅんこ：ああ、そうですか。私も二年前に父をなくしたんです。

ネルソン：全く病気には勝てませんから。鈴木さん達は恋愛結婚ですか。
　　　　　それともお見合いですか。

じゅんこ：あら、恥ずかしいですわ。

すずき：実は順子は妹の親友だったんです。家に何回か遊びに来ていた
　　　　から、何となく知っていたんですが。

じゅんこ：私はお見合いを何回かしたんですけど、なかなか決められな
　　　　　いでいたんです。

すずき：それで、ある日電車の中で順子に偶然に会い、話しはじめて、
　　　　それから付き合いはじめたというわけです。

ネルソン：妹さんには知らせたんですか。

すずき：初めは内緒だったんです。彼女に知らせた時はびっくりしてい
　　　　ましたが、喜んでくれました。

じゅんこ：それで気が付いたら、結婚していたんです。

ネルソン：なるほど。

夕食後、順子はテーブルをかたづけ、一郎に風呂に入るように言う。一郎はファ
ミコンをしたがっている。ネルソン氏は一郎に一ゲーム挑戦する。

ネルソン：一郎君はどんなゲームが得意なの。

いちろう：「マージャン」と言うゲームが一番好きです。

ネルソン：じゃあ、おじさん一ゲーム挑戦するかな。

いちろう：おじさん、ほんとにできるんですか。

ネルソン：大学でそのゲームを毎日していた友達がいて、時々付き合ってたから。

いちろう：じゃあ、始めましょう。いいですか。

ネルソン：はい、いいですよ。

B. 単語

廊下	rooka	hallway	邪魔	jama	disturbance
息子	musuko	son	挨拶	aisatsu	greeting
少々	shooshoo	a little	うるさい	urusai	annoying
住宅地	juutakuchi	residential area	移る	utsuru	to move
増える	fueru	to increase	人口	jinkoo	population
騒々しい	soozooshii	noisy	結婚	kekkon	marriage
電話代	denwadai	phone bill	実際	jissai	actual
実験	jikken	experiment	報告	hookoku	report
大学院	daigakuin	graduate school	卒業	sotsugyoo	graduation
滞在する	taizai suru	to stay	出席する	shusseki suru	to attend
亡くなる	nakunaru	to pass away	勝つ	katsu	to defeat, win
恋愛結婚	ren'aikekkon	"love marriage"	見合い	miai	arranged marriage
親友	shin'yuu	close friend	決める	kimeru	to decide
偶然に	guuzen ni	accidentally, by chance	内緒	naisho	secret
風呂	furo	bathtub	挑戦	choosen	challenge
得意	tokui	strong point			

C. 漢字

予	YO arakaji(me)	previously	予定 予約 予報 予算 予め	よてい よやく よほう よさん あらかじめ	plan reservation forecast, prediction budget, estimate beforehand
定	TEI, JOO sada(meru)	fixed to establish	未定 定価 定期 勘定 定める	みてい ていか ていき かんじょう さだめる	undecided fixed price fixed, regular check to establish

線	SEN	line	中央線	ちゅうおうせん	Chuo Line (train)
			京王線	けいおうせん	Keio Line (train)
			直線	ちょくせん	a straight line
			内線	ないせん	phone extension
失	SHITSU	lose	失礼	しつれい	rude
	ushina(u)		失業	しつぎょう	unemployment
			失敗	しっぱい	failure
			見失う	みうしなう	to lose sight of
			失う	うしなう	to lose
礼	REI	courtesy	礼儀	れいぎ	courtesy
			儀礼	ぎれい	ceremony
			お礼	おれい	thanks, appreciation
見	KEN	see	一見	いっけん	a glance
	mi(ru)		見学	けんがく	visit
			拝見する	はいけんする	to have the honor of seeing
			見る	みる	to see
乾	KAN	dry	乾杯	かんぱい	"Cheers"
	kawa(ku)		乾燥機	かんそうき	clothes dryer
			乾かす	かわかす	to dry
			乾く	かわく	to get dry
杯	HAI, PAI, BAI	glass	一杯	いっぱい	one glassful
静	SEI	quiet	静粛	せいしゅく	quiet
	shizu(ka)		静かな	しずかな	quiet
	shizuma(ru)		静まる	しずまる	to be still
宅	TAKU	house	住宅	じゅうたく	residence
			宅地	たくち	lot
			宅配	たくはい	home delivery

312

地	CHI, JI	land, earth	地図	ちず	map
			地価	ちか	land price
			地震	じしん	earthquake
			番地	ばんち	lot number (used in addresses)
結	KETSU	conclusion	結婚	けっこん	marriage
	musu(bu)	to tie, connect	結果	けっか	result
			結局	けっきょく	after all; in the end
			結ぶ	むすぶ	to tie
婚	KON	marriage	婚約	こんやく	engagement
			結婚式	けっこんしき	wedding ceremony
大	DAI, TAI, OO	large	大学	だいがく	college
			大手	おおて	major companies
	ooki(i)		大会	たいかい	convention
			大きい	おおきい	large
変	HEN	change	大変	たいへん	serious, terrible
	ka(waru)		変化	へんか	change
	kae(ru)		変わる	かわる	to be changed
			変える	かえる	to change

練習問題

A. 次の質問に答えなさい。 (Answer the following questions.)

1. 鈴木さんの家はどこですか。
2. 鈴木さんとネルソンさんは何を飲みますか。
3. ネルソンさんは結婚していますか。
4. ネルソンさんのガールフレンドは今何をしていますか。
5. 一郎は何が一番好きですか。

B. 日本語で書きなさい。 (Write the following in Japanese.)

1. Do you have any plans this Sunday?

2. Shall we have a drink?

3. I cannot drink much, so I'll just have a little bit.

4. Are your parents well?

答え

A. 1. 調布駅の近くです。2. ビールを飲みます。3. いいえ、していません。
4. 大学院に行っています。5. マージャンが一番好きです。
B. 1. 今度の日曜日に何か予定がありますか。2. いっぱい飲みませんか。
3. あまり飲みませんから、少しだけいただきます。4. ご両親はお元気で
すか。

第八課
<ruby>第八課<rt>だいはちか</rt></ruby>

A. 会話
<ruby>会話<rt>かいわ</rt></ruby>

付き合い
<ruby>付<rt>つ</rt></ruby>き<ruby>合<rt>あ</rt></ruby>い

ネルソン<ruby>氏<rt>し</rt></ruby>と<ruby>佐藤嬢<rt>さとうじょう</rt></ruby>はビジテックに<ruby>来<rt>き</rt></ruby>て<ruby>間<rt>ま</rt></ruby>もないので、ボーナスのことを<ruby>知<rt>し</rt></ruby>りたい。<ruby>今晩<rt>こんばん</rt></ruby><ruby>高木部長<rt>たかぎぶちょう</rt></ruby>と<ruby>食事<rt>しょくじ</rt></ruby>をすることになっているので、そのことについて<ruby>聞<rt>き</rt></ruby>いてみることにする。

ネルソン：きれいな<ruby>居酒屋<rt>いざかや</rt></ruby>ですね。

すずき：ええ、<ruby>雰囲気<rt>ふんいき</rt></ruby>もけっこういいし、<ruby>料理<rt>りょうり</rt></ruby>もおいしいんです。<ruby>部長<rt>ぶちょう</rt></ruby>は<ruby>遅<rt>おそ</rt></ruby>いようだから、ビールでも<ruby>飲<rt>の</rt></ruby>み<ruby>始<rt>はじ</rt></ruby>めましょうか。

ネルソン：いいんですか。

さとう：<ruby>遅<rt>おそ</rt></ruby>い<ruby>時<rt>とき</rt></ruby>は<ruby>始<rt>はじ</rt></ruby>めててくれとおっしゃっていました。

すずき：(ウエイターに)ビール<ruby>二三本<rt>にさんぼん</rt></ruby><ruby>お願<rt>ねが</rt></ruby>いします。ああ、<ruby>部長<rt>ぶちょう</rt></ruby>が<ruby>見<rt>み</rt></ruby>えました。

たかぎ：<ruby>遅<rt>おそ</rt></ruby>くなってすみません。<ruby>出<rt>で</rt></ruby>ようとしたら、<ruby>支社長<rt>ししゃちょう</rt></ruby>によばれてしまって。

すずき：いいえ。あっ、ちょうどビールが<ruby>来<rt>き</rt></ruby>ました。<ruby>乾杯<rt>かんぱい</rt></ruby>しましょう。

たかぎ：はい。じゃあ、ネルソン<ruby>君<rt>くん</rt></ruby>を<ruby>歓迎<rt>かんげい</rt></ruby>して。<ruby>乾杯<rt>かんぱい</rt></ruby>。

みんな：<ruby>乾杯<rt>かんぱい</rt></ruby>。

さとう：<ruby>料理<rt>りょうり</rt></ruby>は<ruby>注文<rt>ちゅうもん</rt></ruby>してありますが、<ruby>特<rt>とく</rt></ruby>にご<ruby>希望<rt>きぼう</rt></ruby>があれば<ruby>追加<rt>ついか</rt></ruby>しますから。

ネルソン：はい、<ruby>分<rt>わ</rt></ruby>かりました。それにしても、<ruby>最近忙<rt>さいきんいそが</rt></ruby>しいですね。<ruby>給料<rt>きゅうりょう</rt></ruby>を<ruby>少<rt>すこ</rt></ruby>し<ruby>上<rt>あ</rt></ruby>げてもらいたいですね。(<ruby>笑<rt>わら</rt></ruby>う)

たかぎ：（笑う）賛成。

ネルソン：それでうちの給料制度は変わるんですか。

たかぎ：いや、そういうことは聞いていないけど。どうして。

すずき：部長、それが今年はボーナスが出るという噂ですが。

たかぎ：いや、うちは外資系の会社だから、ボーナスは出さない
　　　給与制度になっているのでね。

すずき：実は、ボーナスがないから、年給で計算したら外の会社より低
　　　いと思いますよ。

たかぎ：そんなことはないはずだが。調査してみよう。

料理がいくつかくる。

ネルソン：おいしそうですね。何ですか。

さとう：ふぐの空揚げです。ここはこれで有名なんです。

たかぎ：これもおいしいけど、この間はフランス料理のすごい所に招待
　　　されましたよ。

さとう：部長はいろいろ素敵な所に行けるんですね。

たかぎ：えっ、ボーイフレンドに連れて行ってもらわないの。

さとう：ボーイフレンドなんかいません。それにそんな素敵なところな
　　　んか行けませんし。

すずき：でも、佐藤さんのように両親の世話になっている人は楽で
　　　しょう。

さとう：そんなことありません。父親ももう引退しているし、そろそろ
　　　結婚のことも考えなくちゃならないし。

すずき：そう言えば、佐藤さん、近いうちに結婚するとか聞きましたが。

さとう：そんなこと、誰から聞いたんですか。

すずき：いつも電話をかけて来る人は。

さとう：あの人は高校時代のクラスメートです。残念ながら恋人なんか
　　　　じゃありません。でも、近いうちに結婚する人を知ってます。

すずき：あっ、話を変えましたね。でも誰かな。

さとう：秘密守れますか。

すずき：大丈夫。言わないから。でも部長はもうご存じなんでしょ。

さとう：飯田さんです。もうすぐゴールインするらしいわよ。

すずき：へえ、ほんと。社内の誰かかな。

さとう：そこまでは分かりません。

すずき：佐藤さんは結婚は。

さとう：私、一人子なんです。だから問題があって。

ネルソン：どうして。ああ、将来は両親の世話をしなければならない訳
　　　　ですか。

さとう：ええ、できればそうしたいと思います。

食事の後で、高木部長が勘定を取る。

ネルソン：わあ、たくさん食べましたね。みんなおいしかったです。

たかぎ：今日はネルソン君の歓迎ということで私がもちます。

すずき：部長、それはどうも。割り勘にしようと考えていたんですが。

たかぎ：たまにはいいでしょう。毎回（まいかい）という訳（わけ）にはいかないけど。

ネルソン：ありがとうございます。

さとう：ご馳走（ちそう）さまでした。

たかぎ：いや、とんでもない。ネルソン君（くん）、何（なに）で帰（かえ）る。

ネルソン：鈴木（すずき）さんと同（おな）じ方向（ほうこう）ですから、鈴木（すずき）さんと電車（でんしゃ）で帰（かえ）ります。

たかぎ：あ、そう。じゃあ、気（き）をつけて。

ネルソン：部長（ぶちょう）もお気（き）をつけて。

B. 単語（たんご）

耳にする	*mimi ni suru*	to overhear	支社長	*shishachoo*	branch manager
雰囲気	*fun'iki*	atmosphere	歓迎	*kangei*	welcome
注文	*chuumon*	order	希望	*kiboo*	desire
追加	*tsuika*	addition	給料	*kyuuryoo*	salary
賛成	*sansei*	agreement	給料制度	*kyuuryoo seido*	salary system
噂	*uwasa*	rumor	外資系	*gaishikei*	foreign owned
給与制度	*kyuuyoseido*	wage system	特別な	*tokubetsu na*	special
計算	*keisan*	calculation	調査	*choosa*	investigation
招待	*shootai*	invitation	素敵な	*suteki na*	wonderful
世話	*sewa*	care	楽な	*raku na*	ease
引退	*intai*	retirement	高校時代	*kookoojidai*	during high school
残念な	*zan'nen na*	regrettable	恋人	*koibito*	lover
秘密	*himitsu*	secret	守る	*mamoru*	to protect
社内	*shanai*	within a company	問題	*mondai*	problem
勘定	*kanjoo*	check, bill			

C. 漢字（かんじ）

酒	SHU *sake, saka,* *zaka*	wine	洋酒 居酒屋 お酒	ようしゅ いざかや おさけ	Western wine bar sake
屋	YA *oku*	shop	パン屋 屋外	パンや おくがい	bakery outside

意	I	will	雰囲気	ふんいき	atmosphere
			意外	いがい	unexpected
			意見	いけん	opinion
			意地	いじ	disposition
遅	CHI	late	遅刻する	ちこくする	to be late for an appointment
	oku(reru)		遅れる	おくれる	to be late
	osoi		遅い	おそい	late
出	SHUTSU	leave	出発	しゅっぱつ	departure
	de(ru)		出張	しゅっちょう	business trip
	da(su)		出る	でる	to leave
			出す	だす	to bring out, send, take out
資	SHI	capital	外資	がいし	foreign capital
			資料	しりょう	data
			資本	しほん	capital
			資格	しかく	qualification
給	KYUU	supply	給料	きゅうりょう	salary
			供給	きょうきゅう	supply
与	YO	give	給与	きゅうよ	salary
	ata(eru)		与える	あたえる	to give
制	SEI	system	制度	せいど	system
			制服	せいふく	school uniform
			制定する	せいていする	to enact
度	DO	times	今度	こんど	this time
	tabi		一度	いちど	one time
			再度	さいど	again
			程度	ていど	degree
			この度	このたび	this time
特	TOKU	special	特別な	とくべつな	special
			特に	とくに	especially
			独特な	どくとくな	unique

別	BETSU	different	別の	べつの	different
			別々の	べつべつの	separate
普	FU	general	普通	ふつう	usual
			普及する	ふきゅうする	to become
					widespread
計	KEI	measure, plan	計算	けいさん	calculation
	haka(ru)		計画	けいかく	plan
			計る	はかる	to measure
算	SAN	calculate	算数	さんすう	arithmetic
			計算器	けいさんき	calculator

練習問題

A. 次の質問に答えなさい。(Answer the following questions.)

1. どんな居酒屋ですか。

2. 部長はどうしておそくなりましたか。

3. この会社はどうしてボーナスを出しませんか。

4. 佐藤さんは何のことを考えていますか。

5. 佐藤さんにいつも電話をかけてくる人は誰ですか。

B. 次を日本語で書きなさい。(Write the following in Japanese.)

1. The atmosphere is really nice, and the food is good, too.

2. Will the salary system be changing at our company?

3. I heard that you are getting married soon.

4. Will you have to take care of your parents in the future?

320

C. 次の下線の漢字をひらがなで書きなさい。(Write the following underlined *kanji* in hiragana.)

1. きれいな居酒屋ですね。
2. 雰囲気がとてもいいです。
3. 外資計の会社です。
4. 日本の給料制度は特別です。
5. 普通の会社と同じです。

答え

A. 1. きれいな居酒屋です。それに雰囲気もいいし、料理もおいしいです。
2. 支社長に呼ばれてしまいましたから。3. 外資系の会社ですから。
4. 結婚のことを考えています。5. 高校時代のクラスメートです。

B. 1. 雰囲気もけっこういいし、料理もおいしいです。2. うちの給料制度が変わるんですか。3. 近いうちに結婚するとか聞きました。4. 将来は両親の世話をしなければなりませんか。

C. 1. いざかや 2. ふんいき 3. がいしけい、かいしゃ 4. にほん、きゅうりょうせいど、とくべつ 5. ふつう、おな

第九課

A. 会話

市場調査

今日は水曜日。ネルソン氏と佐藤嬢は幕張トレードショーに行くことになっている。ネルソン氏、事務所にちょっと遅く着く。

ネルソン：佐藤さん、遅くなってすみません。昨日は久しぶりにリラックスして、ちょっと飲み過ぎてしまったらしいです。

さとう：あら、二日酔いですか。今日幕張へ行くことができますか。

ネルソン：まあ大丈夫でしょう。じゃあ、そろそろ行きましょうか。

さとう：はい。かなり遠いから急ぎましょう。一時間以上かかります。

ネルソン：幕張は初めてですが、電車で行くんですね。

さとう：はい。さっき時刻表で調べたんですが、次の急行は10時です。急げば間に合うかもしれません。

東京駅で。

ネルソン：ふらふらであまり速く走れません。

さとう：でももう少しですから、頑張って。

ネルソン：ああ、間に合った。

さとう：あそこに座りましょうか。

ネルソン：失礼。ちょっとアスピリンを飲みます。幕張メッセでいろいろなショーがあるそうですね。

さとう：はい。東京から遠いけど、とてもきれいな「未来都市」なんです。

ネルソン：そうらしいですね。前に新聞で読みました。今日はいろいろな新製品が出ているらしいですね。

さとう：ええ、競争相手の製品も見られたら、いいですね。

幕張に着く。

さとう：ネルソンさん、着きましたよ。

ネルソン：ああ、すっかり眠ってしまって。いびきかいてたかなあ。

さとう：ええ、ちょっと。

ネルソン：でも大分気分がよくなりました。ごめんなさいね。

さとう：いいえ。ここが会場です。

トレードショーの会場の入口で。

クラーク：何名様ですか。

さとう：二人です。

クラーク：二名様で三千円です。これが本日展示しているブースの案内でございます。

さとう：ありがとう。

ネルソン：わあ、きれいな会場だ。すごい人ですね。ここに寄ってみませんか。

ふるや：こちらにご記名をお願いします。こちらに最新のソフトがいろいろございます。

さとう：この日英翻訳のソフトについてもっと知りたいんですが。

ふるや：これは最も新しいもので、主に手紙の翻訳に使います。普通の書類なら90パーセント正確に翻訳できます。

ネルソン：その残りの10パーセントの訳し方が難しいんでしょう。

ふるや：ええ、そうなんです。人間じゃなくて、機械ですから。このソフトを使って、デモンストレーションしてみましょうか。

ネルソン：はい。

ふるや：どうぞお座りになって下さい。やってみましょう。

ネルソン：なるほど。文章を入れたら、黄色いアイコンをクリックするんですね。そうすると、翻訳が出るというわけですね。うーむ、なかなかいいですね。値段はどのぐらいするんですか。

ふるや：市場に出たばかりで、ちょっと高いですが。ここに価格表がございます。

ネルソン：わあ、かなりいい値段ですね。パンフレット下さい。

ふるや：はい。もちろんインターネットもつなぐことができます。

さとう：なるほど。デモ用をもらえますか。

ふるや：はい、どうぞ。ご質問がありましたら、ここにご連絡下さい。

一時間ほど、他のデモを見ていたら、佐藤嬢、大学時代の友人に偶然に会う。

さとう：ああ、慶子じゃない。

ちば：裕子、久しぶり。元気！

さとう：うん。何してるの。

ちば：NTTで新製品コーディネーターをしているの。

さとう：ブース出してるの。

ちば：うん。あそこなの。

さとう：信じられないわ。こんなところで会うなんて。

ちば：ほんと。裕子は今何してるの。

さとう：ビジテックという外資系の会社に勤めてるの。あっ、紹介する
わ。こちら、本社から来ているネルソンです。ネルソンさん、私の
大学のクラスメートの千葉慶子さん。素敵な方でしょう。

ちば：やめて。

ネルソン：ええ、きれいな方ですね。ネルソンです。どうぞよろしく。

ちば：宜しくお願いします。名刺いただけるかしら。

ネルソン：ああ失礼。これです。

さとう：昼食の予定がなかったら、一緒にしない。

ちば：そうね、是非。

ネルソン：十二時にあの入口で会いましょう。

ちば：はい、楽しみにしている。じゃあ、その時にまたゆっくり。

B. 単語

以上	ijoo	more, above	間に合う	maniau	to be on time
競争相手	kyoosooaite	opponent	走る	hashiru	to run
会場	kaijoo	meeting hall	入口	iriguchi	entrance
展示	tenji	display	案内	an'nai	information
記名	kimei	signature	最新	saishin	newest
書類	shorui	documents	正確な	seikaku na	correct
人間	ningen	human	機械	kikai	machine
文章	bunshoo	sentences	市場	shijoo	market
価格表	kakakuhyoo	list of prices	繋ぐ	tsunagu	to attach, connect
連絡	renraku	contact	是非	zehi	by all means

コンピューター関連語

ファイルを開く	*fairu o hiraku*	Open a file	編集	*henshuu*	Edit
ビュー	*byuu*	View	挿入	*soonyuu*	Insert
ツール	*tsuuru*	Tools	フォーマット	*foomatto*	Format
新規作成	*shinkisakusei*	New	オープン	*oopun*	Open
セーブ	*seebu*	Save	閉じる	*tojiru*	Close
プリント	*purinto*	Print	終了	*shuuryoo*	Exit
ウインドウ	*uindoo*	Window	メニュー	*menyuu*	Menu bar
マウスを使う	*mausu o tsukau*	Use a mouse	ヘルプ	*herupu*	Help

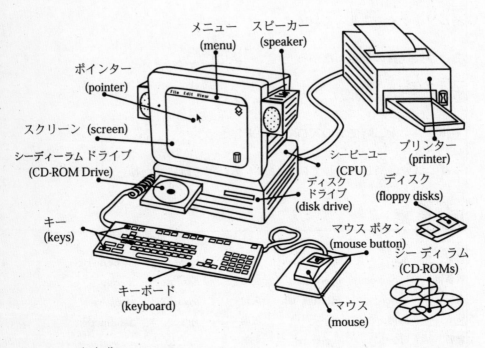

メニュー (menu)
スピーカー (speaker)
ポインター (pointer)
スクリーン (screen)
シーディーラム ドライブ (CD-ROM Drive)
キー (keys)
キーボード (keyboard)
シーピーユー (CPU)
ディスク ドライブ (disk drive)
プリンター (printer)
ディスク (floppy disks)
マウス ボタン (mouse button)
シーディラム (CD-ROMs)
マウス (mouse)

C. 漢字

過	KA *sugi(ru)*	pass, to pass, exceed	過去 飲み過ぎ	かこ のみすぎ	past excessive drinking
酔	SUI *yo(u)*	intoxication	泥酔 二日酔い 酔う	でいすい ふつかよい よう	drunkenness hangover to get drunk

夫	FU, BU *otto*	man, husband	大丈夫 婦人 丈夫	だいじょうぶ ふじん じょうぶ	okay Mrs. strong
未	MI *mada*	not yet, un-	未来 未知 未成年 未だ	みらい みち みせいねん まだ	future unknown minor (underage) not yet
都	TO, TSU *miyako*	capital	都会 都市 都合	とかい とし つごう	big city city convenience
市	SHI *ichi*	city, market	神戸市 市長 市場	こうべし しちょう しじょう	Kobe City mayor market
眠	MIN *nemu(ru)*	sleep	睡眠 眠る	すいみん ねむる	sleeping sleep
分	FUN, BU *wa(karu)* *wa(keru)*	divide, portion	大分 部分 分かる 分ける	だいぶ ぶぶん わかる わける	considerably part understand to divide
場	JOO *ba*	place	会場 場合 職場 場所	かいじょう ばあい しょくば ばしょ	meeting hall case workplace place
寄	KI *yo(ru)*	to give, call at	寄宿舎 寄る	きしゅくしゃ よる	dormitory to stop by
英	EI	English	英語 英訳 和英	えいご えいやく わえい	English translating into English Japanese-English

訳	YAKU	translation,	翻訳	ほんやく	translation
	wake	reason			(written things)
			通訳	つうやく	interpretation
					(spoken words)
			訳	わけ	reason
正	SEI,	right	正確な	せいかくな	accurate
	SHOO		正直な	しょうじきな	honest
	tadashi(i)		正月	しょうがつ	New Year
			正しい	ただしい	correct
確	KAKU	sure	確実な	かくじつな	certain
	tashi(ka)		確かな	たしかな	sure
着	CHAKU	wear	到着	とうちゃく	arrival
	ki(ru)		着物	きもの	kimono
	tsuku		着る	きる	to wear clothes
			着く	つく	to arrive

練習問題

A. 次の質問に答えなさい。(Answer the following questions.)

1. ネルソンさんと佐藤さんはどこへ行きますか。

2. ネルソンさんはなぜ飲みすぎましたか。

3. 日英翻訳のソフトでなぜ正確に訳せませんか。

4. 佐藤さんは会場で誰に会いましたか。

5. 慶子さんはどんな仕事をしていますか。

B. 次を日本語で書きなさい。(Write the following in Japanese.)

1. I'm afraid I had a little too much to drink.

2. I understand that many new products will be on display.

3. I hope we can see some of our competitor's products.

4. If you have any questions, please contact me at this number.

答え

A. 1. 幕張へ行きます。 2. 久しぶりにリラックスしましたから。 3. 人間じゃなくて、機械ですから。 4. 大学時代の友人に会いました。 5. NTTで新製品のコーディネーターをしています。

B. 1. 昨日は飲み過ぎてしまったらしいです。 2. いろいろな新製品が出ているらしいですね。 3. 競争相手の製品も見られたら、いいですね。 4. ご質問がありましたら、ここにご連絡ください。

第十課

A. 会話
かいわ

検診を受ける
けんしん　う

ネルソン氏が日本に来て二か月になる。大変忙しい生活が続き、疲れが出て、
風邪を引く。電話で。

いいだ：ビジテックでございます。

ネルソン：もしもし、ネルソンですが。

いいだ：どうされましたか。元気がないようですが。

ネルソン：今日は休みます。ちょっと気分が悪いから。

いいだ：分かりました。皆さんに伝えておきます。

ネルソン：それで佐藤さんにミーティングは明日すると伝えておいて下
　　　　さい。

いいだ：はい、分かりました。

ネルソン：それで、どこか病院を知っていますか。

いいだ：ちょっと遠いですが、虎ノ門病院 はどうですか。信用があり
　　　　ます。

ネルソン：虎ノ門病院ですか。調布からどう行けばいいんですか。

いいだ：新宿で地下鉄に乗って、虎ノ門で降りるとそこからすぐ見え
　　　　ます。

ネルソン：はい。何かあったら、午後連絡してくださるように言って下
　　　　さい。僕はこれから病院に行ってみますから。

いいだ：はい、お大事に。

ネルソン氏、病院に着いてから、受付と書いてある窓口に行く。

ネルソン：すみません。気分が悪いので、お医者さんに診ていただきたいんですが。

うけつけ：はい。じゃあ、この申込書に書き込んで下さい。保険のカードはありますか。

ネルソン：まだ日本の保険はありませんが。

うけつけ：それでは全額現金で払っていただくことになりますが、よろしいですか。

ネルソン：はい、いいです。大分待たなければなりませんか。

うけつけ：いいえ、十分ぐらいでしょう。
待合室は込んでいたが、十分ほどすると名前が呼ばれ診察室に案内される。

いしゃ：どうしましたか。

ネルソン：気分がよくありません。それに食欲がないんです。

いしゃ：顔色がよくないですね。ちょっと口を開けて下さい。喉がちょっと赤いですね。

ネルソン：そうですか。最近ひどく疲れるんです。実は二か月前にこちらに転勤して来たんですが、休みなしで働いていたものですから。

いしゃ：ああ、そう。めまいがしませんか。

ネルソン：ええ、ちょっと。それに頭が痛いです。

いしゃ：血圧を計りましょう。袖をまくって下さい。アメリカからですか。

ネルソン：はい、シアトルから来ました。

いしゃ：そうですか。去年会議で行きましたよ。きれいな町ですね。

ネルソン：はい。でもちょっと雨が多くて。

いしゃ：あ、そうらしいですね。うん、血圧は平常です。熱がありますか。

ネルソン：ないと思いますが。

いしゃ：計ってみましょう。

医者は体温計をわきの下に入れる。

いしゃ：日本の生活はどうですか。

ネルソン：快適で楽しいです。

いしゃ：日本の生活で困ることがありませんか。

ネルソン：そうですね。電車が込むことと物価が高いことぐらいですね。

いしゃ：ああ、熱はありません。風邪でしょう。二三日ゆっくり休めば治ります。薬を三日分あげますから。それでも気分が悪ければ、また来て下さい。もう一度調べますから。

ネルソン：はい、そうします。

いしゃ：さっきの電車が込む話しですが、政治が悪いんですよ。大都市に何でもつくるから、東京や大阪に人が集まってきます。

ネルソン：世界中みんな同じようです。都会には何か楽しいことがあるとみんな思っているんでしょう。

いしゃ：そのようですね。

ネルソン：どうもありがとうございました。

いしゃ：お大事に。

B. 単語

続く	*tsuzuku*	to continue	疲れ	*tsukare*	fatigue
風邪	*kaze*	a cold	伝える	*tsutaeru*	to tell
病院	*byooin*	hospital	受付	*uketsuke*	receptionist
窓口	*madoguchi*	service window	医者	*isha*	doctor
申込書	*mooshikomisho*	application	診る	*miru*	examine
保険	*hoken*	insurance	全額	*zengaku*	total amount
待合室	*machiaishitsu*	waiting room	現金	*genkin*	cash
診察室	*shinsatsushitsu*	examination room	食欲	*shokuyoku*	appetite
顔色	*kaoiro*	complexion	喉	*nodo*	throat
転勤	*tenkin*	transfer	めまい	*memai*	dizziness
血圧	*ketsuatsu*	blood pressure	計る	*hakaru*	to measure
袖	*sode*	sleeve	まくる	*makuru*	to roll up
平常	*heijoo*	normal	体温計	*taionkei*	thermometer
わきの下	*wakinoshita*	armpit	快適	*kaiteki*	pleasant
困る	*komaru*	to be perplexed, bothered	物価	*bukka*	prices
治る	*naoru*	to get better	薬	*kusuri*	medicine
政治	*seiji*	politics	大都市	*daitoshi*	large city
世界中	*sekaijuu*	all over the world	都会	*tokai*	city

C. 漢字

休	KYUU *yasu(mu)*	rest	休暇 休日 休業 休み	きゅうか きゅうじつ きゅうぎょう やすみ	vacation holiday business closed temporarily rest
悪	AKU *waru(i)*	bad, evil	悪人 悪夢 悪い	あくにん あくむ わるい	bad person nightmare bad
病	BYOO *yamai*	sick	病人 病院 恋の病	びょうにん びょういん こいのやまい	sick person hospital love sickness

院	IN	institution	医院	いいん	clinic
			大学院	だいがくいん	graduate school
			美容院	びよういん	beauty salon
教	KYOO	teach	教室	きょうしつ	classroom
	oshieru		教員	きょういん	teacher
			教える	おしえる	to teach
信	SHIN	trust	信用	しんよう	trust
			信じる	しんじる	to believe
下	KA	below	地下鉄	ちかてつ	subway
	shita		下	した	under
鉄	TETSU	iron	鉄	てつ	iron
			鉄人	てつじん	"expert"
降	KOO	come down	降伏	こうふく	surrender
	ori(ru)		降り口	おりぐち	exit
	fu(ru)		降りる	おりる	to get down
			雨が降る	あめがふる	to rain
書	SHO	writing	書類	しょるい	document
	ka(ku)		書く	かく	to write
保	HO	maintain	保険	ほけん	insurance
	tamot(tsu)		保護	ほご	protection
			保つ	たもつ	to maintain
現	GEN	present, appear	現金	げんきん	cash
	ara(wareru)		現代	げんだい	modern times
			現在	げんざい	at present
			現われる	あらわれる	to appear

払	SHI *hara(u)*	pay	支払い 払う	しはらい はらう	payment to pay
欲	YOKU *ho(shii)*	desire	食欲 欲しい	しょくよく ほしい	appetite want

練習問題

A. 次の質問に答えなさい。 (Answer the following questions.)

1. ネルソンさんはどうしましたか。
2. 何という病院に行きましたか。
3. 何に乗って行きましたか。
4. 保険がありませんでしたから、どうしましたか。
5. ネルソンさんは熱がありましたか。
6. お医者さんはシアトルに何をしに行きましたか。
7. お医者さんはよくアメリカに行きますか。

B. 次を日本語で書きなさい。 (Write the following in Japanese.)

1. Do you know of a hospital somewhere?
2. I'd like to have a doctor examine me.
3. I don't have any health insurance yet.
4. I have been feeling extremely tired lately.
5. If you are still not feeling well, please come back.

C. 次の漢字をひらがなで書きなさい。 (Write the following underlined *kanji* in hiragana.)

1. 今日は気分が悪いから、休みます。
2. 病院を教えて下さい。
3. あのお医者さんは信用があります。
4. 地下鉄でも行けますか。
5. 保険がありませんから、現金で払います。

A. 1. ちょっと気分が悪かったです。2. 虎ノ門病院に行きました。3. 電車に乗って行きました。4. 現金で払いました。5. いいえ、なさそうでした。6. 会議に行きました。7. 一年に一度ぐらい行きます。

B. 1. どこか病院を知っていますか。2. お医者さんに診ていただきたいんですが。3. 日本の保険はありません。4. 最近ひどく疲れるんです。5. それでも気分が悪ければ、また来て下さい。

C. 1. きぶん、わる、やす 2. びょういん、おし 3. しんよう 4. ちかてつ、い 5. ほけん、げんきん、はら

日本人と海外文化

日本人は古くからの独自の文化を維持しながら、海外からの「文化」を好んで取り入れています。

たとえば、毎日の生活で、朝はコーヒーを飲みながら、パンなどを食べます。昼はそばや丼ものなど日本的なものを食べたりします。そして夜は、あるときは洋食、あるときは和食、あるときは中華料理を食べます。休みの日には外国映画を見たり、時代劇の映画を見たり、クラシック音楽会に行ったり、さてはロックのコンサートにも行きます。

スポーツについて考えれば、伝統的な相撲は相変わらず人気がありますが、野球、サッカー、ゴルフ、バレーボールなど欧米で始まったものが盛んに行われています。しかも、これらはごく当たり前のことで、多くの日本人が毎日見たり、自分でもしたりしています。

歴史的に考えてみると、古くは中国から漢字が伝えられ、特に仏教や儒教は日本人の生活や道徳に大きな影響を与えました。その後十六世紀からポルトガル人やスペイン人がヨーロッパの新しい文化を日本に伝え、江戸時代には長崎に住んでいたオランダ人がヨーロッパの医学やオランダ語を教えました。

明治時代になって、多数の日本人はヨーロッパやアメリカに行き、西洋の学問や技術を持ち帰り、産業を発達させました。二十世紀にはアメリカの影響が強く、車や電気製品やコンピューターの技術を取り入れ、又、同時に映画技術とか、音楽などの現代的文化も学びました。もちろんスポーツも歓迎して、普及しました。

というように日本人は外国からたくさんの様々な「文化」を学び、生活に取り入れています。しかし、依然として、自然に対する態度とか神や仏に対する日本古来の考え方をそのまま持ち続け、多くの祭り事などの行事として残しています。

単語

独自	どくじ	unique, individual
維持する	いじする	to maintain
好む	このむ	to like
丼	どんぶり	deep (rice) bowl
洋食	ようしょく	Western food
中華料理	ちゅうかりょうり	Chinese food
伝統的な	でんとうてきな	traditional
時代劇	じだいげき	period drama
相撲	すもう	Sumo
相変わらず	あいかわらず	as usual
野球	やきゅう	baseball
欧米	おうべい	Western, Occidental
ごく		quite, very
当たり前	あたりまえ	natural, of course, reasonable
伝える	つたえる	to pass on, to transmit
仏教	ぶっきょう	Buddhism
儒教	じゅきょう	Confucianism
道徳	どうとく	morals
影響	えいきょう	influence
与える	あたえる	to give, cause
江戸時代	えどじだい	Edo period
長崎	ながさき	Nagasaki
医学	いがく	medicine
明治時代	めいじじだい	Meiji period
多数	たすう	many
学問	がくもん	learning, study
技術	ぎじゅつ	technology
持ち帰る	もちかえる	to take home
二十世紀	にじゅっせいき	twentieth century
電気製品	でんきせいひん	electronics, electric products
映画	えいが	movie
現代的	げんだいてき	modern, modernistic
歓迎する	かんげいする	to welcome
普及する	ふきゅうする	to spread
様々	さまざま	various, many
依然	いぜん	as usual
自然	しぜん	nature
態度	たいど	attitude
仏	ほとけ	Buddha
古来	こらい	from ancient times
祭り	まつり	festival
行事	ぎょうじ	event

第十一課

A. 会話

電話でのアポイント

ネルソン氏は千代田産業の藤井嬢にアポイントを取り付けるために電話する。彼は売り出し中の製品を紹介したいと思っている。ネルソン氏、電話する前に話すことをまとめる。

ネルソン：千代田産業の藤井さんだな。シアトル本社、それから日本
　　　　　電気の小山さんからの紹介のこと。商品のスーパーメールのことを
　　　　　話せばいいんだな。アポイントを取るのを忘れないようにしよう。
　　　　　やってみよう。

電話で。

こじま：はい、小島商事でございます。

ネルソン：すみません。あのう、藤井さんをお願いします。

こじま：藤井さんですか。こちら、小島商事ですが。そういう名前の者
　　　　はおりませんが。

ネルソン：番号は737の4545ですね。

こじま：はい、そうですが。局番は何番ですか。

ネルソン：045です。

こじま：ああ、こちらは054でございます。

ネルソン：ああ、ごめんなさい。間違えました。大変失礼しました。

こじま：いいえ。

ネルソン氏、電話しなおす。

おおしま：はい、千代田産業でございます。

ネルソン：もしもし、藤井さんをお願いします。

おおしま：申し訳ございません。藤井はただいま外出しております。どなた様でしょうか。

ネルソン：ネルソンと申しますが、何時ごろお帰りでしょうか。

おおしま：二時には帰るはずですが。

ネルソン：そうですか。じゃあ、また二時過ぎに電話します。

おおしま：ネルソン様よりお電話があったことを伝えておきます。

ネルソン：よろしくお願いします。

二時間後、ネルソン氏、また電話する。

ふじい：はい、藤井ですが。

ネルソン：もしもし、私、ビジテックのネルソンと申します。

ふじい：ああ、どうも。さきほどお電話いただいたそうで。

ネルソン：ええ。今度シアトルの本社から東京支社に転勤して来ました。日本電気の小山さんからお名前を伺ったのですが。

ふじい：ああ、小山さんからのご紹介ですか。最近彼女には会っていませんが、お元気ですか。

ネルソン：はい、お元気です。実は私とはアメリカの大学の同窓生なんです。

ふじい：どちらの大学ですか。

ネルソン：イリノイ大学です。よろしくとおっしゃっていました。

340

ふじい：ああ、そうですか。実は彼女と私は同郷なんです。

ネルソン：ええ、そう聞きました。長崎だそうですね。

ふじい：ええ、そうです。ネルソンさんはご出身は。

ネルソン：生まれはコロラド州のボールダーです。高校卒業までそこにいました。

ふじい：えっ、そうですか。偶然というか、私、ボールダーのコロラド大学で一年研修したことがあるんです。

ネルソン：ああ、そうですか。何年前ですか。

ふじい：5、6年前です。いろいろ思い出があって、とてもなつかしいです。ボールダーはきれいな町ですね。

ネルソン：はい。でも私は最近行っていないのでよく分かりませんが。

ふじい：まだきれいだと思いますよ。できれば、家族を連れて一度スキーにでも行きたいと思っているんですよ。

ネルソン：それはいいですね。それでお忙しいようですから、用件に入らせていただきますが、実は電子メールのソフトのご紹介をさせていただきたいと思いまして、電話をさしあげたんですが。

ふじい：電子メールですか。

ネルソン：ええ。5年前に日本に進出しまして、いろいろ商品を扱っています。今度スーパーメールという新しい商品を売り出したんです。

ふじい：電子メールは我社ではまだ使っていませんが。

ネルソン：それなら、是非うちの商品を見て下さい。近い将来誰でも使うようになると思います。

ふじい：そうですか。それじゃ、小山さんのご紹介でもあるし、将来のこともありますから。

ネルソン：ありがとうございます。いつ伺ったらよろしいでしょうか。

ふじい：私は明日から二日ばかり出張しますから、月曜日はどうですか。

ネルソン：結構ですよ。午後一時ごろでよろしいですか。

ふじい：いいですよ。

ネルソン：ありがとうございます。月曜日の朝確認の電話をお入れします。

ふじい：お願いします。

ネルソン氏と藤井嬢は電話を切る。ネルソン氏は約束を取り付けることができて大変うれしかった。

ネルソン：やったぞ。

B. 単語

産業	sangyoo	industry	局番	kyokuban	area code
番号	bangoo	number	外出する	gaishutsu suru	to go out
間違える	machigaeru	to make a mistake	伺う	ukagau	to inquire, to hear
伝える	tsutaeru	to convey, to tell	研修	kenshuu	training
偶然	guuzen	chance	なつかしい	natsukashii	nostalgic
思いで	omoide	memories	進出する	shinshutsu suru	to advance
用件	yooken	business	将来	shoorai	future
扱う	atsukau	to handle	確認	kakunin	confirmation
出張	shucchoo	business trip	約束	yakusoku	appointment, promise
切る	kiru	to cut			

C. 漢字

千	CHI *sen*	thousand	千葉県 千円	ちばけん せんえん	Chiba Prefecture thousand en
代	DAI *yo* *ka(waru)* *ka(eru)*	period, cost generation to take the place of to change	電話代 時代 代表 千代田区 代わる 代える	でんわだい じだい だいひょう ちよだく かわる かえる	telephone bill period representative Chiyoda Ward (in Tokyo) to take the place of to change
田	DEN *ta, da*	rice field	田園 田中	でんえん たなか	countryside family name
産	SAN *u(mu)*	produce to give birth	産業 国産 財産 産物 不動産 産む	さんぎょう こくさん ざいさん さんぶつ ふどうさん うむ	industry made in (Japan) property product real estate to give birth
本	HON	origin, book	本社 日本 本屋	ほんしゃ にほん ほんや	main office Japan bookstore
紹	SHOO	introduce	紹介 紹介状	しょうかい しょうかいじょう	introduction letter of introduction
商	SHOO *akina(i)*	trade	商品 商人 商売 商業 商事 商い	しょうひん しょうにん しょうばい しょうぎょう しょうじ あきない	merchandise merchant trade commerce commercial affairs trade

島	TOO *shima*	island	列島 島国	れっとう しまぐに	islands island country
願	GAN *nega(u)*	wish	願望 願い 願う	がんぼう ねがい ねがう	wish desire to wish for
前	ZEN *mae*	before	午前 以前 前	ごぜん いぜん まえ	A.M. in the past before, ago
番	BAN	number	番号 番組	ばんごう ばんぐみ	number program
局	KYOKU	office	局番 郵便局	きょくばん ゆうびんきょく	area code post office
伝	DEN *tsuta(eru)*	transmit	伝言 伝説 伝える	でんごん でんせつ つたえる	message legend, myth to tell, inform
同	DOO *ona(ji)*	same	同窓 同僚 同じ	どうそう どうりょう おなじ	same school coworker same
窓	SOO *mado*	window	同窓生 窓	どうそうせい まど	schoolmate window

練習問題

A. Aの文とBの文をつないで完全な文にしなさい。(Connect each of the expressions in A with the most appropriate expression in B to form a complete sentence.)

A.

a. 間違えました。

b. 鈴木ですが、

c. 彼女に最近会っていませんが、

B.

1. 小山さんをお願いします。

2. よくわかりません。

3. 用件に入ります。

344

d. 最近行っていないので、　　　　4. 大変失礼しました。

e. お忙しいようですから、　　　　5. お元気ですか。

B. 次を日本語で書きなさい。 (Write the following in Japanese.)

1. There is nobody (here) by that name.

2. About what time do you expect him back?

3. I haven't seen her for a while.

4. Our company expanded into Japan about five years ago.

5. I'll call and confirm (the meeting) on Monday morning.

答え

A. a. 4 b. 1 c. 5 d. 2 e. 3

B. 1. そういう名前の者はおりません。 2. (彼は)何時ごろお帰りでしょうか。 3. 彼女に最近会っていません。 4. (我社は)五年前に日本に進出しました。 5. 月曜日の朝確認の電話をお入れします。

第十二課

A. 会話

週末を温泉郷で

ネルソン氏と鈴木夫妻は週末を鈴木氏の友人所有の温泉旅館で過ごす。長いドライブの後、箱根温泉郷にある「石葉」にやっと着く。

すずき：さあ、着きました。景色もなかなかいいでしょう。

ネルソン：わあ、すばらしいですね。「石葉」という名前ですね。

すずき：ええ。この旅館は大学時代の同窓生の家なんです。夏休みや冬休みによくお邪魔しました。

鈴木氏、友人のお母さんの小野寺夫人に挨拶する。

すずき：ごめん下さい。

おのでら：あら、鈴木さん、いらっしゃい。しばらくでございます。

すずき：お母さん、ご無沙汰しています。今日は家内とそれから友人を一人連れて来ました。家内の順子です。それから会社の同僚のネルソンさんです。

じゅんこ：よろしく。主人から大変お世話になったと聞いています。

おのでら：いいえ、とんでもありません。

ネルソン：はじめまして。ネルソンです。よろしく。

おのでら：こちらこそよろしく。さあ、どうぞ。鈴木さん、実はね、息子も帰って来ているんです。

すずき：えっ、そうですか。電話した時は忙しいとのことでしたから。

346

おのでら：はい、そうなんですけど。博、鈴木さん、お着きになりましたよ。

みんな中に入る。鈴木氏と博、再会を喜ぶ。

ひろし：やあ、鈴木。しばらく。元気か。

すずき：うん。銀行勤めはどうだい。

ひろし：サラリーマンも大変だけど、まあなんとかやっている。

すずき：忙しいって言うから、会えないとあきらめていたんだ。

ひろし：うん。忙しいけど、都合つけて飛んで来たよ。

すずき：それはすまないな。

ひろし：この週末は僕の友人も何人か来ることになっている。猿之助と奥さんも今晩いらっしゃる。歌舞伎役者の猿之助、知ってるだろう。

すずき：もちろん。ああ、そう。

みんなさっそく温泉に入る。そして夕食後、一緒に座って雑談する。

じゅんこ：いい湯でしたわ。

ひろし：そうでしたか。それはよかった。

じゅんこ：それにお食事もおいしかったわ。

ひろし：田舎料理ですが。

じゅんこ：そんなことありませんわ。それにこんなに静かな所で生活できる人がうらやましいわ。

ネルソン：本当に静かでいい所ですね。

ひろし：静か過ぎて、ちょっと退屈しませんか。

ネルソン：いや、都会の生活は便利ですけど、うるさくて、時々いやに
　　　　　なりますよ。

ひろし：こういう田舎に住むことでどんないい所がありますかね。

ネルソン：静けさ。簡素な生活。時間の余裕があるから、考える時間だ
　　　　　って持てます。将来会社をやめたら、静かな所で生活したいと考え
　　　　　ています。

すずき：そう。僕だって、出来ることなら、田舎で生活したいですね。
　　　　子供を都会の学校に行かせたいから、今はできませんが。でも定年
　　　　になったら、都会から逃げたいですね。

ネルソン：どうして子供さんを都会の学校に行かせたいんですか。

すずき：やはり都会にいい学校があります。いい大学に入るには都会に
　　　　住んでいた方がいいでしょう。

えんのすけ：私は都会の生活の方が好きですね。東京のような都会の
　　　　　　文化活動は田舎の静かな生活とは比べものにならないと思います。

ネルソン：歌舞伎役者さんとして都会の方がお好きなのは分かります。

すずき：猿之助丈、歌舞伎の台詞を一言お願いできますか。

ネルソン：ええ、是非お願いします。

えんのすけ：では、「忠臣蔵」からひとくさり。「赤穂四七士の一人、
　　　　　　中村勘助は、、、　　」

猿之助、歌舞伎の台詞を披露する。

B. 単語

所有	shoyuu	possession	やっと	yatto	finally
挨拶	aisatsu	greeting	同僚	dooryoo	coworker
再会	saikai	meeting again	喜ぶ	yorokobu	to rejoice
都合	tsugoo	convenience	雑談	zatsudan	chatting
田舎	inaka	countryside	退屈する	taikutsu suru	to get bored
生活	seikatsu	daily life	静けさ	shizukesa	tranquility
簡素な	kanso na	simple	余裕	yoyuu	spare, room
活動	katsudoo	activity	披露する	hiroo suru	to present, introduce
大都市	daitoshi	big cities	中都市	chuutoshi	midsize cities
大都会	daitokai	big cities, metropolitan	都会	tokai	cities
自然	shizen	nature			

C. 漢字

景	KEI	scenery	景色	けしき	scenery
			風景	ふうけい	scenery
			不景気	ふけいき	recession
色	SHIKI	color	彩色	さいしき	coloring
	SHOKU		同色	どうしょく	same color
	iro		色々	いろいろ	various
			赤色	あかいろ	red
館	KAN	building	旅館	りょかん	Japanese inn
			図書館	としょかん	library
学	GAKU	study	大学	だいがく	university
	mana(bu)		学校	がっこう	school
			学歴	がくれき	education history
			学ぶ	まなぶ	to learn
家	KA	house	家族	かぞく	family members
	ie, uchi, ya		家庭	かてい	family, household
			家具	かぐ	furniture
			家賃	やちん	rent
			家	いえor うち	house

夏	KA *natsu*	summer	夏期 夏休み	かき 夏休み	summertime summer break
冬	TOO *fuyu*	winter	冬期 冬休	とうき ふゆやすみ	winter season winter break
友	YUU *tomo*	friend	友人 友達	ゆうじん ともだち	friend friend
連	REN *tsu(reru)*	contact	連絡 連中 連れて行く	れんらく れんちゅう つれていく	contact group to take someone with you
僚	RYOO	companion, official	同僚 官僚	どうりょう かんりょう	colleague bureaucrat
世	SE *yo*	generation world	世話 世界 世の中	せわ せかい よのなか	care world the world
息	SOKU *iki*	son breath	気息 息子 息をする	きそく むすこ いきをする	breathing son to breathe
忙	BOO *isoga(shii)*	busy	多忙 忙しい	たぼう いそがしい	very busy busy
言	GEN, GON *koto, i(u)*	say	言語 方言 言葉 言う	げんご ほうげん ことば いう	language dialect words, language to say
銀	GIN	silver	銀行 銀座 銀河	ぎんこう ぎんざ ぎんが	bank Ginza (district of Tokyo) Milky Way

A. 日本語で書きなさい。 (Write the following in Japanese.)

1. It has been a long time since I saw you last.

2. I am sorry that you haven't heard from me in such a long time.

3. It's too quiet. So you'll probably get bored.

4. When I retire, I want to move somewhere quiet.

B. 次を英語に訳しなさい。 (Translate the following into English.)

1. 主人がいつも世話になったと聞いています。

2. こんな静かな所で生活できる人がうらやましいわ。

3. 都会の生活は便利ですけど、時々いやになります。

4. どうして子供さんを都会の学校に行かせたいんですか。

C. 次の下線の漢字をひらがなで書きなさい。 (Write the following underlined *kanji* in hiragana.)

1. ここはいい景色ですね。

2. この旅館は友だちの家なんです。

3. 夏休みと冬休みに来ました。

4. 息子も忙しいようです。

答え

A. 1. しばらくでございます。 2. 長い間ご無沙汰しています。 3. 静か過ぎて退屈するでしょう。 4. 会社をやめたら、どこか静かな所に行きたいです。

B. 1. My husband is always telling me how good you were to him. 2. I envy people who can live in such a quiet place. 3. Living in the city is convenient, but it's noisy and I get sick of it sometimes. 4. Why do you want your kids to go to school in the city?

C. 1. けしき 2. りょかん、とも、いえ 3. なつやす、ふゆやす、き 4. むすこ、いそが

第十三課

A. 会話

アポイントの取り消し

鈴木氏とネルソン氏は事務所の廊下で話す。

ネルソン：梅雨が上がったと思いましたが、また雨ですね。

すずき：台風ですよ。

ネルソン：7月なのに台風が来るんですか。夏の終わりによく来ると聞いていましたが。

すずき：日本の台風シーズンは長いですから。

ネルソン：今日はアポイントがあるんです。行けるでしょうかね。

すずき：アポイントはどこですか。

ネルソン：横浜です。

すずき：さあ、分かりませんね。テレビで台風速報をしていますよ。聞きましょう。

二人は会議室に行って放送を見る。

アナウンサー：台風5号が関東地方に近づいています。今の状況から推測しますと、台風は夕方 東京及び千葉県に上陸する可能性が強くなっています。台風にともない雨がはげしく降りはじめていますので、十分注意するよう気象庁は警告しております。またJR及び私鉄も運転をとりやめている所もあります。お出かけの際は十分ご注意下さい。

352

ネルソン：この分では出かけられませんね。

すずき：何時のアポイントですか。

ネルソン：一時の約束なんですが。

すずき：乗り物が動いていない所もあるから、無理ですよ。

ネルソン：キャンセルしても構いませんか。悪い印象を与えるかな。

すずき：いいえ、大丈夫でしょう。こんな時はアポイントを取り消した
　　　方がいいですよ。相手も解ってくれますから。日本ではいつもこの
　　　問題があります。心配しないで。

ネルソン：じゃあ、そうします。

ネルソン氏は横浜商事の中野嬢に電話する。

ネルソン：もしもし、ビジテックのネルソンですが、中野さん、お願い
　　　します。

なかの：私ですが。

ネルソン：ああ、中野さん。先週お電話したネルソンですが。

なかの：はい、覚えていますよ。今日のアポイントのことですか。

ネルソン：ええ、台風の関係で、乗り物が動いてない所もあるそうで。
　　　勝手で申し訳ございませんが、アポイントを延期していただきたいの
　　　ですが。

なかの：一応準備はしてあったんですが、仕方がありませんね。

ネルソン：誠に申し訳ありません。

なかの：いいえ。それでどうしますか。

ネルソン：十日あたりはいかがでしょうか。

なかの：十日は木曜日ですねえ。残念ですが、ちょっと無理です。

ネルソン：金曜日午後は。

なかの：ええ、金曜日午後2時にしましょう。都合がつかない時は連絡します。

ネルソン：承知いたしました。アシスタントを2名連れてうかがいますから、よろしくお願いします。

なかの：それで、場所は分かりますか。地図をファックスしましょうか。

ネルソン：いいえ、分かると思います。市役所の隣のビルですね。

なかの：そうです。じゃあ、お待ちしています。

ネルソン：どうもありがとうございます。それでは失礼いたします。
(自分に) これはできた。さあ、電車がないから、どうしてうちに帰るか考えなくちゃ。

B. 単語

事務所	jimusho	office	廊下	rooka	corridor
梅雨	tsuyu	rainy season	台風	taifuu	typhoon
速報	sokuhoo	bulletin	放送	hoosoo	broadcast
状況	jookyoo	situation	推測する	suisoku suru	to assume
上陸	jooriku	to land	可能性	kanoosei	possibility
はげしい	hageshii	intense, violent	注意する	chuui suru	to take caution
気象庁	kishoochoo	The Meteorological Agency			
警告する	keikoku suru	to warn	印象	inshoo	impression
延期する	enki suru	to postpone	準備	junbi	preparation
連絡	renraku	contact	場所	basho	location
地図	chizu	map			

C. 漢字
かんじ

梅	BAI *ume*	plum	梅花 梅雨 梅 梅酒	ばいか つゆ うめ うめしゅ		plum blossoms rainy season plum plum wine
雨	U *ame*	rain	雨期 雨 大雨 小雨	うき あめ おおあめ こさめ		rainy season rain heavy rain drizzle
台	TAI, DAI	stand	台風 台所 一台	たいふう だいどころ いちだい		typhoon kitchen one car (counter)
風	FUU *kaze*	wind, manner	風景 和風 洋風 風	ふうけい わふう ようふう かぜ		scenery Japanese style Western style wind
終	SHUU *o(wari)* *o(waru)*	end	最終 終了 終点 終わる	さいしゅう しゅうりょう しゅうてん おわる		the last end last stop (train) to end
速	SOKU *haya(i)*	fast	速報 早速 速度 快速 速い	そくほう さっそく そくど かいそく はやい		news bulletin immediately speed express train fast
報	HOO	report	報道 情報 予報 報告	ほうどう じょうほう よほう ほうこく		report information forecast report
状	JOO	condition	状況 状態	じょうきょう じょうたい		situation condition

355

況	KYOO	still more	不況	ふきょう	recession
		circumstances	実況	じっきょう	real condition
	mashite		況して	まして	still more
推	SUI	infer	推測	すいそく	conjecture
	o(su)		推薦	すいせん	recommendation
			推論	すいろん	inference
			推す	おす	to infer
可	KA	good	可能	かのう	possible
			許可	きょか	permission
			不可	ふか	bad, wrong

練習問題

A. 次を日本語で書きなさい。　(Write the following in Japanese.)

    1. I thought the rainy season was over.

    2. Is it okay to cancel the appointment?

    3. At times like this, it's better to cancel.

    4. If I can't make it, I will get in touch with you.

    5. Do you know where we're located?

B. 次を英語に訳しなさい。(Translate the following into English.)

    1. 乗り物が動いていない所もあるから、無理です。

    2. 悪い印象を与えるかな。

    3. 日本はいつもこんな問題があります。

    4. 一応準備はしてあったんですが、しかたがありません。

C. 次の下線の漢字をひらがなで書きなさい。(Write the following underlined *kanji* in hiragana.)

    1. 台風速報を聞きましょう。

    2. 梅雨は何月ですか。

    3. 今の状況から推測します。

答え

A. 1. 梅雨が上がったと思いました。2. アポイントをキャンセルしても構いませんか。3. こんな時はアポイントを取り消した方がいいです。4. 都合がつかない時は連絡します。5. (こちらの) 場所は分かりますか。

B. 1. Since the trains aren't even running in some places, it'll be impossible. 2. I wonder if it'll give them a bad impression. 3. We have these problems constantly in Japan. 4. We were prepared, but I guess it can't be helped.

C. 1. たいふうそくほう 2. つゆ、なんがつ 3. いま、じょうきょう、すいそく

第十四課

A. 会話

間違いの処理

佐藤嬢は普段と違って機嫌がよくない。ネルソン氏はどうしたのか考える。

ネルソン：佐藤さんは今日どうしたんですか。あまり機嫌がよくないようですが。

すずき：実は彼女間違ったところにファックスを送ってしまったらしいんですよ。それで今朝お客さんから僕に問い合わせがあって、部長に報告したら、部長がかんかんに怒ってね。

ネルソン：大したことじゃないんじゃないんですか。またファックスすればいいでしょう。

すずき：それが昨日までにするはずだったんです。

ネルソン：今日じゃ遅いんですか。

すずき：遅過ぎるわけではないんですが。

ネルソン：じゃあ、どうしてそんなに大騒ぎするんですか。

すずき：それが違うんですよ。部長は信用の問題だというんです。

ネルソン：まあ。それもそうですが、もう送ってしまったんですから、仕方がないでしょう。

すずき：部長は部の誰かが謝りに行けといっているんですが、どうしようかと考えているんです。

ネルソン：電話では謝れないんですか。

すずき：部長は誠意を示すために、わざわざ行って謝るべきだと言うんです。

358

アメリカ人であるネルソン氏は大した問題じゃないと考えながらも、日本人はこういう場合、どんな処理の仕方をするのかに興味を持つ。そしてネルソン氏は佐藤嬢と話す。

ネルソン：佐藤さん、ファックスの問題のことを聞きました。どうしたんですか。ファックス番号を間違えたんですか。

さとう：いいえ、私は間違えてはいないんです。

ネルソン：じゃあ、誰が間違えたんですか。

さとう：それが分からないんです。番号は紙に書いてありましたから、それで送ったんです。誰がその番号を書いたか私は知りません。でも鈴木さんは私がその番号を書いたように部長に報告したんです。それでちょっと気分を害しています。

ネルソン：なるほど。

さとう：それで部長は私のことをすごく怒っているんです。

ネルソン：それで、どうするんですか。誰が謝りに行くんですか。

さとう：鈴木さんが担当だから、彼が行くべきだと思うんです。私が行ってもかまいませんけど。

ネルソン：そうですね。鈴木さんが行った方がいいかもね。じゃあ、鈴木さんが謝りに行くのが一番いいということを私が上手に言ってあげますよ。番号のことも説明してあげますよ。

さとう：よろしくお願いしますね。

ネルソン：心配しないで。部長もなぜこんなことになったか分かりますよ。

ネルソン氏は信用とか「顔」の問題にまで発展していることに気づく。鈴木氏、明治保険の安藤課長の事務所まで謝りに行くことにする。

あんどう：やあ、どうぞ、お座り下さい。

すずき：この度は大変失礼いたしました。私共の手違いで大変ご迷惑をお掛けしました。

あんどう：それはわざわざ、ご丁寧にありがとうございます。

すずき：注意はしていますが、毎日忙しくしているものですから。

あんどう：いやね。係りのものを待たせておいたし、それにあまり公表したくないものですから。

すずき：そうですか。申し訳ございませんでした。今後絶対にこんな間違いがないように注意いたしますから、お許し下さい。

あんどう：よくあることですよ。あまり気になさらないで下さい。高木部長によろしくおっしゃって下さい。

すずき：分かりました。では失礼します。

B. 単語

普段の	*fudan no*	usual	機嫌	*kigen*	mood
お客さん	*okyakusan*	customer	報告する	*hookoku suru*	to report
怒る	*okoru*	to get angry	大した	*taishita*	great
信用	*shin'yoo*	trust	謝る	*ayamaru*	to apologize
誠意	*seii*	sincerity	示す	*shimesu*	to show
処理する	*shori suru*	to handle	興味	*kyoomi*	interest
担当	*tantoo*	in charge	発展する	*hatten suru*	to develop
手違い	*techigai*	mistake	丁寧に	*teinei ni*	politely
絶対に	*zettai ni*	absolutely	許す	*yurusu*	to forgive

機	KI	occasion machine	機嫌 機会 機械	きげん きかい きかい	mood opportunity machine
彼	HI *kare*	that	彼 彼女	かれ かのじょ	he she
送	SOO *oku(ru)*	send	発送 放送 送る	はっそう ほうそう おくる	dispatch broadcast send
朝	CHOO *asa*	morning	朝食 今朝 毎朝 朝日	ちょうしょく けさ まいあさ あさひ	breakfast this morning every morning morning sun
客	KYAKU	guest	お客様 客観的	おきゃくさま きゃっかんてき	guest objective (adj.)
問	MON *to(u), to(i)*	question	問題 質問 問い合わせ 問う	もんだい しつもん といあわせ とう	problem question inquiry to ask
告	KOKU	report	報告 通告 告げる	ほうこく つうこく つげる	report notice (n.) to tell, inform
怒	DO *oko(ru)*	angry	激怒 怒る	げきど おこる	rage to get angry
昨	SAKU	past, last	昨日 昨年	さくじつ、きのう さくねん	yesterday last year
騒	SOO *sawa(gu)*	noise	騒々しい 大騒ぎ 騒ぎ立てる	そうぞうしい おおさわぎ さわぎたてる	noisy uproar to make a big fuss

題	DAI	topic	話題	わだい	topic
			課題	かだい	theme
			宿題	しゅくだい	homework
起	KI	occur, get up	起源	きげん	origin
	o(koru)		再起	さいき	recovery
	o(kiru)		起こる	おこる	to occur, happen
			起きる	おきる	to wake up
			起こす	おこす	to wake someone up
			早起き	はやおき	early riser
謝	SHA	apologize	感謝	かんしゃ	appreciation
	ayamaru		謝る	あやまる	to apologize
誠	SEI	sincere	誠意	せいい	sincerity
	makoto		誠に	まことに	really
害	GAI	harm	被害	ひがい	damage
			害する	がいする	harm
			災害	さいがい	disaster

練習問題

A. 次を日本語で書きなさい。(Write the following in Japanese.)

    1. That's not (such) a big deal, is it?

    2. Why are they making such a fuss?

    3. The department manager is very upset with me.

    4. I am afraid that our error has caused you a great deal of trouble.

B. 次の下線の漢字をひらがなで書きなさい。(Write the following underlined *kanji* in hiragana.)

    1. 彼の機嫌が良くないですね。

    2. その問題で大騒ぎしています。

    3. 誠意を示すため、謝るべきです。

A. 1. 大したことじゃないじゃないんですか。 2. どうしてそんな大騒ぎするんですか。 3. 部長がすごく怒っています。 4. 私共の手違いで大変ご迷惑をお掛けしました。

B. 1. きげん 2. もんだい、おおさわ 3. せいい、あやま

第十五課

<ruby>第<rt>だい</rt>十<rt>じゅう</rt>五<rt>ご</rt>課<rt>か</rt></ruby>

A．<ruby>会話<rt>かいわ</rt></ruby>

<ruby>京都旅行計画<rt>きょうとりょこうけいかく</rt></ruby>

ネルソン<ruby>氏<rt>し</rt></ruby>は<ruby>行<rt>い</rt></ruby>きつけのすし<ruby>屋<rt>や</rt></ruby>に<ruby>行<rt>い</rt></ruby>く。<ruby>日本滞在<rt>にほんたいざい</rt></ruby>は<ruby>短<rt>みじか</rt></ruby>いにもかかわらず、そこで
は<ruby>皆<rt>みんな</rt></ruby>が<ruby>彼<rt>かれ</rt></ruby>をよく<ruby>知<rt>し</rt></ruby>っている。

シェフ：いらっしゃい。

ネルソン：<ruby>今晩<rt>こんばん</rt></ruby>は。

シェフ：<ruby>毎度<rt>まいど</rt></ruby>どうも。<ruby>今日<rt>きょう</rt></ruby>はお<ruby>一人<rt>ひとり</rt></ruby>ですか。

ネルソン：はい。<ruby>相変<rt>あいか</rt></ruby>わらず、<ruby>込<rt>こ</rt></ruby>んでいますね。

シェフ：おかげさまで。<ruby>和<rt>かず</rt></ruby>ちゃん、お<ruby>一人様<rt>ひとりさま</rt></ruby>。

かずこ：はい。いらっしゃいませ。お<ruby>飲<rt>の</rt></ruby>みものはいつものお<ruby>酒<rt>さけ</rt></ruby>でよろし
いですか。

ネルソン：えーと、<ruby>今日<rt>きょう</rt></ruby>は<ruby>何<rt>なに</rt></ruby>にしようかな。<ruby>今日<rt>きょう</rt></ruby>はビールにします。

シェフ：<ruby>今日<rt>きょう</rt></ruby>はまぐろとうにが<ruby>最高<rt>さいこう</rt></ruby>ですが。

ネルソン：はい、<ruby>適当<rt>てきとう</rt></ruby>にお<ruby>願<rt>ねが</rt></ruby>いします。

シェフ：じゃあ、まぐろの<ruby>刺身<rt>さしみ</rt></ruby>から。

ネルソン：いただきます。わあ、おいしいですね。

<ruby>飲<rt>の</rt></ruby>み<ruby>物<rt>もの</rt></ruby>がきて、<ruby>板前<rt>いたまえ</rt></ruby>はすしをにぎって、ネルソン<ruby>氏<rt>し</rt></ruby>に<ruby>出<rt>だ</rt></ruby>し<ruby>始<rt>はじ</rt></ruby>める。

ネルソン：ところで、<ruby>板前<rt>いたまえ</rt></ruby>さんは<ruby>京都出身<rt>きょうとしゅっしん</rt></ruby>でしたね。

シェフ：僕ですか。いいえ、僕は東京生まれの東京育ちです。和ちゃんのことでしょう。彼女は関西出身ですよ。どうしてですか。

ネルソン：実は来週京都に行く予定なんです。

シェフ：和ちゃん、京都生まれだったよね。

かずこ：はい、京都で生まれて、京都で育ちました。京都のことなら、何でも聞いて下さい。

ネルソン：そうですか。じゃあ、京都についていろいろ教えて下さい。

かずこ：はい。何でいらっしゃいますか。

ネルソン：新幹線です。予約がいりますか。

かずこ：いまは旅行のシーズンじゃありませんから、いらないと思います。

ネルソン：どのホテルがいいですか。

かずこ：何泊なさいますか。

ネルソン：二泊三日です。仕事は半日で終わるので、少し観光でもしようと思って。

かずこ：それなら、都ホテルか京都観光ホテルがいいでしょう。ちょっと高いかもしれませんけど。もっとやすい方がよかったら、旅館もいいでしょう。桂亭という旅館なんかいいですよ。ビールもう一本いかがですか。

ネルソン：はい、お願いします。分かりました。住所はどう調べたらいいですか。

かずこ：みんな京都駅の近くです。

ネルソン：ああ、そうですか。もちろん観光バスがありますね。

かずこ：はい、半日観光、一日観光とかいろいろあります。一日目はバスに乗って、次の日は自分でゆっくり見たい所に行くというのがいいです。

ネルソン：なるほど。京都でおいしいものは何ですか。

かずこ：京都特有のものを何かためしてみますか。もし豆腐が嫌いじゃなかったら、湯豆腐を是非食べてみて下さい。

ネルソン：どうして豆腐が特別なんですか。

かずこ：京都にはお寺が千以上もあって、昔お坊さん達は肉や魚を食べないで、豆腐料理をよく食べたって聞いています。

ネルソン：ああ、それで。おいしい店の名前が分かりますか。

かずこ：あちこちにありますが、えーと、、、

シェフ：次は何にしますか。

ネルソン：海老をお願い。

そこへネルソン氏の隣に座っていた元井という人が会話に加わる。

もとい：お寺とかホテルの近くのどこでもありますよ。都ホテルの近くにもあったと思います。

ネルソン：京都の方ですか。

もとい：いいえ。でも私、仕事でよく行きますから。京都は落ち着いていて、本当にいい町ですよ。金閣寺など有名なお寺もいいですが、無名のお寺や店に行くのもいいですよ。変わったものがあるし、みんな親切にいろいろ教えてしてくれますよ。

ネルソン：なるほど。まだ古い文化が残っているわけですね。

もとい：ええ、何しろ長い間　都でしたから、お寺だけじゃなくて、趣の
　　　　ある美しい建物もたくさん建てられて、それがまだかなり残ってい
　　　　ます。庭園に興味がおありだったら、今は絶好の季節です。どうぞ
　　　　楽しい旅行をして来て下さい。

ネルソン：ええ、本当に楽しみです。

もとい：私はこれで失礼します。板前さん、ご馳走さまでした。おあい
　　　　そ、お願いします。

シェフ：はい、毎度ありがとうございます。

ネルソン：いろいろ教えていただいて、本当にありがとうございました。

もとい：いいえ。じゃあ、お先に。

B．単語

相変わらず	aikawarazu	as usual		刺身	sashimi	sliced raw fish
板前	itamae	chef		にぎる	nigiru	to grip, form
育つ	sodatsu	to grow up		何泊	nanpaku	how many nights
半日	han'nichi	half a day		旅館	ryokan	Japanese inn
観光	kankoo	sightseeing		豆腐	toofu	tofu
特有な	tokuyuu na	unique		寺	tera	temple
特別な	tokubetsu na	special		海老	ebi	shrimp
お坊さん	oboosan	monk		無名な	mumei na	unknown
落ち着く	ochitsuku	to settle down		残る	nokoru	to remain
変わった	kawatta	unusual		趣のある	omomuki no aru	tasteful
都	miyako	old capital		建てる	tateru	to build
建物	tatemono	building		絶好な	zekkoo na	perfect
庭園	teien	garden				

屋	OKU	roof, house,	屋上	おくじょう	roof
	ya	shop	本屋	ほんや	book store
			寿司屋	すしや	sushi restaurant
			部屋	へや	room

| 滞 | TAI | | 滞在 | たいざい | stay |
| | *stay* | | 滞日 | たいにち | staying in Japan |

在	ZAI	exist	存在	そんざい	existence
	a(ru)		在日	ざいにち	staying in Japan
			現在	げんざい	present, current
			在る	ある	to exist

短	TAN	short	短所	たんしょ	shortcoming
	mijika(i)		短気	たんき	short temper
			短い	みじかい	short

相	SOO	mutual	相談	そうだん	consultation
	ai		相撲	すもう	sumo
			相互	そうご	mutual
			相手	あいて	partner

和	WA	peace	平和	へいわ	peace
		Japanese	和食	わしょく	Japanese food
			漢和	かんわ	Chinese-Japanese

京	KYOO	capital	京都	きょうと	Kyoto
	KEI		東京	とうきょう	Tokyo
			京阪神	けいはんしん	Kyoto-Osaka-Kobe

関	KAN	gate	関西	かんさい	Kansai area
	kaka(waru)		関東	かんとう	Kanto area
			関係	かんけい	relationship
			関心	かんしん	interest
			関わる	かかわる	to be related

西	SAI	west	関西	かんさい	Kansai area
	SEI		西洋	せいよう	the West
	nishi		西部	せいぶ	western part
			西	にし	west

| 育 | IKU | grow | 教育 | きょういく | education |
| | *soda(tsu)* | | 育つ | そだつ | to grow up |

思	SHI	think	思想	しそう	thought
	omo(u)		思う	おもう	think
			不思議	ふしぎ	mystery, wonder

泊	HAKU	stay	宿泊	しゅくはく	lodging
	to(maru)		一泊	いっぱく	one night
			泊まる	とまる	to stay overnight

| 仕 | SHI | serve | 仕事 | しごと | work, job |
| | | | 仕方 | しかた | way of doing |

半	HAN	half	半分	はんぶん	half
	naka(ba)		半日	はんにち	half-day
			半ば	なかば	half-way

観	KAN	view	観光	かんこう	sightseeing
	mi(ru)		観光客	かんこうきゃく	tourist
			観点	かんてん	point of view
			観賞	かんしょう	admiration
			観る	みる	to view, look

練習問題
れんしゅうもんだい

A. 次を日本語で書きなさい。 (Write the following words in Japanese.)
つぎ　にほんご　か

1. I'll go with your recommendation.

2. I was born and raised in Tokyo.

3. How should I find the address?

4. I don't eat fish or meat, but I eat a lot of cooked vegetables.

5. Everyone is very kind and helpful.

B. 次の言葉を英語で書きなさい。(Write the following words in English.)

    1. お酒

    2. まぐろ

    3. さしみ

    4. うに

答え

A.　1. 適当にお願いします。2. 東京で生まれ、育ちました。3. 住所はどう探せばいいですか。4. 魚も肉も食べませんが、野菜料理をたくさん食べます。5. みんな親切にいろいろ教えてくれます。

B. 1. sake 2. tuna 3. sliced raw fish 4. sea urchin

読む練習 3

日本人の国民性

国それぞれの「国民性」とか独自の考え方とか文化というものがあると前提して、日本人の国民性を考えてみよう。

第一に考えられることは、日本人が何人か集まると年齢とか社会的地位など、何らかの基準により、お互いの「序列」が意識され、行動も変わることである。その基準が教育だったり、経済的な力だったり、勤めている企業の大きさだったりすることもある。そして他にもさまざまな「基準」を作りだす。しかしながら、その序列を意識しながらも、日本人は調和を見出して生活している。

又、それと同時に日本人は「グループ」で行動する傾向がある。封建時代から集団で行動するよう習慣づけられ、その伝統は依然残っていると考えられているし、独立性に乏しいとも考えられている。

次に、他の人達と違った行動をとることはあまり良くないと考える日本人が多い。「出る釘は打たれる」という諺がある。これは、他の人たちと違う意見をもったり、目立った行動をとる人は、他の人達からあまり好かれないということである。

また、日本人は自分の意見をあまり言わないで、他の人の意見を尊重しながら話を進めていくと言われている。なぜこの自分の考えを強く主張しないかということには色々の説がある。調和を考えて自分を主張しない、という善意に考える説があるし、意見を言うような教育を受けていないから言えないのだという厳しい説もある。

このような日本人特有の国民性も変わりつつある。特に現代っ子は「自由」を謳歌し、コンピューターを使いこなし、伝統的なしきたりに縛られていない。将来は国民性などは失われてしまうのだろうか。

単語

国民性	こくみんせい	national character
前提	ぜんてい	prerequisite, assumption
何らかの	なんらかの	a sort of
基準	きじゅん	standard, foundation
地位	ちい	rank, status
序列	じょれつ	order, rank
意識	いしき	knowledge
傾向	けいこう	tendency
行動	こうどう	action, behavior
封建時代	ほうけんじだい	feudal era
集団	しゅうだん	group
独立性	どくりつせい	independence
乏しい	とぼしい	scarce, lacking
釘	くぎ	nail
諺	ことわざ	proverb
目立った	めだった	striking, standing out
好く	すく	to like
尊重する	そんちょうする	to respect
説	せつ	theory, opinion
調和	ちょうわ	harmony
善意	ぜんい	goodwill
厳しい	きびしい	severe, stern
現代っ子	げんだいっこ	young generation
謳歌する	おおかする	to glorify
仕来り	しきたり	custom, convention
縛る	しばる	to tie, to bind
失う	うしなう	to lose

第十六課
だいじゅうろっか

A. 会話
かいわ

入社試験面接
にゅうしゃしけんめんせつ

ネルソン氏と鈴木氏は入社試験の面接をしているが、適任者を探すのはなかなか難しいことが分かる。

ネルソン：なかなか適当な人がいないですね。

すずき：そうですね。

ネルソン：真面目そうで、やる気のある人はいますが、すぐ仕事ができるという人材が少ないようですね。

すずき：それには理由があるんです。

ネルソン：とおっしゃいますと。

すずき：日本の若い人達は会社に入ってから仕事を学べると考えていますから、スキルを持っている人が少ないんです。

ネルソン：なるほど。アメリカではすぐ仕事ができるようにスキルを持っている人の方が就職しやすいですが。

すずき：大学教育の違いもある訳です。つまり日本の大学生はクラブ活動をしたり、旅行したりして、ネットワーキングや付き合いに力を入れています。勉強は適当にという訳です。

ネルソン：企業はどういう考えなんですか。

すずき：それが面白いんです。実は企業もあまり知識があり、個性の強すぎる人は求めていないようです。むしろ真面目でやる気のある人を採用して企業の方針にしたがって教育し直すという考えです。

ネルソン：今後もそういう体制ですか。

すずき：いや、変わらざるを得ないと思いますよ。国際化しつつある日本はこのままではやって行けませんから。事実もう大分変わりつつあります。

ネルソン：次の人も同じかな。

すずき：いや。経歴がちょっと違うようですから。

ネルソン氏と鈴木氏は会議室に入って来た山下嬢を面接する。

すずき：山下さんですね。どうぞお掛け下さい。

やました：よろしくお願いします。

すずき：経歴を簡単に話して下さい。

やました：千葉に生まれて、高校までそこにいました。神奈川大学の経営学部に入り、三年の時アリゾナ州立大学に留学しました。英語の勉強のつもりで行ったんですが、結局同校に転校して卒業しました。卒業後、東海電気に就職しましたが、今年事情があってやめました。

すずき：さしつかえなければ、その事情というのを話して下さい。

やました：はい。一つの理由は、ご存じのように東海電気は大企業です。

ネルソン：ええ。それで。

やました：毎日することといえば、誰でもできるような仕事で、自分の実力を十分出せるような環境ではなかったんです。

ネルソン：じゃあ、うちのような小さな会社があなたに合うと考えているんですか。

やました：はい。小さい会社なら、企画から営業までいろいろできますから、もっと実力が出せると思います。

ネルソン：なるほど。（履歴書を見ながら）営業の経験は全然ないようですね。

やました：ええ、実際に営業の仕事はしたことはありませんが、東海電気の業務課は営業部と協力して仕事をしていましてから、いろいろ学びました。

ネルソン：営業の仕事をしたいんですね。

やました：はい。人と会って話したりするのが好きですから、やれると思います。

ネルソン：分かりました。この仕事はセールスが主ですが、他のこともしてもらいます。

やました：はい、それは分かっています。

ネルソン：残業なんかどう考えていますか。

やました：やむをえない場合はやります。できればしたくありませんが、時間を有効に使う主義ですから。

ネルソン：この仕事はコンピューター関係で、コンピューターのソフトの販売ですが、インターネットとかオフィスのコンピューター化など、どう思いますか。

やました：すごく興味があります。

ネルソン：コンピューターについての知識は。

やました：アリゾナ州立で勉強しました。家にはマッキントッシュがあります。

ネルソン：はい。じゃあ、二三日して正式に連絡します。

やました：よろしくお願いします。

山下嬢、会議室を出る。

すずき：なかなか積極的で、頼もしいですね。

ネルソン：そうですね。

B．単語

入社試験	*nyuushashiken*	company entrance exam	面接	*mensetsu*	interview
適当な	*tekitoo na*	appropriate	真面目な	*majime na*	serious
やる気	*yaru ki*	eagerness	人材	*jinzai*	talented person
理由	*riyuu*	reason	学べる	*manaberu*	to be able to learn
教育	*kyooiku*	education	違い	*chigai*	difference
活動	*katsudoo*	activity	付き合い	*tsukiai*	association
企業	*kigyoo*	corporation	知識	*chishiki*	knowledge
個性	*kosei*	individuality	求める	*motomeru*	to seek
採用	*saiyoo*	employment	方針	*hooshin*	policy
今後	*kongo*	after this	体制	*taisei*	system
国際化	*kokusaika*	internationalization	事実	*jijitsu*	fact
経歴	*keireki*	work history	経営学部	*keieigakubu*	management department
留学	*ryuugaku*	study abroad	結局	*kekkyoku*	eventually
転校	*tenkoo*	changing schools	東海電気	*Tookaidenki*	Tokai Electric
事情	*jijoo*	circumstances	実力	*jitsuryoku*	capability
環境	*kankyoo*	environment	詳しい	*kuwashii*	detailed
業務課	*gyoomuka*	business department	改善	*kaizen*	improvement
効果的	*kookateki*	effective	合う	*au*	to fit, to suit
企画	*kikaku*	plan	営業	*eigyoo*	sales
履歴書	*rirekisho*	resume	協力	*kyooryoku*	cooperation
残業	*zangyoo*	overtime	場合	*baai*	case
有効な	*yuukoo na*	effective	主義	*shugi*	principle
販売	*hanbai*	sales	興味	*kyoomi*	interest
正式な	*seishiki na*	formal	積極的な	*sekkyokuteki na*	upbeat, positive
頼もしい	*tanomoshii*	reliable			

375

C. 漢字

試	SHI *tame(su)* *kokoro(miru)*	try	試験 入試 試す 試みる	しけん にゅうし ためす こころみる	examination entrance exam to try to experiment, try
験	KEN		経験 体験	けいけん たいけん	an experience personal experience
面	MEN	face	面接 正面 方面	めんせつ しょうめん ほうめん	interview front direction, region
接	SETSU	touch	接待 直接 間接的	せったい ちょくせつ かんせつてき	entertaining a client direct indirect
適	TEKI	suitable	適当な 適任者 適する	てきとうな てきにんしゃ てきする	appropriate qualified person to be suitable
任	NIN *maka(seru)*	duty	任務 責任 着任する 任せる	にんむ せきにん ちゃくにんする まかせる	responsibility, duty responsibility to assume 　responsibility to entrust
真	SHIN *makoto* *ma*	true just	真実 写真 真に 真面目な	しんじつ しゃしん まことに まじめな	truth photo sincerely serious
目	MOKU *me*	eyes	目的 目標 注目 目を通す	もくてき もくひょう ちゅうもく めをとおす	purpose goal attention to glance

由	YU,YUU	reason	理由	りゆう	reason
	yoshi		由来	ゆらい	origin
	yo(ru)		に由る	による	to be based on, depend upon
就	SHUU	settle in	就職	しゅうしょく	finding a job
	tsu(ku)		就く	つく	to take a position
職	SHOKU	employment	職業	しょくぎょう	occupation
			職員	しょくいん	staff
			職場	しょくば	place of work
			職歴	しょくれき	occupational history
育	IKU	raise	教育	きょういく	education
	soda(tsu)		発育	はついく	growth
			育つ	そだつ	to be raised
企	KI	plan	企画	きかく	plan
			企業	きぎょう	corporation
知	CHI	knowledge	知識	ちしき	knowledge
	shi(ru)		知人	ちじん	acquaintance
			知恵	ちえ	wisdom
			知る	しる	to know
採	SAI	accept	採用	さいよう	employment
	to(ru)	employ	採決	さいけつ	adoption or rejection, vote
			採る	とる	to adopt, hire

A. 次を日本語で書きなさい。(Write the following in Japanese.)

1. There just aren't any people who are well suited for the job.

2. Describe briefly your career history.

3. Could you explain it a little more in detail?

4. You mean you were frustrated with the job?

5. I have never actually had a sales job.

B. 次を英語に訳しなさい。(Translate the following into English.)

1. 日本の若い人達は会社に入ってから仕事を学べると考えています。

2. 国際化しつつある日本はこのままではやって行けません。

3. 小さい会社なら、企画から営業までいろいろできます。

4. 残業なんかどう思いますか。

答え

A. 1. なかなか適当な人がいないですね。 2. 経験を簡単に話して下さい。
3. もうちょっと詳しく話して下さい。 4. 思うように仕事ができなかった
という訳ですか。 5. 実際に営業の仕事をしたことはありません。

B. 1. Young Japanese think that they will be able to learn the job once they enter a company. 2. Japan, continuing in its internationalization, cannot continue to operate in the same way. 3. In a small company, one can do various things, from planning to marketing. 4. How do you feel about overtime?

第十七課

A. 会話
かいわ

プレゼンテーション

ネルソン氏、小林産業の和田部長に電話して、新製品を紹介するために、その
し こばやしさんぎょう わだぶちょう でんわ しんせいひん しょうかい
面会のアポイントを取る。
めんかい と

ひしょ：和田部長、ネルソンさんという方からお電話です。
わだぶちょう かた でんわ

わだ：はい。総務部の和田ですが。
そうむぶ わだ

ネルソン：もしもし、JTCの山中専務からご紹介いただいたネルソンと申
やまなかせんむ しょうかい もう
しますが。一度お時間をいただけましたらありがたいと思いますが。
いちど じかん おも

わだ：失礼ですが、ご用件は何なのでしょうか。
しつれい ようけん なん

ネルソン：実は「スーパーメール」という新製品をご紹介させていただ
じつ しんせいひん しょうかい
きたいと思いまして。
おも

わだ：それはどういったものですか。

ネルソン：Eメール、即ち電子メールのソフトでございます。
すなわ でんし

わだ：なるほど。

ネルソン：それで、そちら様の方でもコンピューター化されつつあると
さま ほう か
伺っておりますが。
うかが

わだ：みんな使ってはいるんですが、全員ではありません。
つか ぜんいん

ネルソン：それでしたら、ぜひ当社の製品をご説明させていただけませ
とうしゃ せいひん せつめい
んか。使いやすくて、事務能力が向上すること、間違いありません。
つか じむのうりょく こうじょう まちが

379

わだ：山中専務からのお話でもあるし、聞くだけでも聞いてみましょう。

ネルソン：本当にありがとうございます。早速ですが、来週の末ごろはいかがでしょうか。改めてご連絡させていただきますが。

わだ：いや、問題ないと思いますから、木曜日の午後に決めましょう。

ネルソン氏、プレゼンテーションをする。

ネルソン：ビジテックのネルソンでございます。本日は、お忙しいところをお集りいただき、ありがとうございます。これから、私どもで扱っております商品「スーパーメール」のご紹介をさせていただきますが、その前に当社について簡単にご説明したいと思います。それから商品説明の後で皆様のご質問をお受けしたいと思います。どうぞよろしくお願いします。弊社ビジテックは1980年にシアトルに設立され、主にコンピューターのソフトの開発販売の業務を行っています。社員は今のところ百人ほどですが、海外進出のため今年は大分増える予定です。日本支社は三年前にJTC社と業務提携して設立されました。顧客リスト、取引銀行、売上高などについては、こちらの資料をご覧下さい。本日ご紹介いたします「スーパー　メール」は、社内の連絡を総て電子メールでするためのソフトでございます。これを使いますと時間と紙の節約が出来ますし、一度にたくさんの方々に短時間で連絡できます。もちろん外部の方々とも簡単に連絡し合えます。外部と言いますのは世界中の方々と会話できることです。この製品のいいところは英語でも日本語でも使うことができて、インターネットともつなげることです。日本でも大分インターネットが盛んになっているようですが、今後もっともっと盛んになると思いますから、時間的にタイムリーだと言えます。価格は色々な機能があるにもかかわらず、他の製品と大差ありません。

以上、簡単ですが、概要を申し上げました。これからプロモーション
ビデオをご覧いただきたいと思います。
それから詳しくは商品カタログをご覧下さい。後は皆様のご質問にお
答えしながら補足していきたいと思います。

ありがとうございました。

B. 単語

面会	*menkai*	meeting	総務部	*soomubu*	general affairs department
用件	*yooken*	business	電子	*denshi*	electron, electric
全員	*zen'in*	all employees	当社	*toosha*	our company
事務	*jimu*	office work	能力	*nooryoku*	ability
向上	*koojoo*	increase	間違い	*machigai*	mistake
早速	*sassoku*	abrupt	改めて	*aratamete*	again
決める	*kimeru*	to decide	準備	*junbi*	preparation
商品	*shoohin*	product	競争会社	*kyoosoogaisha*	competitors
比較	*hikaku*	comparison	好都合な	*kootsugoo na*	convenient
氾濫	*hanran*	flood	機能	*kinoo*	function
強調	*kyoochoo*	emphasis	年配	*nenpai*	age, older
なるべく	*narubeku*	as much as possible	分かりやすい	*wakariyasui*	easy to understand
扱う	*atsukau*	to handle, treat	質問	*shitsumon*	question
受ける	*ukeru*	to receive	設立	*setsuritsu*	establishment
開発	*kaihatsu*	development	支社	*shisha*	branch office
業務	*gyoomu*	work, business	海外	*kaigai*	overseas
業務提携	*gyoomuteikei*	joint venture	顧客	*kokyaku*	customer
進出	*shinshutsu*	expansion	銀行	*ginkoo*	bank
取引	*torihiki*	transaction	売上高	*uriagedaka*	sales
節約する	*setsuyaku suru*	to economize	外部	*gaibu*	outside
世界中	*sekaijuu*	worldwide	盛んに	*sakan ni*	actively
価格	*kakaku*	price	大差	*taisa*	big difference
概要	*gaiyoo*	overview	補足	*hosoku*	supplement

C. 漢字 <ruby>漢字<rt>かんじ</rt></ruby>

総	SOO	general	総務	そうむ	general affairs	
			総合	そうごう	composite	
			総会	そうかい	general meeting	
			総轄	そうかつ	general control	
務	MU	work	勤務	きんむ	work, service	
	tsuto(meru)		事務	じむ	office work	
			専務	せんむ	managing director	
			勤める	つとめる	to work, serve	
件	KEN	matter	用件	ようけん	business	
		item	要件	ようけん	important matter	
			事件	じけん	incident	
全	ZEN	all	全員	ぜんいん	all members	
	matta(ku)		全体	ぜんたい	all	
			全部	ぜんぶ	all	
			全国	ぜんこく	the entire country	
			全く	まったく	completely	
員	IN	member	社員	しゃいん	employee	
			銀行員	ぎんこういん	bank employee	
			工員	こういん	factory worker	
当	TOO	this, right	当社	とうしゃ	this company, our company	
			当人	とうにん	the said person	
			当日	とうじつ	the appointed day	
	a(taru)	to strike	当たる	あたる	to hit	
	a(teru)		当てる	あてる	to guess correctly	
能	NOO	ability	能力	のうりょく	ability	
			知能	ちのう	intelligence	
向	KOO	face forward	向上	こうじょう	improvement	
	mu(ku)		傾向	けいこう	tendency	
			向く	むく	to turn toward	

382

改	KAI	reform	改革	かいかく	reform
			改定	かいてい	reform
			改正	かいせい	revision
	arata(mete)		改めて	あらためて	anew, again
決	KETSU	decision	決定	けってい	decision
	ki(meru)		決心	けっしん	resolution
	ki(maru)		決める	きめる	to decide
			決まる	きまる	to be decided
準	JUN	semi-, aim	準備	じゅんび	preparation
			準急	じゅんきゅう	semi-express train
備	BI	provide	整備	せいび	adjustment
	sona(eru)		備品	びひん	fixtures
			備える	そなえる	to provide
競	KYOO	compete	競争	きょうそう	competition
	kiso(u)		競技	きょうぎ	sports competition
			競う	きそう	to compete
比	HI	compare	比較	ひかく	comparison
	kura(beru)		比率	ひりつ	ratio
			比べる	くらべる	to compare

練習問題

A. 次を日本語で書きなさい。 (Write the following in Japanese.)

1. I would be grateful if you could spare some time.

2. I am sorry to ask, but what does this concern?

3. It is easy to use and there is no doubt that your office productivity will increase.

4. Thank you very much for taking time out of your busy schedules to meet here today.

B. 次の下線の漢字をひらがなで書きなさい。(Write the following underlined *kanji* in hiragana.)

1. 在宅勤務は全員ではありません。

2. ご用件は何でしょうか。

3. 事務能力が向上します。

4. 競争のために準備しなければなりません。

答え

A. 1. お時間をいただけましたら、ありがたいと思います。 2. 失礼ですが、ご用件は何でしょうか。3. 使いやすくて、事務能力が向上すること、間違いありません。4. お忙しいところお集りいただき、ありがとうございます。
B. 1. きんむ、ぜんいん 2. ようけん、なん 3. じむのうりょく、こうじょう 4. きょうそう、じゅんび

384

第十八課

A. 会話

接待ゴルフ

鈴木氏とネルソン氏は先週のプレゼンテーションの話を続けるため、小林産業の和田部長と浜中課長をゴルフに招待する。練習場にいた和田部長に鈴木氏が近づく。

すずき：先日はありがとうございました。

わだ：いいえ。こちらこそ。わざわざお出でいただきまして。

すずき：いいえ、ご無理をお願いしまして。

わだ：それにしましても、新しい時代になりましたね。我々も本格的にコンピューター導入を考える時期に来ていると感じました。

すずき：そうですね。将来はいわゆる「テレワーク」が普及して、通勤問題や事務所のスペース問題が緩和されると思います。

わだ：在宅勤務が効率的かもしれません。

すずき：全くです。ところで、部長、ゴルフの方はよくされますか。

わだ：月二回ですね。前はもっと多かったんですが、最近少しひかえています。

すずき：なるほど。

わだ：運動不足ですから、もっとやった方がいいんでしょうが、時間がとれません。それに費用も馬鹿になりませんから。

すずき：はい。ところで、このコースは初めてとか。

わだ：ええ、よく聞きますが、プレイするのは初めてです。

すずき：この箱根ゴルフコースは一応名門コースで、かなり難コースです。

わだ：よく来られるんですか。

すずき：たまに。実は友人がこのコースの役員をしていますので、時々無理して予約をとってもらってます。

わだ：それは何かと便利ですね。ゴルフの予約はなかなか大変ですからね。

すずき：平山というんですが、ご紹介しましょう。便宜をはかってくれるように頼んでおきます。

わだ：それはありがたいですね。急な時など予約が取れなくて困る時がありますから。

そこにネルソン氏と浜中課長が着く。

ネルソン：先日はどうもありがとうございました。

わだ：いいえ、こちらこそ。わざわざご足労をおかけしまして。

ネルソン：いいえ。

皆練習を始める。

はまなか：やあ、ネルソン君は腕が良さそうですね。

すずき：彼は大学でゴルフ部に入っていたそうで、飛ばすことは飛ばします。

ネルソン：でも最近やっていませんので、さっぱりいいショットが出ません。

はまなか：コーチして下さい。

ネルソン：こちらこそ、教えていただきたいくらいです。それに日本の
　　　　コースはフェヤーウエイが狭くできていますから、ちょっと苦手
　　　　です。

わだ：まあ、いいスコアが出るよう頑張りましょう。

ネルソン：はい、よろしく。

数時間後 ゲームが終わってから。

ネルソン：部長、お上手ですね。

わだ：数だけはやっていますから。勝たせていただきました。ところで、
　　　　朝話した件ですが、浜中君とも話したんですが、お宅のソフトを使
　　　　って、コンピューター化する方向に進んでいます。よろしく頼み
　　　　ます。

ネルソン：ありがとうございます。お宅の会社に合うようなプログラム
　　　　を工夫させていただきます。お値段の方もぎりぎりまで勉強させて
　　　　いただきます。

わだ：詳しくは浜中君、それに技術部長と相談しながら話を進めて下さい。

ネルソン：はい、恐縮です。来週中にでもご連絡して、お伺いします。

わだ：これで、当社も一流企業に仲間入りができるかもしれません。

ネルソン：名実共にですね。

わだ：ありがとう。

B. 単語

練習場	*renshuujoo*	practice range	近づく	*chikazuku*	to draw closer
わざわざ	*wazawaza*	on purpose	無理な	*muri na*	impossible
時代	*jidai*	generation, era	本格的	*honkakuteki*	basically
導入	*doonyuu*	introduction	時期	*jiki*	time period
普及	*fukyuu*	diffusion	通勤	*tsuukin*	commuting
緩和	*kanwa*	ease	控える	*hikaeru*	to refrain, ease up
運動	*undoo*	exercise	不足	*fusoku*	lack of
費用	*hiyoo*	expenses	難コース	*nankoosu*	hard course
役員	*yakuin*	officer	便宜	*bengi*	convenience, assistance
急な	*kyuu na*	urgent	飛ばす	*tobasu*	to make fly
狭い	*semai*	narrow	苦手	*nigate*	weak point
勝つ	*katsu*	to win	件	*ken*	matter
方向	*hookoo*	direction	工夫	*kufuu*	ingenuity
相談	*soodan*	consultation	一流	*ichiryuu*	first-rate
			名実共	*meijitsutomo*	in fact and name

C. 漢字

練	REN	polish	練習	れんしゅう	practice
			練習張	れんしゅうちょう	workbook
			訓練	くんれん	training
習	SHUU	practice	学習	がくしゅう	learning
	nara(u)	learn	自習	じしゅう	self-study
			習字	しゅうじ	calligraphy
			習う	ならう	to learn (by practice)
導	DOO	guide	導入	どうにゅう	introduction
	michibi(ku)		指導	しどう	instruction
			導く	みちびく	to guide
将	SHOO	from now, lead	将来	しょうらい	future
			将来性	しょうらいせい	prospects
			将棋	しょうぎ	Japanese chess

388

緩	KAN	loosen	緩和	かんわ	relief
	yuru(mu)		緩む	ゆるむ	to become loose
	yuru(meru)		緩める	ゆるめる	to loosen
和	WA	peace	平和	へいわ	peace
			調和	ちょうわ	harmony
	yawa(ragu)		和らぐ	やわらぐ	to soften
	yawa(rageru)		和らげる	やわらげる	to soften
運	UN	transport	運動	うんどう	(physical) exercise
	hako(bu)	fortune	運転	うんてん	driving
			幸運	こううん	good luck
			運ぶ	はこぶ	to transport, carry
動	DOO	move	自動	じどう	automatic
	ugo(ku)		自動車	じどうしゃ	car
			動物	どうぶつ	animal
			動く	うごく	to move
難	NAN	difficult	難コース	なんコース	difficult course
	muzuka(shii)		困難	こんなん	difficulty
			難しい	むずかしい	difficult
役	YAKU	office	役員	やくいん	director
			役所	やくしょ	government office
			役人	やくにん	government official
宜	GI	all right	便宜	べんぎ	convenience
	yoro(shii)		宜しい	よろしい	good
			宜しく	よろしく	regards
腕	WAN	arm	腕力	わんりょく	physical strength
	ude		手腕	しゅわん	ability
			腕	うで	arm
飛	HI	fly	飛行機	ひこうき	airplane
	to(bu)		飛ぶ	とぶ	to fly

苦	KU	suffering	苦労	くろう	suffering
	kuru(shimu)		苦難	くなん	difficulty
	niga(i)		苦しむ	くるしむ	to suffer
			苦しい	くるしい	painful
			苦い	にがい	bitter
勝	SHOO	win	勝利	しょうり	winning
	ka(tsu)		勝敗	しょうはい	victory or defeat
			必勝	ひっしょう	sure victory
			勝つ	かつ	to win

練習問題

A. 次を日本語で書きなさい。 (Write the following in Japanese.)

1. Working at home might be efficient.

2. I don't get enough exercise; I should play (golf) more.

3. Getting golf reservations is so difficult.

4. I will try to make a program that will suit your company.

5. We'll also do our best to make it as inexpensive as possible.

B. 次の下線の漢字をひらがなで書きなさい。 (Write the following underlined *kanji* in hiragana.)

1. コンピューターを将来導入します。

2. 役員で、便宜をはかってくれます。

3. 苦労して勝ちました。

答え

A. 1. 在宅勤務は効率的かもしれません。 2. 運動不足ですから、もっとやった方がいいです。 3. ゴルフの予約はなかなか大変です。 4. お宅の会社に合うようなプログラムを工夫します。 5. お値段もぎりぎりまで勉強させていただきます。

B. 1. しょうらい、どうにゅう 2. やくいん、べんぎ 3. くろう、か

390

第十九課

A. 会話

日本の宗教

事務所から駅に行く途中、ネルソン氏は佐藤嬢に昨日神社で見た白い紙について聞く。

ネルソン：昨日、散歩していたら、神社があって、白い紙が小枝にたくさんぶら下がっていましたけど、あれ、何ですか。

さとう：みんな、何か願いごとをしているんです。あれは人々がそうなってほしいというようなことを紙や板に書いてあそこにぶら下げるんです。

ネルソン：願いごとですか。

さとう：ええ、迷信と分かっていても、いわゆる神を信じたがっている訳です。

ネルソン：なるほど。例えばどんなことですか。

さとう：例えば、健康な子供が生まれるようにとか、志望校に入学できるようにとか、いろいろあります。

ネルソン：神を信じていないこともないんでしょう。

さとう：それはどうですかね。信じている人もいるでしょうが、「苦しい時の神頼み」という人もいると思います。

ネルソン：それはどういう意味ですか。

さとう：普通は神を信じていないのに、困った時にだけ神にお願いする訳です。

ネルソン：でも京都で有名なお寺や神社でたくさん人を見かけましたよ。

さとう：そうですよね。私の両親なども神社によくお参りに行っています。ネルソンさんはどうなの。

ネルソン：子供の時、両親に連れられて、教会に行くことは行ったけど、最近はほとんど行ってません。

さとう：教会と言えば、私の友達で一人クリスチャンがいたわ。とってもいい人だったわ。どうしているかな。

ネルソン：でも日本にはクリスチャンは少ないんでしょう。

さとう：長崎とかに多いらしいけど、普通は少ないみたい。

ネルソン：日本人は神道と仏教を両方信じていると聞いたけど。

さとう：まあ、お祝いの時は神道で、お葬式は仏教でというのが普通です。

ネルソン：ああ、そうですか。両方を使い分けるんですね。なるほど。宗教に対しての考え方が欧米の人達と違うんですね。

さとう：はい、日本人は神を信じているというか、一種の哲学みたいに考えている人が多いみたいです。

ネルソン：ああ、ちょっと分かりませんが。

さとう：簡単には説明できませんが、多くの日本人は知らず知らず仏教などから学んだ知恵を哲学のように生活に活用しているようです。それにはスーパーナチュラルつまり「神」を必要としない訳です。

ネルソン：なるほど。

駅の近くで占い師を見る。

さとう：あそこに占い師がいるわ。見てもらったら。

ネルソン：そうね。来年はどんな年になるか見てもらおう。（占い師に）運勢を見て下さい。

うらないし：はい。来年ですが、健康は上々でしょう。女性関係は決断をしなければなりませんね。仕事は「大吉」と出ています。大いに新しいことを企画して、どんどん進めて行くべきです。迷ってはいけません。

電車だ。

ネルソン：本当に当たるんですか。

さとう：さあ、どうでしょう。でも、あんなことを聞いたら、勇気とやる気が出るんじゃない。

ネルソン：それもそうですが、悪いことばかりだったら、どうしますか。

さとう：そういう時は気をつけるようになるから、またいいのよ。

ネルソン：なるほどね。それぞれ効用があるという訳ですね。

B. 単語

途中	tochuu	on the way	散歩	sanpo	stroll
小枝	koeda	twig	下がる	sagaru	to hang down
板	ita	wooden board	神	kami	gods
信じる	shinjiru	to believe	健康	kenkoo	health
生まれる	umareru	to be born	志望校	shibookoo	school of choice
意味	imi	meaning	困る	komaru	to be perplexed, troubled
両親	ryooshin	parents	教会	kyookai	church
両方	ryoohoo	both	お祝い	oiwai	celebration
葬式	sooshiki	funeral	宗教	shuukyoo	religion
欧米	oobei	America and Europe	一種	isshu	kind, sort

哲学	*tetsugaku*	philosophy	知らず知らず	*shirazushirazu*	unconsciously
生活	*seikatsu*	life	活用	*katsuyoo*	use
占い師	*uranaishi*	fortune-teller	運勢	*unsei*	fate
決断	*ketsudan*	decision	企画	*kikaku*	plan
迷う	*mayou*	to get lost	勇気	*yuuki*	courage
効用	*kooyoo*	use			

C. 漢字

神	JIN, SHIN	god	神社	じんじゃ	Shinto shrine
			神学	しんがく	theology
			神秘	しんぴ	mystery
			神父	しんぷ	priest
	kami		神	かみ	god
散	SAN	scatter	散歩	さんぽ	stroll
	chi(ru)		解散	かいさん	to break up
			散る	ちる	to disperse
歩	HO, PO	walk	徒歩	とほ	on foot
	aru(ku)		歩道	ほどう	sidewalk
			歩く	あるく	to walk
紙	SHI	paper	和紙	わし	Japanese paper
	kami		用紙	ようし	form
	gami		紙	かみ	paper
			手紙	てがみ	letter
迷	MEI	perplexed	迷信	めいしん	superstition
	mayo(u)		迷惑	めいわく	annoyance
			迷う	まよう	to get lost
健	KEN	health	健康	けんこう	health
			健全な	けんぜんな	healthy
志	SHI	will	志望	しぼう	wish
			意志	いし	will
			同志	どうし	comrades

望	BOO	wish	希望	きぼう	hope
	nozo(mu)		有望な	ゆうぼうな	promising
			欲望	よくぼう	desire
			望む	のぞむ	to wish
頼	RAI	ask, trust	信頼	しんらい	trust
	tano(mu)		依頼	いらい	request
	tano(moshii)		頼む	たのむ	to ask
			頼もしい	たのもしい	promising
参	SAN	participate	参加	さんか	participation
			参列	さんれつ	attendance
			参考	さんこう	reference
祝	SHUKU	celebration	祝日	しゅくじつ	holiday
	iwa(u)		祝辞	しゅくじ	congratulatory address
			祝う	いわう	to celebrate
式	SHIKI	ceremony	葬式	そうしき	funeral
			正式	せいしき	formal
			卒業式	そつぎょうしき	graduation ceremony
宗	SHUU	sect	宗教	しゅうきょう	religion
			宗派	しゅうは	denomination
欧	OO	Europe	欧州	おうしゅう	Europe
			欧米	おうべい	Europe and America
哲	TETSU	wisdom	哲学	てつがく	philosophy
			哲人	てつじん	wise person

A. 次を訳しなさい。 (Translate the following into English.)

1. 日本人は神道と仏教を両方信じていると聞いた。
2. お祝いの時は神道で、お葬式は仏教でというのが普通です。
3. 宗教に対しての考え方が違うんです。
4. 女性関係は決断しなければなりませんね。

B. 次の下線の漢字をひらがなで書きなさい。

1. 神社は神道です。
2. 散歩しませんか。
3. 宗教と哲学は関係があるでしょう。

答え

A. 1. I heard that the Japanese believe in both Shintoism and Buddhism.
2. Usually it's Shintoism for times of celebration and Buddhism for funerals.
3. The views on religion are quite different. 4. As for your relationships with women, you will have to make a decision.

B. 1. じんじゃ、しんとう 2. さんぽ 3. しゅうきょう、てつがく、かんけい

第二十課

A. 会話

忘年会

日本では十二月はとても忙しく、忘年会の季節でもある。

さとう：鈴木さん、今年の忘年会はどうしますか。

すずき：ああ、忘年会ね。そろそろ年末ですね。すっかり忘れていました。

さとう：まだ準備してないんですか。仕方ないですよね。忙しかったんですからね。

すずき：でも部長には僕がすると言ってあるんです。

さとう：ああ、そう。じゃあ、私ちょうど仕事の区切りがついたから、お手伝いしましょうか。

すずき：そうですか。それはありがたい。

さとう：今年の予算はいくらぐらいがしら。

すずき：一人一万円ぐらいかな。

さとう：一万円ですか。ほんと。じゃあ、いい所が見つかるかも。

すずき：じゃあ、幹事をお願いできますか。

さとう：ええ、いいわ。適当な所が探せたら、お知らせします。

すずき：頼りにしています。

さとう：楽しいのを企画したいけど、どうかしら。うん、今年は「酒なしの忘年会」にしようかな。

すずき：えっ、本当ですか。

さとう：いいえ、冗談ですよ。でも少し趣向を変えてもいいですか。

すずき：ええ、去年までのと違ってもいいですよ。いつもと同じじゃ、
　　　　あきますから。

さとう：どうなるか分かりませんが、計画してみます。

すずき：じゃ、お願いします。部長によると、一次回の費用は会社がも
　　　　つそうですから。

さとう：じゃあ、豪華にやりましょうか。

すずき：いや一応予算はあると思います。

さとう：分かりました。

次の日。

さとう：鈴木さん、例の忘年会の件ですが、今年は洋食でしようと思い
　　　　ますが、どうかしら。

すずき：いいですけど。高くつくんじゃないですか。

さとう：ちょっとね。一人一万円ぐらいになります。

すずき：それぐらいなら、大丈夫でしょう。

さとう：有楽町駅前のアルプスという高級レストランでキャンセルがあ
　　　　って、15名ぐらいなら、大丈夫だということです。一応予約してお
　　　　きました。

すずき：何時開始ですか。

さとう：七時半にしました。ちょっと遅いですか。

すずき：年末で皆忙しいからちょうどいいですよ。

さとう：カラオケは二次会でしていただくということで、準備していません。

すずき：いいですよ。じゃあ、二次会は僕のいきつけのスナックにでも行きましょう。最新式のカラオケがありますから充分楽しんでもらえます。でも、一次回でカラオケがないとすると、時間をもてあますんじゃないですか。

さとう：それが問題なんですが、支社長にスピーチでもお願いするか、だれか講師を招いて話をしてもらうか、ミュージシャンを雇うか、などいろいろ検討しています。

すずき：まかせます。

忘年会が近づいたのに、皆、仕事が終わらない。

すずき：あすは忘年会というのに、仕事が終わりそうもありませんよ。

ネルソン：僕だってそうです。でもAP社の契約が取れそうだから、年が越せそうです。

すずき：それはよかった。我々の例のプロジェクトも順調に進んでいるから、ほっとしているところです。

ネルソン：全く新しいソフトを作り出すのはなかなかの苦労でしょう。

すずき：ええ。でも幸いにも提携先がテクノロジーの優秀な人材をもっているので、うちの技術と組み合わせるとすごいソフトができるはずです。

ネルソン：それは素晴しいですね。本社も喜ぶでしょう。

すずき：そう言えば、クリスマスに帰国するんですね。

ネルソン：ええ、二週間ばかり行って来ます。ついでに本社にも寄って来ます。そしてこちらの状況をいろいろ説明して来ます。

B. 単語

忘年会	*boonenkai*	year-end party	季節	*kisetsu*	season
区切り	*kugiri*	end	予算	*yosan*	budget
頼り	*tayori*	reliance	冗談	*joodan*	joke
あきる	*akiru*	to get sick of	計画	*keikaku*	plan
費用	*hiyoo*	expenses	豪華	*gooka*	extravagant
洋食	*yooshoku*	Western food	高級	*kookyuu*	high-class
開始	*kaishi*	beginning	最新式	*saishinshiki*	newest type
充分な	*juubun na*	enough	講師	*kooshi*	lecturer
雇う	*yatoo*	to hire	検討する	*kentoo suru*	to examine
契約	*keiyaku*	contract	順調な	*junchoo na*	smooth, favorable
進む	*susumu*	to progress	優秀な	*yuushuu na*	excellent
技術	*gijutsu*	technology, technique	状況	*jookyoo*	situation

C. 漢字

忘	BOO *wasu(reru)*	forget	忘年会 忘れる	ぼうねんかい わすれる	year-end party to forget
季	KI	season	季節 四季	きせつ しき	season four seasons
節	SETSU	season, moderation	節度 節約 節分	せつど せつやく せつぶん	moderation economizing last day of winter
末	MATSU *sue*	end	年末 月末 週末 末	ねんまつ げつまつ しゅうまつ すえ	end of the year end of the month weekend end
区	KU	ward, part	区切り 区役所 区画	くぎり くやくしょ くかく	ending ward office division
幹	KAN	main part	幹事 幹部	かんじ かんぶ	coordinator leaders, executives

400

談	DAN	conversation	冗談	じょうだん	joke
			相談	そうだん	consultation
			会談	かいだん	conference
豪	GOO	magnificence	豪華	ごうか	splendor
			豪奢	ごうしゃ	luxury
華	KA	flower	中華	ちゅうか	Chinese
			華道	かどう	flower arranging
講	KOO	lecture	講師	こうし	lecturer
			講義	こうぎ	lecture
			講座	こうざ	lecture
師	SHI	teacher	師匠	ししょう	teacher
			教師	きょうし	teacher
雇	KO	employ	雇用	こよう	employment
	yato(u)		雇う	やとう	to hire
契	KEI	pledge	契約	けいやく	contract
			契約書	けいやくしょ	contract
約	YAKU	promise	約束	やくそく	promise
			予約	よやく	reservation
順	JUN	order	順調な	じゅんちょうな	smooth
			順番	じゅんばん	turn (chance)
			順序	じゅんじょ	order
優	YUU	superior	優秀な	ゆうしゅうな	superior
			優先	ゆうせん	priority
			優勝	ゆうしょう	victory

A. 次を日本語で書きなさい。(Write the following in Japanese.)

    1. I wonder what our budget is this year.

    2. Can I ask you to be the coordinator?

    3. Once I find an appropriate location, I'll let you know.

    4. It doesn't look like I'm going to finish my work.

    5. It must be really tough creating completely new software.

B. 次の下線の漢字をひらがなで書きなさい。(Write the following underlined *kanji* in hiragana.)

    1. 忘年会の季節です。

    2. パーティを豪華にやりましょう。

    3. 講師をお願いしましょう。

    4. 順調に契約できました。

こた
答え

A. 1. 今年の予算はいくらぐらいかしら（でしょうか）。

2. 幹事をお願いできますか。 3. 適当な所が探せたら、お知らせします。

4. 仕事が終わりそうにありません。 5. 全く新しいソフトを作りだすのは
なかなかの苦労でしょう。

B. 1. ぼうねんかい、きせつ 2. ごうか 3. こうし、ねが 4. じゅんちょう、
けいやく

日本的雇用制度

日本で今まで実行されてきた日本的雇用制度がだんだん変わりつつあるし、現に変わっていると言われている。

最近の調査によると（共同通信）、新入社員の多くは、苦労して就職した会社にはあまり長くいるつもりはなく、大体社員の半分は二年から五年位しかいるつもりはないという。65%は理由があれば転勤してもいいという。これは一旦就職したら定年まで同じ会社に勤めるという、いわゆる「終身雇用制」が崩れている表われと思われる。

また、今までの年齢や経験による給料より、業績や能力を中心にした給与体系を望む、という社員が70%を超えているという。これも、いわゆる「年功序列」制をとってきた企業や官庁に勤めるサラリーマンが欧米の能力主義を望む表われで、古い制度になれた日本人には革命的な考えと取られている。

このことから、勤め先に対する忠誠心は薄れているし、また同時に欧米の能力主義の雇用制度を望んでいるのではないかということが推測されているが、これらの社員はどこまで本気でこのことを考えているのだろうか。統計の解釈に間違いがないか、統計に「落し穴」がないだろうか。

というのは、統計では多くの社員が転職することを望んでいる。しかしどういう企業に勤めている社員かははっきりしていない。中小企業に勤める社員が転職したいのはすぐ分かるが、大企業に勤める社員まで転職を望んでいるだろうか。少ないはずである。

なぜかというと、大企業のイメージや給与制度、それに他の条件も中小企業よりずっといい。それに依然として一流大学への大学入試は大変だ。一流大学を目指す理由は大企業に勤められるチャンスが大きいからではないか。

能力中心主義についてはどうか。何年か勤めた社員が年功序列がいいとか、能力主義がいいというのは意味があるが、若い新入社員が年功序列を望むというのはそもそもおかしいことであって、この数字がどこまで統計的な意義があるかは疑わしい。

したがって、日本的雇用制度が変わってきているのは事実だが、数字に出ているほど変わっていないのではないかという結論にもなる。どうだろう。全く「数字」だけでは分からないこともあるし、統計の解釈もそうやさしいものではない。

B. 単語

現に	げんに	actually
調査	ちょうさ	research, investigation
共同通信	きょうどうつうしん	Kyodo News
転職する	てんしょくする	to change jobs
定年	ていねん	retirement age
終身雇用	しゅうしんこよう	life-time employment
崩れる	くずれる	to break down
表われ	あらわれ	sign, expression
業績	ぎょうせき	achievements
能力	のうりょく	ability
体系	たいけい	system
超える	こえる	to exceed
年功序列	ねんこうじょれつ	seniority system
官庁	かんちょう	government office
革命的な	かくめいてきな	revolutionary, radical
勤め先	つとめさき	place of employment
忠誠心	ちゅうせいしん	allegiance, loyalty
薄れる	うすれる	to be become faint, dwindle
推測する	すいそくする	to guess, assume
本気	ほんき	serious, earnest
統計	とうけい	statistics
解釈	かいしゃく	interpretation
間違い	まちがい	mistake
落し穴	おとしあな	pitfall, trap
目指す	めざす	to aim at
意義	いぎ	meaning, significance
そもそも		to begin with
疑わしい	うたがわしい	suspicious, questionable

GLOSSARY

JAPANESE–ENGLISH

Please note that the numbers in the right-hand columns refer to the lesson(s) in which the word is introduced.

A

abunai *dangerous*	4
achikochi *here and there*	15
achira *there*	1
agaru *to go up, rise*	7
ageru *to give, raise*	10
aikawarazu *as usual*	2
aikon *icon*	9
aida *interval, period*	6
aidia *idea*	5
ainiku *unfortunately*	1
aisatsu *greeting*	2
aite *partner, opponent*	9
akai *red*	10
akarui *light, bright*	3
akeru *to open*	10
akirameru *to give up, to abandon*	12
akiru *to be sick of, to get tired of*	20
amari *remainder, very much, not very*	2
ame *rain*	10
amerika *America*	11
an *plan, draft*	5
anguru *angle*	5
an'nai *guidance, information*	2
ano *that*	1
anoo *well, uh, hmm*	11
anshin *relief*	5
anzen *safety, safe*	4
anzensei *safety*	9
apaato *apartment*	3
apointo *appointment*	10
ara *hey, look*	12
arashi *storm*	13
arashi ga kuru *storm is coming*	13
aratameru *to renew*	17
aratamete *again*	17
arau *to wash*	5
araware *sign, expression*	4
arigatoo *thank you*	1
aru *to exist, to have*	1
arubaito *side business, part-time job*	2
aru hi *one day*	7
aruku *to walk*	3
asa *morning*	5
Asahi *brand of beer*	7
ashisutanto *assistant*	13
ashita *tomorrow*	3
asobu *to play*	7
asoko *over there, that place*	4
asu *tomorrow*	5
asupirin *aspirin*	9
atama *head*	10
atama ga itai *have a headache*	10
atarashii *new*	3

atari *around, neighborhood*	13
atarimae *natural, of course, reasonable*	2
ataru *to hit, to prove true*	3
ato *after, afterwards*	2
atsukau *to handle, to treat*	11
atsumaru *to gather, to convene*	2
au *to fit, to suit*	3
au *to meet*	1
awaseru *to put together, to match, to collect*	5
ayamaru *to apologize*	14

B

baai *occasion, case*	14
baka *fool*	18
bakari *just, only*	4
bangohan *dinner*	5
bangoo *number*	11
banmeshi *dinner*	5
basho *place, location*	3
basu *bus*	15
bengi *convenience*	18
bengi o hakaru *to assist, help*	18
benkai suru *to defend, rationalize*	14
beki *should*	14
benkyoo *study*	2
benri na *convenient*	1
bentoo *lunch*	6
bikkuri suru *to be surprised*	7
biiru *beer*	7
bijinesu *business*	1
biru *building*	13
boku *I (male speech)*	10
boodo *board*	6
booifurendo *boyfriend*	8
boonasu *bonus*	7
boonenkai *year-end party*	20
bu *division*	2
buchoo *chief of a department, division*	2
buka *a subordinate*	2
bukka *prices*	10
bukken *thing, article*	3
bukkyoo *Buddhism*	19, 2
bunka *culture*	15
bunka katsudoo *cultural activity*	12
bunpoo *grammar*	1
bunsho *sentences, composition*	9
burasageru *to hang*	19
buusu *booth*	9
byooin *hospital*	10
byooki *sick*	7

C

chichi *father*	2
chichioya *father*	8

gaishikei *foreign-owned*   8
gaishutsu suru *to go out*   11
gaiyoo *overview*   17
gakubu *school department*   16
gakumon *learning, study*   2
gakusei *student*   4
gakushuusha *learner, student*   1
gaman *restraint, perseverance*   5
ganbaru *to try one's best, hang in there*   2
gaarufurendo *girlfriend*   7
gawa *side*   1
geemu *game*   7
gendaiteki na *modern, modernistic*   2
gengo *language*   1
genjitsuteki na *realistic*   6
genki na *healthy, well*   2
genkin *cash*   10
gensoku *principle*   1
getsuyoobi *Monday*   2
ginkoo *bank*   4
gijutsu *technology, skills*   20, 2
girigiri *lowest (possible), last (possible)*   18
giron *argument*   1
-go *after*   4
gobusata *long time no see (polite form)*   12
gochisoo ni naru *to be treated*   8
gochisoo sama *thanks for treating me*   8
gochisoo suru *to treat*   8
gogo *afternoon*   10
gohan *cooked rice, food, meal (general)*   5
gokai *misunderstanding*   14
gokai suru *to misunderstand*   14
gomen kudasai *excuse me, is anybody home*   14
gomen'nasai *I am sorry*   14
gooka na *extravagant*   19
goran kudasai *please take a look (def.)*   17
gorufu *golf*   2
gorufukoosu *golf course*   18
gosokuroo *asking you to come*   18
gotsugoo *convenience (polite)*   17
gozonji *to know (deferential)*   16
gurai *about, around*   1
gurasu *glass*   7
guuzen (ni) *by chance, by accident*   7
gyoomu *work, business*   6
gyoomubu *business department*   2
gyoomuka *business section*   16
gyoomu teikei *joint venture*   17
gyooseki *achievements*   6, 4

H

hachi *eight*   1
hageshii *intense*   13
haha *mother*   7
hairu *to go into*   2
haitekku *high tech*   6
hajimemashite *nice to meet you*   12
hajimeru *to begin*   1
hakaru *to measure*   10
hakike *nausea*   10
hakike ga suru *to feel like vomitting*   10
hakkiri *clearly*   3
hanashiai *discussion*   5
hanashichuu *on the phone, busy line*   11
hanasu *to talk, speak*   5

hanbai *sales, selling*   5
han'nichi *half day*   6
hanran *flood*   17
hantai *disagreement, opposition*   6
hantai suru *to oppose*   6
harau *to pay*   6
hare *sunny*   13
hareru *to be clear*   13
hashiru *to run*   9
hataraku *to work*   10
hatten *expansion, development*   14
hatten suru *to develop*   14
hatsuon *pronunciation*   1
hayai *early, fast*   4
hayame *earlier than normal*   1
hawai *Hawaii*   14
hazu *expected*   5
hazukashii *shy*   7
heijoo *normal, usualness*   10
heisha *our company*   5
heiten *closed*   1
hen *side, area*   3
henshuu *editing, edit (computer function)*   9
herupu *Help (computer function)*   9
heya *room*   3
hi *day*   10
hikaeru *to refrain, ease up*   18
hikaku *comparison*   17
hikakuteki *comparatively*   8
hikkoshi *removing*   4
hikkosu *to move (homes)*   4
hiku *to pull, to catch (i.e., a cold)*   10
hikui *low*   9
hima *free time*   6
himitsu *secret*   8
hinshitsu *quality*   6
hinshitsu kanri *quality control*   6
hiroi *wide*   6
hiroo suru *to present*   12
hirugohan *lunch*   5
hirumeshi *lunch*   5
hisashiburi *long time no see*   1
hito *person*   5
hitobito *people*   5
hitokoto *one thing, one word, one message*   12
hitori *one person*   8
hitotachi *people*   5
hitsuyoo *need, requirement, necessity*   5
hiyoo *expenses*   18
hochoo *pace*   5
hodo *degree*   1
hogo *protection*   5
hoka *another*   16
hoken *insurance*   10
honjitsu *today*   17
honkakuteki na *full-scale, real*   18
honki *serious, earnest*   4
honsha *head office*   1
hontoo *real*   3
hontoo ni *really*   5
hon'yaku *translation (of written things)*   9
hoo *direction*   6
hoo *as to, in regards to*   5
hoohoo *way, method, means*   5

juutaku *dwelling, housing* 3
juutakuchi *residential area* 7

K

ka *section* 1
kabuki *kabuki (Japanese drama)* 12
kabushikigaisha *a joint-stock company* 2
kachoo *manager (section head)* 2
kado *corner* 4
kaado *card* 10
kaeru *to return* 4
kaeru *to change* 7
-kai *floor (of a building)* 2
kaigai *overseas* 17
kaigi *formal meeting* 2
kaigi o hiraku *to hold a conference* 9
kaigai ryokoo ni iku *to travel abroad* 15
kaigishitsu *meeting room* 2
kaigoo *meeting* 2
kaigyooi *general practitioner (doctor)* 10
kaihatsu *development* 17
kaihatsubu *development department* 1
kaijoo *meeting place, venue* 9
kaisha *company* 2
kaishaku *interpretation* 4
kaishamei *name of a company* 2
kaishi *beginning, start* 19
kaiteki na *comfortable, pleasant* 10
kaitenchuu *open (for business)* 1
kaiwa *conversation* 1
kaizen *improvement* 16
kakaku *price* 9
kakakuhyoo *list of prices* 9
kakaru *to take (time), to cost (money)* 1
kaku *to write* 6
kakunin *recognition, confirmation* 11
kamau *to be concerned with* 14
kami *paper* 5
kami *god* 19
kamidanomi *praying for the gods' help* 19
kaminari *thunder* 13
kaminari ga ochiru *lightning strikes* 13
kaminari ga naru *to thunder* 13
-kan *period (of time)* 1
-kana *(I) wonder if ~* 3
kanai *wife (humble)* 7
kanari *rather, fairly* 5
kanashii *sad* 14
kanchigai *misconception* 14
kanchoo *government office* 4
kangae *thought, idea* 5
kangaeru *to consider, think* 6
kangei suru *to welcome* 8, 2
kanji *organizer, coordinator* 20
kanjiru *to feel* 18
kanjoo *bill, check* 8
kankei *relationship* 1, 1
kankoo *sight-seeing* 1
kankyoo *environment* 5
kanojo *she* 2
kanoosei *possibility* 13
kanpai *toast, "Cheers!"* 7
kanrishoku *management position* 5
kanso na *simple* 12
kansoo *impression* 1
kantan na *simple* 6

kantoo chihoo *Kanto area (eastern Japan)* 13
kanwa suru *to ease* 18
kao *face* 5
kaoiro *complexion* 10
-kara *because* 5
kara age *deep-fry* 8
karaoke *karaoke, sing-along* 4
kare *he* 11
karera *they* 5
kariru *to borrow* 3
kata *person* 11
katagata *all people* 2
katagaki *position* 2
katamichi *one-way* 15
katsu *to win, to be victorious, to defeat* 7
katsudoo *activity* 2
katte *selfishness* 13
kau *to buy* 5
kawari *in place of, substitute* 5
kawaru *to change* 7
kawatta *unusual* 15
kaze *cold (illness), wind* 10
kaze o hiku *to catch a cold* 10
kazoku *family* 11
kazu *number* 18
kedo *but* 8
keiei suru *to manage* 16
keieigakubu *management department* 16
keigo *honorifics* 1
keikaku *plan* 5
keiken *experience* 16
keikoku *warning* 13
keikoo *tendency, trend* 6
keireki *work history, career* 16
keisan *calculation* 8
keisatsu *police* 4
keisatsukan *police officer* 5
keiyaku *contract* 5
keiyaku o musubu *to make a contract* 5
keizai *economics* 9
keizaiteki na *economical* 9
kekkon *marriage* 7
kekkon suru *to get married* 6
kekkoo na *fine, adequate* 2
kekkyoku *eventually, after all* 16
kenkoo na *healthy* 19
kenshin *medical examination* 10
kenshuu *corporate training* 2
kentoo suru *to examine* 20
kesa *this morning* 14
keshiki *view, scenery* 12
kesu *to put out, extinguish* 13
ketsuatsu *blood pressure* 10
ketsudan *decision* 19
ketten *defect, weak point* 3
ki *air, care, spirit* 4
kibishii *sever, stern* 3
kiboo *wish, desire, hope* 8
kibun *mood* 9
kibun ga ii *to feel well* 14
ki ga suru *to have the feeling that . . .* 3
ki ga tsuku *to notice, to realize* 7
kigen *temper, mood* 14
kigyoo *business, enterprise, company* 5
kiiroi *yellow* 9

410

M

maajan *mahjong* 7
maakettingu *marketing* 5
machi *town* 10
machiaishitsu *waiting room* 10
machigaeru *to make a mistake* 4
machigai *mistake* 14
machigai denwa *wrong number* 11
mada *yet* 1
made *until* 5
madoguchi *service window* 10
mae *before, front* 5
maguro *tuna* 15
maido *each time, thank you* 14
mainichi *every day* 7
mairu *to come, to go (humble)* 19
majime na *serious* 16
makaseru *to leave it up to someone* 20
makkintosshu *Macintosh (Apple computer)* 16
makoto ni *sincerely* 13
makuru *to tuck up, to roll up* 10
mamoru *to keep, to guard* 8
man *ten thousand* 3
manaberu *to be able to learn* 16
manabu *to learn* 16
maneejaa *manager* 5
maneku *to invite* 20
maniau *to be on time* 9
manshon *Western-style apartment* 3
massugu *straight* 4
mattaku *completely, quite* 5
matomeru *to gather, to pile* 6
matsu *to wait* 1
matsuri *festival* 2
mausu o tsukau *to use a mouse* 9
mayou *be at a loss, confused* 4
mazu *first* 3
medatta *striking, standing out* 3
meijitsutomoni *in fact and name* 18
meimon *distinguished* 18
meeru *mail (computer term)* 5
meiji jidai *Meiji period* 2
meishi *business card* 1
meishin *superstition* 19
meiwaku o kakeru *to bother someone* 14
memai *dizziness* 10
memo *memo* 5
menkai *meeting* 17
menkyoshoo *license* 1
mensetsu *interview* 15
menyuu *menu* 9
messeiji *message* 11
mezasu *to aim at* 4
mezurashii *rare* 5
miai kekkon *arranged marriage* 7
mibun *social status* 4
mibun shoomeishoo *identification card* 4
michi *road* 4
mieru *to be seen, can see* 8
mijikai *short* 14
mikkabun *for three days* 10
mimi ni suru *to overhear* 8
min'na *all, everyone* 2
mirai *future* 9

miru *to see* 1
miru *to examine* 10
mise *shop* 3
miseru *to show* 5
miitingu *meeting* 10
miyako *large city, old capital* 15
mizu *water* 15
mochikaeru *to take home* 2
mochiron *of course* 9
modoru *to return* 6
mokuyoobi *Thursday* 13
mon *gate* 10
mondai *question, problem* 1
mono *thing, object* 4
moo *already* 5
mooshikomisho *application form* 10
mooshiwake arimasen *I am very sorry* 14
moosu *to tell (humble)* 14
morau *to receive* 3
moshi *if* 4
moshi moshi *hello (on the phone)* 4
moteamasu *to find unmanageable* 20
motomeru *to seek* 16
motsu *to hold, to have* 4
motto *more* 5
mottomo *the most, the best* 5
muda na *useless* 2
mukaeru *to meet, to welcome* 1
mukashi *a long time ago* 15
mumei na *unknown* 15
mura *village* 10
murasaki *soy sauce (for sushi), purple* 15
muri na *impossible, unreasonableness* 2
muri suru *to overwork oneself* 1
musuko *son* 7
musuu *countless* 2
muzukashii *difficult* 6

N

nagai *long* 1
nagasaki *Nagasaki* 2
naisen *extension (telephone)* 11
naisho *secret* 7
naka *inside* 7
nakama *companion* 18
naka naka *rather, quite, not easily* 4
nakunaru *to pass away* 7
namae *name* 1
nanakai *seventh floor* 1
nan (nani) *what* 1
nani ka *something, anything* 4
nanji *what time* 13
nankai *what floor* 2
nankai *how many times* 2
nankoosu *difficult course* 18
nanpaku *how many nights* 15
nan toka *somehow* 12
naoru *to be fixed (i.e., get over a cold)* 10
naosu *to correct, to fix* 16
narabu *to stand in a line* 6
narau *to learn* 4
nareru *to get used to* 5
naru *to become* 1
narubeku *as much as possible* 17
naruhodo *I see* 2
natsu *summer* 7

natsukashii *nostalgic, longed for* 11
naze *why* 14
nedan *price* 6
negau *to desire, wish for* 1
neemuburando *name brand* 6
nemui *sleepy* 9
-nen *year* 3
nendai *era, age* 6
nenkoo-joretsu *seniority system* 5
nenkyuu *annual salary* 8
nenpai *older, elder* 5
nenreiteki *age-wise* 1
nerau *to aim* 2
netsu *heat, fever* 10
nettowaakingu *networking* 16
-nichi *day* 1
nigate *weak point* 18
nigeru *to flee* 12
nigiru *to grasp, grip, form* 14
nihon *Japan* 1
nihongo *Japanese* 4
nijusseiki *twentieth century* 2
nikaidate *two-story house* 3
niku *meat* 15
ningen *human being* 9
nodo *throat* 10
nodo ga itai *have a sore throat* 10
nokoru *to remain, be left over* 9
nomihajimeru *to start drinking* 8
nomimono *a drink* 15
nomu *to drink* 7
nonbiri suru *to relax* 5
nooryoku *ability, capacity* 17, 4
nooryokushugi *principle of ability, merit-based system* 5, 4
norimono *vehicle* 13
noru *to get on, to ride* 4
nozoku *to peep, spy* 4
nyuugaku *entrance to a school* 19
nyuukoku suru *to enter a country* 1
nyuukokukanri-jimusho *immigration office* 1
nyuusha shiken *company entrance exam* 16

O

oboeru *to remember* 13
oboosan *monk* 15
ochitsuku *to settle down, relax, calm down* 5
ofisu *office* 15
ogoru *to treat, buy someone a meal* 8
ohashi *chopsticks* 15
ohiya *cold water, a cup of cold water* 15
oishii *delicious* 8
oiwai *celebration* 19
oka *hill* 4
okane *money* 1
okonau *to perform, to take place* 5
okoru *to happen, occur* 14
okoru *to get angry* 14
oku *to place, to put* 11
okurimono *a present* 7
okuru *to send* 4
okusan *someone's wife* 7
okyakusan *customer* 14

omawarisan *policeman* 4
omiyage *souvenir* 7
omocha *toy* 2
omoide *memory* 11
omomuki *effect, taste* 15
omomuki no aru *tasteful* 15
omo ni *mainly* 9
omoshiroii *fun, interesting* 16
omou *to think* 1
onaji *the same* 7
onaka ga itai *have a stomachache* 10
onegai suru *to please, to ask, to beseech* 6
onsen *hot spring* 12
onsha *your company* 5
oobei *America and Europe, Western, Occidental* 19, 2
ooeru *OL, "office lady"* 16
oofuku *round-trip* 15
ooi *many, much* 2
ooka suru *to glorify* 3
ooku *many* 5
oopun *open (computer term)* 9
ooshin *doctor's visit, house call* 10
ooshin-jikan *hours for visiting patients* 10
oriru *to get off, descend* 4
oru *to exist, to be (humble form)* 11
oshare *sophistication, high fashion, upbeat* 3
oshieru *to instruct, to teach* 2
osoi *late, slow* 4
ossharu *to say (deferential)* 16
otaku *you, your home* 18
oto *sound* 3
otoshiana *pitfall* 4
ou *to pursue* 6
owari *end, finish* 13
oyobi *and, also* 13
oyurushi kudasai *please forgive me* 14

P

paasento *percent* 9
paatonaa *partner* 5
panfuretto *pamphlet* 9
pasupooto *passport* 4
purei *play* 18
purezenteeshon *presentation* 17
purinto *printed material, copy* 9

R

raishuu *next week* 1
rainen *next year* 4
raku *ease, enjoyment, relaxation* 8
reigai *exception* 1
reikin *reward, key money* 3
ren'ai kekkon *love marriage* 7
renraku *contact* 5
renshuujoo *practice range* 18
repooto *report* 5
resutoran *restaurant* 3
rirakkusu suru *to relax* 9
rirekisho *résumé* 16
riron *theory, logic, reason* 1
risuto *list* 3
riyuu *reason* 16
rooka *corridor, hallway* 7
ryokan *inn, Japanese-style hotel* 12

ENGLISH–JAPANESE

A

a lot *takusan*
ability *nooryoku*
ability-oriented *nooryoku-shugi*
to be able to find *sagaseru*
to be able to learn *manaberu*
to be absent *rusu ni suru, yasumu*
about *ni tsuite*
about, around *gurai*
absolutely *zettai ni*
accident *jiko*
achievement *gyooseki*
actively *sakan ni*
activity *katsudoo*
actor *yakusha*
addition *tsuika* (extra), *tashizan* (mathematics)
address *juusho*
to advance *shinshutsu suru, susumu*
advantageous *yuuri (na)*
after, afterward *ato*
after *-go*
after a long time *hisashiburi*
afternoon *gogo*
again *aratamete*
age *nendai* (generation), *nenrei* (of a man or animal)
to agree *sansei suru*
agreement *sansei*
to aim *nerau*
air *kuuki, ki*
airport *kuukoo*
airline company *kookuugaisha*
all over *-juu*
all over the world *sekaijuu*
already *moo, sude ni*
all right *daijoobu (na)*
always *itsumo, zutto*
America *Amerika*
America and Europe *oobei*
ancient times *mukashi*
and *soshite, to, toka, ya*
and also *oyobi*
angle *anguru*
annual salary *nenkyuu*
another *moo hitori (no)* (person), *moo hitotsu (no)* (thing)
to answer *kotaeru*
anxiety *shinpai*
anybody *dare demo*
apartment *apaato*
to apologize *ayamaru*
appetite *shokuyoku*
application *mooshikomisho*
appointment *apointo*
to make an appointment *yakusoku o suru*
to approach *chikazuku*
appropriate *tekitoo (na)*
acquaintance *shiriai*
area code *kyokuban*
arm *ude*

armpit *wakinoshita*
arranged marriage *miai kekkon*
to arrive *tsuku*
arrival *toochaku*
article *bukken*
asking someone to come *gosokuroo*
to ask *kiku, tazuneru, shitsumon suru, onegai suru, ukagau*
aspirin *asupirin*
assistant *ashisutanto*
as usual *aikawarazu*
at once *sassoku, sugu (ni)*
atmosphere *fun'iki*
to attach *tsukeru tsunagu*
to attain *eru*

B

bad *warui*
bad weather *tenki ga warui*
bank *ginkoo*
bashful *hazukashii*
bath *furo, yu*
to be *iru* (people, animals), *aru* (things)
to be (humble) *de gozaru*
beautiful *utsukushii*
because *-kara, -node*
to become *naru*
beer *biiru*
before *mae*
to begin *hajimeru, hajimaru*
to begin to rain *furihajimeru*
beginning *hajime*
behind *ushiro*
being at home *zaitaku*
being refreshed *sappari*
to believe *shinjiru*
besides *shikamo, sore ni*
best *zekkoo (no), saikoo (no)*
bicycle *jitensha*
big *ookii*
big difference *taisa*
bill *kanjoo*
birth *umare*
blood pressure *ketsuatsu*
blowfish *fugu*
board *boodo, ita*
bonus *boonasu*
to be bored *taikutsu suru*
boring *tsumaranai*
to be born *umareru*
to borrow *kariru*
boss *jooshi*
both *ryoohoo*
to bother someone *meiwaku o kakeru*
boyfriend *booifurendo*
branch manager *shitenchoo*
branch office *shisha*
bright *akarui*
broadcasting *hoosoo*
Buddhism *bukkyoo*
budget *yosan*

to build *tateru*
building *biru, tatemono*
bullet train *Shinkansen*
bus *basu*
business *bijinesu*
business card *meishi*
business trip *shucchoo*
business, work *gyoomu*
business department *gyoomubu*
business section *gyoomuka*
busy *isogashii*
busy telephone line *hanashichuu*
but *demo, kedo*
to buy *kau*
by the way *tokoro de*

C

calculation *keisan*
to call *yobu* (someone's name); *denwa suru* (phone)
campaign *kyanpeen*
to cancel *kyanseru suru*
cancellation *torikeshi*
can do *dekiru*
capability *jitsuryoku*
card *kaado*
care *sewa*
career woman *kyaria-uuman*
to be careful *ki o tsukeru*
cash *genkin*
to catch (i.e., a cold) *hiku*
celebration *oiwai*
certain *tashika (na)*
certainly *zehi*
challenge *choosen*
by chance *guuzen (ni)*
chance meeting *deai*
to change *kawaru, kaeru*
to change schools *tenkoo suru*
chatting *zatsudan*
cheap *yasui*
chef *itamae, shefu*
child *kodomo*
to choose *erabu*
chopsticks *ohashi*
Christian *kurisuchan*
church *kyookai*
circumstances *jijoo*
city *tokai, toshi*
city hall *shiyakusho*
classmate *dookyuusei, kurasumeeto*
to clear up (weather) *hareru*
clearly *hakkiri*
clerk *jimuin* (office), *ten'in* (store)
to click *kurikku suru* (computer term)
climate *kishoo*
to close *tojiru, shimeru, shimaru*
close friend *shin'yuu*
closed (shop, office) *heiten*
cloudy *kumori*
club *kurabu*
coach *koochi*
cold *kaze* (virus), *samui* (weather, temperature), *tsumetai* (to the touch, unfriendly)
colleague *dooryoo*
college student *daigakusei*

to come *kuru, mairu*
to come, to go (deferential) *irassharu*
to come out *deru*
comfortable *kaiteki (na)*
communication *tsuushin*
to commute *tsuukin suru*
companion *nakama*
our company *heisha, toosha*
company *kaisha, -sha*
company entrance exam *nyuushashiken*
to compare *kuraberu, hikaku suru*
comparison *hikaku*
comparatively *hikakuteki*
competition *kyoosoo*
competitor *kyoosoosha* (person), *kyoosoogaisha* (company)
completely *mattaku, sukkari*
complexion *kaoiro*
computer *konpyuutaa*
computer game system *famikon*
to confirm *tashikameru, kakunin suru*
confirmation *kakunin*
to consider *kangaeru, kooryo suru*
considerably *daibu*
consulate general *sooryoojikan*
consultation *soodan*
consumer *shoohisha*
to contact *renraku, suru*
to continue *tsuzuku, tsuzukeru*
contract *keiyaku*
to make a contract *keiyaku o musubu*
convenience *benri, tsugoo*
convenient *benri (na), kootsugoo (na)*
conversation *kaiwa*
cooking *ryoori*
cooperation *kyooryoku*
corner *kado*
correct *tadashii, seikaku (na)*
to correct *naosu* (fix)
corridor *rooka*
countryside *inaka*
couple, husband and wife *fusai*
courage *yuuki*
course (golf) *koosu*
to cross, pass *kosu*
to be crowded *komu*
cultural activity *bunka katsudoo*
culture *bunka*
customer *kokyaku, kyaku, okyakusan*
custom *shuukan*
customs (office) *zeikan*
to cut *kiru*

D

danger *kiken*
dangerous *abunai, kiken (na)*
data *deeta, shiryoo*
day *hi, -nichi*
decision *ketsudan, kettei, kesshin*
deep-fry *kara age*
defect *ketten*
to defend *mamoru* (protect), *benkai suru* (justify)
degree *hodo*
delicious *oishii*
demonstration *demonsutoreeshon, demo*

418

deposit *shikikin*
detailed *kuwashii*
to develop *hatten suru*
development *kaihatsu*
development department *kaihatsubu*
device *kufuu*
difference *chigai*
to be different *chigau*
difficult *muzukashii*
diffusion *fukyuu*
dinner *yuushoku, bangohan*
direction *hookoo*
disadvantageous *furi (na)*
disagreement *hantai*
discussion *hanashiai*
disposal *shori*
distinguished *meimon (no)*
distributor *dairiten*
disturbance *(o)jama*
division *bu*
dizziness *memai*
to do *suru, itasu* (humble), *saseru* (causative form), *yaru*
doctor *isha*
doctor's office *iin*
doctor's visit *ooshin*
document *shorui*
dollar *doru*
downtown *toshin*
to draw closer *chikazuku*
drink *nomimono*
to drink *nomu*
driving *unten*
duty *kinmu* (work), *gimu* (obligation)
dwelling *juutaku*
dynamic *dainamikku (na)*

E

each *sorezore*
each time *maido*
eagerness *yaru ki*
early *hayai*
earlier than expected *hayame ni*
earthquake *jishin*
an earthquake was felt *jishin ga atta*
to ease *kanwa suru*
easy *yasui, raku (na)*
to eat *taberu*
economical *keizaiteki (na)*
economics *keizai*
to economize *setsuyaku suru*
to edit *henshuu suru*
education *kyooiku*
effective *kookateki (na), yuukoo (na)*
efficiency *kooritsu*
eight *hachi*
electric, electronic *denshi*
electricity *denki*
elementary school *shoogakkoo*
e-mail *e-meeru*
emphasis *kyoochoo*
employee *juugyooin, shain*
all employees *zen'in*
employee training *shain-kyooiku*
employment *saiyoo*
encounter *deai*

end *kugiri, owari, sue*
English *eigo*
to enter *hairu*
to enter a country *nyuukoku suru*
entrance *iriguchi*
entrance into a school *nyuugaku*
to entrust *tanomu, makaseru*
environment *kankyoo*
especially *toku (ni), wazawaza* (purposely)
establishment (i.e., of a business) *setsuritsu*
evening *yuugata*
this evening *konban*
event *ibento*
eventually *kekkyoku*
everybody *dare mo*
every day *mainichi*
everyone *min'na*
everything *subete*
to examine *choosa suru kentoo suru* (scrutinize), *shinsatsu o suru* (medical)
examining room *shinsatsushitsu*
example *rei*
for example *tatoeba*
to exceed *kosu, sugiru*
to excel *sugureru*
excellent *yuushuu (na)*
to be excited *koofun suru*
excitement *koofun*
excuse me *sumimasen*
excuse me, but *shitsurei desu ga*
excuse me, is anybody home? *gomen kudasai*
exercise *undoo*
exhibition *tenji*
to exist *aru, iru*
expansion *kakudai, hatten* (development)
as expected *sasuga, yahari, yappari*
expense *hiyoo*
expensive *takai*
experience *keiken*
experiment *jikken*
explanation *setsumei*
express *kyuukoo* (train), *sokutatsu* (mail)
extension (phone) *naisen*
extravagant *gooka (na)*

F

face *kao*
fact *jissai, jijitsu*
in fact and name *meijitsutomo*
faculty *gakubu*
fairly *kanari*
fairway *feyaauei*
family *kazoku*
family name *myooji*
famous *yuumei (na)*
far *tooi*
fashion *ryuukoo*
fashion-conscious *oshare*
fast *hayai*
fate *unsei*
father *chichi, chichioya*
fatigue *tsukare*
fax *fakkusu*
to feel *kanjiru*
to feel well *kibun ga ii, kimochi ga ii*
feeling *kimochi* (emotion), *kanji* (impression)

female *josei*
female university student *joshidaisei*
fever *netsu*
few *sukunai*
finally *yatto*
to find unmanageable *moteamasu*
finding employment *shuushoku*
fine *kekkoo (na)*
to finish *owaru, oeru, sumasu*
first *daiichi, mazu, saisho*
first day *ichinichime, shonichi*
first party *ichijikai*
first-rate *ichiryuu*
to fit *au*
to be fixed, be healed *naoru*
to flee *nigeru*
flood *hanran*
floor *yuka* (surface), *kai* (story)
to fly *tobu*
focus *shooten*
fog *kiri*
foggy *kiri ga ooi*
fool *baka*
foreigner *gaikokujin*
foreigner registration card *gaikokujin-toorokusho*
foreign-owned *gaishikei*
to forget *wasureru*
to forgive *yurusu*
formal *seishiki (na)*
format *foomatto* (computer term)
fortune-teller *uranaishi*
four-night stay *yonpaku*
France *furansu*
free *jiyuu (na)*
free of charge *tada*
free time *hima*
Friday *kin'yoobi*
friend *tomodachi, yuujin, shin'yuu* (close friend)
full *ippai*
fun *tanoshii*
function *kinoo*
funeral *sooshiki*
futile *muda (na)*
future *mirai, shoorai*

G

game *geemu*
garden *niwa* (private), *teien* (public)
gate *mon*
to gather *atsumaru, matomeru*
general affairs department *soomubu*
general practitioner *kaigyooi*
in general *zenpan (ni)*
geography *chiri*
to get angry *okoru*
to get cloudy *kumoru*
to get off *oriru*
to get on *noru*
to get used to *nareru*
girlfriend *gaarufurendo*
to give *ageru, kudasaru, kureru*
to give up *akirameru*
glass *gurasu*
to go *iku*
to go into *hairu*

to go out *dekakeru, gaishutsu suru*
to go up *agaru*
god *kami*
"going dutch" *warikan*
golf *gorufu*
golf course *gorufu koosu*
good *ii, yoi, yoroshii* (formal)
government office *yakusho*
gradually *dandan*
a graduate *sotsugyoosei, doosoosei*
graduation *sotsugyoo*
graduate school *daigakuin*
to grasp *nigiru*
great *taishita*
greeting *aisatsu*
to grow up *sodatsu*
guarantor *hoshoonin*
to guess *suisoku suru*
to guess correctly *ataru*
guidance *an'nai*

H

half-day *han'nichi*
to handle *atsukau, shori suru*
to hang down *sagaru*
to happen *okoru*
happy *ureshii*
harm *gai*
to have *aru, motte iru*
to have a headache *atama ga itai*
to have a hunch about *ki ga suru*
to have a previous appointment *sen'yaku ga aru*
to have a sore throat *nodo ga itai*
to have a stomachache *onaka ga itai*
he *kare*
head *atama*
head office *honsha*
healthy *genki (na), kenkoo (na)*
to hear *kiku*
hello (when answering telephone) *moshi moshi*
help *tetsudai, herupu* (computer term)
to help *tetsudau, tasukeru*
to be helpful *tasukaru*
here *koko*
here and there *achikochi*
hey *ara*
high-class *kookyuu*
high school *kookoo*
high school days *kookoojidai*
high-tech *haitekku*
hill *oka*
to hire *yatou*
hobby *shumi*
to hold *motsu*
to hold a conference *kaigi o hiraku*
hometown *shusshin*
hospital *byooin*
hot spring *onsen*
hotel *hoteru*
hours for visiting patients *ooshin-jikan*
house *ie, uchi*
how *ikaga, doo*
how many *ikutsu*
how many nights *nan paku*

how many times *nan kai*
how much *dore gurai, ikura*
human being *ningen*
hundred *hyaku*
to hurry *isogu*
husband *shujin*

I

I *watakushi* (polite), *watashi; boku, ore*
(male speech)
I am sorry *gomen'nasai, shitsurei shimashita*
icon *aikon* (computer term)
idea *aidia, kangae*
identification card *mibun shoomeisho*
to be idle *furafura suru*
immigration office *nyuukokukanri-jimusho*
impolite *shitsurei (na)*
important *daiji (na), taisetsu (na)*
impossible *muri (na)*
improvement *kaizen*
in charge *tantoo*
to be in charge of *tantoo suru*
in order to *tame (ni)*
incident *jiken*
to increase *fueru*
indeed *naruhodo*
individual *kojin*
individualism *kojinshugi*
industry *sangyoo*
to inform *tsutaeru*
inn (Japanese-style) *ryokan*
insert *soonyuu* (computer term)
inside *naka*
insurance *hoken*
to intend *suru tsumori (da)*
intense *hageshii*
interest *kyoomi*
interesting *omoshiroi*
international telephone call *kokusai
denwa*
internationalization *kokusaika*
Internet *intaanetto*
interval *aida*
interview *mensetsu*
to be intoxicated by *ni you*
intra-company *shanai*
to introduce *shookai suru*
introduction *shookai*
investigation *choosa*
to investigate *shiraberu*
invitation *shootai*
to invite *shootai suru, maneku*
issue (matter for discussion) *yooken*
it *kore, sore are*

J

Japan *nihon*
Japanese *nihongo* (language), *nihonjin*
(person)
joint-stock company *kabushikigaisha*
joint venture *gyoomuteikei*
joke *joodan*
junior *koohai*
junior high school *chuugakkoo*
just, only *bakari*
just in time *girigiri*

K

Kanto area (eastern Japan) *kantoo chihoo*
to keep *motsu* (have), *mamoru* (protect)
kind *isshu, shurui* (type), *shinsetsu (na)*
(kindhearted)
kindergarten *yoochien*
kindness *shinsetsu*
to know *shiru, zonjiru* (honorific)
knowledge *chishiki*

L

lack of *fusoku*
land *tochi*
to land *jooriku suru* (ship, storm), *chakuriku
suru* (plane)
landlord *yanushi*
large city *daitoshi*
large company, corporation *daikigyoo*
last month *sengetsu*
last night *sakuya*
last week *senshuu*
last year *kyonen, sakunen*
late *osoi*
to learn *narau, manabu*
to leave a country *shukkoku suru*
lecturer *kooshi*
lethargic *darui*
letter *tegami*
letter of guarantee *hoshoosho*
license *menkyoshoo*
lifestyle *seikatsu*
lightning strikes *kaminari ga ochiru*
to like *ki ni iru, konomu, suki (da)*
likewise (not at all) *kochira koso*
line (from a play) *serifu*
list *risuto*
list of prices *kakakuhyoo*
to listen *kiku, ukagau* (humble)
a little *chotto, shooshoo, sukoshi*
to live *sumu* (reside), *ikiru* (have life)
living expenses *seikatsuhi*
lonely *sabishii*
long *nagai*
long-distance call *chookyori denwa*
long time no see (polite form) *gobusata*
to lose *mayou*
lost item *wasuremono*
"love marriage" *ren'ai kekkon*
lover *koibito*
low *hikui*
lucky *saiwai (na)*
lunch *chuushoku, hirugohan, hirumeshi, bentoo*
(boxed lunch)

M

machine *kikai*
Macintosh (Apple computer)
makkintosshu
magazine *zasshi*
mahjong *maajan*
mail *meeru* (computer term)
mainly *omo ni*
to make *tsukuru*
to make fly *tobasu*
to make noise *sawagu*

to make convenient for someone *bengi o hakaru*
to make a mistake *machigaeru*
male *dansei*
man *otoko, otoko no hito*
management *keiei*
management department *keieigakubu*
management position *kanrishoku*
manager *maneejaa, kachoo* (section head)
managing director *senmu*
in this manner *kore de*
to manufacture *seizoo suru*
many *ooi, ooku, takusan*
map *chizu*
market *maaketto, shijoo*
marketing *maakettingu*
marriage *kekkon*
to get married *kekkon suru*
math *suugaku*
matter *koto*
meal *shokuji*
meaning *imi*
to measure *hakaru*
meat *niku*
medical examination *kenshin*
medicine *kusuri*
to meet *au*
meeting *kaigi, menkai, kaigou*
meeting hall *kaijoo*
meeting room *kaigishitsu*
memo *memo*
to memorize *oboeru*
memory *omoide* (recollection), *kioku* (faculty of remembering)
menu bar *menyuu* (computer term)
message *dengon, messeeji*
the Meteorological Agency *kishoochoo*
method *shikata*
metropolitan *daitokai (no)*
mid- and small (size) *chuushoo*
midsize and small-size corporations *chuushookigyoo*
midsize cities *chuutoshi*
in the middle of *tochuu*
middle management *chuukenshain*
misconception *kanchigai*
Miss *-san, -joo*
mistake *machigai, techigai*
misunderstanding *gokai*
Monday *getsuyoobi*
money *okane*
monk *oboosan*
mood *kibun*
more *motto*
more and more *dondon*
more than *ijoo*
this morning *kesa*
morning *asa*
mortifying *kuyashii*
mother *haha, hahaoya*
mouth *kuchi*
to move *ugoku* (change position), *hikkosu* (change abode)
movement *shindoo*
moving (homes) *hikkoshi*
Mr. *-san, -shi*

Mr., Mrs., Miss *san, sama*
as much as possible *narubeku*
to mutter *tsubuyaku*

N

name *namae, shimei*
name brand *neemuburando*
name of a company *kaishamei*
narrow *semai*
nature *shizen*
nausea *hakike*
near *chikai*
nearly *hotondo*
need *hitsuyoo*
negotiation *kooshoo*
neighbor *kinjo no hito, rinjin*
to be nervous *kinchoo suru*
networking *nettowaakingu*
new *atarashii*
new employees *shin'nyuushain*
newly manufactured goods *shinseihin*
newest type *saishinshiki*
newspaper *shinbun*
next *tsugi*
next door *tonari*
next time *kondo*
next week *raishuu*
next year *rainen*
nice to meet you *hajimemashite*
no *iie, iya*
nonreserved seat *jiyuu-seki*
normal *heijoo (na)*
no smoking *kin'en*
no-smoking room *kin'enshitsu*
noisy *soozooshii, urusai*
nostalgic *natsukashii*
not at all *zenzen*
not in the slightest *tondemo nai*
to notice *kizuku, ki ga tsuku*
now *ima*
from now on *kongo*
number *bangoo, kazu, ken, suu*
number one *ichiban*

O

obstacle *jama*
occasion *baai*
of course *mochiron*
to offer (honorific) *sashiageru*
office *jimusho*
"office lady" *ooeru (OL)*
office work *jimu*
old *furui*
old capital *miyako*
older *nenpai (no)*
to be on time *maniau*
at once (immediately) *sassoku*
one *ichi*
one day (a certain day) *aru hi*
one person *hitori*
one thing *hitotsu, hitokoto*
one-way *katamichi*
one week *isshuukan*
only *dake*
to open *akeru, oopun suru* (computer term)
open (for business) *kaitenchuu*

to open a file *fairu o akeru* (computer term)
opinion *iken*
opponent *kyoosooaite, aite*
to oppose *hantai suru*
order *chuumon* (request), *meirei* (command)
ordinary *futsuu*
outside *gaibu, soto*
to overhear *mimi ni suru*
overseas *kaigai*
overtime *zangyoo*
overview *gaiyoo*
to overwork oneself *hataraki-sugiru, muri suru*
owner *shoyuusha*

P

pace *hochoo*
painful *itai, kurushii*
pamphlet *panfuretto*
paper *kami*
parents *ryooshin*
partner *aite, paatonaa*
part-time job *arubaito*
to pass away *nakunaru*
passport *pasupooto*
to pay *harau*
to pay attention *chuui suru*
payment *shiharai*
pediatrician *shoonikai*
people *hitobito, hitotachi*
percent *paasento*
to perform *okonau*
period *jidai* (epoch), *kikan* (portion of time)
perseverance *gaman*
person *hito, kata*
personality *kosei*
personnel department *jinjibu*
philosophy *tetsugaku*
phone bill *denwadai*
place *basho, tokoro*
in place of *kawari (ni)*
to place, put *oku*
plan *keikaku*
planning *kikaku*
planning department *kikakubu*
to play *asobu, purei suru* (computer term)
please (go ahead) *doozo*
please forgive me *oyurushi kudasai*
please take a look *gorankudasai*
point *ten*
police *keisatsu*
police box *kooban*
policeman *omawarisan*
police officer *keisatsukan*
policy *hooshin*
politely *teinei ni*
politics *seiji*
to pour *tsugu*
population *jinkoo*
position *ichi, basho* (location), *chi'i* (social standing)
positive *sekkyokuteki (na)*
possession *shoyuu*
possibility *kanoosei*
to postpone *enki suru*
postponement *enki*
practical *jissenteki (na)*

practice range *renshuujoo*
praying for the gods' help *kamidanomi*
to present *hiroo suru*
preparation *junbi, yooi*
present (gift) *okurimono*
a present to bring on visits *temiyage*
presentation *purezenteeshon*
pretty *kirei (na)*
previous appointment *sen'yaku*
price *kakaku, nedan, bukka*
principle *gensoku, -shugi* ("-ism")
to print *purinto suru*
priority *yuusen*
private railway *shitetsu*
probably *tabun*
problem *mondai*
product *seihin, shoohin*
production *seisan*
profit *rieki*
promise *yakusoku*
prompt report *sokuhoo*
proposal *teian*
protection *hogo*
psychiatrist *seishinkai*
pub (Japanese-style) *izakaya*
public announcement *koohyoo*
public (pay) phone *kooshuu denwa*
to pursue *ou*
to put in *ireru*
to put on *tsukeru*
to put out (extinguish) *kesu*
to put together *awaseru, kumiawaseru*

Q

quality *hinshitsu, shitsu*
quality control *hinshitsu kanri*
question *shitsumon*
quiet *shizuka (na)*

R

railroad tracks *senro*
rain *ame*
rainy season *tsuyu*
rare *mezurashii*
rate *wariai*
rather *kanari, nakanaka*
to read *yomu*
real *hontoo (no), honkakuteki (na)*
realistic *genjitsuteki (na)*
really *hontoo ni*
realtor *fudoosan-ya*
reason *riyuu, wake*
to receive *morau, ukeru, uketoru, itadaku* (humble)
recently *saikin*
receptionist *uketsuke*
red *akai*
to refrain *hikaeru*
registration *tooroku*
regrettable *zannen (na)*
to rejoice *yorokobu*
relation *kankei*
relationship *kankei, tsukiai*
to relax *nonbiri suru, rirakkusu suru*
reliable *tanomoshii*
reliance *tayori*

relief *anshin*
to remain *nokoru*
remainder *nokori, amari*
to remember *oboeru*
to renovate *aratameru*
rent *yachin*
report *hookoku, repooto*
to report *hookoku suru*
to request *tanomu*
reservation *yoyaku*
reserved seat *shitei-seki*
residential area *juutakuchi*
to rest *yasumu*
restaurant *resutoran*
résumé *rirekisho*
retirement age *teinen*
to return *kaeru* (home), *modoru* (something)
reunion *saikai*
rice *kome* (uncooked), *gohan* (cooked)
to ride *noru*
road *michi*
room *heya*
round-trip *oofuku*
rumor *uwasa*
to run *hashiru*

S

sad *kanashii*
safe *anzen (na)*
safety *anzensei*
salary *kyuuryoo*
salaryman *sarariiman*
sales *hanbai, eigyoo, seerusu, uriage*
sales network *seerusu nettowaaku*
salt *shio*
same *onaji*
same town *dookyoo*
sample *sanpuru*
Saturday *doyoobi*
save *seibu,* (computer term)
to say *iu, ossharu* (deferential)
school of choice *shibookoo*
score *tokuten sukoa*
to search for *sagasu*
season *kisetsu, shiizun*
secret *himitsu, naisho*
section *bubun* (separate part), *ka* (of
    an organization or company)
to see *miru*
to seek *motomeru*
self *jibun*
to sell *uru*
seminar *seminaa*
to send *okuru*
senior *senpai*
seniority system *nenkoo-joretsu*
sentence (group of words) *bun*
serious *majime (na)*
service *saabisu*
service window *madoguchi*
to settle down *ochitsuku*
seventh floor *nanakai*
several *ikutsuka (no)*
she *kanojo*
Shintoism *shintoo*
shop *mise*

short *mijikai*
show *shoo*
to show *miseru, shimesu*
shrimp *ebi*
shrine *jinja*
sick *byooki*
to be sick of *akiru*
side *gawa*
sight-seeing *kankoo*
simplicity *kanso sa*
since *irai* (time), *node* (reason), *kara* (reason)
sincerity *makoto, seii*
to sit down *suwaru*
situation *jitai, jookyoo*
size *saizu* (clothes), *ookisa* (dimensions or
    extent)
ski *sukii*
skill *sukiru*
skillful *joozu (na)*
sleepy *nemui*
sleeve *sode*
slowly *yukkuri*
small *chiisai*
smoking room *kitsuenshitsu*
smooth *junchoo (na)* (free from difficulties)
snack bar *sunakku*
snore *ibiki*
snow *yuki*
to snow *yuki ga furu*
so *soo*
so-called *iwayuru*
social status *mibun*
soft *yawarakai, sofuto (na)*
software *sofuto*
somehow *nantoka*
someone *dareka*
something *nanika*
sometimes *tama ni, tokidoki*
son *musuko*
soon *sugu, sorosoro*
sophistication *oshare*
sound *oto*
souvenir *omiyage*
soy sauce *shooyu, murasaki* (for sushi)
special *tokubetsu (na)*
specialty *senmon, tokui*
splitting the bill *warikan*
staff *sutaffu*
to stand in line *narabu*
to start drinking *nomihajimeru*
station *eki*
to state clearly *meiji suru*
to stay *taizai suru* (reside temporarily), *tomaru*
    (overnight)
to stop *tomaru* (cease moving), *yameru* (quit)
storm *arashi*
storm is coming *arashi ga kuru*
strategy *senryaku*
stroll *sanpo*
strong *tsuyoi*
student *gakusei*
study abroad *ryuugaku*
to study *benkyoo suru, manabu*
subordinate *buka*
subsidiary *kogaisha*
subway *chikatetsu*

suddenly *totsuzen*
sufficient *juubun (na)*
suitable *tekitoo (na)*
suitable person *tekininsha*
summer *natsu*
sunny *hare*
superior *jooshi*
supernatural *suupaanachuraru*
superstition *meishin*
supper *bangohan, banmeshi, yuushoku*
to supplement *hosoku suru*
to be surprised *bikkuri suru*
sushi restaurant *sushiya*
system *seido*

T

table *teeburu* (furniture), *hyoo* (chart)
to take *toru* (into possession), *tsureru*
    (someone with you), *kakaru* (cost)
talented person *jinzai*
to talk *hanasu*
tall *se ga takai*
tasteful *omomuki no aru*
taxi *takushii*
to teach *oshieru*
technology *gijutsu, tekunorojii*
telephone *denwa*
telephone card *terehon kaado*
telephone charge *denwa ryookin*
telephone number *denwa-bangoo*
telephone operator *kookanshu*
television *terebi*
to tell *iu, moosu* (honorific), *oshieru* (inform),
    tsutaeru
temper *kigen*
temple *tera*
temporarily *shibaraku*
temptation *yuuwaku*
tendency *keikoo*
tentatively *ichioo*
ten thousand *man*
terrible *taihen (na)*
than *yori*
thank you *arigatoo, doomo*
thanks for treating me *gochisoo sama*
that *ano, sono*
that place *asoko*
then *soreja* (so), *sorekara* (next in order)
there *achira, sochira*
thermometer *ondokei* (standard), *taionkei*
    (clinical)
they *karera*
thief *doroboo*
thing *mono, koto*
to think *omou*
this, this one *kore*
thought *kangae*
thousand *sen*
three *san*
throat *nodo*
thunder *kaminari*
to thunder *kaminari ga naru*
Thursday *mokuyoobi*
ticket *kippu*
tiger *tora*
time *ji, jikan, jikoku, tabi, toki*

timely *taimurii (na), taimingu ga ii*
time difference *jisa*
time period *jiki*
time-wise *jikanteki*
to be tired *tsukareru*
toast ("Cheers") *kanpai*
today *kyoo, honjitsu*
together *issho (ni)*
tomorrow *ashita, asu*
tools *tsuuru* (computer term)
total amount (money) *zengaku*
town *machi*
toy *omocha*
trade *torihiki*
trading company *shooji*
trade show *toreedo shoo*
train *densha, kisha*
limited express train *tokkyuu*
training *kunren, kenshuu*
tranquility *shizukesa*
transaction *torihiki*
transfer (job) *tenkin*
translation *hon'yaku, yaku*
travel *ryokoo*
to travel *ryokoo suru*
traveler's checks *ryookoo-yoo-kogitte*
to travel abroad *kaigai ryokoo ni iku*
to treat *atsukau* (deal with), *gochisoo suru,*
    ogoru (to a meal)
to be treated *gochisoo ni naru*
trend *ryuukoo* (fashion), *keikoo* (tendency),
    torendo
to be in trouble *komaru*
trust *shin'yoo*
truth *shinjitsu, hontoo*
to try one's best *ganbaru*
to tuck up *makuru*
tuna *maguro*
twig *koeda*
two homes *futabukken*
two-story house *nikaidate*
typhoon *taifuu*

U

unconciously *shirazu shirazu*
to understand *wakaru, rikai suru*
understanding (agreement) *ryookai*
unfortunately *ainiku*
unique *tokuyuu (no)*
university *daigaku*
unknown *mumei (no)*
until *made*
unusual *kawatta, mezurashii*
up-to-date *saishin (no)*
urgent *kyuu (na)*
urgent business *kyuuyoo*
use *shiyoo*
to use *tsukau*
to use a mouse *mausu o tsukau* (computer
    term)
useless *dame (na)*
usual *fudan (no), itsumo (no), futsuu (no)*

V

vacation *yasumi*
vacationer *ryookoosha*

various *iroiro (na)*
vegetables *yasai*
vehicle *norimono*
very *sugoku, totemo, zuibun*
view (landscape) *keshiki*
village *mura*
to vomit *haku*
to feel like vomiting *hakike ga suru*
voyeur *nozoki*

W

wage system *kyuuyo seido, kyuuryo seido*
to wait *matsu*
waiting room *machiaishitsu*
to walk *aruku*
want *hoshii*
ward office *kuyakusho*
to warn *keikoku suru*
warning *chuui, keikoku*
to wash *arau*
water *mizu, ohiya*
way (manner) *hoohoo*
we *watashitachi, watakushi-domo, wareware*
weather *tenki*
Wednesday *suiyoobi*
this week *konshuu*
welcome *kangei, yookoso, irasshaimase*
    (interjection)
well *genki (na)* (healthy), *yoku* (excellently)
well, then *saa*
well (uh, hmm) *anoo, eetto, jaa*
Western food *yooshoku*
Western-style apartment *manshon*
Western-style clothes *yoofuku*
what *nan, nani*
what floor? *nankai*
what kind of *don'na*
what time *nanji*
when *itsu*

where *doko*
which *dono, dore, dochira* (polite)
while *aida ni, uchi ni*
a while ago *sakki*
white *shiroi*
who *dare*
why *dooshite, naze*
wide *hiroi*
wife *kanai* (one's own wife), *okusan* (someone
    else's wife)
to win *katsu*
window *mado* (glass), *uindoo* (computer
    term)
wisdom *chie*
wish *kiboo*
within (a certain time, distance) *inai*
woman *josei, onna, onna no hito, joshi,*
(I) wonder if *kana*
wonderful *subarashii, sugoi, suteki (na)*
work *shigoto*
to work *hataraku, shigoto suru*
to work for *tsutomeru*
work history *keireki*
to write *kaku*
wrong number *machigai denwa*

Y

year *toshi, ~nen*
this year *kotoshi*
year-end party *boonenkai*
yellow *kiiroi*
yen *en*
yes *hai, ee, un, yaa*
yesterday *kinoo*
yet *mada*
you *anata, otaku, kimi*
young *wakai*
younger sister *imooto*
your company *kisha*

INDEX

427